TongBible Story Guide

TongBible Story
Guide

806, Seolleung-ro, Gangnam-gu, Seoul, Korea 06014
http://www.tongbooks.com

writer: Byoungho Zoh
publisher: TONGDOKWON

Printed in South Korea

ISBN 978-89-92247-86-3 03230

TongBible Story Guide

by. Byoungho Zoh

Tongdokwon

• Prologue •

Leading 'Tong Bible Story' camps for the past 25 years has been my greatest joy and honour. Through the years, I have come to discover a few things. The first is that the more time one spends in reading or listening to the Word, the more one starts to understand and feel the Heart of God. The second is that when approaching the Word, it helps to have a thought-out guide or method.

So I bring to my readers this book which attempts to explore the whole Bible in the 'Tong' method. Broadly speaking, 'Tong' encompasses the concept of 'whole'. In other words, reading it and consuming it in its wholesome form as opposed to dissecting it into parts and segments. This book is a result from various steps and projects of mine of which includes my previous publications; 'Reading through the Bible like this 2004' and 'Reading through the Bible (revised version) 2008'. Also, I was one of the co-representatives for the Seoul Declaration of 140 Korean Theologians in 2008 for Reorientation through the Bible. From these stages, I have developed a guide which takes the reader through a method whereby they can chronologically and fully explore the Bible.

I would like to broadly introduce five steps which is the formula for 'Tong Bible'.

This book is step 3 within the formula.

I pray that this book helps Christians today to approach the Living Word in its 'whole' by using the 'Tong Bible Story' method.

Byoungho Zoh

• Contents •

Track 6 - 30 Years of Acts

16 The Disciple Era

17 Extension of the Gospel with no Boundaries

18 Eternal Crown and handed-down Request

Track 7 - The 9 Epistles

19 Letters for the Righteous Fight

20 Song of Victory Pre-received

* Tong Bible Story Orientation

1. What is Tong Bible Story?

Before all, there is a need to clarify the meaning of 'Tong'.

I have a few thoughts concerning the Bible as a book of which I will share with you all here.

The Bible is a thin book

Even if the sky were used as scroll and sea as ink, that eternal love and truth cannot be recorded, and in that sense the Bible is a thin book. This is why it should be read in whole and not in parts.

The Bible is the one book worth reading aloud

The Bible is the product in text of God's spoken words. This is why it should be read as both text and speech. When reading the Bible out loud, the Words come to life more vividly.

The Bible is the one book worth hearing 10 times in one year

The more we hear the Bible, the more our faith matures. This is why it should be repeatedly heard 10 times in one year.

The Bible is the one book that contains the Heart of God

The Bible contains the whole universe, not to mention the Heart of God in all parts of history. This is why it should be read chronologically using the Tong Method. Also, it has to be interpreted canonically with Shimjung(the Heart of God). Diachronic and synchronic reading through the Bible using the Tong Method whilst taking into consideration the dissective Western way and the intuitive Eastern way should also be used.

The Bible is the one book that contains the story of a person, family and all nations

This is why it should be read from God feeding, healing, teaching, forgiving and praying for one individual and family to managing the whole universe through the A Kingdom of Priests and the Kingdom of God using the Tong Method.

The Bible must be taught to our children

Parents' work of teaching the Bible to their children will become the only way of transmitting faith to the next generation and beyond.

2. The concept of "reading through the Bible?"

- To read as a 'whole' and not in 'part'

What I mean by "reading through the Bible" is that we read all 66 books as a whole rather than into separate episodes or parts.

While each verse and book carries a great message, the whole Bible carries an even greater and more united message. A 'partial' or 'selective' reading of the Bible can lead to a fragmented understanding of God's management of the world as well as reducing the effectiveness of meditation. Let me give you an example. Let's say one's diet consists mainly of carbohydrates. No one can say that is a healthy or advisable diet. Likewise, reading the Bible in parts is similar to an unbalanced diet; we need to consume the whole Bible in order to understand and grasp the Heart of God. I believe that reading the whole repeatedly is the best and most effective way to grasp the overall flow of the whole text.

If you read all 66 books of the Bible once, twice and repeatedly, you come to experience a wonderful intuition about the Bible: Tsunami of the Word and Grace.

● To read in chronological order

As the title would suggest, "reading through" encourages to read the Bible in chronological order. The Bible takes the form of arrangements by theme and genre. The books of law are categorised in one place, the historical parts in another, the poems in another etc. However, reading in chronological order enables the reader to grasp the story in terms of its relationship to the generation before and after as well as in regards to world history.

Since God is the master of history and manages the world in history, it is important that we study and consume the Bible in chronological order in order to understand God's management within history. From doing so, we can further understand and feel how God is managing our lives today.

● To focus on the Heart of God

Another important part of "Reading through" and "Tong" is focusing on feeling the Heart of God. From reading each word, phrase, sentence, paragraph and eventually the whole Bible, you come to read the mind and heart of God which flows through the entire Bible. Thus, it enables us to feel how the Bible is God's love-letter.

The purpose of reading through the Bible is not to stock up knowledge but more so to figure out the heart of God and establish a deeper relationship with Him. The Bible is the Word of God that should become the standards of our life and thoughts today.

3. The Old Testament: Tong Bible Story

● Traditional classification of the Old Testament

So far we have traditionally classified the Old Testament (total 39 volumes) as follows:

1) The books of law (5 volumes)
: Genesis, Exodus, Leviticus, Numbers, Deuteronomy

The books of law are the five volumes of law Moses wrote. We commonly refer to them as 'Pentateuch'. They explain the creation of the universe and the world and the origin of the nation of Israel through a variety of events from the creation to Moses' times. The Sadducees in Jesus' days authorized only these five books as the Bible.

2) Historical books (12 volumes) : Joshua, Judges, Ruth, I Samuel, II Samuel, I Kings, II Kings, I Chronicles, II Chronicles, Ezra, Nehemiah, Esther

Historical books are books which contain record of historical events. They contain the historical story starting from the time the nation of Israel who came out of Egypt conquered Canaan and settled there, through the times of the rule of the kings such as David and Solomon, down to the time the nation of Israel completed captivity in Babylon and Persia and then returned.

3) Poetical books (5 volumes) **: Job, Psalms, Proverbs, Ecclesiastes, Song of Songs**

Poetical books (Written books) are the collection of books that have poetical characteristic. They record the languages and understanding of deep faith one individual confesses to God rather than deal with historical events. Particularly, Ecclesiastes and Song of Songs are included in the five scrolls among poetical books and these five scrolls were read by the Jews on every important feast. It is said that Song of Songs was read on Passover, Ruth on Pentecost, Lamentations on the Fasting day of the ninth day of the month of Abib in order to lament and remember the fall of the temple in Jerusalem, Ecclesiastes on the feast of Tabernacle and Esther on Purim.

4) Prophetical books (17 volumes) **: Major Prophets - Isaiah, Jeremiah, Lamentations, Ezekiel, Daniel**

Minor Prophets - Hosea, Joel, Amos, Obadiah, Jonah, Micah, Nahum, Habakkuk, Zephaniah, Haggai, Zechariah, Malachi

These were written by prophets. They were divided into Major Prophets and Minor Prophets. This classification does not deal with the contents of prophets' prophecy but is only the standard for quantity of their prophecy. Unlike high priests, the position of prophets was not succeeded. They were called by God in His sovereign will. Prophets sharply asked if God's law were kept perfectly in their ages and pointed out any violations and played the role of giving the people God's plan and will.

● Re-arrangement of the Old Testament in chronological order

Imagine there is a saga written in a total of ten volumes. If you read the first volume today, the sixth volume tomorrow, the third volume the day after tomorrow, the ninth volume the next day and read on like this, disregarding the numerical order, it would be difficult for you to understand the story and human relationship properly even after you have read all. Unfortunately, this is the case as we read 39 books of the Old Testament. What is worse, we do not finish even one volume but just pick up and read only the verses we like in it.

As we have already observed, the Bible we now have is edited according to theme or genre. Therefore, however many times we read in the present system of editing, it is not easy to put in order the historical flow of the Bible. Since the books of law from Genesis to Deuteronomy and Joshua, Judges, Ruth, I Samuel, II Samuel are in the order of Chronological flow, it is not particularly hard to read through them. But if you come to I Kings and II Kings and then prophetical books, you may feel that it is quite difficult because they are put together not in the order of history but according to quantity (major prophets and minor prophets).

Here is one easy example: Ezra and Nehemiah were the people who appeared after Babylonian captivity. Yet in the Bible they are laid ahead of Isaiah and Jeremiah who lived much earlier. If we are going to read in the right order of time, we should read Isaiah and Jeremiah first and then follow up with Ezra and Nehemiah. But, since most believers read through the Bible without doubt of its order, they come to think that despite reading the Bible over and over again, it is a book difficult to understand.

(1) Classification of the Old Testament Age

From now on let's rearrange 39 books of the Old Testament in the order of history. First, the Old Testament age is largely divided into the following four eras.

1) Primeval history, History of Patriarchs, the era of Moses and Exodus

2) Era of Canaan conquest and Judges

3) Era of King's Rule

4) Era of Babylon and Persia

(2) Arranging Historical books

Now, let us properly put five volumes of 'the books of law' and twelve volumes of

'Historical books,' which we saw in the previous classification by theme, into these four periods. First, if we put them just by book, they are as follows.

1) Primeval history, history of Patriarchs, the era of Moses and Exodus

: Genesis, Exodus, Leviticus, Numbers, Deuteronomy (5 volumes)

2) Era of Canaan conquest and Judges

: Joshua, Judges, Ruth (3 volumes)

3) Era of Kings' Rule

: I Samuel, II Samuel, I Kings, II Kings, I Chronicles, II Chronicles (6 volumes)

(Since I Samuel ends with the story of Samuel who worked as the last Judge, strictly speaking, it contains both period of Judges and that of Kings' rule. And most contents of I Chronicles are overlapped with the books of Samuel while II Chronicles is overlapped with the books of Kings.)

4) Era of Babylon and Persia

: Esther, Ezra, Nehemiah (3 volumes)

(3) Arranging Poetical books

Next, let's arrange poetical books. Psalms is the book that has collected poems written by lots of people over a period of more than 1,000 years but about half of Psalms are officially referred to as the Psalms of David. Therefore, it is beneficial to read Psalms together with I Samuel and II Samuel that show the story of David. And, regarding the central author of Proverbs, Song of Songs and Ecclesiastes as Solomon, we can read them together with the story of Solomon appearing in the first half of I Kings. Finally, the chronological background of Job was the period of Patriarchs. He was roughly a contemporary of the times when Abraham lived. Therefore, we may read it together with Genesis. But, considering the overall flow, it is better to read it after reading Ecclesiastes which is a poetical book we come to read the latest due to the flow of time among the poetical books except Job. After that, we read the remaining Psalms.

- **Psalms .... with I Samuel, II Samuel/continued from Job**

- **Proverbs, Song of Songs, Ecclesiastes .... along with I Kings chaps. 1-11**
- **Job .... continued from Ecclesiastes**

(4) Arranging Prophetical books

Now the remaining are 17 volumes of prophetical books, and this part can be said to be difficult. As said already, the Bible we have is not edited in the order of time. Instead, books of larger quantity are placed in front after classified as Major Prophets, and the books of smaller quantity are placed behind them after classified as Minor Prophets. Therefore, the prophetical books whose contents are about seeing and lamenting destroyed Israel are followed by the books whose contents were about shouting to the people for repentance because of Israel's imminent destruction. Therefore, reading the prophetical books in the order of the Bible we have, it is natural that get confused about the times and cannot know which prophet worked first. Now, when we read through the Bible, we should ignore the method of classification by quantity and think according to the order of the times when prophets worked.

All the prophetical books were written only during the era of Kings' rule and captivity. The era when the prophets who left behind prophetical books worked are the era of Kings' rule and captivity. We can classify the prophets of era of Kings' rule and prophets of captivity period and then classify prophetical books in the order of activity as follows. Parenthesis is the collection of prophets who worked in the similar period.

- **Prophetical books of the era of Kings' rule** **(12 volumes)**
  : (Amos. Hosea. Jonah) (Isaiah. Micah) (Zephaniah. Nahum. Habakkuk) Joel (?) (Jeremiah. Lamentations. Obadiah)
- **Prophetical books of the period of Babylon and Persia** **(5 volumes)**
  : (Daniel. Ezekiel) (Haggai. Zechariah) Malachi

period classification	Prophetical book	Main period of prophet's activity
Prophetical books of era of Kings' rule	Amos	During the rule of Jeroboam II, Northern Israel
	Hosea	During the rule of Jeroboam II, Northern Israel
	Jonah	During the rule of Jeroboam II., Northern Israel (in Nineveh, capital of Assyria)
	Isaiah	During the rule of Uzziah, Jotham, Ahaz, Hezekiah of Southern Judah
	Micah	During the rule of Jotham, Ahaz, Hezekiah of Southern Judah
	Zephaniah	Presumed during the rule of Josiah of Southern Judah
	Habakkuk	Presumed during the rule of Jehoiakim of Southern Judah
	Nahum	During the rule of Josiah of Southern Judah(declared to Nineveh)
	Joel	Not clear but we think 'before Jerusalem's fall'
	Jeremiah	During the rule of Josiah, Jehoahaz, Jehoiakim, Jehoiachin, Zedekiah of Southern Judah
	Lamentation	Written by Jeremiah after Jerusalem's fall
	Obadiah	Not clear but we think 'after Jerusalem's fall'
Prophetical books of era of Babylon and Persia	Daniel	During the rule of Jehoiakim, Jehoiachin, Zedekiah of Southern Judah, Babylonian Nebuchadnezzar, Persian Cyrus
	Ezekiel	During the rule of Jehoiachin, Zedekiah of Southern Judah, Babylonian Nebuchadnezzar
	Haggai	During the rule of Darius I, after Persian Cyrus
	Zechariah	During the rule of Darius I, after Persian Cyrus
	Malachi	During the rule of Darius II of Persia (ministered with Nehemiah)

(5) Rearranging the whole Old Testament chronologically

By now, you may have grasped the overall flow. The above chart is the most basic framework of rearranging the Bible. If you have correctly understood the flow, now it is time to see a more detailed order.

In the book of the Kings are recorded the stories of the Kings who ruled Israel. When a particular king ruled, a particular prophet appeared, pointed out the rights and wrongs about the king's rule and gave him God's will. Therefore, in the flow of the books of Kings are activity periods of prophets. Thus, only when we read by inserting prophetical books into books of Kings in keeping with the time, we can know which prophets were contemporaries with which kings, how the country was and what the prophets said.

Accordingly, if the activity periods of prophets appear here and there among the stories of books of Kings, their prophetical books have been inserted right in there and rearranged. It may be complicated more or less but we can say that 'regrouping" the Bible books in the order of history like this is the merit of reading through the Bible.

If you read this way by matching the books of Kings and Chronicles with prophetical books of the prophets who were active at their given periods, you can read the Old Testament chronologically. There may be difference more or less from person to person in reading the whole Old Testament. But if you concentrate on reading the Bible intensively, you can read through the entire Old Testament in about 36 hours. The order is as follows. If you keep this order on the front and back of your Bible, it will help you read while reviewing the flow of history.

The order of reading through the Old Testament	
Primeval history & History of Patriarchs	Gen.chap.1-11 → Gen.chap.12-50
Moses and Exodus age(1)	Exo. → Lev.
Moses and Exodus age(2)	Num. → Deu.
Canaan conquest age & Judges age	Jos. → Jud. → Rut.
King's rule period(1) United kingdom period 1	I Sa. → (I Ch.chap.1-10) → II Sa./(I Ch.chap.11-29) → I Ki.chap.1-2
King's rule era (2) United Kingdom Period 2	I Ki.chap.3-11/(II Ch.chap.1-9) → Pro. → Son. → Ecc. → Job → Psa.
King's rule era (3) Divided Kingdom Period	I Ki.chap.12-22/II Ki.chap.1-14/(II Ch.chap.10-25) → Amo. → Hos. → Jon. → II Ki.chap.15-20/(II Ch.chap.26-32) → Isa. → Mic.
King's rule era (4) Southern Judah declining Period	II Ki.chap.21-23/(II Ch.chap.33-35) → Zep. → Hab. → Nah. → Joe. → II Ki.chap.24-25/(II Ch.chap.36) → Jer. → Lam. → Oba

Babylon Captivity period	Eze. → Dan.
Persian Period	Ezr.chap.1-4 → Hag. → Zec. → Ezr.chap.5-6 → Est. → Ezr.chap.7-10 → Neh. → Mal.

An overview of the Old Testament

I have put in order the whole Old Testament in the form of a total of ten sessions and 24 lessons by rearranging it chronologically. And since I arranged the intermediate history between the Old and New Testaments in the form of one session and two lessons and the whole New Testament in the form of nine sessions and 14 lessons, the entire Bible has been put in order in the form of 20 sessions and 40 lessons. It has been arranged in such a way that if you study a lesson a day, you can read through the Bible in 40 days.

I have put in order each session's author, writing times, chronological background, and historical, geographical and cultural backgrounds that are necessary for us to understand the session while reviewing its whole and parts so that you can read the contents of whole reviewing, ground and annual ring, wind and soil and the like while actually reading through the Bible. I have also put in order the major outline of each Bible book appearing in the session. In addition, each session has concepts to help grasp it. This shows an important viewpoint of how to read the Tong points.

I have tried not to miss important Bible scenes that are to be included in the contents of each lesson. My hopes are that you gain the "Tong Bible Story" concept as you read through the whole Bible.

Session 1 God expresses His Heart Primeval History & Era of Patriarchs	Lesson 1 Primeval History	Gen.chap.1-11
	Lesson 2 The History of Patriarchs	Gen.chap.12-36
	Lesson 3 Entering Egypt and Birth of the Nation	Gen.chap.37-50

Session	Lesson	Scripture
Session 2 A Dream for all Nations Era of Moses and Exodus(1)	Lesson 4 Exodus and Empire	Exo.chap.1-18
	Lesson 5 The dream of World Mission - A Kingdom of Priests	Exo.chap.19-40
	Lesson 6 Textbook for the school of Holy Citizens	Lev.
Session 3 The Manna Generation Era of Moses and Exodus(2)	Lesson 7 Growth of Manna Generation	Num.
	Lesson 8 Graduation sermon for Manna School	Deu.
Session 4 Succession of Faith Era of Canaan conquest and Judges	Lesson 9 Entering the Promised Land	Jos.
	Lesson 10 The Period when Judges ruled	Jud.
	Lesson 11 Successful case of education	Rut.
Session 5 A Model for a Thousand Years Era of Kings' rule(1) Era of United Kingdom 1	Lesson 12 Birth of Mizpah Generation	I Sa.chap.1-7
	Lesson 13 The beginning of Kings' rule	I Sa.chap.8-31
	Lesson 14 God's servant David	II Sa., I Ki.chap.1-2
Session 6 Mind and Wisdom Era of Kings' rule(2) Era of United Kingdom 2	Lesson 15 Solomon and Poetical books	I Ki.chap.3-11, Pro., Son., Ecc., Job., Psa.
Session 7 Line of Love, Line of Mission Era of Kings' rule(3) Era of Divided Dynasties	Lesson 16 Divided Dynasties of South and North	I Ki.chap.12-22, II Ki.chap.1-14, Amo., Hos., Jon.
	Lesson 17 Destruction of Northern Kingdom Israel	II Ki.chap.15-20, Isa., Mic.
Session 8 Hope Standing before Despair Era of Kings' rule(4) Era of Weakened Southern Judah	Lesson 18 Weakening of Southern Kingdom Judah	II Ki.chap.21-23, Zep., Hab., Nah., Joe.
	Lesson 19 Brief discipline	II Ki.chap.24-25, Jer., Lam., Oba., I&II Ch.
Session 9 Punishment, a Stepping Stone of Hope Era of Babylonian captivity	Lesson 20 Persuading captives	Eze.
	Lesson 21 The rough sketch of change of Empire	Dan.

Session 10 A Community of Reconstruction Persian Era	Lesson 22 Rebuilding the Temple Lesson 23 Rebuilding the Wall of Jerusalem Lesson 24 Confession and Silence	Ezr., Hag., Zec., Est. Neh. Mal.

4. The New Testament: Tong Bible Story

● The traditional classification of the New Testament

The traditional classification of the New Testament we are using is as follows;

1) The Gospels (4 volumes) : Matthew's Gospel, Mark's Gospel, Luke's Gospel, John's Gospel

Since they are four separate accounts about Jesus, they are also called Four Gospels. As four writers wrote about Jesus from each different viewpoint, the order of writing or aspect of emphasis is a little different from one another depending on each writer's character. However, the Gospels of four volumes are complementary to one another. The Gospels were recorded for the purpose of preaching the Gospel of God who saved mankind through Jesus Christ. That is why we call this book "Gospel (Blessed news)."

2) Historical book (1 volume) : The Acts of the Apostles

The Acts of Apostles is very important as it records the history of early Christianity. It vividly records the ministry of the disciples who started evangelistic activity upon receiving the Holy Spirit after Jesus was resurrected and taken up to heaven. Its central theme is the start of church and how Christianity was preached to the Gentile world. Particularly the course of Apostle Paul's missionary journey is recorded in detail.

3) Paul's letters (13 volumes)

Paul's letters which were written for the early churches are called 'Paul's letters'. The early churches needed the care of the Apostles. However, when Paul, who took care of many churches in Asia and Europe, could not visit them in person, he cared for the saints and natured them through letters.

A. Prison letters : **Ephesians, Philippians, Colossians, Philemon**

Around A.D.61-63 when Apostle Paul was in prison he wrote and sent these letters.

B. Pastoral letters : **I Timothy, II Timothy, Titus**

These letters were written by Paul to Timothy and Titus, the two fellow workers he trusted and cared for. They contain the contents of his instruction given to them so that they would lead the local churches.

C. Ordinary letters : **Romans, I Corinthians, II Corinthians, Galatians, I Thessalonians, II Thessalonians**

These are other letters of Paul which were written to the early church.

4) General letters (8 volumes) **: Hebrews, James, I Peter, II Peter, I John, II John, III John, Jude**

They are called General letters, first, in that they were the documents recognized by the whole church, and second, in that recipients were not particular people but all kinds of readers. They were the letters written by Peter and John who were the disciples of Jesus, James the brother of Jesus (by flesh) and Jude. They include the letter to the Hebrews whose author is not clearly known.

5) The Prophetical Book (1 volume) **: Revelation**

Revelation deals with the word of prophecy about the last days and is also called 'Apocalypse'. This book was written by John, who was a disciple of Jesus and cared for the saints and ministered the longest among Jesus' disciples, to give hope for the new heaven and new earth. It talks about the second coming of Jesus, all the events of future in history to be accomplished and its fulfillment.

● Re-arrangement of the New Testament in chronological order

In the New Testament, we attempt to solve two problems; how we should combine and read the book of Acts and Paul's letters.

(1) Classification of the New Testament

The timescale covering the New Testament is a century (Jesus' birth B.C. 4 - A.D 95-96). Dividing the New Testamament into four parts as follows is not only divided by theme but also reflects the historical flow of time.

1) Jesus' ministry

2) The start of church and ministry of twelve Apostles

3) Ministry of Apostle Paul and his letters

4) General letters and the book of Revelation

(2) Arranging the New Testament

Now we will arrange 27 volumes of the New Testament Bible in accordance with the four classifications.

1) Jesus' ministry (4 volumes)

: Matthew, Mark, Luke, John

2) The start of church and ministry of twelve apostles (first half of Acts)

: Acts chapters 1-12

3) Ministry of Apostle Paul and his letters (second half of Acts and 13 volumes)

a. The first missionary journey : Acts chapters 13-15:35

b. The second missionary journey : Acts 15:36-18:22,
I & II Thessalonians, Galatians

c. The third missionary journey : Acts 18:23-chapter 19,
I & II Corinthians

d. Paul's journey to Jerusalem: Acts chapters 20-26, Romans

e. Paul in Rome : Acts chapters 27-28, Ephesians, Philippians, Colossians,
Philemon, I & II Timothy, Titus

4) General letters and Revelation **(9 volumes)**

: Hebrews, James, I & II Peter, I , II & III John, Jude, Revelation

(3) Rearranging the whole New Testament chronologically

The quantity of the New Testament is as much as we can read through in one day or two. Particularly, as the background of those times was not complex, just reading it helps us understand the contents without much difficulty. As Paul's letters also have a clear message in each letter and it is all right to read each independently, there is tendency that people make less effort to review the historical flow compared with the Old Testament. However, it helps for us to read through the New Testament with a thought into history during the flow of those times. There clearly existed senders and recipients of the Letters which form the main body of the New Testament. If we read Paul's missionary journey and his letters together, it will help us to figure out and understand why the letters were written, circumstances of those times and Paul's state of mind within the letters.

The order of reading through the New Testament	
Jesus' ministry (1)	Matthew
Jesus' ministry (2)	Mark
Jesus' ministry (3)	Luke
Jesus' ministry (4)	John

The start of church and ministry of twelve apostles	Acts chap.1-12
Ministry of Apostle Paul & his letters (1)	Act.chap.13-18:22 → I Th. → II Th. → Gal. → Act.18:23-chap.19 → I Co. → II Co.
Ministry of Apostle Paul & his letters (2)	Act.20:1-6 → Rom. → Act.20:7-chap.28 → Eph. → Phil → Col. → Phi. → I Ti. → Tit. → II Ti.
General Letters & Revelation	Heb.→ Jam.→ I Pe. → II Pe. → Jud. → I Jo. → II Jo. → III Jo. → Rev.

An overview of the New Testament

The New Testament introduces Our Saviour Jesus Christ, who broke the 400 years of silence of the intermediate period.

Session 12 A Joyful Birth Jesus' ministry	Lesson 27 Jesus' birth	Mat.
Session 13 Love for One Soul Jesus' ministry	Lesson 28 Three year public life	Mar.
Session 14 Passion towards Forgiveness Jesus' ministry	Lesson 29 The last week	Luk.
Session 15 Invitation to Glory and Peace Jesus' ministry	Lesson 30 Victory of the Cross	Joh.
Session 16 The Disciple Era The start of church and ministry of twelve apostles	Lesson 31 The Disciple Era	Act.chap.1-12
Session 17 Extenstion of the Gospel with no Boundaries Ministry of Apostle Paul & his letters(1)	Lesson 32 Paul's first missionary journey Lesson 33 Paul's second missionary journey Lesson 34 Paul's third missionary journey	Act.chap.13-15:35 Act.15:36-18:22, I&II Th, Gal. Act.18:23-chap.19, I&II Co.

Session	Lesson	Scripture
Session 18 Eternal Crown and handed down Request, Ministry of Apostle Paul & his letters(2)	Lesson 35 Paul's journey to Jerusalem	Act.chap. 20-26, Rom.
	Lesson 36 Ecclesiology and love letters	Act.chap. 27-28, Eph., Phi.
	Lesson 37 Christology and miracle letters	Col., Phm.
	Lesson 38 Letter left to sons of faith	I Ti., Tit., II Ti.
Session 19 Letters for the Righteous Fight General letters	Lesson 39 Letters for the Righteous Fight	Heb., Jam., I&II Pe., Jud.
Session 20 Song of Victory Pre-recieved Revelation	Lesson 40 Song of Victory	I&II&III Jo., Rev.

Track 1
Pentateuch

Tong Track 1 - The atmosphere of the Pentateuch

The atmosphere of the Pentateuch is that of God's kingdom of Priests being set up from the time of Abraham to the era of Moses.

In order to set up a kingdom of Priests through Abraham's descendants, God ordered them to leave the plagued Canaan and enter Egypt in its abundance. And during the 400 years of residence in Egypt, God increased their numbers which resulted in the Egyptians calling them the Hebrew 'Nation'.

"'Now if you obey me fully and keep my covenant, then out of all nations you will be my treasured possession. Although the whole Earth is mine, you will be for me a kingdom of priests and a holy nation.' These are the words you are to speak to the Israelites." (Exodus 19:5-6)

God made the Hebrews (who were a nation but without a country/land) experience the proud and restraining Egypt that was on its way to build an empire, thus training them to differentiate between Imperialism and a kingdom of Priests through His covenant with them.

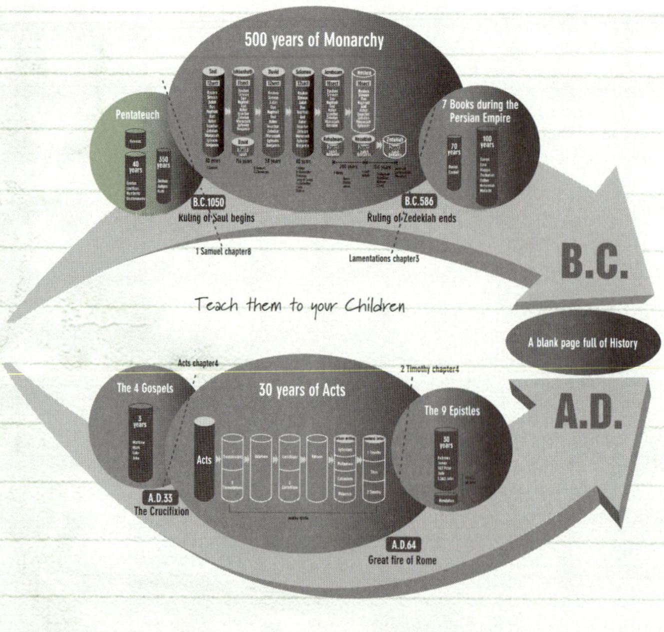

Session 1

God expresses His Heart

Tong Map

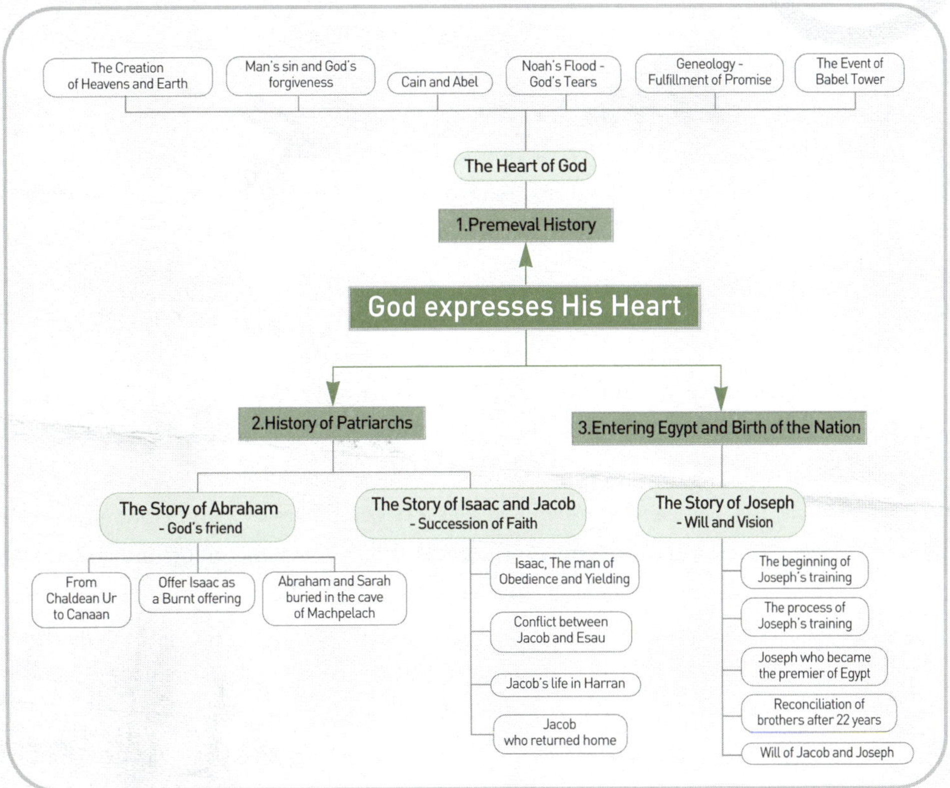

Tong Concept

Let's figure out "God's heart."

Figuring out 'God's heart' is the final goal of our "reading through the Bible". 'Figuring out God's heart' is the most important viewpoint in reading through not only the first part of the Bible but also the whole Bible. As we read through Genesis, let's study with focus on 'God's heart'.

Tong At a glance

＊ Looking around the forst Genesis is the first book of five books Moses wrote(Genesis, Exodus, Leviticus, Numbers, Deuteronomy). Genesis that tells us the beginning of everything sets a stage for the rest of the Bible by describing God's creation, man's fall, origin of the world's nations and covenant relationship God established with Israel. Genesis chapters 1-11 are called "primeval history", which is the record of events of which time and place are not exactly known. Such events as creation, man's fall, the Flood, the tower of Babel and the like are recorded. The history of patriarchs starts from Genesis chapter 12. God's endless love for Abraham, Isaac, Jacob and Joseph, who form the beginning of the nation of Israel and their obedience to him with sweat and tears, form the foundation.

＊ Land and annual ring There are diverse opinions about the supposed fact that the location of the Garden of Eden is near the water source of rivers of Euphrates and Tigris of the highland of Armenia. The location is still unknown. Although there is an opinion that the tower of Babel was built in the Sinai plain of ancient Babylon (south of Mesopotamia), this is also still under research.

However, we can know the time and geographical background of the events from the time of Abraham, who lived around B.C.2000. The stories appearing in Genesis chapters 37-50 about Joseph and his brothers took place about 200 years after Abraham's time. Patriarchs lived in the mountainous areas of Canaan and their vicinities between B.C.1700 and B.C.2000 which is the middle period of the Bronze age.

＊ Wind and climate Chaldean Ur in Babylon was a city in the lower part of Mesopotamia and its civilization was highly developed. Abraham left the benefits of the civilization behind and departed for Canaan via Harran of Mesopotamia, in order to obey the word of God. In those days the Near East region was succeeding a well developed civilization. The Code of Hammurabi of ancient Babylon which is one of the three greatest codes of the world is a great legacy of Patriarchal times. In order to understand the era of patriarchs we need to understand the inheritance laws and marriage contract of those days. According to the inheritance laws back then, the couples who did not have children were able to adopt a son. That was why Abraham was going to appoint his servant Eliezer of Damascus as his heir.(Gen.15:2) However, if the couple gave birth to their own son later, the adopted son had to give up the right to inherit.

This was applied to Eliezer of Damascus. According to the marriage contract back then, a wife who could not bear a child for her husband was required to arrange one of her slaves to bear a child for him. We can see that according to this law Sarai gave Hagar to Abraham and Rachel gave Bilhah to Jacob.(Gen.30:1-8)

Tong Seeing the forest

Genesis God created all things and made man in His image. However, by committing sins, which lead God to regret that He created them, human beings failed to keep their promise with God. Yet, even while judging all things He created with water, He extended the grace of salvation through Noah's ark. He chose Abraham among Noah's descendants and let him be the father of one nation in order to use him as a channel of blessing for many people. The rest of Genesis deals with the story of Abraham the father of faith, Sarah and Isaac, his grandson Jacob and Joseph and ends with the scene in which seventy family members of Jacob settled in Egypt on the foundation that Joseph laid.

01 Lesson

Primeval History

Genesis. chap.1-11

Accumulative reading amount 0.87% 1189

The One Year Tongdok Bible Days 1-4 | Reading time 25 minutes

TongBible Story overview

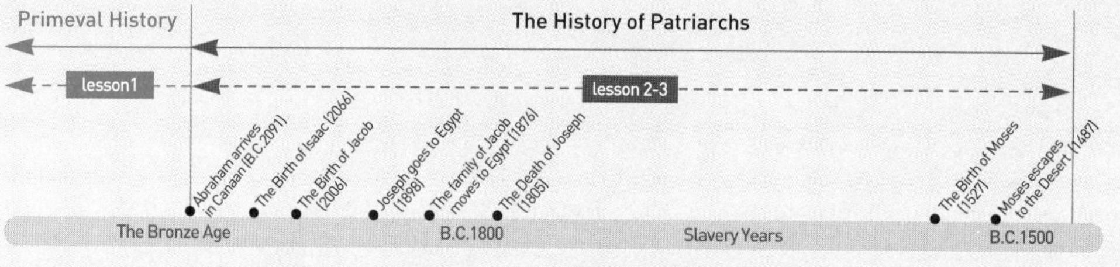

Reading the Old Testament in detail in the order of history (1)

Genesis chapters 1 to 11 is referred to as 'Primeval history.' Although its exact era and space are not known, it records important events such as the beginning of all things and human race and the like. What is the most important in this part is to figure out 'the Heart of God.'

How to read Primeval history

This part contains God's creation; the universe, man's fall, the Flood, the incident of Babel Tower and so on. When reading Genesis, we should aim to focus on how God felt as He created the world and also as humans started to commit sin.

Tong Point

Chapters 1 to 11 of Genesis are primeval history. I want you to read through the Bible on the basis of following contents with focus on figuring out 'the heart of God.'

1. The Creation of Heavens and Earth Gen. chap.1

Have you ever looked up at the shining stars in the sky that look like they are going to fall into your chest in a solitary quiet countryside field one summer night? Just by looking at the stars in the sky, it is not difficult to understand that there was a 'creator' of these wonders.

Our God made Heaven and Earth in the beginning. On the first day He created light and on the second and third days created the firmament (heavens), seas and land. On the fourth day He made the sun, the moon and stars in the already made firmament. On the fifth and sixth days He filled heavens, seas and land with living things. He made man in His image as well. God created His creatures to be natural and beautiful so that they could maintain harmony and balance. Seeing all He created, God was very pleased.

After God created heavens and earth, He blessed what He had created. Blessing fish and birds, he told them to multiply and prosper(Gen.1:21-22). God gave human beings the responsibility to enjoy, rule and manage all these and was pleased to bless humans. In Genesis chapter 1 we can fully feel the Heart of God who created the universe with pleasure and particularly was pleased to make us and bless us among all things.

The Creation

- The first day : created the light and divided day and night
- The second day : created firmament (heavens)
- The third day : created land, seas and all plants
- The fourth day : created the sun, the moon and stars
- The fifth day : created birds and fish according to their kind
- The sixth day : created animals and man
- The seventh day : blessed and sanctified the seventh day and rested

2. Man's sin and God's forgiveness Gen. chap.2-3

God made the Garden of Eden for Adam and Eve. He gave human beings the blessing "Be fruitful and increase in number and fill the Earth" and then gave them the ground of life which is fit for it. There was the tree of knowing good and evil among the trees in the Garden of Eden.

And the LORD God commanded Adam, "You are free to eat from any tree in the garden; but you must not eat from the tree of the knowledge of good and evil, for when you eat of it you will surely die"(Gen.2:16-17). God's word, 'You are free to eat from any tree in the garden...' meant that He gave human beings freedom. However, God also made restrictions. We should see that God declared man's limit in commanding: 'You may eat as you please, but also don't eat' which was requiring humans to be responsible for what he does and to obey the word of God. **Every time Adam saw the fruit of knowing good and evil, at least he could be aware that man as a creature is fundamentally different from God the Creator.**

And then one day the serpent came up to Eve and asked, "Did God really say, 'You must not eat from any tree in the garden'?" The serpent's question is ambiguous. At that, Eve answered, "We may eat fruit from the trees in the garden, but God did say, 'You must not eat fruit from the tree that is in the middle of the garden, and you must not touch it, or you will die.'" Though God said, 'Don't eat.' Eve says that God said, 'Neither eat nor touch.' There is complaint against the commandment in her answer. Also Eve slightly distorts the word, 'will surely die' and says 'lest you die.' We can see that

Blessing God gave human race

- Gave rest (Gen.2:3)
- Beautiful ground of life (Gen.2:8)
- Freedom to choose (Gen.2:9)
- Had man share God's ministry of creation (Gen.2:15)
- Fellow worker to help one another (Gen.2:24)

Life and death
God's plan was changed due to the disobedience of Adam and Eve. The issue of death caused by Adam's disobedience was solved by the victory (victory of Adam's descendant) of Jesus' cross on Calvary, and was extended to the last victory in new Jerusalem.

Eve had doubts of the commandment God had given.

The serpent changed the word of God completely, 'You will surely die' into 'You will never die.' The serpent tempted Eve by saying, 'Your eyes will be opened, become like God and know good and evil.' This is one of Satan's strategies and characteristics. Satan perverts the word of God by changing it slightly and similarly.

"When the woman saw that the fruit of the tree was good for food and pleasing to the eye, and also desirable for gaining wisdom, she took some and ate it. She also gave some to her husband, who was with her, and he ate it. Then the eyes of both of them were opened, and they realized they were naked; so they sewed fig leaves together and made coverings for themselves" (Gen.3:6-7).

After they committed sins, what was not in their mind came into being. What happened to them as soon as their eyes were opened? None other than feeling shame and fear. Since their relationship with God was destroyed, eventually they came to fear upon hearing the voice of God. As such, sin isolates us from God.

Adam and Eve, who took and ate the fruit of knowing good and evil, paid their price for their sins. Adam had to experience painful toil. Eve had to experience pain in childbearing. All human beings had to return to dust. The Earth was cursed due to man's sin.

After God clearly talked about the sins of human beings and their punishment, He took pity on Adam and Eve who sinned and put leather garments on them. This reveals how God forgives and pities even sinners.

3. Cain and Abel Gen. chap.4-5

After some time, Cain, the eldest son of Adam and Eve became jealous of his brother Abel and then for the first time in human history, a murder took place. The Heart of God, who was so pleased after creating the universe, grieved in front of the mind of evil human beings.

God made the genealogy of the righteous be continued by giving Adam and Eve another son (Seth) of theirs in place of Abel who was killed by Cain. This was a preparation for God to work out his work of salvation.

We can feel God's great grace also through the genealogy of Genesis chapter 5. We can confirm that the blessing given to Adam did not end during his lifetime but was being handed down to his descendants continually.

Justice and love
That the God of justice loves man to the end even while disciplining him is a theme flowing constantly from Genesis and throughout the whole Bible.

4. Noah's Flood - God's Tears Gen. chap.6-9

Genesis chapter 6 records that the sins of human beings originated by the sins of Adam and Cain came to fill the Earth and all the plans human beings were thinking in their minds were evil.

However, despite the diappointment in humans, He chose a man called Noah and implemented an important plan through him; He had Noah build a large ark. Noah started the tough work by carrying the heavy cypress woods on his shoulder for a long period of time. We can presume that he was laughed at by people around him. Enduring all this, he built a huge ark with cypress woods and pitch. The eight family members of Noah and all kinds of animals (two each for male and female) entered the completed ark.

At last it began to rain and some time later all the land went into waters. When the shrieks of those who shouted for help filled the world, I think that he would have first felt very pitiful when he saw a countless number of people and animals dying. **The drops of rain that came down ceaselessly and covered the world were God's tears. The whole world was full of God's tears.**

Finally the flood came to an end and the land was revealed. Getting out of the ark, Noah chose some animals and sacrificed burnt offerings to God. God gave His rainbow for Noah's family members, as a sign of promise that He would not destroy the Earth with flood again and blessed them, saying "Be fruitful and increase in number and fill the Earth."

Ark

The ark Noah built was 135m long, 22.5m wide and 13.5m high. It had three floors. Scholars guess that this size ship could contain more than 43,000 tons.

5. Genealogy – Fulfillment of Promise Gen. chap.10

The contents of Genesis chapter 10 are the genealogy which we often come across in various parts of the Bible. "Be fruitful and increase in number and fill the Earth." The names of so many people in Genesis chapter 10 are the evidence that the word of that promise was fulfilled.

6. The Event of Babel Tower Gen. chap.11

God wanted to fill the whole Earth with people, but they planned, on the contrary, not to be scattered but to make their name known by building high cities and towers and to want to go up as high as the heavens. God scattered them by force by creating different languages. This was the event of Babel Tower. However, we can see God's firm plan of salvation through Shem's genealogy in the second half of Genesis chapter 11. **We come to expect Abraham, a man prepared in the midst of the event of Babel Tower.**

The meaning of 'Babel'
'Babel' has the meaning of 'vain sound.'
Vain sound 1: "We will have the top of the tower reach heaven."
Vain sound 2: "We will make a name for ourselves."
Vain Sound 3: "We can avoid being scattered."

Write down the contents of this lesson in the form of Tong Story

Let's pray in a loud voice so that we may be able to teach the contents of this lesson to our children

- Teach them to your children, talking about them when you sit at home and when you walk along the road, when you lie down and when you get up……so that your days and the days of your children may be many……as many as the days that the heavens are above the earth (Deuteronomy 11:19-21).
- you know those from whom you learned it, and how from infancy you have known the holy Scriptures(II Timothy 3:14-15).

02 Lesson History of Patriarchs

Genesis chap.12-36

Accumulative reading amount 3.3% 1189

The One Year Tongdok Bible Days 5-12 | Reading time 70 minutes

TongBible Story over view

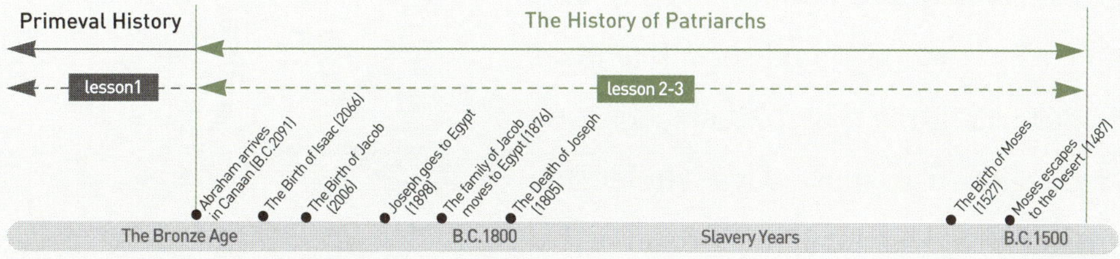

Reading the Old Testament in detail in the order of history (2)

We go on to read Genesis chapters 12 to 36. It is about the story of the era of patriarchs. Abraham was chosen to fulfill God's plan to bless all things through one man. The story is unfolded through the lives of Isaac and Jacob.

How to read the history of patriarchs

Chaldean Ur where Abraham lived was a place located at the lower part of Mesopotamia. Civilization was highly developed. Leaving behind all the benefits of the civilization, Abraham moved to the land of Canaan. God chose Abraham and his descendants and established a relationship with them and had the plan to bless all the nations of the earth through them.

It is not easy for us to relate to Abraham's faith. He was the man who left his home by believing in the word of God. Also, when he was ordered by God to offer Isaac, he obeyed focusing on the fact that it was God who ordered him rather than hesitating with personal agony. The fact that Isaac was born was God's miracle. Reading down Genesis, we can observe how Abraham experienced God through his long journey of life and on what basis of relation he could become a 'friend of God.'

Tong Point

Abraham who became God's friend!!
Let's carefully review the process until Abraham was called God's friend.

1. From Chaldean Ur to Canaan Gen. chap.12

One day God came to Abram (his previous name) and commanded him to leave the land and go to the land He would show. He lived in Chaldean Ur, a city where civilization was highly developed in those days. He left his hometown for the land of promise by obeying the word of God.

Abram's journey

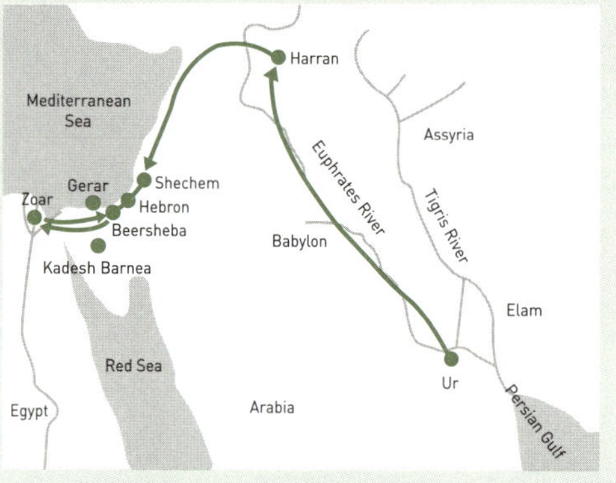

The lineal distance from Chaldean Ur to Haran was about 1,000km, which is quite a long distance in consideration of 444.3km (general railroad) from Seoul to Busan. It was about 800km from Haran to Canaan. Abram traveled the total linear distance of about 1,800km (he must have traveled crooked roads.)

God gave Abram two promises about 'descendants' and 'land.' First was that God would make Abraham's descendants as many as stars of the sky and sands of beaches. The second was that the land of Canaan where he would stay would be given to his descendants. **This promise about 'descendants and land' is an important core for understanding the Pentateuch and Joshua and also an important foundation for understanding God's world management.**

2. Offer Isaac as a Burnt offering Gen. chap.13-22

Abram who moved to Canaan had time to deeply fellowship

The way of obedience
For Abraham the way to Mt. Moriah was the "way of suffering"(Via Dolorosa) as the way to Calvary was for Jesus. However, he also obeyed the word of God without complaining or questioning.

with God for 25 years trusting the promise about descendants. Abram who lived walking with God through a variety of training courses was circumcised at the age of 99, and his name was changed from 'Abram' to 'Abraham.' God also changed his wife's name from 'Sarai' to 'Sarah.' Abraham means the 'father of many nations' and Sarah means 'mother of many nations.'

After a long waiting, at last their son Isaac was born. Abraham must have loved and held dear Isaac born at his age of 100. One day God commanded Abraham, "Take your son, your only son, Isaac, whom you love, and go to the region of Moriah. Sacrifice him there as a burnt offering on one of the mountains I will tell you about" (Gen.22:2). Isaac was the son of promise God mentioned, but He asked Abraham to surrender the son to God.

However, Abraham made up his mind to obey the word of God because he paid attention to the fact that it was God who asked him to do so, rather than to God's request and its contents.

The moment Abraham held a knife in his hand toward Isaac at Mt.Moriah, God made Abraham his friend. **Abraham gave his only son to God while 2000 years later God gave His only son Jesus Christ for the descendants of Abraham.** Abraham and God became friends by sharing the experience of giving their most precious sons for each other.

3. Abraham and Sarah buried in the cave of Machpelah Gen. chap.23-25

Time passed and Abraham's wife Sarah died. When Sarah died who had come together in Abraham's journey of faith from Chaldean Ur, he bought Machpelah cave in Hebron and buried her there. And then he planned to find a wife for Isaac after losing his mother.

Abraham entrusted his servant Eliezer from Damascus with the duty of bringing a bride for Isaac. Eliezer from Damascus was both Abraham's faithful servant and trusted friend of faith while he lived the life of faith and had been with him all along. He lived up to his master's expectation by going as far as Harran and brought Rebekah as bride for Isaac.

Abraham was called by God and died at the age of 175 and was buried beside Sarah in Machpelah cave.

The land of Hebron

Hebron which Abraham bought as burial place of Sarah became a very important land from generation to generation in the history of Israel. Later it became the base of Caleb of the tribe of Judah and the central place where David was anointed as king of the tribe of Judah.

Tong Point

The story of Isaac (Gen.25:12-chap.26) : The succession of faith from Abraham to Isaac.

The story of Jacob (Gen.27-chap.35) : The succession of faith from Isaac to Jacob the younger, not Esau the elder out of the twins.

4. Isaac, The man of Obedience and Yielding Gen. chap.26

Now Isaac unfolded his age by being handed down the life of faith and obedience of Abraham. However, his wife Rebekah

The obedience of Isaac

Obeying his father

- When he was bound as burnt offering(Gen. chap.22).
- Command about his future bride (Gen. chap.24).

Obeying God

-Obeyed the word of God who told him not to leave the land even during famine(Gen. chap.26).

did not become pregnant even twenty years after their marriage. God who heard the earnest prayer of Isaac and his wife gave them twin children called Jacob and Esau at his age of sixty.

A famine came upon the land of Canaan during the days of Isaac. God told Isaac not to go down to Egypt while giving him the promise about 'descendants and land'(Gen.26:2-5). Isaac accepted God's command and stayed in the land of Gerar and sowed seeds in a barren soil. As a result, even though the farming was done during the years of extreme famine, he reaped a hundredfold. God saw Isaac's obedience and blessed him greatly.

Then an unfortunate event occured; the people of Gerar covered every well Isaac dug with dirt. They became jealous of Isaac who suddenly became rich. In order not to quarrel with them Isaac dug wells again. As a result, they recognized that Isaac was a good man and God was with him and therefore came to Isaac and made a treaty with him.

5. Conflict between Jacob and Esau Gen. chap.27

When the prayer of Isaac and Rebekah for children was answered, God said, "The older will serve the younger"(Gen. 25:23). Accordingly, Isaac and Rebekah had to deal with this matter considerately and maturely.

However, neglecting the will of God, Isaac was going to bless Esau. Realizing this, Rebekah omitted the right procedure of reminding Isaac of the word of God and then made Jacob receive his father's blessing by deceiving him. Jacob cooperated with his mother about this wrong method and then was blessed by his father. At this, Esau thought that previously he had been deprived of his birthright by his brother Jacob (Gen. 25:29-34) and now Jacob stole from him his father's blessing. So naturally, Esau became very angry at Jacob.

6. Jacob's life in Harran Gen. chap.28-31

Running away from his elder brother Esau who became extremely angry, eventually Jacob had to flee to the house of Laban (his mother's brother) in Harran. Jacob began to work in Laban's house. He worked hard for a wife and wealth that he became the head of family of four wives, twelve sons and one daughter. However, there was always anxiety and quarreling in Jacob's household due to the conflict between Leah and Rachel, the two wives who were constantly jealous of each other. Jacob experienced conflict with Laban who was also his father-in-law

Jacob's way of life
Even though there was the way of life of obeying and yielding his grandfather and his father had discovered and the way of life of serving God that the fathers of faith had laid down, he failed to accept and inherit them positively. As a result Jacob's life was struck by much conflict and suffering.

Tong Point

Jacob's family

No	Name	Meaning	Mother
1	Reuben	See, a son	Leah
2	Simeon	God hears	
3	Levi	Attach	
4	Judah	Let's praise Him	
5	Dan	Judge	Bilhah (Rachel's servant)
6	Naphtali	Struggle	
7	Gad	Fortune	Zilpah (Leah's servant)
8	Asher	Joy	

No	Name	Meaning	Mother
9	Issachar	Hire	Leah
10	Zebulun	Abundant gift	
11	Joseph	Hope He will add	Rachel
12	Benjamin	Right hand's son, Rachel named him 'Benoni' meaning, Son of sorrow	
13	Manasseh	Forget	Manasseh & Ephraim were Joseph's sons but Jacob adopted them after moving to Egypt.
14	Ephraim	Fruitful	

over the matter of property. This became the turning point that Jacob ended his twenty year life in Harran and left for Canaan his home town.

7. Jacob who returned home Gen. chap.32-36

Esau

Esau was someone who chose specific interest rather than good name. He sold his birthright for one bowl of lentil soup thinking that his position as the first born was not meaningful compared with substance. However, the genealogy of Esau's descendants in Genesis chapter 36 once again proves that God loves all people indiscriminately. Between Esau and Jacob God had Jacob be able to inherit His promise given to Abraham. However, he was not indifferent to Esau.

Even while Jacob walked toward the land of Canaan (according to the word of God) who told him to return home, his mind was full of fear of his brother, Esau. However, God had already moved the mind of Esau and prepared a sincere table of reconciliation. Jacob met with Esau by the grace of God and was reconciled with him.

Jacob lost his wife Rachel near Bethel. Isaac became so old that he died in Hebron and Esau and Jacob buried their father together. The genealogy of the descendants of Esau in Genesis chapter 36 shows the origin of the people of Edom. Seen from the whole Bible, the genealogy of Esau's descendants later becomes the background of the books of prophecy including Obadiah.

Write down the contents of this lesson in the form of Tong Story

Let's pray in a loud voice so that we may be able to teach the contents of this lesson to our children

- Teach them to your children, talking about them when you sit at home and when you walk along the road, when you lie down and when you get up……so that your days and the days of your children may be many……as many as the days that the heavens are above the earth (Deuteronomy 11:19-21).
- you know those from whom you learned it, and how from infancy you have known the holy Scriptures(II Timothy 3:14-15).

03 Lesson

Entering Egypt and Birth of the Nation

Genesis chap.37-50

Accumulative reading amount 4.86% 1189

The One Year Tongdok Bible Days 13-17 | Reading time 45 minutes

TongBible Story over view

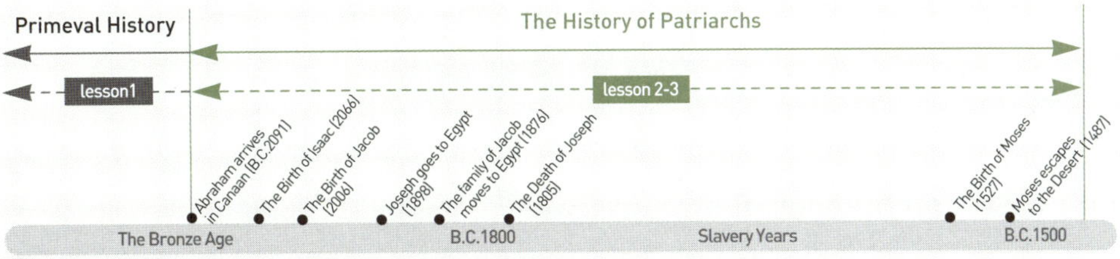

Reading the Old Testament in detail in the order of history (3)

We go on to read Genesis chapters 37 to 50. The story of Joseph is unfolded. There exists the interval of over 200 years between Genesis chapter 50 that ends with the death of Joseph and Exodus chapter 1 where 'a new king who did not know Joseph' appears.

How to read the story of Joseph

The portion from Genesis chapters 37-50 is filled with the stories of Joseph and his brothers. This was the time when about 200 years passed since God had told Abraham to go to the land He would show him. Joseph lived a total of 110 years. He served as prime minister for at least 14 years after he was appointed the position at age 30 and his power of influence in Egypt even after that was indeed great. Joseph's father Jacob arrived in Egypt at the age of 130 and died at the age of 147. Although it was when much time passed after the seven year famine was over, Jacob's funeral was a seventy day funeral which was the magnitude of Egyptian national funeral. From this we can know that Joseph's power of influence in Egypt was tremendous. Therefore, our emphasis on the shape of seventeen year old Joseph wearing a richly ornamented robe and thirty year old Joseph as prime minister of Egypt could not be enough for us to see the total flow of Joseph's life. Joseph carried out the important role of stepping stone in the process of his family, who originated from Abraham, becoming the great nation.

Tong Point

The story of Joseph - will and vision

The story of Joseph is very important as the household of faith that started from a man called Abraham was connected to the becoming of a nation in Exodus. Jacob's will became Joseph's vision and then Joseph's will became the vision of Exodus. Jesus' will had become the vision of not only his disciples but also us today. Let's connect 'Genesis' the first story of the Bible to the 'vision' that makes possible the 'will', which is the last word of humans and their new beginning.

1. The beginning of Joseph's training Gen. chap.37-38

The story of Joseph

Much portion of Genesis is about the story of Joseph(Gen. chap. 37-50). Joseph connected family and nation.

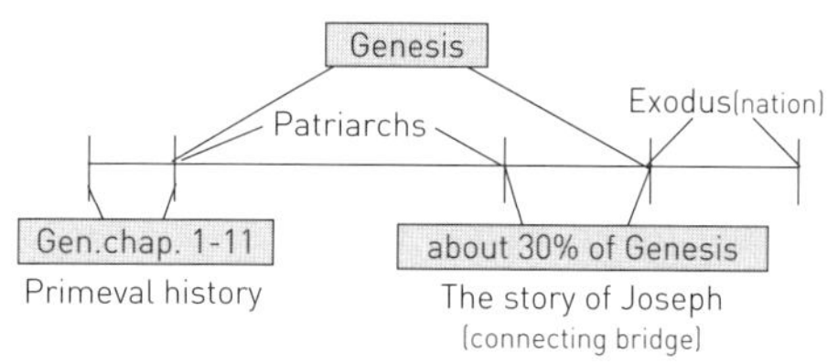

Jacob's obsession of material and love was more extreme than anybody else's. Such act of Jacob could not help but be a great pain to the other family members who were excluded from his love. When his dear wife Rachel died, he began to pour out his favoritism intensively on Joseph who was born from Rachel. As a result, Joseph was sold as slave to the remote foreign land of Egypt by his elder brothers who were jealous of him. And Jacob, who thought that Joseph was dead, came to love Bemjamin (Joseph's younger brother) wholly.

Joseph was sold as slave to the house of Potiphar the captain of Egyptian palace guard. From then on, Joseph went through the training slavery for about twelve years.

2. The process of Joseph's training Gen. chap.39-40

Joseph's life as slave, which started when he was 17 years old, was grueling and tough. His language was not communicated, his body was very tired everyday and above all, possibly he cried every night because of his yearning for home, his father and his younger brother. However, Joseph thought about what plan and providence God sent him to Egypt in, even in the midst of his suffering whose reason he could never figure out. Since he harbored his trust in God and the dream He gave him, he endured the tough life of slavery in Egypt.

Joseph's training
- Potiphar Home School
  - market economy education
- Prison school
  - politics administration education

Aware of Joseph's smartness, integrity and excellent ability to handle matters, Potiphar entrusted Joseph with the duty of family manager to control all his possessions. One day Potiphar's wife asked Joseph to sleep with her because he was very handsome. Joseph rejected it firmly. Joseph was put in prison because of the lie of Potiphar's wife who had a grudge against him for running away from her. **While Joseph was going through this process of training in the house of Potiphar and prison, he was being equipped with qualification for a greater duty.**

Even in prison Joseph was taken note of by the warden and was made to be in charge of all affairs of prison. There Joseph came to know chief baker and chief cup bearer of Pharaoh and interpreted their dreams. The chief baker died and the chief cup bearer was restored to his job, as interpreted by Joseph. From the day the chief cup bearer got out of prison, everyday Joseph expected to be released from prison with the help of the chief cup bearer, but nothing happened for two years.

3. Joseph who became the premier of Egypt Gen. chap.41

One morning, there was a commotion in the palace over the matter of interpreting the dream Pharaoh dreamed the previous night. The chief cup bearer who had forgotten Joseph's request for favor two years earlier suddenly remembered Joseph who was still in prison. Called out of prison and standing in front of Pharaoh and hearing all the detail of the king's dream, he said: "the dreams are one." Then he interpreted the dreams very clearly in detail. One step further, Joseph presented answers for the seven year great abundance and seven year famine. Immediately aware that Joseph was an excellent man fit to be a partner in ruling Egypt, Pharaoh jumped out of his throne and appointed Joseph as premier, entrusting him with managing the country in connection with the famine and great abundance.

4. Reconciliation of brothers after 22 years Gen. chap.42-47

About nine years passed since Joseph became premier. The famine struck not only Egypt but also Canaan. The family of Jacob had to come to Egypt in search of food two years after famine struck them.

The ten brothers met Premier Joseph and bowed down to

Judah and Benjamin

Judah	Benjamin
• Fourth brother Judah	• Youngest brother Benjamin
• David of the tribe of Judah	• Jonathan of the tribe of Benjamin
• Southern Judah(Kingdom): tribe of Judah + tribe of Benjamin	
• Jews in danger of destruction	• Queen Esther of tribe of Benjamin
• Jesus of the tribe of Judah	• Apostle Paul of the tribe of Judah

him. Unlike Joseph who recognized his elder brothers immediately, they failed to recognize him. Unable to find Benjamin in the group, Joseph put them into a dilemma by branding them as 'spies' in order to solve the friction among brothers. He imprisoned one of his brothers (Simeon) and said to them, "Bring your youngest brother to me" and sent the remaining nine elder brothers back.

Jacob's sons went to Jacob and conveyed the message of the Egyptian premier to him that they were to bring Benjamin to Egypt. However, Jacob absolutely refused to send Benjamin. It was because of his attachment to Benjamin. If Jacob had abandoned his attachment to Benjamin quickly, the day when he could see his son Joseph would have been expedited much faster.

When his eldest son Reuben persuaded him, Jacob did not change his mind. But when his fourth son Judah earnestly persuaded him, Jacob gave in and said, "If I am bereaved, I am bereaved." When the father gave up his greed and attachment, the foundation of his family was established again.

Benjamin and his elder brothers who came to Egypt again to get food met with Joseph. Joseph gave them a final test. He created a situation in which Benjamin stole his precious silver cup, and threatened to make him his slave. It was the order of Egyptian premier nobody could dare to violate. In the midst of the dire situation nobody could do anything about, the fourth brother Judah stood up and said, "Please don't be angry with your slave." Judah's saying which began with this word showed that their father and youngest son were not simply "father and son", but life and death was connected between them. Therefore, he said that he would remain in place of Benjamin and pleaded with Joseph to send suspect Benjamin back to their father. Confirming Judah's sincere love for his younger brother Benjamin and his father and Judah's deep devotion for their family community, Joseph cried loudly. With the confession, "I am Joseph. It is God who sent me here," he relieved the guilt that the elder brothers had. Joseph cried as much as he wanted as if he were venting out all tears he had spared until then.

5. Wills of Jacob and Joseph Gen. chap.48-50

Jacob's family emigrated to Egypt according to Joseph's proposal and God's permission. Holding the position of premier, Joseph excellently carried out the duty of having the family community settle in the land of Goshen and solved the problem of the seven year famine, which was the grand national disaster.

Time went by and the day of Jacob's death approached. Calling together his sons, Jacob blessed them according to the standard of their lives he had observed until then. And as his last will he told them to bury him in the cave of Machpelah in Canaan. Joseph held his father Jacob's funeral for 70 days in the scale of Egyptian national funeral. And with the permission of Pharaoh, Joseph went down to Canaan to hold his father Jacob's funeral along with not only his family but also lots of

Fulfillment of promise about descendants
The theme of who is the heir of the kingdom of God first appeared in Genesis chapter 12. Once Genesis comes to an end and the cover is opened, the conclusion was 70 family members of Jacob. The heirs of God's kingdom increase from 70 to about two million between Genesis and Exodus.

Egyptian subjects. Seen from the flow of the Old Testament Bible, this was like rehearsal of Exodus out of Egypt to happen later.

Joseph came to die at the age of 110. Joseph was the man who walked with God and realized God's dream and vision all his lifetime. He was cool in head and warm in heart. His will that his body be buried in his homeland showed that God's promise was not over but under way(present progressive tense).

Write down the contents of this lesson in the form of Tong Story

Let's pray in a loud voice so that we may be able to teach the contents of this lesson to our children

- Teach them to your children, talking about them when you sit at home and when you walk along the road, when you lie down and when you get up……so that your days and the days of your children may be many……as many as the days that the heavens are above the earth (Deuteronomy 11:19-21).
- you know those from whom you learned it, and how from infancy you have known the holy Scriptures(II Timothy 3:14-15).

Session 2

A Dream for All Nations

Tong Map

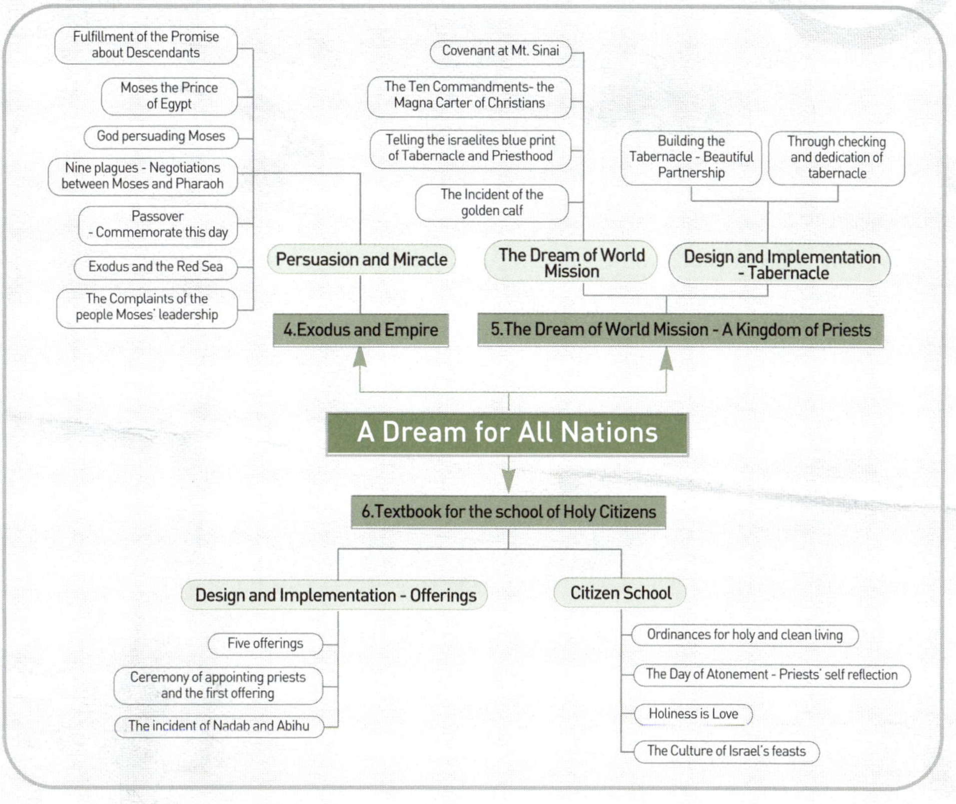

Tong Concept

- **God called the nation of Israel to make them A Kingdom of Priests and holy nation.'**

We can see a change that while in Genesis God called a man Abraham, in Exodus he called a nation who were his descendants. He proposed to them (who became a nation) that they were to have the dream of becoming ' A kingdom of priests and holy nation' for world mission. Let's study while meeting with God who dreamt toward the nation of Israel on the basis of 'dream for all nations.'

- **One year at Mt.Sinai when the greatest foundation was laid!**

During the period of one year at Mt.Sinai since Exodus the most important foundation of the nation of Israel was laid. Let's study while remembering the Ten Commandments, various laws, tabernacle, offerings and the like were aimed at making them 'A kingdom of priests and holy nation.'

Tong At a glance

* Looking around the forst

In Exodus 1:6-7 we come across the background against which Jacob's descendants ended up becoming slaves. In Genesis is revealed God's calling a man whereas in Exodus the nation of Israel is revealed as tool for God's world management. The event of Exodus is crucially important when studying the Old Testament.

During this period the laws including Ten Commandments were given. Israel enjoyed the privilege of being educated and trained directly by God for 3400 years ago.

* Land and annual ring

Assuming the time of Exodus according to the record of the Bible, we come up with B.C.1446, 480 years earlier than B.C.966 when they started building Solomon's temple, on the basis of I Kings 6:1 which says the temple construction was started 480 years after Exodus.

* Wind and Climate

Around B.C.1500-1200 Egyptian Pharaohs built huge pyramids as their tombs. Moses was in that position of succeeding the brilliant civilization. Palaces, shrines and tombs were very majestic and decorative. But these were the result of cruelly oppressing slaves and having them put into forced labor. Education, commercial prosperity and political position were only for a few people of privileged class.

Tong Seeing the forest

Exodus

A very tough negotiation between Moses and Pharaoh took place for around six months and eventually the nation of Israel came out of Egypt. God lead them to Mt. Sinai and there trained them for about a year. In Exodus was the covenant in which God made the people of Israel 'A kingdom of priests and holy nation.' The laws, regulations and statutes given to the people by God were recorded there. Here we can also see the scene where the people of Israel obeyed in making the tabernacle, which symbolized God's presence, according to the design God gave them.

Leviticus

Leviticus was God's warm love letter sent to human beings. It is like a manual of explanation from God who made human and also made to help them so that they could live healthily and rightly in this world. It records five kinds of sacrificial methods that the people of Israel should do in order to meet God deeply in the tabernacle they completed over a period of about six months, and detailed responsibility of priests and the tribe of Levi who were to lead in carrying out the work.

These complicated and troublesome procedures were actually the love of God who opened the way human beings could come to Him and ask Him for forgiveness when they sinned against Him. From Leviticus chapter 11, we see the requirement of God which was 'holiness' from human beings. He gave necessary principles so that people could respect each other and keep establishing their relationship rightfully. Through Leviticus, we can learn that protecting the weak, caring for the sick and comforting the poor are true 'holiness'.

04 Lesson

Exodus and Empire

Exodus chap.1-18

Accumulative reading amount 6.6% 1189

The One Year Tongdok Bible Days 18-24 | Reading time 50 minutes

TongBible Story overview

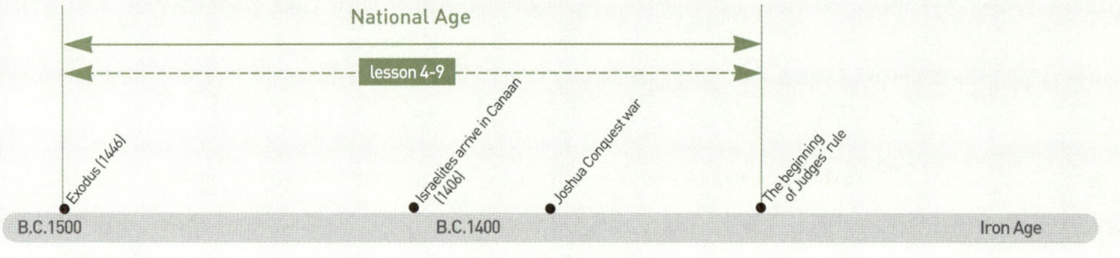

Reading the Old Testament in the order of history (4)

Exodus chapters 1 to 4 are the record of happenings from the birth of Moses to him being called by God at Mt.Sinai at the age of 80. The following chapters 5 to 11 are the story of events happening for six months when he had breathtaking negotiations with Pharaoh after his return to Egypt. And eventually in chapter 12, Israel carried out the ceremony of Passover that was to be commemorated forever and then came to get out of Egypt; a remarkable historic event. The story appearing in Exodus chapters 12 to 18 are about what happened for three months from Israel's Exodus to their arrival at Mt.Sinai.

How to read the event of Exodus

The Israel people who were treated as precious guests by the Egyptians in the days of Joseph ended up being slaves due to the changes in Egyptian dynasties. If we review the historical background a little more, we find that the age when Joseph lived and worked in Egypt was during the 12th dynasty of Egypt. Afterward, the Hyksos dynasty came to power in Egypt dethroning the previous 12th dynasty. A new king who did not know Joseph, who was honored highly during the 12th dynasty, came to rule Egypt. He prohibited the Hebrews from moving their residential location from one place to another and deprived them of the freedom to choose jobs and further made them slaves.

Then later the Hyksos dynasty was destroyed and then came 18th dynasty which was the most powerful empire in Egyptian history. This 18th dynasty tormented the Hebrews to such an extent that they planned to kill all Hebrew male babies. Right this time Moses was raised by a woman called Hasepsut who was Pharaoh's daughter.

Tong Point

Persuasion, miracle and judgment
The whole process of Exodus can be summarized as 'persuasion and miracle.' Expressed otherwise, compromise is 'persuasion.' And the nine plagues were God's miracles and judgment. The miracle of God was not so much about the miracle itself, but a grave method to persuade the Egyptians.

1. Fulfillment of the Promise about Descendants Exo. chap.1

Covenant and fulfillment
We can know that God's promise about descendants among His promises to Abraham was fulfilled in Exodus chapter 1 over 500 years later and His promise about land was fulfilled after Joshua chapter 10. As such, God's promises and plans are long and far-reaching.

After Jacob and his 70 family members came down to Egypt, the descendants of Israel gradually "were fruitful, multiplied and prospered and became very powerful, filling the whole earth." However, the new king, who did not know Joseph, was afraid of the prosperity of the Israel people and made the people of Israel slaves. He gave a fearful order that if male babies were born by an Israelite, all be killed. Watching down on the agony of Israel who were to be wiped out, God prepared Exodus.

2. Moses the Prince of Egypt Exo. chap.2

Egypt Daily page one

Moses, a new Hebrew politician who has been taken note of, Fled during night with accusation of murder and abandoning dead body!

"Seemingly his political life ended, A reliable source says He fled to Midian desert......"

About this time a man was being prepared. A baby, who was doomed to die upon his birth because he was a Hebrew boy, floated down the Nile River. It was a very tough measure of the parents who could no way keep the child. This male child who was delivered by Pharaoh's daughter was named 'Moses' which meant being 'saved out of water.'

Living as an Egyptian prince until the age of 40, Moses received the best education given to the Egyptian royal family. However, he never forgot that he was an Israelite. One day he went outside of the palace and happened to see an Israelite and an Egyptian fighting each other. He killed the Egyptian and hid the body. He soon learned however, that this was disclosed to the public and left everything that night and fled to Midian, because he was in danger of being killed. The headline of (Egypt Daily) the next morning probably was filled with the news of Moses' defection.

3. God persuading Moses Exo. chap.3-4

Moses, who was suddenly turned into a shepherd of sheep in the desert from the position of Egyptian prince, spent 40 years as a shepherd. One day he was tending to sheep as he was reaching Mt. Horeb where he went everyday. God came to him. Telling Moses His plan of Exodus, God said that He would entrust him with this duty.

However, Moses did not hear God at first because he was afraid of Egypt he had experienced and did not know well about God. **God persuaded Moses who was exhausted through his 40 year desert life. By showing miracles and even getting angry, God succeeded in persuading him.** Finally Moses was persuaded by God's will because he came to realize and believe that God's power was greater than that of Egypt.

4. Nine plagues
- Negotiations between Moses and Pharaoh Exo. chap.5-10

The outward appearance of Moses who reemerged in the political stage of Egypt with a staff in his hand 40 years later, was extremely shabby.

Egypt Daily **Society page**

"Last night Moses who had defected 40 years before, returned"

Yet, as a courtesy to Moses who lived once in the Egyptian palace, Pharaoh met with Moses. Moses told Pharaoh that since the people of Israel served God, they should go on a three day journey and offer sacrifices to Him and if not, God would punish them with pestilence or sword. However, it was no surprise that Pharaoh did not allow this to happen and stop the labor of as many as 600,000 strong men.

From this time on, God's power began to appear through various plagues. Every time there were plagues such as blood, frogs, lice, flies, hailstones, and the like, Moses told Pharaoh that Israelites should go to offer sacrifice to God. Pharaoh refused to release the labor power of Israel by all means saying; only male Israelites will go for sacrifice, take children but not animals, and so on.

Egypt's Disobedience and God's punishment

Contents	Pharaoh's Response	Other things
1.Blood	Unyielding Heart	Egyptian Magicians also did
2. Frogs	Unyielding Heart	Egyptian Magicians also did
3.Gnats	Unyielding Heart	Egyptian Magicians could not
4. Flies	Permitted Exodus, changed mind	Except Goshen
5. Death of livestock	Hardened heart	Except Israel's livestock
6.Boils	Hardened heart	
7.Hail	Confesses, "The LORD is just and I and my people are evil."	Except Goshen
8.Locusts	Let only men leave Egypt	
9.Darkness	Permitted Exodus except livestock	Except Goshen
10.Death of the firstborn	Exodus of all Israel	All Egypt

5. Passover
- Commemorate this day Exo. chap.11-12:36

God attempted nine negotiations with Pharaoh through Moses for six months but they were not accomplished due to Pharaoh's refusal. Now the last plague was to come. The last plague which was to kill all the first born of Egypt was to hold Pharaoh responsible for disobeying the word of God and to ask the people of Israel for minimum practical obedience. The minimum obedience was that the people of Israel were to believe the word of God spoken by Moses,which was to kill lambs and smear the blood on the top and both sides of the doorframe.

'Passover' was the day when the people of Israel rejoiced the most in hundreds of years. This was the day of new start when they ended a long period of slavery and was the day they were to commemorate forever. God also considered this day important and made this day the first year of the history of Israel.

Passover
- Passover is one of the three greatest Jewish feasts along with the Feast of Weeks and the Feast of Tabernacles. It is 'Pesah' in Hebrew and Passover in English, which means "go over" "pass".
- Take one year old purse male sheep or goat on the tenth day of month of Abib (Solar Calendar March - April) and keep it until the 14th and around the sunset put its blood on the top and both sides of the doorframe. Roast its meat over fire and eat it with unleavened bread and bitter herbs, with belts around their waist and sandals on their feet and staff in their hands and eat in haste. The leftover is to be burned.
- Do this seven times every year, seven days each time and worship God on the first and last days.

6. Exodus and the Red Sea Exo.12:37-chap.15

Finally, God sent signals and the people of Israel went out of Egypt quickly. However, not long afterwards, the Egyptian army pursued them with horses and chariots. Trembling with fear, the people of Israel complained to Moses.

The moment Moses raised his staff and extended his hand over the seas saying, **"The LORD will fight for you ; you need**

Exodus path

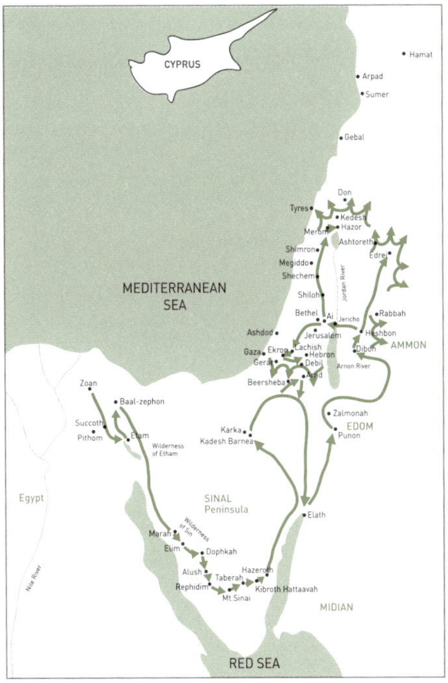

only to be still." (Ex.14:14), the Red Sea which stood in their way was split into two and the seas became dry land. The people of Israel were able to cross the Red Sea quickly. When the people of Israel all had crossed the sea, God destroyed Pharaoh and his army in the middle of the Red Sea. In Exodus chapter 15 is recorded the song Moses and the people of Israel sang giving praise and glory to God after watching all this.

7. The Complaint of the people Moses' leadership Exo. chap.16-18

The people of Israel who got out of Egypt arrived in the desert of Sin in one and a half months. Here they ran out of food and complained to Moses. God had already been preparing Manna but unfortunately, the people of Israel began to complain non-stop from here.

Israel who left the desert of Sin came to Rephidim. There they could not find water to drink and complained to Moses again. God commanded Moses to "strike the rock with his staff." Normal people would find it difficult to obey this word. However, **Moses believed that water would come out if he obeyed God's command to strike the rock and so he struck it. It was Moses who took God for His word.**

Following the advice of his father-in-law Jethro, Moses appointed captains of thousand, hundred, fifty and entrusted them with relevant work. Indeed, Moses was the man who

God's nicknames

- Jehovah(Ex.3:14)
  - I am who I am
- Jehovah Jireh(Gen.22:14)
  - God will provide
- Jehovah Nissi(Ex.17:15)
  - Jehovah is my banner
- Jehovah Salom(Jud.6:24)
  - God who gives peace
- Jehovah Chidkenu(Jer.23:6)
  - Jehovah is our righteousness
- Jehovah Chbauth(Ps.24:10)
  - Jehovah Almighty
- Jehovah Samma(Ezk.48:35)
  - God is there

deserved to be called an 'unparalleled leader.'

Write down the contents of this lesson in the form of Tong Story

Let's pray in a loud voice so that we may be able to teach the contents of this lesson to our children

- Teach them to your children, talking about them when you sit at home and when you walk along the road, when you lie down and when you get up……so that your days and the days of your children may be many……as many as the days that the heavens are above the earth (Deuteronomy 11:19-21).
- you know those from whom you learned it, and how from infancy you have known the holy Scriptures(II Timothy 3:14-15).

05 Lesson The dream of World Mission - A Kingdom of Priests Exodus chap.19-40

Accumulative reading amount 8.69% 1189

The One Year Tongdok Bible Days 25-32 | Reading time 60 minutes

TongBible Story overview

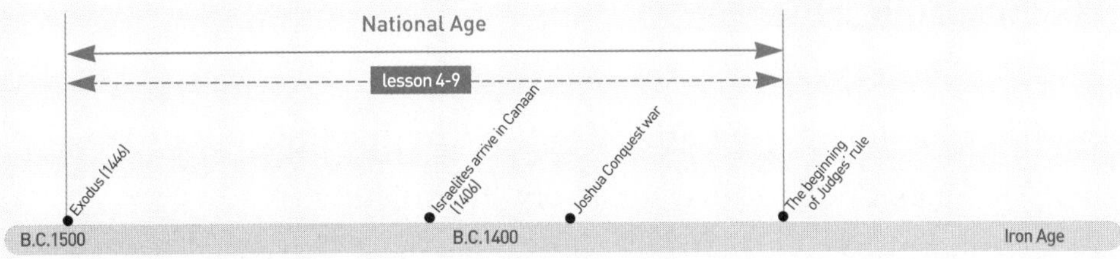

Reading the Old Testament in the order of history (5)

The record from Exodus chapters 19 to 40, Leviticus chapters 1 to 27 and Numbers chapter 1 to 10:10 are about the incidents that took place during the year while Moses and the Exodus generation were staying at Mt. Sinai. Knowing this fact alone is very helpful for us to understand the Pentateuch. While the Exodus generation were staying in the foothills of Mt. Sinai, they received the laws of God and built the tabernacle.

How to read the record of Mt. Sinai

The people of Israel arrived at Mt.Sinai about three months after Exodus and came to reside there for about a year. The events that happened at this time are recorded from Exodus chapter 19 to the end of Exodus, all of Leviticus and up to Numbers 10:10.

God led the nation of Israel out of Egypt, to deliver them suffering from the persecution and oppression of Egyptians. He called them to become 'A kingdom of priests and holy nation.' Obeying God, the people of Israel established a covenant, which was called 'Covenant of Mt.Sinai.' After the covenant was established, God taught them the laws including the Ten Commandments over a period of a year when they resided at Mt. Sinai. God had them build the tabernacle so that He could meet with them anytime. He made them engrave the names of the people of Israel, which were written on the documents of Egyptian slavery on precious stones stuck into the robes of priests.

Tong Point

The dream of missions

During the one year at Mt.Sinai the foundation of God's 'dream of world missions' was laid. 'A kingdom of priests and holy nation' were the foundational stones of world missions. God's dream for all nations is the thought we should always harbor in our heart as we read through the whole Bible.

1. Covenant at Mt. Sinai Exo. chap.19

About three months passed after Exodus. The Iraelites resided at Mt. Sinai. God prepared for a very important work with the people of Israel.

God first spoke. It was about becoming 'A kingdom of priests and holy nation.' God meant that they should become the holy nation of God and become the leader in doing God's work as kingdom of priests for the whole world.

The people of Israel answered, "Yes, we'll do so." This meant that a promise was established between God and the people of Israel. **In Exodus chapter 19, all of Leviticus and Numbers chapters 1-10 records God's word of how the people of Israel were to live as God's people on the basis of this promise.**

Dream for nations
"All nations"(Gen.12:1-3).
"The world is mine"(Exo.19:5).
"In Jerusalem, all Judea and Samaria and to the ends of the world"(Act.1:8).

Six months(Ten plagues) Three months(Arrive at Mt.Sinai)

Egypt → Exodus (Left Rameses) → Mt.Sinai

Stayed at Mt.Sinai for a year
(Exo.chap.19-40, Lev., Num.chap.1-10:10)

Two streams of law

1. Laws about the attitude toward God
2. Laws about the attitude toward neighbors

2. The Ten Commandments - The Magna Carta of Christians Exo. chap.20

God began to tell the people of Israel the laws; the Ten Commandments included. **The core of what God asked the people of Israel for through the Ten Commandments was 'love for God and neighbors.'** We can say that these were basic principles and the most essential.

However, hearing the voice of God at Mt. Sinai directly, the people were afraid to meet with God. The people of Israel did not realize the love of God who wanted to meet with them face to face. Asked by the people, Moses was to hear the word of God alone himself and convey it to them. From this time on, going up and down Mt. Sinai, Moses carried out the duty of playing the role of mediator between God and the people.

3. Telling the israelites blueprint of Tabernacle and priesthood Exo. chap.21-31

Luxurious uniform

God gave Aaron sacred garments and then made him carry out the duty as priest. Aaron's garments were luxurious but in fact they were also working uniform which he was to wear while carrying out various duties.

Asking the people of Israel to wait, Moses went up Mt. Sinai and met with God. **The word God gave Moses on Mt. Sinai can be largely summarized into 'Building the tabernacle' and 'Appointment and mission of priests.'** Explaining the blueprint of the tabernacle where God would meet with the people of Israel, God additionally told the details of tabernacle utensils, altar of burnt offering, patterns of tabernacle courts and the like. God planned to have continual meetings with the people of Israel through the tabernacle.

Also, God appointed Aaron and his sons as chief officiators of sacrifice in the tabernacle. From then on, the officiators of sacrifice of Israel were priest Aaron and his descendants from generation to generation.

The priest had a lot more duties do carry out. The roles were various; ranging from killing sheep and cattle and sacrificing them to burning incense painstakingly. God has separated Aaron and his sons in order to give them mission.

4. The Incident of the golden calf Exo. chap.32-34

● Moses' 40 days vs. 40 days of the people of Israel

40 days did not pass since Moses was called by God and went up on Mt.Sinai before the people of Israel committed a great sin. God was telling the people of Israel the blueprint of 'tabernacle' that He would give them. Tabernacle symbolized God's presence. However, the people did not wait for this deep preparation of God but ended up making the idol of golden calf.

God who saw this ridiculous sight happening below the mountain became very angry and said He would destroy the people of Israel. Moses knelt before God and asked for His mercy while praying to Him. **Moses worried about God's prestige.** It meant that he was afraid that the Egyptians, might mock God because of this matter, saying "Their God took His people into the desert and just killed them."

● The prayer of Moses who thought about both the nation and God's prestige

Hearing Moses' earnest prayer, God cancelled His will to destroy Israel. Then Moses came down the mountain and saw the shameful sight before him. He was so angry that he broke down the two stone tablets by throwing them down and had them burn the golden calf, crush it and made it into flour. Then he mixed it with water and made all the people drink the 'gold flour tea.' In addition, as punishment for that sin, about 3,000 people were killed.

The next day Moses went to God and repented of the sin of the people on their behalf. He pleaded with God to forgive the people telling Him he was willing to have his name erased out of the LORD's book. Knowing very well how much God loved and spared the people of Israel, Moses held on to that Heart of God and asked Him to forgive.

Then the people of Israel waited again for Moses for 40 days patiently who went up on Mt.Sinai. God and the people of Israel were made to be close to each other again through this event.

Tong Point

Design and implementation - Tabernacle

During the one year at Mt.Sinai two important things were established. They were none other than 'tabernacle' and 'sacrifice.' Let's remember that 'design' was the work of God who was the expert and 'implementation' was obedience, participation and devotion of the people of Israel. Design had purpose as well.

5. Building the Tabernacle
- Beautiful Partnership Exo. chap.35-39:31

Under the leadership of Moses who came down the mountain in 40 days the work of Israel's building tabernacle was launched. Repenting of the sin of making the golden calf, the people of Israel gave in their treasures for the work. **Through the blue print that was given by God, the tabernacle was completed with the obedience and participation of the people and their practice. This was a beautiful partnership between God and Israel.**

Moses appointed Bezalel and Oholiab as the ones specifically responsible for building the tabernacle and as implementers. They did their best and finished building the tabernacle. Also, they made sacred garments for Aaron and his sons. God had them attach the breast plates, which had 12 precious stones, on these garments to be worn by priests who was to be used before God. And He had them inscribe the names of the 12 tribes of Israel on the precious stones.

Design and Implementation
- Design : God's providence, management
- Implementation : Human efforts, sweat, devotion, loyalty, service

Designer	Implementer	Creature
God	God	The Garden of Eden
	man	The ark
	man	The ark of testimony
	man	Temple
	God	New heavens and new earth

6. Thorough checking and dedication of tabernacle
Exo. 39:32-chap.40

After the tabernacle and sacred garments were all completed, Moses took time to check and verify that all utensils had been made as instructed by God. As soon as Moses finished the last check and said, "All is finished!"; we can assume that all the people immediately shouted the sound of joy and embraced one another. The great work which took about six months was completed.

Now the tabernacle where they met with God had been completed and priests were ready to mediate between God and human. The official channel through which God could meet with the people of Israel had been opened.

Here let us briefly put in order what happened at Mt.Sinai during the one year.

- March - first year .... arrived at Mount Sinai(Exo.19:1)
    - Moses' first Mount climbing : God gave laws regarding slave, murder, restitution, morality, justice and welfare, feast and so on along with Ten Commandments (Exo. chap. 20-23).
    - Moses' first going down: God established covenant with people, reading aloud written covenant (Exo.24:1-11).
    - Moses' second climbing: God gave him ordinance on blueprint of tabernacle and priest (for 40 days) (Exo. chap.24:12-chap.31).
    - Moses' second going down: Moses broke down stone tablet in front of the people who made golden calf (Exo. chap. 32-33).
    - Moses' third climbing: climbed Mount Sinai to receive tablets again(for 40 days). Established covenant again (Exo. 34:1-28).
    - Moses' third going down: As Moses came down, his face was radiant (Exo.34:29-35).
    - Building tabernacle: collected gifts willingly given by the people, appointed workers like Bezalel and Oholiab and began making tabernacle and sacred garments for priests. Finished in about six months (Exo. chap. 35-39).

- January 1, second year .... Dedicating tabernacle (Exo.40:17)
    - The word of Leviticus was given for a month and 20 days till

they left Mt.Sinai after the tabernacle was built.

- January 14, second year .... second Passover (Num.9:1-3)

- February, 1. second year .... first census (Num.1:1)

- Feb. 20, second year .... left Mount Sinai, moved toward the Desert of Paran (Num.10:11-12)

Write down the contents of this lesson in the form of Tong Story

Let's pray in a loud voice so that we may be able to teach the contents of this lesson to our children

- Teach them to your children, talking about them when you sit at home and when you walk along the road, when you lie down and when you get up……so that your days and the days of your children may be many……as many as the days that the heavens are above the earth (Deuteronomy 11:19-21).
- you know those from whom you learned it, and how from infancy you have known the holy Scriptures(II Timothy 3:14-15).

06 Lesson

Textbook for the school of Holy Citizens

Leviticus

Accumulative reading amount 11.12% 1189

The One Year Tongdok Bible Days 33-42 | Reading time 70 minutes

TongBible Story over view

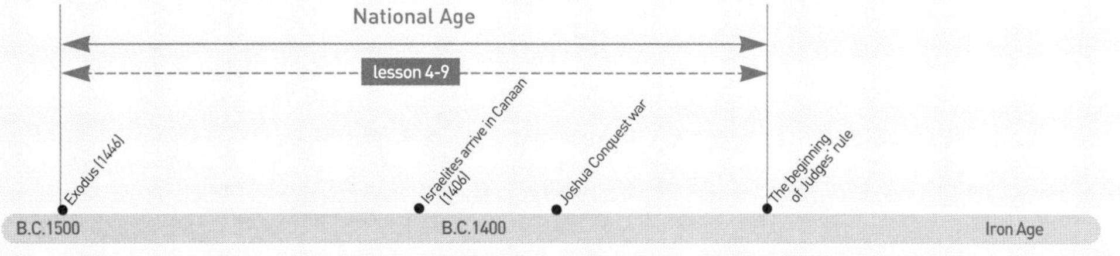

Reading the Old Testament in detail in the order of history (6)

In Leviticus chapters 1 to 27 is the continuous record of the year when Israel resided at Mt. Sinai.

How to read Leviticus

Cain and Abel, (two sons of Adam and Eve) were the first human beings to built altars and worship God. Afterwards, coming out of the ark, Noah built an altar to God and worshipped. Abraham, the man of faith built the altar wherever he moved for living and worshipped God. So did Isaac and Jacob.

Leviticus is the book which records intensively how people should worship God. However, it is not a reference book on methods of sacrifice that only priests were to read. A variety of sacrifices shown in Leviticus were instituted not to trouble people but in order to show how to be forgiven when people sinned against God. It explains in detail various methods for how people should serve God well and live healthily in this world.

Tong Point

Design and implementation - offering
Formerly in Exo. chap.35-40 we observed the design and implementation of the 'tabernacle.' Now God gave five methods of offering through the book of Leviticus. These five offerings were proposals for deeper fellowship between God and the people of Israel. Let's remember that offerings were intended not to trouble people but was a positive expression of God that He would forgive people who sinned and give them another chance.

1. Five offerings Lev. chap.1-7

Once the tabernacle had been completely built, God told them five methods of sacrifice in the tabernacle in thorough detail. These five types of sacrifice were procedures of God and people meeting with each other. In them were deeply rooted the Heart of God for His people. Therefore, to review the meanings contained in these methods of sacrifice is absolutely necessary for Christians today who are living the 21st century.

First, **the burnt offering** was an offering in which one offered fragrance to God with the attitude of offering oneself by taking cattle, sheep, goats, doves and placing one's hands on their heads and burning them on behalf of them.

The grain offering in which grain was offered had the meaning of offering property. It was to offer to God gratefully the grain people got as the result of working faithfully. The people of Israel were able to offer to God gladly the crops they attained as the result of working faithfully. On the other hand, **the fellowship offering** to be offered when gratitude happened was the offering in which God specially desired shared with neighbors. He had them offer its internal organs to Him by

Five offerings

- **The Burnt Offering**
  - burnt by fire and offered with the offering that has life. It meant redeeming one's life(life commitment)
- **The Grain Offering**
  - bake, fry or boil grain flour mixed with oil and incense and offer it
  - It meant committing wealth to God(wealth commitment)
- **The Fellowship Offering**
  - burns only fat, liver and kidney and the remaining part is to be eaten by priest and him who offers.
  - When there was an event of thankfulness, God ordered them to share food with neighbors.
- **The Sin Offering**
  - Priest lays his hand on the offering and sprinkles its blood on the altar
- **The Guilt Offering**
  - When one inflicted damage on what belongs to God or neighbor, he added one fifth more to it and offered it to God or paid back to neighbor and offered it.

burning it and eat the remaining meat with neighbors.

The sin offering was the offering to rectify the wrong when the people of Israel had committed sins and caused problems in relation with God. This was the blessed news that God wanted to convey through Leviticus. We can feel the Heart of God who till this day intends to forgive us.

The guilt offering was the offering in which the people asked God to forgive them for the wrongs committed by mistake when they unconsciously violated the word of God or did wrong to neighbors. Even though people were forgiven if they repented of their sins, God educated them to be responsible people by making restitution without fail.

Through the five offerings shown in Leviticus we can read the Heart of God who wanted to establish a holy relationship with His people.

2. Ceremony of appointing priests and the first offering Lev. chap.8-9

Aaron and his sons were appointed as priests to be responsible for offering. They were appointed new leaders and all Israel promised to follow them.

Aaron offered the first offering as priest. Presummably all the people of Israel including Moses watched Aaron with hands sweating, not to mention Aaron himself. God accepted the first offering with pleasure which Aaron was officiating. It was an impressive moment.

Leadership

That a leader is appointed who will lead the nation is no small matter. Especially all the more so it was for Israel who lived as slaves in Egypt. As Israel was under the leadership of Egypt and were not allowed any leadership of their own, God called Moses as their leader and appointed priests as new power group of leadership of Israel after liberating them out of Egypt.

3. The incident of Nadab and Abihu Lev. chap.10

However, a shocking incident happened that all Israel as well as the family of Aaron were surprised at after the ceremony of appointing priests and the first offering. God's fire came down upon and burned Nadab and Abihu, first and second sons of Aaron. Although the exact cause was not revealed, we guess from the immediately following word that they excessively drank wine and went to the sanctuary with fire other than the designated one. They got drunk and neglected their responsibility and then suffered the punishment. This event clearly showed what a great responsibility the mission given to priests was accompanied by.

Tong Point

The School of Holy Citizens
One year at Mt.Sinai was the period of education aimed at making the people of Israel, who had been just freed from slavery, no longer slaves but responsible citizens. It was the School of Holy Citizens for them. One of the important characteristics of this school was that it had the contents of education. Leviticus which was given for a month and 20 days after the tabernacle was built and until they left Mt.Sinai was the best textbook of 'the School of Holy Citizens' for them to become holy citizens.

4. Ordinances for holy and clean living Lev. chap.11-15

- Leviticus chap.11: foods the people of Israel were to eat and foods there were not to eat.

You may feel, "Wow, God intervened even in these small

things!" But these were the crucial details God had to let them know for their health in the environment of those days when they were not able to keep foods in refrigerators we use now. God who made human bodies became the best nutrition specialist.

● Leviticus chap.12: Restoring woman's body after delivery

God also educated about the period of a woman's time of restoring her body after baby delivery(Lev. chap.12). He gave the law that stipulated that women who gave birth to babies do not carry out hard work but spend time to meditate on the mystery of birth of life and God while resting comfortably.

● Leviticus chap.13-14: Ordinance about leper

Regarding leprosy, God educated about the symptoms in the long story of as many as 116 verses. He conferred on priests the right and duty to discern the symptoms and stipulated how to discern in detail(Lev. chap.13-14). Leviticus chapter 14 which stipulated the procedure of returning to the community of Israel when they were healed must have been no doubt the 'gospel' for the lepers.

Points priests were to memorize without fail
An important role of priests: to meet lepers and diagnose them. There were to be no mistake in diagnosis because it was the moment when the patient's life was at stake. Perhaps Leviticus chapter 13 was what priests had to memorize underlining the sentences repeatedly.

● Leviticus chap.15: Gift for life

The blessing of being fruitful and prosperous God promised and the peace and stability of homes were able to be realized through sound sex life. God told a variety of ordinances in order to prevent in advance the indiscriminate abuse of sex which was given as blessing by Him (Lev. chap.15).

5. The Day of Atonement - Priests' self reflection Lev. chap.16

Nadab and Abihu, the two sons of Aaron were killed for the sin of offering fire God did not designate and now two other sons remained. They had to make sure that priests would not get killed like them again while offering sacrifices to God. So God had priests offer sin offering for themselves first before they came into the sanctuary. This meant that the priests had an opportunity to reflect themselves beforehand.

God designated July 10 each year as the day when priests were to enter into the holy of holies once a year and had them observe it as 'day of atonement' when mediation was done for sins of all the people. **Day of atonement was the day of joy and gratitude when the people of Israel reflected themselves and all the people repented and got cleansed.**

6. Holiness is Love Lev. chap.17-22

Leviticus shows the list of 'sins for which the sinners must be killed without fail.' God proclaimed that as people distribute rotten fruit to the good fruits, so should the community of Israel likewise for the sinners. Otherwise, just as one rotten fruit can contaminate the rest of the fruits in the box rot, so can the community of Israel.

What is holiness? God told people to leave the corner of the field not harvested and not to pick all fruits of vineyard(Lev.19:9-10). It was ordered for the sake of the poor

The best textbook for citizens movement
Though God loves the weak, he does not take the side of the weak unconditionally. God who has the nature of justice along with love told people not to take sides in trials but to do the right thing.(Lev.19:15) In this sense, Leviticus is the best textbook which was absolutely necessary for citizens movement in this age.

and the foreigners. Holiness is love and that love should be followed by 'acting'. It is important for us to remember that holiness is not done by mouth alone but is practice as action through 'loving neighbors.'

7. The Culture of Israel's feasts Lev. chap.23-27

7 of Leviticus

- -Sabbath every 7 days
- -Sabbatical year every 7 years
- -Jubilee in the next year after 7 multiplied by 7
- -Pentecost 7 weeks after Passover
- -Pentecost and Passover were continued 7 days respectively
- -Feast of Trumpet in the 7th month
- -Feast of Tabernacle in the 7th month
- -Day of Atonement in the 7th month

In Leviticus chapter 23 God stated the various feasts Israel were to observe. They were Sabbath, Passover, Feast of Unleavened bread, July 1 Sabbath, July 10 day of Atonement and Feast of tabernacle. The culture of feasts God proposed was 'resting culture' and 'culture for the weak.' God ordered them not to work at all during feasts. This way the weak of society were made to rest sufficiently and all the people of Israel had time to think of God deeply. In Leviticus chapter 25 He explained laws about sabbatical year and Jubilee. And in chapter 26 He said two futures, namely; what will happen when the people of Israel live according to the word of God and when they do not. Blessing or curse were to be decided depending on the choice of the people of Israel.

Tong Point

The feasts of Israel

(Dates recorded in the Bible differ slightly from today's calendar)

Feast name	Date	Related verses	Meaning	Feast-ceremony
Passover (Day of Unleavened bread)	Jan. 14	Exo.chap.12-13	Commemorate liberation from Egypt	Put the blood of lamb on the doorposts and eat unleavened bread.
Pentecost (Feast of Weeks)	Mar. 6	Num.28:26	Celebrate each year's crop	Read through Exodus to commemorate the day they received the law at Mt. Sinai.
Feast of trumpets	July 1	Lev.23:23-25	Commemorate by blowing trumpets	Eat honey bread blowing the horn trumpet of sheep.
The Day of Atonement	July 10	Lev.23:26-32	The day for redeeming the sin of the nation	Fast all day and confess sins.
The day of tabernacle (Feast of Tabernacles)	July 15	Num.29:12-40	Commemorate sojourner's life in wilderness	Build tabernacle with palm tree or poplar and dwell inside.
The feast of Purim	Dec. 14	Est.9:21	Commemorate salvation from Haman's plot to massacre the Jews	Read the book of Esther. Exchange gifts each other and relieve the poor.

Write down the contents of this lesson in the form of Tong Story

Let's pray in a loud voice so that we may be able to teach the contents of this lesson to our children

- Teach them to your children, talking about them when you sit at home and when you walk along the road, when you lie down and when you get up……so that your days and the days of your children may be many……as many as the days that the heavens are above the earth (Deuteronomy 11:19-21).
- you know those from whom you learned it, and how from infancy you have known the holy Scriptures(II Timothy 3:14-15).

Session 3

The Manna Generation

Tong Map

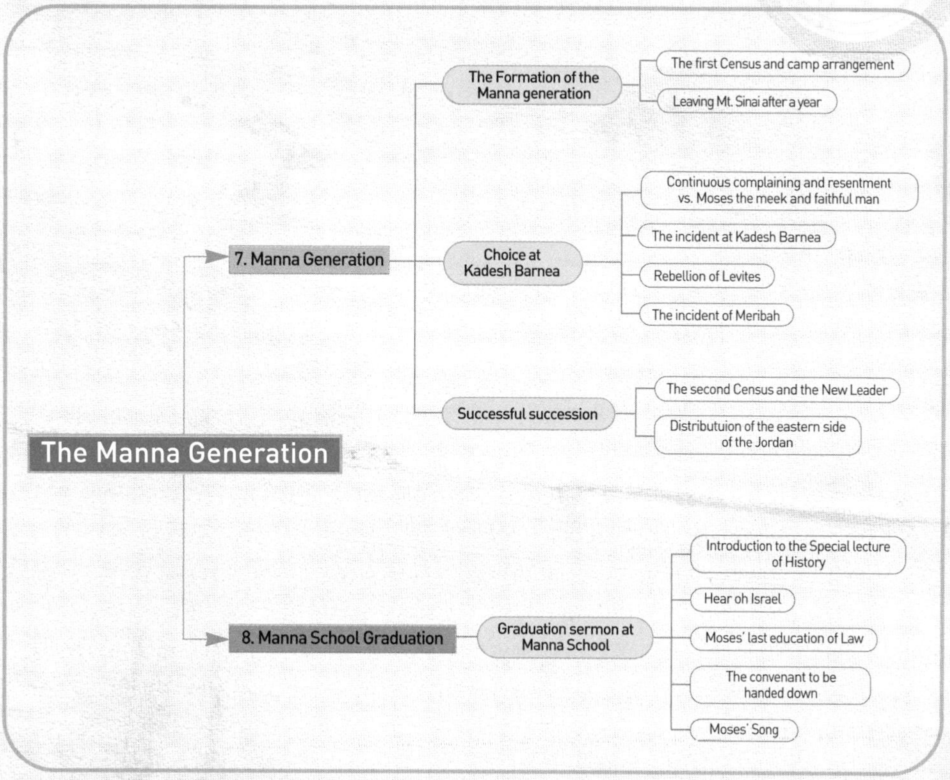

Tong Concept

- **The Manna generation as a result from the 40 year desert life!**

The 40 year desert life was decided by the worst choice made at Kadesh Barnea. Let's study while remembering that generation change was made from Exodus generation to Manna generation through this 40 year desert school.

- **The Manna generation different from Exodus generation! Due to education!**

Manna generation who grew eating Manna given by God from birth in the desert were taught God's law in detail by Moses. This was the greatest reason for Manna generation being able to be different from the former Exodus generation. After putting in order in a big frame the 'education' being made between the first census of Numbers chapter one and the second census of Numbers chapter 26, let's study while filling in specific contents.

Tong At a glance

* Looking around the forest

Finally the people of Israel who departed from Mt.Sinai for Paran desert reached Kadesh Barnea of Paran Desert. However the Exodus generation who heard the report of spies sent to Canaan were unable to move ahead toward Canaan and ended up all dying in the desert after spending 40 years there. Then there was the taking of the census of the Manna generation; their children. The second Exodus generation' who grew eating Manna in the desert (Num. chap.26). The book of Numbers ends with them preparing to cross the Jordan to enter Canaan.

Deuteronomy was a special lecture of history Moses gave the Manna generation to prepare them for entering Canaan.

* Land and annual ring

Kadesh Barnea is the area at the southern border of Canaan. It leads directly to Canaan if you go north from there. There is also a northern road called 'big road of king' through the south of Dead Sea after moving east. Though it was a detour compared with 'northern straight course', the people of Israel took 'big road of king' and moved ahead. However, in order to go through 'big road of king' they had to go through territories of Edom and Moab which were located south east of Dead Sea.

Moses sent a messenger to the king of Edom to ask him to let them go through but was rejected. Although Moses sent a team of envoys to Sihon king of the Amorites and Og king of Bashan, saying, "If you allow us to go through your land, we will never cause any damage but just pass," they attacked Israel rather than helping. However, through this unexpected war, Moses and the people of Israel came to capture the land (Num.21:21-35). We may say that Moses' sermon of Deuteronomy was delivered right before the Manna generation (who were staying in Arabah desert of Moabite Plain near the Jordan) crossed the Jordan.

* Wind and Climate

A typical document of treaty of the latter Bronze Age always includes historical prologue explaining the past relationships of the treaty signatories. Deuteronomy also takes that form. Moses remembered the 40 years from the time when the law was given the first time at Mt.Sinai (Deu.1:6). He briefly summarized the contents already dealt with in detain through Exodus, Leviticus and Numbers. In order to let the people of Israel know what God expected of them, Moses remembered the important events which became the historical turning points.

Tong Seeing the forest

Numbers The first part of Numbers began about one month after the ending of the book of Exodus. Israel took the first census in the desert of Sinai and marched toward Kadesh Barnea. They were equipped with a complete system and army almost 14 months after their departure from Egypt. However, the report of ten spies sent from Kadesh Barnea to Canaan discouraged the mind of people and eventually the Exodus generation who disobeyed God's plan all came to die while spending 40 years in the desert. This 40 year desert period was the time of testing and training for them and the time they were being equipped with the shape of God's army both in name and reality. About 40 years later, Moses took the second census of Manna generation who were the children of Exodus generation and carried out the work of distributing the land of Gilead they conquered in the east of the Jordan to the tribes of Reuben, Gad and the half tribe of Manasseh.

Deuteronomy 'Deut' of Deuteronomy means 'repeat' and 'watch.' Moses preached the word of God at Mt. Sinai 40 years prior to his death. This was a collection of sermons he concludedly preached to his beloved people of Israel. This can be said to be 'Moses' special lecture on history'. He began with briefly summarizing and recollecting the previous history and then once again explained God's law Manna generation were to keep and live on after entering and settling in Canaan. He finally asked them eagerly to choose the way of life on the crossroads of blessing and curse and to 'love God.'

07 Lesson

Manna Generation

Numbers

Accumulative reading amount 14.94% 1189

The One Year Tongdok Bible Days 43-57 | Reading time 110 minutes

TongBible Story overview

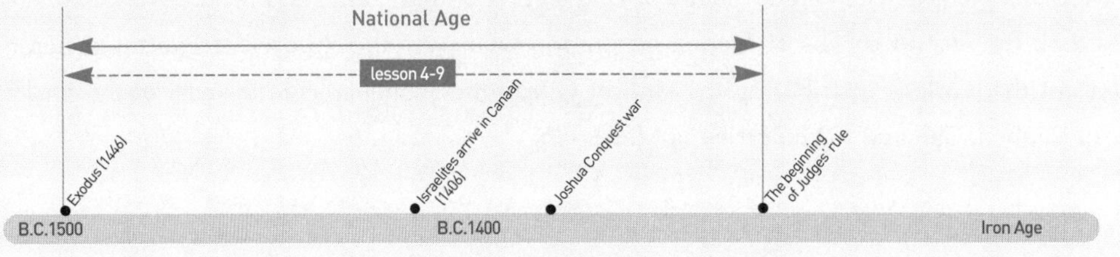

Reading the Old Testament in detail in the order of history (7)

In Numbers chapter 1 to 10:10 is the continuous record of what happened for a year when Israel resided at Mt. Sinai. We go on to read from 10:11 to the end of Numbers. Here are contained the period of 40 years spent in wilderness. This period was the second half of Moses' 120-year life and at the same time was the time when 'Manna generation' (who were new generation not born in Egypt but in wilderness) were being formed.

How to read Numbers

In Numbers are recorded two censuses of the people of Israel. While they stayed in the desert for forty years, they had censuses taken in the beginning and later parts. Surprisingly, the two results were about the same. Though they stayed in the desert where a plant could not grow nor farming could be done for forty years, the fact that the population of Israel were not reduced but rather maintained would have been impossible if God had not cared for them.

Tong Point

The formation of Manna generation
The census of Num.chap.1 specifically shows how God's promise to Abraham in Genesis about his descendants was realized, in addition to Exo.chap.1. Two censuses were taken throughout Numbers and their objects were different.

1. The first Census and camp arrangement

Num. chap. 1-8

● The first census

About the time they stayed in Mt.Sinai for almost a year, God ordered Moses to count the number of all Israelites who were 20 or older and were able to go to wars. The census in Numbers chapter 1 shows how God's promise made to Abraham about descendants in Genesis was realized and continued from Exodus chapter 1.

A total of two censuses were taken throughout Numbers. They appear in chapters 1 and 26. People for each census were different respectively.

- Numbers chap.1: First census - those out of Egypt; the number of Exodus generation
- Numbers 26: Second census - those to enter Canaan; the number of Manna generation

Arrangement of Israel's camp
(Number of People)

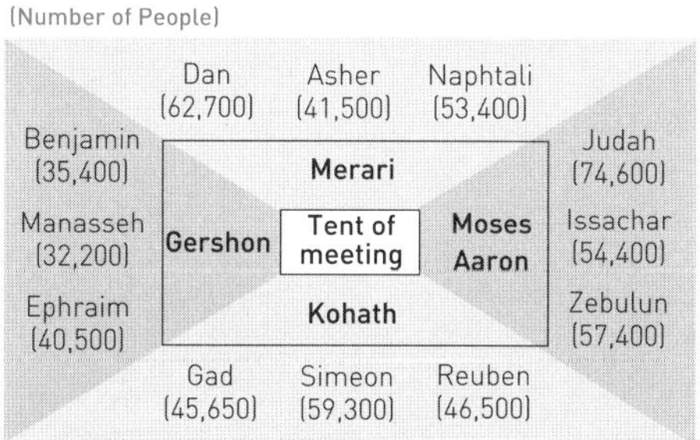

● Camp establishment

After counting was done by the tribe, camps were ready. By locating three tribes each in the east, west, south and north, Israel had come to have an organized army. **Here what was important was that the tabernacle of meeting was placed along with the tribe of Leviticus in the center of these tribes in the east, west, south and north. This was the difference the camp of Israel had from camps of other nations.**

Meanwhile, in Numbers chapter 8 were Levites separated for the work of God. During the last plague right before Exodus the people of Israel obeyed the word of God that told them to put the blood of lambs on the top and both sides of the doorframe and then could spare the life of their eldest sons. The tribe of Levi were chosen as the group on behalf of the eldest sons of the 12 tribes. From this time on Levites were made to help priests in the tabernacle.

Separating Levites

Males of other tribes were divided into two groups of above and below age 20. But males of Levi older than a month were separated and among them those above age 30 and below 50 were separated again. Males of other tribes at the age of 20 worked for the nation. However, males of Levi needed to prepare ten years more from age 20 to be able to work. If Levites were as old as a month, they were counted. Then they prepared 30 years, work 20 years and then had to retire. After they had become 50 years old, perhaps they taught preliminary participants who were younger than age 30.

2. Leaving Mt. Sinai after a year Num. chap.9-10

Exactly a year passed since Exodus. Recalling their past time, the people of Israel observed the second Passover. During the past year they built the tabernacle and experienced the glory of God coming upon it. The absolutely necessary ordinances for living as the holy people of God were instituted for them.

At last on February 20 of the second year it was time to leave Mt.Sinai. Clouds rose up on the tabernacle of testimony and the sound of trumpets for marching resounded dynamically in the camp of Israel.

Tong Point

Choice at Kadesh Barnea

Two choices were made at a place called 'Kadesh Barnea.' Ten leaders made a faithless choice and two, Joshua and Caleb, made a choice of faith. Because of the choice the people of Israel made that day, an extremely different road unfolded for them.

3. Continuous complaining and resentment vs. Moses the meek and faithful man Num. chap.11-12

It seems that Israel was not entirely ready yet. The people complained to Moses over food and then even those who were closest to Moses spoke evil of him. When Moses took a Cushite woman as his wife, Miriam and Aaron exposed his faults downgrading his leadership. This caused Miriam to become a leper and stay outside the camp for seven days. Moses meekly endured such complaining and evil speaking against him and God let him stand on his such authority. Moses was indeed meek and faithful.

4. The incident at Kadesh Barnea Num. chap.13-14

At last they arrived at Kadesh Barnea near Canaan. At this time, 12 promising young leaders from each tribe were chosen and sent as spies to Canaan. They were leaders equal to the level of Joshua and Caleb in qualification.

They travelled throughout Canaan as spies forty days and returned. There was too much difference between the two of them and the ten among the 12 who finished spying. Seeing Canaanites who were giants and their fortified cities, the ten leaders were so discouraged that they insisted that was better for them to return as slaves to the Egyptian. Caleb and Joshua shouted at the top of their voice, "we will devour them. Their protection is gone, but the LORD is with us. Do not be afraid of them"(Num.14:9). **That night the choice of the people of Israel was as if they forgot about the great Exodus. God could not help postponing the plan of conquering Canaan until 40 years later due to this incident.**

Journey of complaining

1. Taberah
Complained in the hearing of God → the LORD's fire consumed the outskirts of the camp.(Num.11:1-3)
2. Kibroth Hattaavah
Complained as they said they wanted meat → died of great plague before they chewed meat.(Num.11:4-35)
3. Hazeroth
Miriam talked against Moses for marrying a Cushite → Miriam became a leper seven days.(Num. chap.12)
4. Kadesh Barnea
Hearing the report on spying, they tried to kill Moses proposing that they return to Egypt → They came to wander in the desert forty years.(Num. chap.13-14)
5. Hormah
Korah, Dathan, Abiram and On formed a faction and opposed Moses and Aaron → The masterminds and their family were buried alive.(Num.16:1-35)
6. Zin Desert Kadesh
Complained about no water to Moses → In haste Moses had the rock produce water by striking it, not by ordering it. Moses and Aaron could not enter Canaan.(Num.20:2-13)
7. The land of Edom
They complained about rough roads → Many were bitten and killed by venomous snakes.(Num.21:4-9)

5. Rebellion of Levites Num. chap.15-19

Hearing that they were not to enter Canaan, the people of Israel complained to leader Moses just over the result of them being unable to enter Canaan rather than reflecting deeply upon their sins. Some Levites who were coveting the priesthood agitated some people, formed a party against Moses and rebelled. Thinking the priesthood as a kind of privilege, they tried to take it.

The families of Korah, Dathan, Abiram who agitated people eventually suffered the terrible punishment of being swallowed up by the earth which opened its mouth. That was the tragic

God who adjusts the height of eyes
What was the reason for God who created heavens and earth to make the long-dead staff bud and produce flowers? It was because he intended to confirm that he established priesthood painstakingly and it was the precious evidence of promise that he gave it to the people of Israel as a gift. In other words, Aaron's staff that budded was not what God wanted but his care of adjusting the height of eyes to the low level of Israel who lacked faith.

end of those who resisted against God.

In order to establish the authority of priest Aaron after this incident, God performed the miracle of having his staff blossom and bear the fruit of almond.

6. The incident of Meribah Num. chap.20-21

- Stern standard

The people again began to grumble against Moses and Aaron. "Why did you take us out of Egypt? Why make us suffer like this? There are no figs, no grapes. We don't have this and that..." Of course, what they said was technically the truth. However, God gave manna down from heaven everyday. Despite so, the Hebrews were grumbling against God and Moses counting only what they did not have.

God told Moses to 'order' the rock to produce water. However, Moses made the rock produce water by raising his arm and 'striking' it twice with his staff. At this, God made an important declaration onto Moses; since he did not reveal God's holiness, Moses and Aaron could not enter Canaan. Seeing this scene, we may think, "How can he get so extreme when Moses made just one mistake, is not there just a little difference between speaking and striking twice?" However, **the standard God demanded from Moses was different. God applied a strict standard which did not allow even that much disobedience.** Later Moses pleaded with God to let him cross the Jordan and see the beautiful land, but God said, 'Your mission is up to this' and just let him be satisfied with seeing the land of Canaan from afar.

● Moses who did his best up to the last minute

Yet, knowing that he could not enter Canaan, Moses did not neglect his remaining duties. As Israel approached Canaan, they had to wage wars with various Gentile peoples. When they occupied the eastern side of the Jordan, Moses led the battle (Num. chap.21). Through this battle they gained the land that belonged to Amorite king Sihon and Bashan king Og. From then on, the Bible called this region 'the east of the Jordan' or "land of Gilead."

Tong Point

Successful succession

The Manna generation who grew up in the desert eating Manna given by God for 40 years were taught the law of God through Moses thoroughly. Unlike the Exodus generation (their parents generation) they were well educated and trained. It was literally a 'successful succession.'

7. The second Census and the New Leader

Num. chap.22-31

● Case of successful succession : The story of Balak the Moabite king

God trained Israel in the desert and had them organize the system for forty years. Therefore, around the time Israel approached Canaan, they were turned into the army of God who deserved to enjoy fame among surrounding countries.

Population change by tribe
(number of people)

tribe	1st census	2nd census	population change
Reuben	46,500	43,730	-2,770
Simeon	59,300	22,200	-37,100
Gad	45,650	40,500	-5,150
Judah	74,600	76,500	+1,900
Issachar	54,400	64,300	+9,900
Zebulun	57,400	60,500	+3,100
Ephraim	40,500	32,500	-8,000
Manasseh	32,200	52,700	+20,500
Benjamin	35,400	45,600	+10,200
Dan	62,700	64,400	+1,700
Asher	41,500	53,400	+11,900
Naphtali	53,400	45,400	-8,000
Total	603,550	601,730	-1,820

● The second census

About this time, God had them take the second census(Num. chap.26). The total population was 601,730, which did not show much difference from the first census, 603,550. It was the result of God being with and keeping them in spite of the desert life which had various unfavorable conditions.

● Moses' last mission

Meanwhile, Moses who was informed of his death appointed Joshua as new leader and empowered him by shifting all his honor to him. In Numbers chapter 31 Moses waged a war with the Midianites which can be said to have been his last mission. Since Moses did not work for his greed but devoted himself as the servant of God, he was satisfied with his role and did his best to the last minute.

8. Distribution of the eastern side of the Jordan

Num. chap.32-36

The land where Israel settled was divided into two: the east and west of the Jordan. The east was already occupied (Num. chap. 21) and the west was yet to be occupied. Then some came to say that they wanted to live in the east before they occupy the west. They were none other than the Reubenites and Gadites. Seen from the big picture, it was not time to distribute the land but to occupy it. Their proposal that they would like to stay in the east of the Jordan might discourage the people. Therefore, upon hearing their proposal, Moses became very angry.

They said to Moses, "We'll have only our children and livestock stay here. Our men who are able to fight will go to the west side and fight alongside other tribes' men until they have occupied all the land of the west. When we fight, we'll go first to fight on the front line and will not return home until the war is over." Hearing this, Moses permitted their proposal. Then he distributed the land in the east also to the half tribe of Manasseh. This way the people of the two and a half tribes who were given the east of the Jordan ahead of other tribes came to lead in battles to come.

Numbers chapter 34 shows the specific scale and area of the land of Canaan they were to enter and settle in. This land was the land that had been kept in the Heart of God over 500 years since Abraham.

Wars during the 40 year Desert life

Scriptures	Adversary	Battlefield
Exo.17:8-16	Amalekites	Rephidim
Num.14:45	Amalekites & Canaanites	Hormah
Num.21:1-3	Arad	Hormah
Num.21:21-25	Amorites	Jahaz
Num.21:33-35	Bashan	Edrei
Num.31:1-12	Midianites	Midian

People who are scattered for mission

Land was not given to the Levites. Instead they were given 48 cities and pasture-lands surrounding them. (Num. chap.35). These 48 cities were not located in a certain place together but widely scattered in the regions where the people of Israel lived. They taught the people in each region and played the role of helping each tribe be able to live a God-centered life. This was also the fulfillment of what Jacob prophesied (Gen.49:5-7).

Write down the contents of this lesson in the form of Tong Story

Let's pray in a loud voice so that we may be able to teach the contents of this lesson to our children

- Teach them to your children, talking about them when you sit at home and when you walk along the road, when you lie down and when you get up……so that your days and the days of your children may be many……as many as the days that the heavens are above the earth (Deuteronomy 11:19-21).
- you know those from whom you learned it, and how from infancy you have known the holy Scriptures(II Timothy 3:14-15).

08 Lesson

Manna School Graduation

Deuteronomy

Accumulative reading amount 18.41% 1189

The One Year Tongdok Bible Days 58-70 | Reading time 100 minutes

Tong Bible Story overview

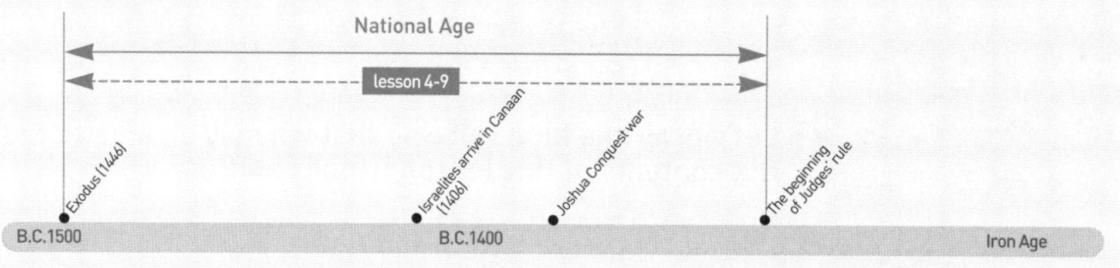

Reading the Old Testament in detail in the order of history (8)

We now read Deuteronomy. This is the portion that contains the 40 years Israel spent in wilderness. Deuteronomy is a written sermon left behind by Moses for Manna generation(the children of Exodus generation) in Arabah desert of Moabite plains before he died. From the perspective of Moses who preached Deuteronomy, we also read Psalm 90 written by him.

How to read Deuteronomy

Moses preached Deuteronomy to Manna generation right before they crossed the Jordan River. The covenant between God and the people had been already established at Mt. Sinai. However, now when all the people who were in the venue of establishing covenant with God had died and a new generation had to take up the mission of history, Moses realized the need to renew the covenant. Therefore, Moses explained the items of the covenant including the Ten Commandments to Manna generation again and made them establish the covenant with God for themselves.

Moses told them again all of how God had cared for and loved the people of Israel in the desert for forty years.

Tong Point

Graduation sermon at Manna School

Deuteronomy was Moses' four 'Graduation sermons at Manna School' delivered over a period of two months in Arabah desert of Moab Plain near the Jordan where they were staying, right before they crossed the Jordan to conquer Canaan. The core of this graduation message was to teach the children the wonderful way of A kingdom of priests. Forty years ago the dream of A kingdom of priests at Mt.Sinai was the joy of only one man called Moses, whereas now in Deuteronomy it was revealed as the joy of the 600,000 Manna generation.

1. Introduction to the Special lecture of History

Deu. chap.1-4

Educate

In order for a man to live properly in community, education is essential. That Moses was now preaching the word of Deuteronomy was part of this education. The contents were that when they settled in the land of Canaan for living, they were to not forget the experiences of Exodus and the desert life and make God's laws the basis of their life. Moses did not forget to ask them to teach their children as they were taught.(Deu.4:9-10)

Moses gave his last special lecture of history to the people of Israel as his will. He stressed that the reason God delivered the people of Israel out of Egypt and made them enter Canaan was not simply because their forefathers lived there in the past. Nor was it because they were righteous before God. **The reason they were able to enter Canaan was only because God remembered His covenant with Abraham and gave the land to them.**

Telling them again the previous incident of Kadesh Barnea in which all the people were in crisis, Moses asked them to keep their mind firm and to not be shaken. He also stressed that they were not to serve idols but serve only God who had led them so far.

2. Hear oh Israel Deu. chap.5-11

Moses taught the Manna generation the dream of A

kingdom of priests that contained Ten Commandments about the love for God and the love for neighbors which God Himself engraved on the stone tablets forty years ago.

Particularly the word of Deuteronomy chapter 6 verses 4-9 which begins with the phrase "Hear, Israel" is called 'Shema,' which meaning is very deep and important. "Hear, O Israel: The LORD our God, the LORD is one. Love the LORD your God with all your heart and with all your soul and with all your strength"(Deu.6:4-5).

"Teach them to your children, talking about them when you sit at home and when you walk along the road, when you lie down and when you get up. Write them on the doorframes of your houses and on your gates, so that your days and the days of your children may be many in the land that the LORD swore to give your forefathers, as many as the days that the heavens are above the earth"(Deu.11:19-21).

This was the word in which Moses who loved God in the past earnestly asked Manna generation again to love God. The core of the word preached by Moses who deeply loved God throughout his whole life was 'the Love of God.'

Shema
The sentences of Deuteronomy chapter 6 verses 4-9 are called "Shema"(Hear) in Hebrew. This is the core text of the Bible, which became the foundation of Judaism. The families of Israel meditated on Shema every morning and evening.

3. Moses' last education of Law Deu. chap.12-26

It can be said that the contents of the word from Deuteronomy chapters 12 to 26 were teachings about how specifically Manna generation were to live in the land of Canaan. God who already knew the culture of the land of Canaan wanted Israel to create God's culture to replace

Canaanite culture.

- Designated place of worship (Deu. chap.12)

Israel were to worship God as the people of God at the place of promise chosen and designated by God.

- The year for cancelling debts (Deu. chap.15)

God who delivered Israel out of the place where they were slaves ordered the year for cancelling debts to be observed. He told the people of Israel, who experienced what the joy of freedom was, to give freedom to those who still remained as slaves.

- Distribution of wealth through feasts (Deu. chap.16)

The feasts God commanded Israel to observe were the periods when people were to care for slaves, foreigners, Levites and weak neighbors so that they too can have benefits.

- Cities of Refuge (Deu. chap.19)

When someone did not intend to kill but actually killed a person by accident, God granted him cities of refuge where he could flee to.

- Right use of all produce of the land and tithe (Deu. chap.26)

When the people of Israel were made to live in Canaan, God commanded them to bring tithe of their produce to Him. That tithe was used to be shared with the fatherless, the widows, the foreigners, and the Levite so that they may also have a livelihood.

4. The covenant to be handed down Deu. chap.27-30

Moses proclaimed what Manna generation were to do first in Canaan after entering it was to set up large stones, write the laws there, build the altar and then sacrifice burnt offerings and fellowship offerings to God. God established a special covenant with the people of Israel that God became Israel's God and Israel become His people. He stressed that this special relationship between God and Israel should not be changed over the passing of time.

Tong Point

Moses' ministry finished.
In Deuteronomy chapters 31-34 are recorded the final request, song and blessing of Moses and Deuteronomy which ends with his death. There are two things Moses did as he finished his ministry. The first was to appoint Joshua as leader after him and the second was to tell the people of Israel what they were to do when they entered Canaan. After carefully reviewing this contents we together read Psalm 90 which was the song Moses sang with past history.

5. Moses' Song Deu. chap.31-34/ Psalm 90

Moses, who was the messenger between God and the people of Israel as God's servant and lived as a great leader for the past 40 years, now encouraged Joshua and again stressed the laws to be observed by Israel (Deu.31:7-13).

Moses' song(Deu. chap.32) that followed was summarization of the history of Israel until that point. The song of Moses was the song the people of Israel that was to be remembered forever. As the life of Moses who was an unparalleled leader came to end, the desert period of Israel's history came to the grand finale and the new history in Canaan with Joshua began.

Write down the contents of this lesson in the form of Tong Story

Let's pray in a loud voice so that we may be able to teach the contents of this lesson to our children

- Teach them to your children, talking about them when you sit at home and when you walk along the road, when you lie down and when you get up……so that your days and the days of your children may be many……as many as the days that the heavens are above the earth (Deuteronomy 11:19-21).
- you know those from whom you learned it, and how from infancy you have known the holy Scriptures(II Timothy 3:14-15).

4 Session

Succession of Faith

Tong Map

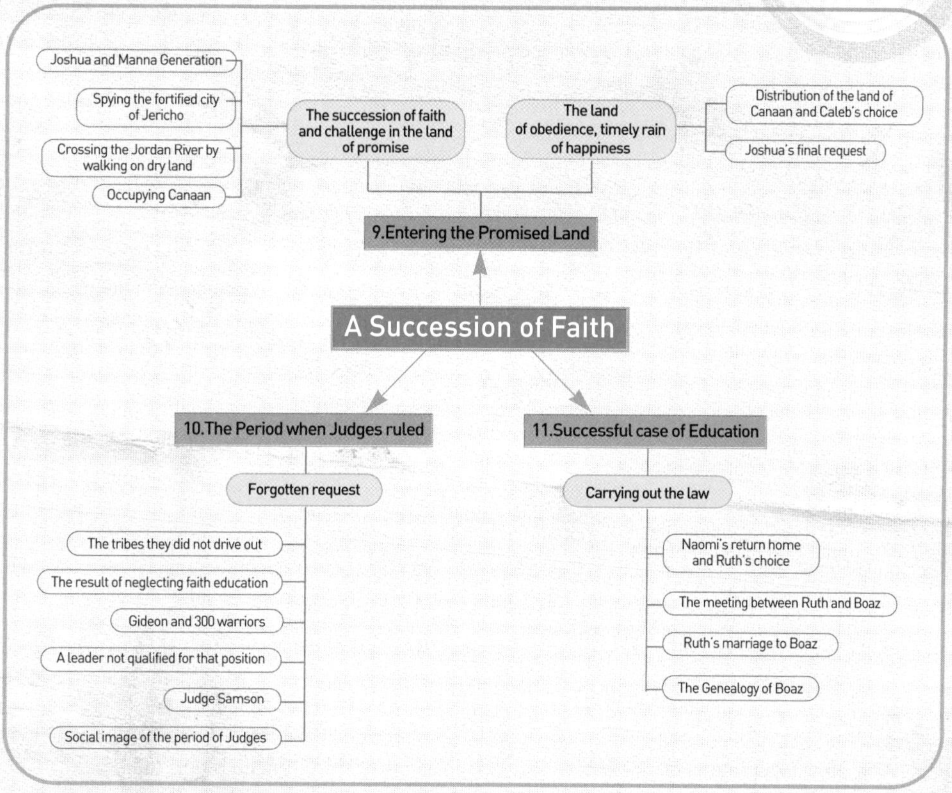

Tong Concept

- **From the viewpoint of success and failure in faith succession! Success, Joshua! Failure, Judges!**

The book of Joshua contains the Manna generation who accomplished the promise on land with faith. This is a case of good succession of faith. On the contrary, Judges shows us what kind of dark era came when faith succession failed. Meanwhile the book of Ruth is a story that happened in a small community in which faith succession was done well even amid the darkness of the ear of Judges.

- **Success and failure of faith succession, 'Faith education'!**

Success or failure of faith succession depends on 'faith education.'

Tong At a glance

* Looking around the forest

Joshua who became the new leader of Israel accomplished the historic task of 'Entering Canaan' with the Manna generation.

However, Israel failed in educating their children on faith. Therefore, during the era of Judges (lasting about 350 years) evil and arrogance of Israel forced God to send Judges to persuade them from serving idols and committing sins. The book of Ruth (amidst the dark times) was like an oasis which satisfied God's heart. The story of Ruth who became an ancestor of king David and Jesus occupies a very important place when seen from the overview of the whole Old Testament.

* Land and annual ring

Israel entered Canaan around B.C.1406. The land of Canaan was about 290km long and 65km wide. On its south was Shin desert and on its north were Lebanon mountains. On its east was Arabian Desert and on its west lies Mediterranean Sea. Canaan can be said to a geographically important area in that the continents of Europe, Asia and Africa meet together. Some part of Joshua and the second half of Judges chapter one show us that there was land yet to be conquered.

* Wind and Climate

It seems that around B.C.2500 Canaan was subject to Mesopotamia and accepted their language and civilization. Later, it ruled Egypt. Canaan probably flourished in culture from these influences.

That was why Israel came to settle in Canaan by being successful militarily but they were significantly influenced by Canaanites culturally and also impacted by Baal worship in terms of religion. The culture of ancient Near East was a morally corrupt and vulgar one due to the obscene immoral and cruel rituals of religions of Canaanites. Israel kept being warned by God not to follow such evil of Canaanite peoples.

Tong Seeing the forest

Joshua The Manna generation and Joshua who were trained in the desert with the Word by Moses over 40 years continued conquering the land of Canaan waging fierce battles for about five years. Various parts in the Book of Joshua witness the fact that this war was not just a conquering war but the war which gave them victory through their obedience to God. The people of Israel distributed the land by keeping with the scale of each tribe after defeating all the 31 kings in the west side of Canaan. It was to fulfill the repeated promise of God about the land since God promised to Abraham to give him the land in Genesis chapter 12.

Judges Judges shows what Israel looked like after the people of Israel conquered Canaan through the leadership of Joshua. However, they did not conquer all of that land. We can see that there were still Canaanites in various parts of the land. As a result, as time went by, Israel began to serve the idols Canaanites had been serving. In order to make them realize their sins and return to Him, God disciplined Israel by raising up neighboring nations. Israel sought God only when afflictions came upon them. God saved the people of Israel by sending 'judges' such as Gideon, Jephthah and Samson. However, Israel repeated the foolishness of returning to the previous sinful state when the afflictions stopped. God's sorrowful discipline and saving ministry of love for them were repeated continually.

Ruth The background of Ruth was the period of Judges. Elimelech and Naomi emigrated to Moab from Bethlehem with two sons to avoid the famine which was God's discipline. Eventually losing her husband and her two sons there, Naomi realized God's will and returned home to Bethlehem, accompanied by Ruth who was her Moabite daughter-in-law. The meeting between the faithful woman Ruth (who had a great filial piety and kept increasing her faith in the living God) and Boaz who practiced the law faithfully was never an accident. Through the genealogy shown at the last part of Ruth we come to confirm God's wonderful providence which was continued from Obed, the son of Boaz and Ruth to David.

09 Lesson

Entering the Promised Land

Joshua

Accumulative reading amount 20.49% 1189

The One Year Tongdok Bible Days 71-78 | Reading time 60 minutes

TongBible Story Overview

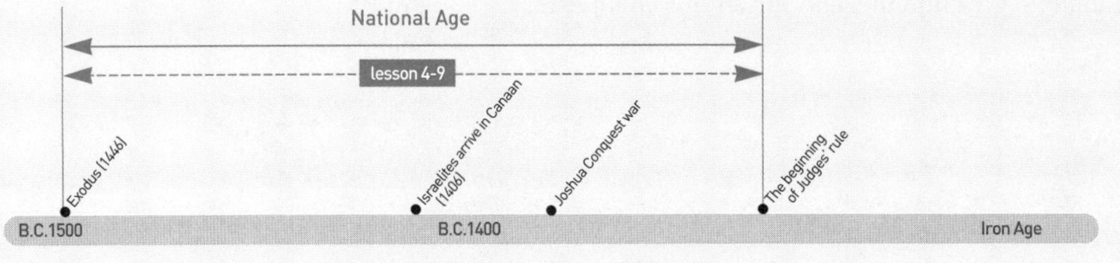

Reading the Old Testament in detail in the order of history (9)

And so continued the march on toward Canaan. Joshua chapters 1 to 12 contain the story of conquest war Joshua and Manna generation fought for about five years. The major contents of the following chapters 13-24 are the story of Israel distributing and settling in the land of Canaan.

How to read Joshua

The book of Joshua records the wars of conquering Canaan, the land distribution and the process of Israel's settlement in Canaan. Manna generation who were trained by Moses for forty years began to obey the word of God. They were different from their parents' generation who complained endlessly. Through the Manna generation, we are able to understand the successful results from.

Tong Point

The succession and challenge in the land of promise
The contents of Joshua chapters 1-12 are about the Canaanite Conquest battle. Let's review how the laws ordered through Moses were handed down to their community and what kind of challenge they faced.

1. Joshua and Manna Generation Jos. chap.1

Joshua
The original name of Joshua was 'Hosea'. Since he was from the tribe of Ephraim and his father's name was 'Nun', he was called also 'son of Nun'. After Exodus he was an assistant to Moses. He was chosen as a spy for the land of Canaan and insisted on the possibility of conquering Canaan along with Caleb. Eventually he became the leader of Israel after Moses.

Now the leadership of Israel was handed down to Joshua from Moses and the history of Manna generation (who graduated from the desert school) began. However, Joshua who was faced with occupying Canaan trembled. God said to Joshua who was afraid, "Be strong and courageous" and promised to him that He would be with Joshua wherever he went.

Comforted and encouraged by God, Joshua appointed the advance party of war. They were the tribes of Reuben, Gad and the half tribe of Manasseh to whom land was already distributed in the east of the Jordan. They promised to Moses that they would become advance party when other tribes would go to occupy the west of the Jordan. Joshua reminded them of that promise. At that, they said, "We will do all you have commanded us to do and will go wherever you command us to go. Just as we obeyed leader Moses in everything, we'll follow you." **This is the scene where we can see how excellently the Manna Generation were trained.**

2. Spying the fortified city of Jericho Jos. chap.2

They gathered their energy and began the war of conquering Canaan. Deeply considering before occupying the city of Jericho, Joshua sent two spies to Jericho. However, not long after these two spies went to spy the city, they were disclosed to the enemy. Fortunately, they came to overcome the crisis safely with the help of a woman called Rahab who was living in Jericho. At this time Rahab made a confession before the two spies.

She already heard and knew that God made the Red Sea dry during the Exodus and destroyed two kings Sihon and Og of the east of the Jordan and therefore said that she believed that God was God in heaven above and on the earth below. She confessed that not only she but also all the people of the land became afraid and trembled when they heard it(Jos.2:9-11). And then she asked the spies to spare the lives of her and her family. Accepting Rahab's request, the spies made a treaty with her. Finishing the spying with the help of Rahab, they returned to Joshua and gave him the report. This report became a great strength to Israel who had the conquering war to fight ahead.

3. Crossing the Jordan River by walking on dry land Jos. chap.3-5

The Israelites who came out of Egypt over forty years ago experienced the miracle of crossing the Red Sea by walking on dry land. Now forty years later Manna generation also came to

The miracle that happened again

While in the Red Sea the people of Israel crossed over after the sea was split and dry land was exposed(Exo.chap.14), in the Jordan River a dry road was made when the feet of priests who carried the ark of covenant stepped into the waters. Seeing that it was when the waters of the Jordan were full, we can discover that the faith of the people in God was full. The people of Israel came to advance boldly with faith in God through the 40 year education of law.

cross the Jordan River, the first gateway to the land of Canaan promised by God, by walking on dry land. This time Joshua was commanded by God, and the priests who were carrying the ark of the covenant marched ahead of the people. When they crossed the Jordan River, the desert period was over and the Canaan period began. Right at this time the people of Israel again performed the circumcision they had not done for forty years and observed the first Passover in the land of promise.

4. Occupying Canaan Jos. chap.6-12

The five year war of conquest was launched. Although lots of wars were waged during the periods of Judges, David and kings, no other period compared to this. Israel captured Jericho, which was the first city in the war of conquering Canaan, not by using swords and spears but by the way God instructed them. **During this period was established the principle of faith, 'War belongs not to man but to God.'**

In Joshua chapter twelve is recorded the list of the two kings of the east of the Jordan Moses conquered and 31 kings of the west of the Jordan Joshua conquered. **Faith and obedience to the word of God and sweats and labor of the people of Israel combined together to produced 33 victories in the wars.**

Manna generation occupied the land of Canaan with the faith and obedience that wars belonged to God. It meant that

The peoples who lived in Canaan in those days

People	Location
Hittites	Region stretching from the desert and Lebanon up to Euphrates
Canaanites	Shores of Phoenician region and valleys of the Jordan River
Philistines	Shores of Palestine
Hivites	Northern mountain area of Palestine and Gibeon
Jebusites	Jerusalem and its surrounding mountain area
Perizzites	Mainly outskirts or mountain area
Girgashites	The western side of the Jordan

faith wins the battle. "Faith overcomes. Faith overcomes. Faith in the LORD Jesus overcomes the world!"

Tong Point

The land of obedience, timely rain of happiness
The story of distribution of land is recorded in Joshua chapters 13-24. Perhaps 'land' was not so significant for them during their times of slavery in Egypt and their life in the desert. But, 'land' which was the most important foundation for not only their generation but future generations to come, was distributed to each tribe.

5. Distribution of the land of Canaan and Caleb's choice Jos. chap.13-22

- The story of Caleb

After finishing conquest of Canaan to some degree, each tribe started to choose the land there were to live in in the sense of 'lottery'. It was the method prescribed by God. However, only Caleb was an exception in this principle. It was a privilege God gave Caleb who chose God faithfully in Kadesh Barnea 45 years ago. At the time when distribution of the land was implemented, Caleb brought his family and all his relatives and had them stand next to him and then reminded Joshua of his privilege conferred on him in the past.

"Now give me this hill country the LORD promised that day. Indeed there are the Anakites there and their cities are big and firm. However, if the LORD is with me I can drive them out as the LORD has said" (Ref. Jos.14:6-12).

Caleb could have chosen the place of best locaton which was

Lottery
Distributing through lottery method did not mean that a stronger person was able to possess a better land. Lottery method was a means for the people to understand God's rights and blessing.

already conquered. However, when Caleb said, "Give me this hill country" while looking at the land of Hebron which they had not yet conquered, we can assume that Joshua truly appreciated Caleb who was his long time friend.

As requested by Caleb, Hebron which was the hill country not conquered yet was given to him as inheritance and that land became the land of Caleb and his descendants.

- War hero Joshua who chose not to become king

After Joshua distributed the land to everybody, he had land distributed to him and his descendants the latest. It can be said that Joshua also was a great leader after Moses.

Distribution
Although the conquest of Canaan was not finished yet, land was distributed to other tribes except the tribe of Levi. In Joshua chapter 12 are listed the lands conquered by Moses and Joshua but in chapter 13 distribution was made for the land not conquered yet.
This was the actualization of God's promise to Abraham over 500 years later as said, "To your descendants I give this land, from the river of Egypt to the great river, the Euphrates" (Gen.15:18).

- The tribe of Levi scattered for mission

After the land was distributed to all of the twelve tribes of Israel, it was also distributed to the tribe of Levi. The descendants of Levi to whom land was distributed came to live scattered among each tribe of Israel, because Levites had to teach the word of God while living scattered. Meanwhile, the tribes of Reuben, Gad and the half tribe of Manasseh, who were advance party in the war with Canaan returned to the east of the Jordan (as promised with Moses).

6. Joshua's final request Jos. chap.23-24

Joshua, who finished the conquest war of Canaan and the distribution of land efficiently as the leader of Israel after Moses, was near the age of death. When his life was almost over, Joshua asked the people with all his heart as Moses did; **"So be very careful to love the LORD your God"(Jos.23:11).** It was the same message that previous leader Moses left with the people of Israel. The two leaders' common request, "Love God" became the direction of future life of Israel.

Distribution of the land of Canaan

Jos.chap.13	The story of three tribes already allotted the eastern land of the Jordan. (Reuben, Gath, eastern tribe of Manasseh)
Jos.chap.14	Caleb chose and occupied Hebron
Jos.chap.15-17	Judah, Ephraim, western tribe of Manasseh were allotted western land of the Jordan
Jos.chap.18-19	Seven remaining tribes were allotted the land yet to be conquered.
Jos.chap.20-21	The tribe of Levi was allotted 48 towns including cities of refuge

Write down the contents of this lesson in the form of Tong Story

Let's pray in a loud voice so that we may be able to teach the contents of this lesson to our children

- Teach them to your children, talking about them when you sit at home and when you walk along the road, when you lie down and when you get up……so that your days and the days of your children may be many……as many as the days that the heavens are above the earth (Deuteronomy 11:19-21).
- you know those from whom you learned it, and how from infancy you have known the holy Scriptures(II Timothy 3:14-15).

10 Lesson

The Period when Judges ruled

Judges

Accumulative reading amount 22.75% 1189

The One Year Tongdok Bible Days 79-86 | Reading time 65 minutes

TongBible Story Overview

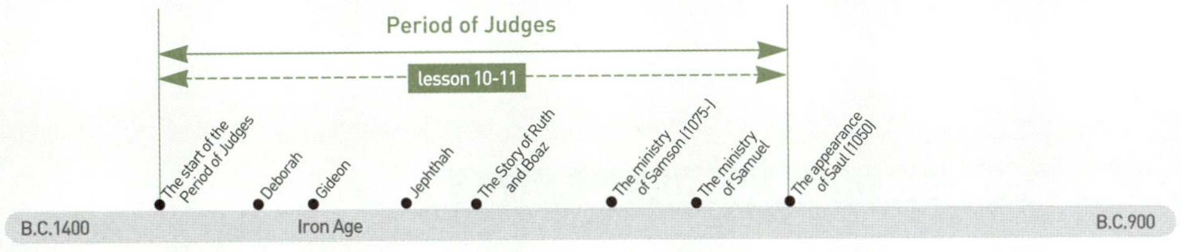

Reading the Old Testament in detail in the order of history (10)

We go on to read Judges. It is the story of the unfortunate period of Judges which lasted about 350 years.

How to read Judges

The Manna generation who were the children of the Exodus generation promised with both Moses and Joshua that they would educate their children with "Shema" but they unfortunately did not. The Manna generation put education for children about God behind them after settling in Canaan and instead began to serve the idols of Canaan. Therefore, the period of Judges which lasted over about 350 years was very gloomy. The 12 tribes did not cooperate with one another in the distributed land and the judges who were regarded as leaders were below the level of expected judges.

In Judges there were repetitions of evil deeds and arrogance of Israel who nullified God's expectation and plan for them along with repetition of the hand of God who judged them, loved and saved them again.

Tong Point

Forgotten request

The dark era called the era of Judges which lasted about 350 years unfolded. The most important foundation was laid for the nation of Israel for a year at Mt.Sinai during the days of Moses. It was the tabernacle and offerings which were the core contents for the sake of their mission of becoming A kingdom of priests and holy people. The core of the tabernacle and offerings was the law and the priest. During the era of Judges these two were decisively broken down. It was a society where this important foundation was broken down. Let's remember that it was the result of their neglecting 'faith education' which both Moses and Joshua so eagerly asked them to do.

1. The tribes they did not drive out Jdg. chap.1-2:10

The Israelites were trained well while enduring the desert life for 40 years well. They also carried out the five year war of conquest well by risking their lives. After Caleb's heroic choice about land, they did a good job about distributing the land by the lottery method. Although their life in Canaan was not completely stable, it was incomparable to their previous life. They no longer had to travel carrying tents and loads. They enjoyed the joy of farming and harvesting. Indeed they came to be able to live the life of A kingdom of priests.

However, in Judges chapter 1 verses 27-36 appear the names of the peoples who still lived in Canaan who had not been yet driven out by the people of Israel. In other words, there were Canaanite peoples who had not been conquered. This was an important task yet to be handled by the Manna generation.

Land still to be conquered

There was still land Israel had not conquered(Jos.13:1-6; Jud.3:1-3): from north western part of the Mediterranean Sea where the Philistines lived to the entire region of the north of Galilee, and the land of Geshur in the shape of coin on the right side with the Sea of Galilee and so on. The Philistines were extremely hostile people living by the sea. The giants of the mountains north of Galilee (Nephirim, Anak descendants) were strong nations who possessed iron tools and chariots.(Jud.1:19) These regions were not conquered completely until the period of David.

2. The result of neglecting faith education

Jdg. 2:11-chap.5

"The people served the LORD throughout the lifetime of Joshua and of the elders who outlived him and who had seen all the great things the LORD had done for Israel....After that whole generation had been gathered to their fathers, another generation grew up, who knew neither the LORD nor what He had done for Israel"(Jud.2:7-10).

"The other generation who emerged after that," that is, the generation who had not yet seen the great works of God did not know the LORD. **It meant that the Manna generation neglected faith education for their children. This was a decisive cause of dark shadow in the Judges' period.**

Absence of education
Moses stressed education for the children along with the word, "Love God"(Deu.6:5) and entreated the people to pay attention to it. However, the generation who witnessed the great works of God, who led Israel into Canaan, failed to teach God to their descendants. The result was depravity and went astray of the next generations.

In order to enlighten and establish these people, God repeated discipline and forgiveness. However, only when Israel was under maltreatment and oppression of another Gentile people, they seeked God. But if they thought there was no more crisis, immediately they returned to the way of evil.

3. Gideon and 300 warriors Jdg. chap.6-9

The descendants of Israel did evil again in the sight of God and were made to be oppressed by Midianites for seven years. At this time, God called Gideon and appointed him Judge.

The fear of the people of Israel including Gideon was towards the Midianite army whose number was as many as grass hoppers. However, if God was with them, the number of troops was no longer important. Out of 32,000 who gathered to participate in the battle against Midian, God chose only 300 and made all the others return.

Israel's Judges

Judge's name	His tribe	duration of service	Gentile nation(king) he defeated
Othniel	Judah	40 years	Mesopotamia (Cushan-Rishathaim)
Ehud	Benjamin	80 years	Moab (Eglon)
Shamgar	?	?	Philistines
Deborah	Ephraim	40 years	Canaan (Jabin)
Gideon	Manasseh	40 years	Midian (Abimelech's rebellion)
Tola	Issachar	23 years	
Jair	Gileadite	22 years	
Iphtah	Gileadite	6 years	Ammon
Ibzan	Judah	7 years	
Elon	Zebulun	10 years	
Abdon	Ephraim	8 years	
Samson	Dan	20 years	Philistines

When Gideon and the 300 warriors blew the trumpets with torches in their hands, God fought for them. Eventually, Gideon and the 300 warriors defeated the Midianite Army and Israel enjoyed a peaceful period after a long time.

In spite of that, the people who did not want to have God as their king intended to make Gideon their king while he was alive. When he died, they served Baal again instead of God. The misery of the period of Judges was deepened.

4. A leader not qualified for that position

Jdg. chap.10-12

There was a judge called Jair whose resume was as follows; "He had thirty sons, who rode thirty donkeys. They controlled thirty towns"(Jud. 10:4). As leader who should have led the people according to the word of God, his resume was indeed disappointing.

On the other hand, another judge (Iphtah) delivered Israel out of the hand of Ammonite descendants by the power of God. However, for the victory in the battle, he made a rash oath

All kinds of idols
Here is a list of the names of idols Israel served during the period of Judges(Jud.10:6) Baal, Ashtoreth, Aramaic gods. Sidonian gods. Moab's gods. Ammon's gods. Philistines' gods.

saying. "whatever comes out of the door of my house to meet me when I return in triumph from the Ammonites will be the LORD's, and I will sacrifice it as a burnt offering." As a result he had to sacrifice his only child and daughter as burnt offering. But sacrificing the person as burnt offering was prohibited by God already through the laws of Moses. This incident shows us very well how ignorant even judges, who were appointed as leaders, were of the word of God.

5. Judge Samson Jdg. chap.13-16

Samson, one of the famous judges was blessed by God and the spirit of the LORD was with him. There were two tasks for Samson: first, to liberate Israel out of the Philistines. Second, to remove idols out of Israel and reform Israel into a nation to serve only God. In battles with the Philistines Samson brought about victory various times but he did not amount to God's expectation despite being a Judge for as long as 20 years. As we know well, he came into conflict between God's promise and a Philistine woman named Delilah. He gave into Delilah which as a result lead him to his death.

6. Social image of the period of Judges Jdg. chap.17-21

The story of a person called Micah shown in Judges chapters 17-18 tells us how much the society in those times fell apart. A Levite who was wandering looking for a place to live in came to visit Micah's house, and Micah appointed him his personal priest and asked him to pray for him. Here we can see how Levites lived in the period of Judges. The people of Israel did not give their wealth for Levites to be able to make a living. Therefore, priests and Levites had to wander around or look for other jobs to make a living themselves.

Lesson of the book of Judges
The law which was the way of life of Israel God had shown through Moses. The book of Judges teaches us what kind of result people's choice against the word of God brought.

The incident of Judges chapters 19-21 is even gloomier. One Levite and his concubine entered the region called Gibeah belonging to tribe of Benjamin, and his concubine was killed by gangsters of the area. Seeing the body of his concubine at the door, the Levite who thought of retaliation cut her body into twelve parts and sent them everywhere in Israel. Due to this incident the society of Israel fell into a great confusion. A war broke out between the tribe of Benjamin and the remaining 11 tribes and over 25,000 young men of the tribe of Benjamin were killed so that the tribe was in danger of extinction. While the battle raged, they devoted themselves to killing one another. After the stormy time passed, the only thing that was left was misery.

The events and characters introduced in Judges show the condition of those days when many people lived according to their views and thoughts. The basics that the people of God were to maintain was not observed and Israel during this period, brought about much disappointment and regret to God.

Write down the contents of this lesson in the form of Tong Story

Let's pray in a loud voice so that we may be able to teach the contents of this lesson to our children

- Teach them to your children, talking about them when you sit at home and when you walk along the road, when you lie down and when you get up……so that your days and the days of your children may be many……as many as the days that the heavens are above the earth (Deuteronomy 11:19-21).
- you know those from whom you learned it, and how from infancy you have known the holy Scriptures(II Timothy 3:14-15).

11 Lesson

Successful case of Education

Ruth

Accumulative reading amount 23.1% 1189

The One Year Tongdok Bible Day 87 | Reading time10 minutes

TongBible Story Overview

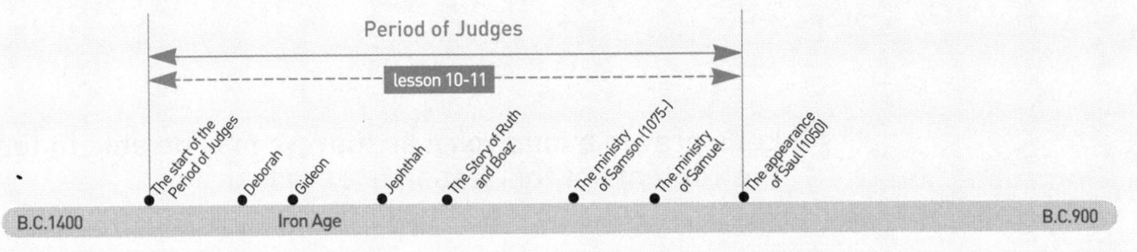

Reading the Old Testament in detail in the order of history (11)

We read the book of Ruth. Ruth records an event like 'Oasis of desert' during the period of Judges.

How to read Ruth

Ruth is like a cool oasis in the middle of a desert. When famine came upon Israel during the period of Judges, Naomi (who lived in Bethlehem) emigrated to Moab, a neighboring country with her family to avoid the famine. About ten years passed and both her husband and two sons came to die. Naomi returned home with her daughter-in-law Ruth. Ruth was a Moabite woman. Great was her love for her mother-in- law and her desire to serve the God her mother-in-law served. She later came to marry a man called Boaz and formed a blessed family.

Meanwhile, Boaz, who married Ruth, was a son of Rahab (who lived in Jericho) and was a man of God who studied 'holiness' of Leviticus and lived practicing it. We can think about the importance of faith education through him.

Tong Point

Carrying out the law
In the book of Ruth the process of people solving difficulties in a community according to the law of God unfolds in the form of a beautiful story. Let's remember that people were able to form this kind of beautiful community due to the laus given by God.

1. Naomi's return home and Ruth's choice

Rut. chap. 1

A famine came upon the land during the period of Judges. Famine was a way of God to discipline Israel. However, one family who lived in the land of Bethlehem, namely, Elimelech, Naomi and their two sons emigrated to the land of Moab to avoid God's discipline. The sons married Moabite women who were Gentiles but their happiness did not last long even despite fleeing from the famine. Losing her husband and two sons in the land of Moab and thinking deeply, Naomi came to realize that only God was the one she had to rely on. Therefore, she made up her mind to put in order her life in Moab and return home. She told her daughter-in-laws her determination. "I am going back home. You return to your parents." She told them to return to their parents and start a new life. Orpah who wept together with them for a while eventually went back to her parents. However, the other daughter-in-law Ruth refused and remained with her mother-in-law.

Even though there was no guarantee that good things would happen if she followed her old mother-in-law and it

Naomi
The name Naomi meant 'My joy.' Naomi was the wife of Elimelech who emigrated to Moab because famine struck Bethlehem during the period of Judges. Although he had a considerable amount of great wealth in Bethlehem, he lost all in the Gentile land of Moab and then was helped by God after he returned to Bethlehem.

was expected that she would face a difficult situation of being responsible for caring for her mother-in-law, she strongly insisted on following her.

2. The Meeting between Ruth and Boaz Rut. chap.2

Although Naomi returned to her long cherished hometown, they had no food to eat. The reason why Naomi was made to be in this situation was: about 10 years ago when famine struck Bethlehem, Naomi and Elimelech sold the right of cultivation of the land they were handed down from ancestors, and with the money they emigrated to Moab. Land was distributed to the people of Israel by tribe during the times of Joshua and they lived in the land from generation to generation. They were able to buy and sell only the 'the right of cultivation' every Jubilee(50 years). They could not sell or buy the right of 'possession' of the land itself. Because the owner of all land was God and the land was given to each tribe of Israel equally as a perpetuating gift. God prohibited the land of one tribe to be transferred to other tribes by people's buying and selling the right of possession of the land so that he could prevent the gap between the rich and the poor from being fixed within the community. Therefore, they were able to sell and buy only 'the right of cultivation' and there was a principle that this right also be returned to the original owner when Jubilee came. Therefore, Naomi calculated the remaining years until Jubilee in money value and sold their

The law revealed in Ruth

Contents	Ruth	Books of law
About greeting	Rut.2:4	Num.6:24-26
About Gentiles & the poor	Rut.2:15-16	Lev.19:9-10

right of cultivation and had gone to Moab. There was much time left until Jubilee, so she had no land to cultivate. She had to buy again the right of cultivation she had sold in order to cultivate but she was unable to do so.

In this situation her daughter-in-law Ruth went out to the field of other people to look for food for her and her mother-in-law. She went to glean in the field overcoming her embarrassment. The field she reached was none other than that of Boaz.

Here, we meet a man called Boaz, who greeted the reapers in his field saying, "The LORD be with you." Hearing that greeting of blessing, the reapers also answered, "The LORD bless you." Have you ever seen this kind of beautiful relationship between employer and employees who bless each other in the name of God? Furthermore, considering that it was the period of Judges, this was a truly amazing scene.

Boaz cared for Ruth. Saying that he heard that Ruth was a good woman taking care of her mother-in-law who was left alone after her husband died, he encouraged her with kind words (Rut.2:12). He also gave Ruth bread and roasted grain. He told the harvesting boys to pull out the grains purposely and leave them on the field. This was the scene in which he remembered and observed the law of Leviticus, "When you reap the harvest of your land, do not reap to the very edges of your field or gather the gleanings of your harvest. Do not go over your vineyard a second time or pick up the grapes that have fallen. Leave them for the poor and the alien" (Lev.19:9-10).

3. Ruth's marriage to Boaz Rut. chap.3-4:17

It is recorded that Naomi and Ruth arrived at Bethlehem when it was time to begin to reap barley(Rut.1:22). Around the time when the reaping period was almost over which usually lasted two weeks, mother-in-law Naomi called Ruth and said that Boaz was the kinsman who was to redeem her family. Redeeming as kinsman was that when a brother died childless, a close relative married the dead brother's widow so that the family's descendants may not be cut off. This was also called 'generation succeeding marriage'. Another duty of the man who was redeemed as kinsman was that when somebody sold his right of cultivation to make a living due to poverty, he became the person who would redeem what was sold and pay the price to the man who bought and restore the property of his family. Naomi thought Boaz was the person who was suitable for carrying out this duty.

Ruth went to the field of Boaz. Lying down in the tent at night, Boaz felt something touching his feet. Ruth, in a feeble voice said, "I am your servant Ruth," and said "Spread the corner of your garment over me, since you are a kinsman-redeemer." However, Boaz comforted Ruth who came to his bedroom with a fearful mind in the middle of the night, saying, "The LORD bless you, my daughter. All my fellow townsmen know that you are a woman of noble character." Then he told her that there was a relative closer than he who could redeem Naomi's family as a kinsman. So in order to observe the laws of God rightly, Boaz and Ruth spent that night separately and at dawn Ruth went out of the tent

Redeemer of property

The system of a relative redeeming property was one of ordinances given through Moses(Lev.25:24-28). It was to pay the price for the relative who lost the property and to restore it. Although the closest relative had the duty to redeem the property, the order was handed down to the next closest relative because this system was not a duty but was applied to the one who wanted it. The purpose of this system was to care for the relative who lost economic power. But it was also implemented for such deep purposes as descent preservation and helping the family of the one who suffered unfair death be continued and so on.

secretly without anybody seeing her.

The next day Boaz called the elders of the city and the relative who was closer to Elimelech than he and told him to redeem Naomi as kinsman. The closest kinsman said he could not do so and this matter was handed over to Boaz. Boaz accepted the responsibility and took Ruth as his wife.

4. The Genealogy of Boaz Rut.4:18-22

During the period of Judges when Boaz lived, most of the people lived in the way in which they wanted. But, unlike others, Boaz lived holding on to the word of God. First, it was the grace of God. Second, we can guess the reason through his genealogy.

At the end of Ruth is recorded the genealogy of Boaz. The father of Boaz was Salmon. "Salmon was the father of Boaz, who was the father of Obed," Here let's briefly see Matthew chapter 1 verse 5: **"Salmon the father of Boaz, whose mother was Rahab, Boaz the father of Obed, whose mother was Ruth, Obed the father of Jesse, and Jesse the father of King David": Who was the wife of Salmon? She was none other than Rahab, the woman of faith who hid spies in Jericho.**

Rahab was a woman who had an insight to see the history and could see God. When all the people in Jericho perished, she saved the lives of her and her family and at the same time was able to witness the city of Jericho being destroyed by the power of God. What do you think Rahab taught her son Boaz most passionately while raising him? We can presume she taught him the 'Living God' telling him the story of how she was able to save her life in the middle of the sudden destruction of the city of Jericho, which was her greatest experience. So, Boaz lived memorizing and practicing the word of God. Indeed, it was a beautiful home that deserved to be **"a shining successful case of faith education."**

Like this, in Ruth are described the obedience and faith of Boaz who carried out responsibility according to the word of God. The story of Ruth, which clearly showed that the Law of God was not simply restriction but the best way to be able to truly keep cultivating the level of the human life and the community most beautifully and honorably, is indeed like a stream of cool living water during the period of Judges.

Write down the contents of this lesson in the form of Tong Story

Let's pray in a loud voice so that we may be able to teach the contents of this lesson to our children

- Teach them to your children, talking about them when you sit at home and when you walk along the road, when you lie down and when you get up……so that your days and the days of your children may be many……as many as the days that the heavens are above the earth (Deuteronomy 11:19-21).
- you know those from whom you learned it, and how from infancy you have known the holy Scriptures(II Timothy 3:14-15).

Track 2
500 years of Monarchy

Tong Track 2 - The atmosphere of the 500 years of Monarchy

The atmosphere of the 500 years of Monarchy is that of opposition and cooperation between kings and prophets. God wanted the Israelites to become a nation that could take on the mission of being A Kingdom of Priests, rather than a nation under the rule of a king. However, whilst residing in the Promised Land, the Israelites required a king like all the other nations in Canaan.

The atmosphere of the 500 years of Monarchy starting from I Samuel 8 is a complete contrast to the atmosphere of the Pentateuch.

"But when they said, "Give us a king to lead us," this displeased Samuel; so he prayed to the LORD. And the LORD told him: "Listen to all that the people are saying to you; it is not you they have rejected, but they have rejected me as their king" (I Sa.8:6-7).

God through Samuel explained the abuse they would have to undertake in having a Monarch, but the Israelites refused to listen. And then the 500 years of Monarchy unravels.

From this point, whenever the Israelites practiced idol worship and positioned themselves far from God, He sent His prophets. The kings and the prophets constantly went from opposition and cooperation during these years between the Monarchy and A Kingdom of Priests.

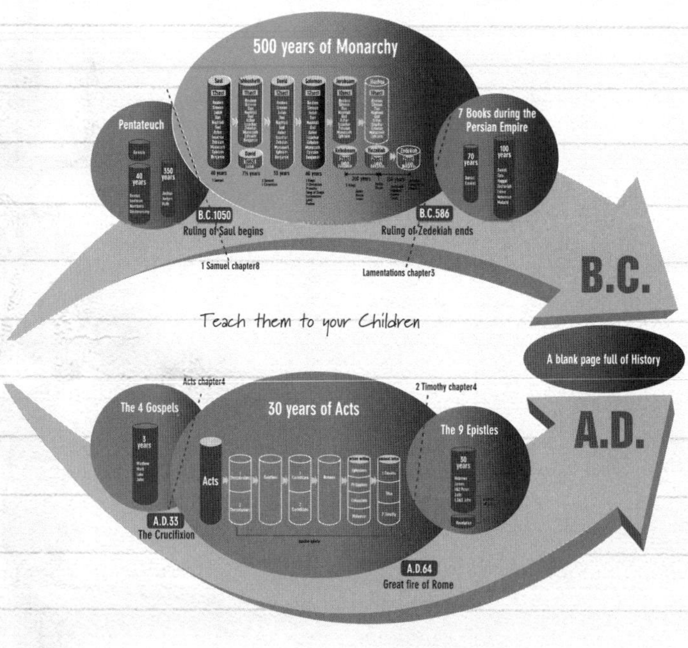

Session 5

A Model for a Thousand Years

Tong Map

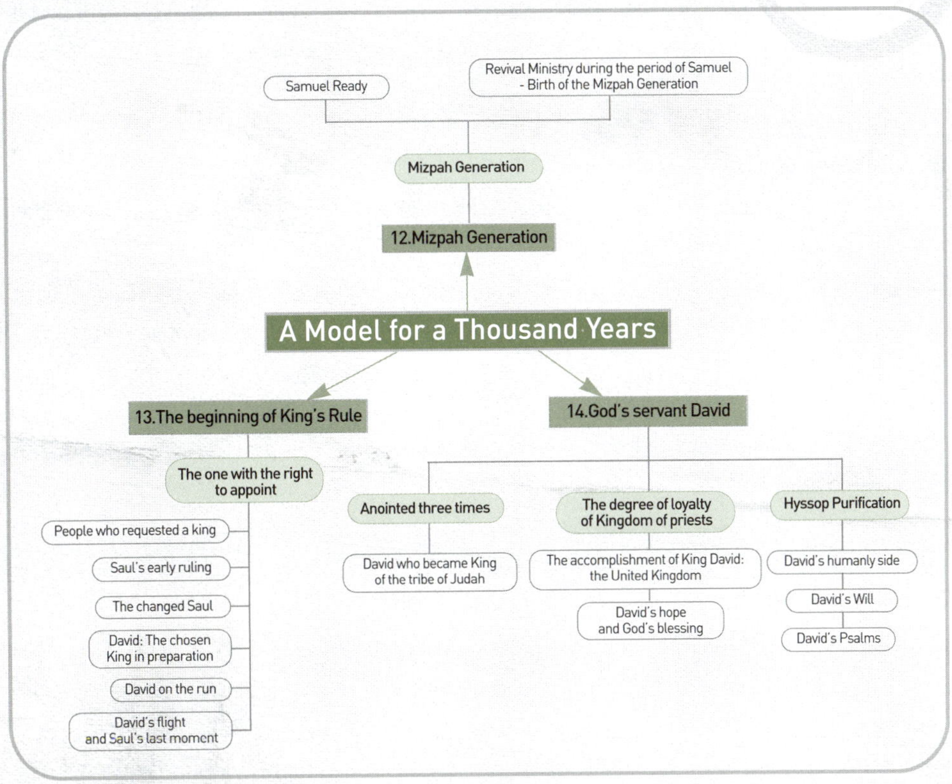

Tong Concept

- **The birth of Mizpah Generation through the ministry of Samuel**

Samuel broke through the darkness of the 350 year long Judges era and reestablished the era with the law of God. The generation that was born became the Mizpah generation. Let's study while remembering that the substance of Mizpah generation consisted of the fact that the law and priesthood broke down during the era of Judges was established again.

- **Why was David the model for a thousand years?**

David who was born on the basis of Samuel's ministry ruled the country with justice and righteousness and became the most exemplary model for a thousand years remaining as the rest of the Old Testament history. Let's study with focus on what kind of training course he went gone through until he became the model for a thousand years and what he specifically did as the model for a thousand years.

Tong At a glance

* Looking around the forest

Samuel played an important role in transferring Israel from the era of Judges to that of kings' rule. Israel began to get restored through him who was prepared as a man of God after being born of Hannah, known as the praying mother.

God who accepted the request of the people who wanted a king had Samuel prepare Saul. Yet, Saul got alienated from God by disobeying Him and so God chose David to replace Saul. But David had to spend a long period of hardship and training under Saul's government until he became the king of Israel.

* Land and annual ring

David became the one thousand year stepping stone between Abraham who lived in B.C.2000s' and Jesus who was the crossroad of B.C. and A.D.

David did not neglect fellowshipping with God even while he lived a life of escape. Particularly, Psalms 3,7,18,34,51,52,54,56,57,59,60,63,142(13 psalms) are closely connected to particular situations of David's life. Therefore, reading the Bible by connecting his life to his Psalms is a good opportunity for us to study his life.

After this, Jerusalem was designated as 'place chosen to bear the name of God' and became the most important city in history.

* Wind and Climate

The Philistines was a federation of what they called 'Pentapolis', that is, five cities (Ashdod, Ashkelon, Ekron, Gath, Gaza). These showed a much stronger power of union militarily than Canaanites. They were advanced in metal industry and Israel had to depend on them to have metal tools made. The backbreaking life of the people of Israel threatened by them constantly was only gone after David became king. II Samuel and the most of I Chronicles contain the record about David's rule.

Tong Seeing the forest

I Samuel I Samuel deals with a transitional situation starting from the time the society of Israel from the period of Judges to the period of king's rule, from the birth of Samuel (the last Judge of Israel) to the death of Saul (first king of Israel). This book can be divided into three parts with the characters as standard; the first part focuses on Samuel, the second part on Saul and the third part on David. Samuel was a great leader who carried out the significant role of disconnecting the flow of the dark period of Judges and turning Israel to God. However, when Samuel became old, the people of Israel came to request rule by king and in that flow Saul was anointed as the first king. In the beginning, Saul was a good leader in many ways but when he got drunk with power, he disobeyed the will of God. Then God chose David in advance to be the next king.

II Samuel If I Samuel shows David's preliminary contest, II Samuel deals with his main contest. In other words, while I Samuel showed with what faith and patience David overcame the period of training before becoming the king of Israel; II Samuel shows how he ruled the country as king with God's justice. David, who ruled in Hebron seven and a half years as king of only the tribe of Judah, waited for the unification of the nation. As a result, he was enthroned as king of the unified kingdom by attaining the approval of all the Northern tribes. Deciding Jerusalem as new capital, David (who moved the ark of God to Jerusalem) was not only a possessor of deep faith in God but also an excellent king who ruled the entire country with justice and righteousness. He was also a man who committed mistakes and sins but each time he confessed his sins and was humble enough to get on his knees before God.

I Kings I Kings can be divided into three parts; the first part is about the story of David's death and Solomon who succeeded his throne(chap.1-2), the second is about Solomon's reign and achievements (particularly building the temple) (chap.3-11). The third part is about stories of various kings who appeared in each dynasty after Solomon died and how the kingdom of Judah was divided into the south and Israel in the north(chap.12-22). The standard of God who evaluated kings was whether they followed the way of King David or the way of Jeroboam who introduced the idol of golden calf in Northern Israel.

12 Lesson

Mizpah Generation

I Samuel chap.1-7

Accumulative reading amount 23.97% 1189

The One Year Tongdok Bible Days 88-89 | Reading time 25 minutes

TongBible Story Overview

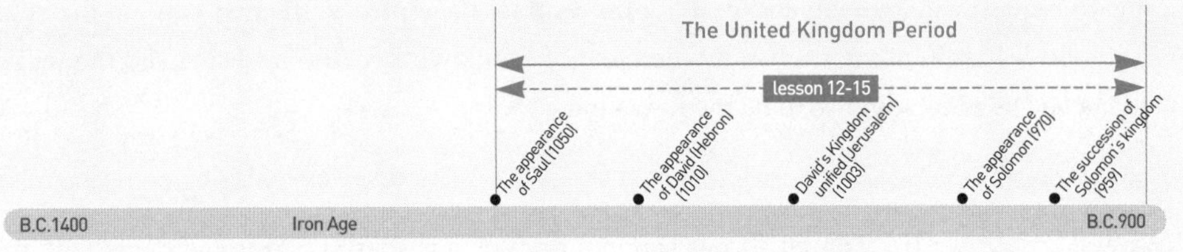

Reading the Old Testament in detail in the order of history (12)

The outstanding achievements of Samuel (the last judge) appears in I Samuel chapters 1-7.

How to read the story of Samuel

History changes only when people are ready. After God led the people of Israel out of Egypt who were living as slaves, God waited. Now we reach the period when God prepared a new lader, Samuel to put an end to the dark and gloomy period of the judges. Through Samuel who was born of Hannah (the mother of prayer) Israel began to get restored again. Before Saul became king, Samuel played the role of actual ruler(Judge), prophet and priest of Israel. Only Samuel held these three positions at the same time in the Old Testament.

Tong Point

Mizpah Generation
Samuel was faithfully educated and became a prepared leader who came to learn the word of God. Let's observe 'Mizpah generation' with a focus on the fact that it was the era which, followed by the 'Manna generation,' showed the supremacy of rule of A kingdom of priests.

1. Samuel Ready 1Sa. chap.1-3

Preparation that removes darkness:
Samuel, a man who cut off the dark history of the period of Judges was under preparation. At the same time, the marriage of Boaz and Ruth that took place in a small village called Bethlehem was a great providence of God who was preparing David who would cut off the dark period of Saul.

The story of Hannah

After Joshua died, the people of Israel fell into idolatry of Canaan and spent dark times rather than following God and observing His law. At this time God took note of a woman while watching that period. It was Hannah, a woman who prayed tearfully in the temple of God with the pain of being barren.

Unable to pray loudly in the temple where there were many people, she prayed in a feeble voice. She prayed with the pledge that if a son would be given, she would give him to God. She prayed so earnestly that her face turned red. Watching this from afar, priest Eli came up to her and advised her to stop drinking wine. Hannah told him her prayer subject. Hearing all the story, Eli told her that God heard all her prayer. Believing the word of Eli, she returned home.

Indeed, Hannah gave birth to a son and gave the son the name 'Samuel' which meant 'I asked God.' When the child was weaned, Hannah entrusted priest Eli with Samuel just as she pledged and had the child live in the temple all his life time serving God. We can learn here how deep Hannah's faith in

God was.

- Samuel who was a prepared man

Samuel began to get prepared as a man of God living apart from his parents. Although Eli did not educate his own sons well, he was a good teacher for Samuel. Seeing evil deeds of Hophni and Phinehas (the two sons of Eli) Samuel learned the wisdom of guarding his own behavior. Also, his mother Hannah's eager prayer became a significant support.

As Samuel grew up, all Israel came to know that not one of his words fell to the ground and he was appointed as prophet of God. Now Samuel came to play the role of cutting off the dark history of over 350 years.

2. Revival Ministry during the period of Samuel - Birth of the Mizpah Generation I Sa. chap.4-7

- Battle with the Philistines

One day a war broke out between the Philistines and Israel, and Hophni and Phinehas were killed in this battle. However, (Israel who carried God's ark of covenant to the battle fields) were foolish enough to let the enemy take it away. Hearing that his two sons died and even God's ark of covenant was taken away, priest Eli was shocked and died by falling. However, lots of plagues happened due to God's ark and the Philistines sent it back by cart after seven months. From this time on this ark was kept in a village called Kiriath Jearim for a long time.

Circuit education of Samuel

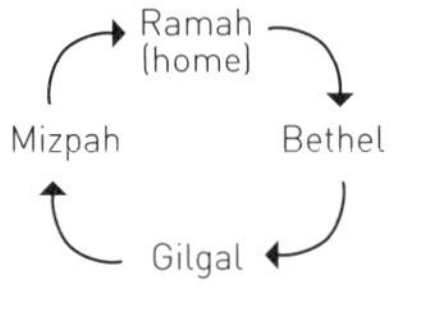

● Samuel's circuit education

Meanwhile, appointed as leader of all Israel, Samuel did his best to wipe out the dark past of the period of Judges and to turn Israel again into the nation who served God during his time. He traveled around the whole country proclaiming the word, having people remove such idols as Baal and Ashtoreth and teaching the people to serve only the LORD God.

● The birth of Mizpah Generation

All the people of Israel gathered in Mizpah through Samuel's earnest ministry. Those who gathered in Mizpah repented truly. Even though the Philistines (who heard that Israel gathered in Mizpah all together) invaded Israel, the people of Israel defeated them by praying together with one mind. **We can call these people 'Mizpah generation.' We can say that if Manna generation were educated by Moses and experienced the wonderful event of entrance into Canaan in common, Mizpah generation were educated by Samuel and experienced the power of God in Mizpah in common.**

Tong Point

Putting in order the era of Samuel
The era of Samuel differs from that of Judges. First, there was no king during the era of Samuel. Second, there was no internal national conflict. It meant that there was no conflict among tribes. Third, there was no invasion by foreign enemies. Thus, the era of Samuel was a time when the truth and love of God blossomed in all the world due to God's rule.

Write down the contents of this lesson in the form of Tong Story

Let's pray in a loud voice so that we may be able to teach the contents of this lesson to our children

- Teach them to your children, talking about them when you sit at home and when you walk along the road, when you lie down and when you get up……so that your days and the days of your children may be many……as many as the days that the heavens are above the earth (Deuteronomy 11:19-21).
- you know those from whom you learned it, and how from infancy you have known the holy Scriptures(II Timothy 3:14-15).

13 Lesson

The beginning of King's Rule

I Samuel chap.8-31

Accumulative reading amount 26.75% 1189

The One Year Tongdok Bible Days 90-100 | Reading time 80 minutes

TongBible Story Overview

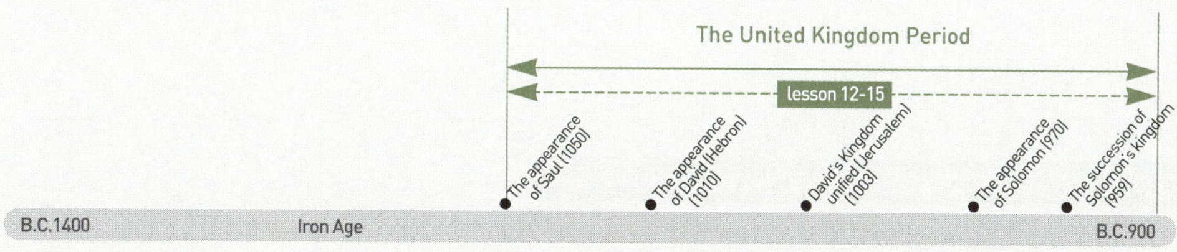

Reading the Old Testament in detail in the order of history (13)

In I Samuel chapters 8-31 are contained the contents in which the story of Saul (the first king of Israel) was anointed by Samuel as God accepted the request of the people who asked for royal rule. Also, the story of David (the second king) are overlapped. Here it would be beneficial if you also read Psalms of David directly related to his life. They are Psalms 34, 52, 54, 56, 57, 59, 142 and the like. The Chronicles applicable in this period are I Chronicles chapters 1 to 10, where have recorded the genealogy from Adam to the return of Babylonian captivity and the scenes in which the royal power of Saul (the first king) was handed over to David.

How to read the story of David

Saul, David and Solomon all ruled Israel for 40 years. David was the grandson of Obed (the son of Boaz and Ruth) whom we met in the book of Ruth and the eighth and youngest son of his father Jesse. He was anointed by Samuel in Bethlehem his hometown. Though he was chosen in advance to be the next king, he had to spend much time of suffering and training until he became the king of all of Israel. Unlike Saul who devoted himself to killing David and pursued David with 3,000 soldiers, David did not kill Saul despite many opportunities to kill him. No wonder God favored David because he admitted the fact that it was God who anointed Saul as king.

Tong Point

The one with the right to appoint

I Samuel chap.9 to 31 deals with Saul's 40 year rule. First, Saul was appointed king and then next was David. An important word here is 'appointed.' When God appointed someone, it meant that He expected something from that person. The substance and contents were none other than 'law.' In order not to repeat Saul's failure, David had to go through training by doing his best with the 'contents of being appointed.' He spent time thinking about the role of king and further a king's identity. Let's compare Saul and David bearing in mind 'the one who has the right to appoint.'

1. People who requested a king I Sam. chap.8

Time passed and Samuel (the man of God) grew old and was unable to carry out the mission of leader. However, somehow, Samuel did not succeed in educating his own children. "But his sons did not walk in his ways. They turned aside after dishonest gain and accepted bribes and perverted justice" (I Sa. 8:3).

With this as a turning-point, the people and elders of Israel said that they wanted king's rule like other countries. The political system God gave the people of Israel was that each tribe was to live forming a community and all people establish an equal and free relation and live serving God according to the law with priests and Levites in their center. However, the people of Israel rejected God's rule.

Samuel was very disappointed with this request of the people. God also was very disappointed at their decision. God had Samuel explain that king's rule was not beneficial for

Difference between King's Rule system and Priestly System

King's Rule system	Priestly System
King's rule	God's rule
Royal authority centered	People centered
Classes system	United community
The strong centered command system	Care for the weak in society comes first

Because of love

Everyone who has loved somebody knows that when a person who has more love and another who has less love quarrel, the latter defeats the former. It is natural that children defeat their parents and pupils defeat their teachers. Therefore, they say that no parents can defeat their children. The same was true with the relationship between Israel and God. God who loved Israel, gave into their request for a king.

Israel at all. He said that if kings ruled, eventually the people would become the 'king's servants.' Still, the people stubbornly wanted king's rule.

Despite so, our God accepted the request of the foolish and stubborn people.

2. Saul's early ruling 1 Sa. chap.9-12

The people of Israel thought that if a king was appointed, the country would become stable and he would be at the head to save the country out of every crisis. However, this was only their hope and short thought.

When God appointed Saul as the first king of Israel, He did so because Saul was qualified at that time. He was tall and handsome and was a son of filial duty who knew how to worry about his parents. Even having the insight to read the flow of the times, he went back to his home, worked on the farm as usual and waited for the optimum time to exercise his leadership though he was appointed as king rather than immediately building the palace and gathering his subjects.

Not long afterward, that 'time' approached. The Ammonites attacked Jabesh Gilead. The region called Jabesh in the territory of Gilead was relatively a remote place unlike other regions of Israel. It was fragile against attack from Ammonites in the south and Arameans in the north. This time also an Ammonite called Nahash attacked and harassed them. Although the people of Jabesh Gilead proposed that they make a treaty, Nahash threatened the people of Jabesh, "I will made a treaty with you only when all your right eyes have been pulled out." The elders of Jabesh who became desperate sent word to all Israel asking for help. Hearing this news in his hometown Gibeah, Saul immediately took a pair of the oxen, cut them into pieces and sent them to all tribes, strongly asking the people to participate in this battle. Exercising his excellent leadership and uniting all tribes in one mind, Saul enjoyed great victory in the war against the Ammonites. This event solidified Saul's position as king. Like so, in the beginning Saul was a man who knew how to serve God and how to care for the people.

3. The changed Saul I Sa. chap.13-15

Over 20 years passed after Saul became king and the country became strong. A mission of God was given to Saul. It was to attack the Amalekites and totally destroy the people and their possession. The Amalekites plundered and tormented the weak who could not help marching behind the ranks when all Israel were getting out of Egypt over 400 years earlier. However, even now after much time passed God saw them still maintaining that kind of lifestyle and ordered Saul to make them pay for their sins.

At this time one of the words Saul should have listened to very attentively was 'totally destroy.' Since the possession of the Amalekites was not what they worked for honestly but rather what they took from the weak by unrighteous

Process of Saul's failures

Failure Process	Contents	Text
Disobeying God's order	Sacrificed burnt-offering without Samuel in the battle with the Philistines	I Sa. chap.13
Greed for wealth	Did not totally destroyed the Amalekites but took plunders	I Sa. chap.15
Superstition	Went to a female shaman of Endor	I Sa. chap.28

methods, God ordered Saul to totally destroy them. However, Saul did not obey this word. Saul spared king Agag of the Amalekites and did not destroy the best plunders. Seeing this, God greatly regretted that He made Saul king.

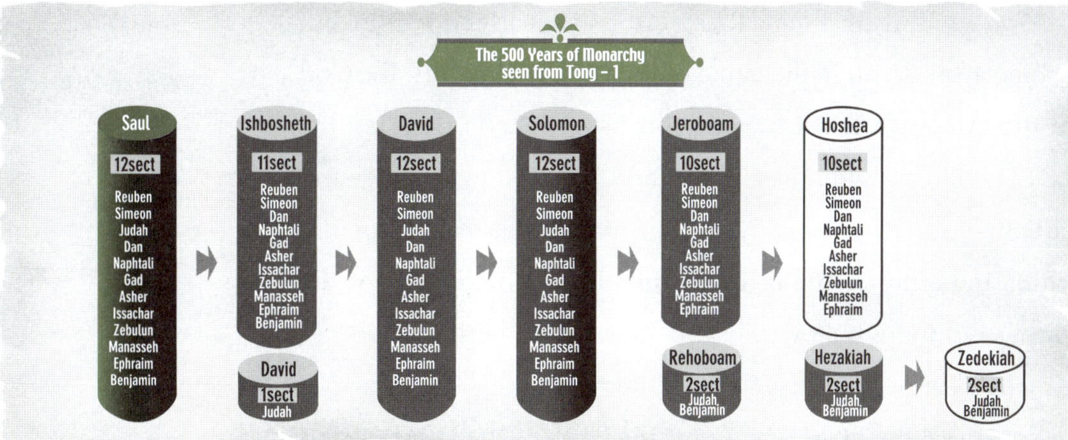

4. David: The chosen King in preparation 1Sa. chap.16-17

Returning to Ramah, Samuel became very sad. Right at this time God told Samuel to fill a horn with oil and go to Jesse (a man of Bethlehem) because He chose David as king in advance. God chose David because God looked at man's heart, not appearance. Avoiding the eyes of Saul who watched every action of his, Samuel went to Bethlehem risking his life and anointed David there.

Some time later, a great crisis came upon the country. The army of Israel and the army of the Philistines had camped in the valley of Elah for 40 days, ready to fight. David was sent by his father on an errand of meeting his elder brothers and came to the valley of Elah. Seeing the situation, he made up his mind to fight Goliath. He believed that God's name should not be insulted, and he had the passion to love God's name more than his life. Advancing toward Goliath the giant general of the Philistine, David shouted:

"You come against me with sword and spear and javelin, but I come against you in the name of the LORD Almighty, the God of the armies of Israel, whom you have defied. This day the LORD will hand you over to me, and I'll strike you down and cut off your head. Today I will give the carcasses of the Philistine army to the birds of the air and the beasts of the earth, and the whole world will know that there is a God in Israel. All those gathered here will know that it is not by sword or spear that the LORD saves; for the battle is the LORD's, and he will give all of you into our hands" (I Sa.17:45-47).

This victory at the valley of Elah made David a hero who saved Israel. He became very famous.

Guarding what belongs to God

God took note of David who repeatedly practiced the skill of turning around the sling to protect his father's sheep and fought the lions and bears. It seems that God expected David to guard what belonged to Him faithfully as he guarded what belonged to his father with all his passion. Reviewing David's confession and faith shown when he volunteered to fight Goliath(I Sa.17:45-47), we can know that David was ready to guard what belonged to God with all his life.

5. David on the run I Sa. chap.18-26

Many people was thoroughly impressed when they saw David defeating Goliath. Prince Jonathan, the son of Saul, came to clearly see at the valley of Elah 'How much David loves God' and 'How much God also loves David.' From this time on, Jonathan loved David as his own life.

Although Saul appointed David a commanding general of the army and made him his son-in-law, his jealousy for David became deeper and deeper day after day. At last David was put

David and Psalms

Psalms	David's situation	The books of Samuel
Psa.59	When Saul sent people to watch David's house to kill him	I Sa. chap.19
Psa.34	Wrote after pretending to be crazy and being driven out from before Abimelech	I Sa. chap.21
Psa.56	When David was caught by the Philistines at Gath	I Sa. chap. 21
Psa.52	When Edomite Doeg came to Saul and told him that David was in Ahimelech's house	I Sa. chap.22
Psa.57	When David was in the cave to avoid Saul	I Sa. chap.24
Psa.142	When David was in the cave	I Sa. chap.24
Psa.54	When a man of Ziph informed Saul of David's whereabout	I Sa. chap.23, 26

in a situation where he had to run away to avoid Saul's sword. Neither Michal (who was Saul's daughter and David's wife) nor Prince Jonathan could protect David's life(at this time, David wrote Psalms 59).

Fleeing from Saul to the land of Nob, the town of priests, David got Goliath's sword and a little bread from priest Ahimelech. And he moved again and went to king Gath of the Philistines. Unfortunately, the subjects of the Philistines recognized David and told the king that he had killed Goliath. In order to avoid the crisis David pretended to be crazy. How agonizing David must have felt that he had to pretend to be crazy to survive! Driven away from before king Achish and made to save his life narrowly, David sang to God. That song was Psalms 34 and 56.

"This poor man called, and the LORD heard him; He saved him out of all his troubles …… The lions may grow weak and hungry, but those who seek the LORD lack no good thing" (Psa.34:6-10).

The course of David's escape

Places for escape	Incident	Related verses
Nob	Got some bread and Goliath's sword from Ahimelech. Doeg the Edomite informed.	I Sa.21:1-9
Achish king of Gath the Philistine	Pretended to be crazy	I Sa.21:10-15
Adullam Cave	All those who were in distress or in debt or discontented, 400 formed a new political power group.	I Sa.22:1-2
Moab	Defected to Mizpah only to be asked by God to return to Judah through prophet Gad.	I Sa.22:3-5
Desert of En Gedi	Cut off a corner of Saul's robe	I Sa. chap.24
Desert of Ziph	Let Saul live twice	I Sa. chap.26

David who fled to the cave of Adullam met 400 people who were situated in a similar situation to his. Although it was difficult for him even to take care of himself, David decided to embrace them and go together. Defecting to the country of Moab in the east of

Israel and taking rest after a long time, David was visited by prophet Gad. He told David not to stay there but to return to Judah.

David obeyed his word and returned to Judah. However, Saul committed a terrible evil of killing 85 priests of Nob, people, both young and old, male and female and even livestock for the reason of having given David Goliath's sword and some bread (at this time David wrote Psalm 52). Saul had shown a firm will that anyone who helped David would be punished.

But God was with David. Though Saul's sword came as close as under his nose, his life was within God's protection. Rather, David had two opportunities to kill Saul. But every time he had the chance, he did not kill Saul for the reason that Saul was 'anointed by the LORD.' David felt guilty for even his act of cutting off a part of Saul's clothes and agonized. Perhaps God came to watch David with greater expectation, who respected and exalted God's to such an extent.

Saul and David seen from the viewpoint of Him who had the right to appoint

<table>
<tr><th></th><th>Saul</th><th>David</th></tr>
<tr><td>Possession</td><td>Subjugated two things Samuel established, which was the law and priest to himself.
(ex.) He offered up to the end burnt offering himself(I Sa.chap.13)
He called the people 'my people.'(I Sa.chap.15)</td><td rowspan="2">Honored the appointer</td></tr>
<tr><td>Ground for</td><td>Ground for judging depended on keeping his throne
(ex.) even to the extent of killing priests</td></tr>
<tr><td>Close persons</td><td>Close aids for keeping his political power</td><td>The poor, debtors
(So he could wait 7.5 years though he became king of tribe of Judah.)</td></tr>
</table>

6. David's flight and Saul's last moment

I Sa. chap.27-31 / II Sa. chap.1 / I Ch. chap.1-10

Unable to stand Saul's pursuit any longer, David attempted to defect again and came to spend some time under king Achish of the Philistines because this time God permitted him to do so. During this period a war broke out between Israel and the Philistines and the Philistines won. Saul was wounded greatly and killed himself at the age of 80. Three sons of Saul including Jonathan were killed as well. The Philistine soldiers found the bodies of Saul and the princes, cut off Saul's neck and brought it to the Philistine land. They hung the three bodies and Saul's body without neck on the wall of Beth Shan near Mt. Gilboa. In the midst of this terrible situation the people of Jabesh Gilead who remembered the good deeds of Saul (who helped them 40 years earlier) picked up the bodies and held a funeral ceremony for them. This was the heart-warming story of this sad scene.

People who left to repay the favor (I Sa. 31:11-13)
The people of Jabesh Gilead received the favor of Saul 40 years ago.(I Sa. chap.11) Seemingly they taught their descendants the fact that in the year when Saul was made king, they could avoid the crisis thanks to the help of rescuing army of Israel who were mobilized and led by Saul. They also knew that Saul exercised an extremely monstrous politics for forty years. However, they remembered the favor they received long ago deep in their hearts. There is a saying that enmity is engraved on stones and favor on water. However, the people of Jabesh Gilead came to the wall of Beth Shan near Mt. Gilboa to bury Saul's body with neck cut off by traveling all night over mountains and waters so that they might repay the favor. They were the beautiful who engraved the favor deep in their inner tombstone.

Write down the contents of this lesson in the form of Tong Story

Let's pray in a loud voice so that we may be able to teach the contents of this lesson to our children

- Teach them to your children, talking about them when you sit at home and when you walk along the road, when you lie down and when you get up……so that your days and the days of your children may be many……as many as the days that the heavens are above the earth (Deuteronomy 11:19-21).
- you know those from whom you learned it, and how from infancy you have known the holy Scriptures(II Timothy 3:14-15).

14 Lesson : God's servant David

II Samuel, I Kings chap.1-2

Accumulative reading amount 29.87% 1189

The One Year Tongdok Bible Days 101-112 | Reading time 90 minutes

TongBible Story Overview

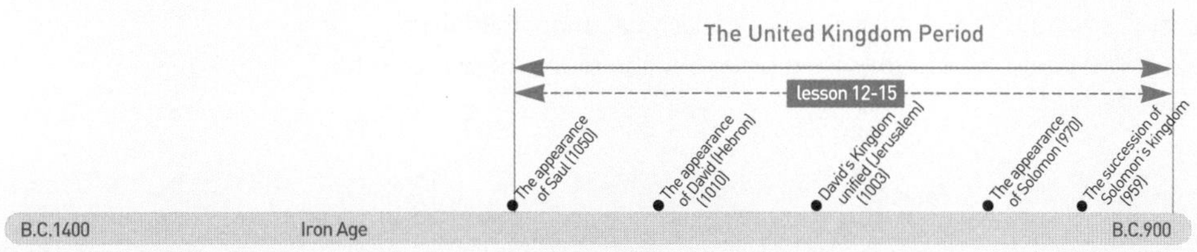

Reading the Old Testament in detail in the order of history (14)

After Saul died, the story of king David is unfolded. When we finish reading all of II Samuel and I Kings chapters 1 and 2, the story of David is over. The Scriptures applicable in this period are I Chronicles chapters 11 to 29 and David's Psalms 3, 7, 18, 51, 60 and 63.

SENSE! How to read the story of David

I Samuel ends with the death of Saul and his sons and II Samuel begins with the story of David. The records about David's rule started this way form the most part of II Samuel and I Chronicles.

Since David was made king of the tribe of Judah at age 30 until he returned to the God at age 70, he was pleased with living as God's servant and lived as a great statesman who served the people of God. Recognized as the greatest king in the history of Israel, David was named by God continually as the standard of good kings.

Psalms is the book filled with inspiration that contains hope and passion of the nation of Israel who loved to worship God. While young, David was a shepherd and later became a soldier, politician and king. Though his position kept changing, his lips always praised God and were with him. Even when he was in the position of giving orders, he ordered himself (his soul) to praise God.

Tong Point

Anointed three times

So far we have observed David who had lived as a fugitive since he was first anointed. Now II Samuel begins with what happened in the year when he was 30 years old, right after Saul died. At this time David was anointed by the tribe of Judah for the second time. Then seven and a half years later he was anointed by all Israel as king the third time. Regarding the contents of II Samuel chapter 1-10 we will observe the following three questions with a focus on his 'being anointed three times.'

-First, what did David do in Hebron whilst waiting for seven and a half years? What was the purpose of his waiting like this?

-Second, what did David do to firmly establish the united kingdom?

-Third, what did David think when he was made to live in peace? What did he confess?

1. David who became King of the tribe of Judah

II Sa. chap. 1-4

Hearing that Saul and Jonathan were killed, David sadly wept and fasted. He wrote sad songs for them and had the people of the tribe of Judah sing them after him and restored the honor of Saul.

In the midst of the confusing situation of the times a man called Abner (who was a subject of Saul) established the government of the eleven tribes in Mahanaim in the north. And David became king of only the tribe of Judah in Hebron. That way time went by with the nation divided into the South and North for seven years and six months.

One day while David waited for the right time hoping peaceful unification rather than a war, Abner who held actual power of Northern Israel came to Hebron to hand over the government of the eleven tribes to David. Rejoicing that he was

David who was anointed three times

The first: was anointed by Samuel

The second: was anointed by the tribe of Judah

The third: was anointed as king of all Israel.

able to fulfill the unification of the South and North peacefully without shedding blood, David finished negotiation with Abner and sent him back. However, on his way back Abner was assassinated by Joab who was David's right arm and the second strongman of his kingdom. Joab killed him because of personal grudge for Abner's having killed his younger brother Asahel and in the midst of the consciousness of crisis that if David and Abner worked together, the position of him who was the second strongman would be threatened.

It was such a very dangerous situation, where unless they were careful, David could have been misunderstood to have ordered Joab to kill Abner. A war could have broken out between the South and North. David wept very loudly. He wrote and sang lamenting songs and did not eat. Only then all the people of the South and North came to believe that David did not kill Abner but Joab committed the crime on his own. This way David was able to overcome the crisis.

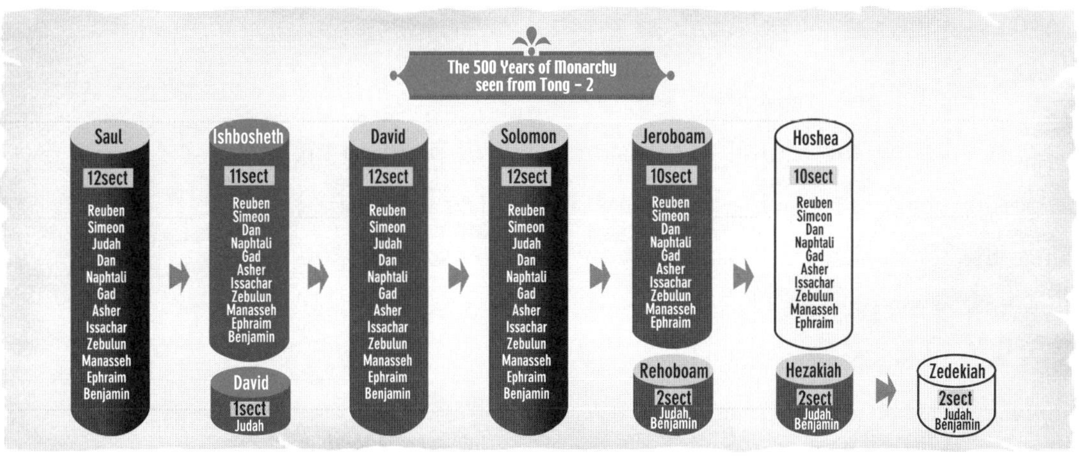

Tong Point

The degree of loyalty of A Kingdom of priests

The reason David's 40 year rule out of the 500 year royal rule was considered highly as "the way of David" was because David drew out intense devotion on A kingdom of priests. Although royal rule had fatal flaws as shown by many kings like Saul, David enhanced the degree of loyalty of A kingdom of priests by using that royal rule as a tool. Let's observe with this in mind.

2. The accomplishments of King David: the United Kingdom II Sa. chap.5-6/(I Ch. chap.11-16)

● Jerusalem

At last the representatives of the eleven tribes in the North came up to David in Hebron, anointing him as king. After a long wait David was set up officially as king of all the twelve tribes. Becoming king of the United Kingdom of Israel, David planned to move the capital to Jerusalem. David occupied Jerusalem, the city of natural fortress, where the Jebusites were still lived, and made it new capital.

Jerusalem
From long ago in Jerusalem were living the Jebusites, one of seven peoples in Canaan. Jerusalem is 640-770m above sea level. Even Manna generation who occupied Canaan under the leadership of Joshua could not conquer it.

● Moving the ark of covenant

After moving the capital to Jerusalem, David planned an important matter of moving the ark of covenant to the capital. Since the ark, which was taken away by Philistines during the last days of the period of judges, was returned to Israel, it had been left in Kiriath Jearim without being watched. Feeling sorry for this situation, David tried to move the ark to capital Jerusalem. For this work David mobilized 30,000 soldiers throughout the country, made a good cart and began to move the ark on the cart. Then the oxen which pulled the cart became shocked at the sound of the threshing floor of Nakon and stumbled. At that time, a man called Uzzah who reached out and took hold of the shaken ark was killed immediately.

Stopping the event and returning to the palace, David realized after much agony and reflection that although his zeal was good, his method was not God's. He did not observe the ordinance of God who said about the ark, "the Kohathites of the tribe of Levi are to come to do the carrying on their shoulders"(Num.4:15).

About three months later, David had Kohathite descendants carry the ark according to the word of God and walk six steps very carefully. When it was confirmed that God permitted the ark to be moved, David killed an oxen, sacrificed fellowship offering and burnt offerings and then rejoiced dancing before God.

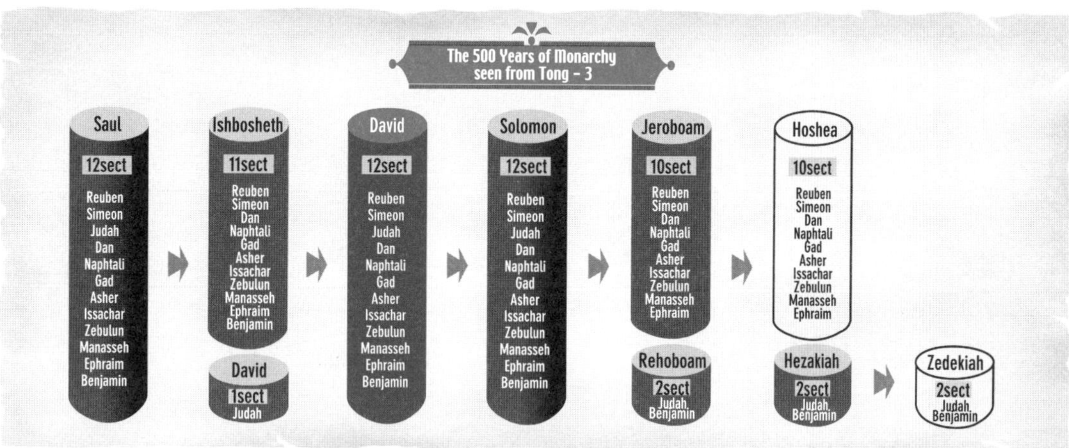

3. David's hope and God's blessing

II Sa. chap.7-10/ (I Ch. chap.17-19)

Moving the ark this way, David came to live in the palace peacefully. Right this time in the deepest of David's mind settled his precious wish to build the temple of God.

Accepting this mind of David and being very pleased, God gave the promise, "The temple will be built not by you but by your son Solomon but I have received such mind of yours with pleasure. I will keep your house forever and have your throne be continued." David who received this promise humbled himself as 'servant' before God and prayed the prayer of thanksgiving which is recorded in II Samuel chapter 7 verses 18-29.

Wherever David went, God was with him and gave him great victory. II Samuel chapter 10 shows what a high standing Israel came to gain in the relation of international diplomacy during the period of David.

The list of David's Cabinet
(II Sa. chap.8, 20)
Commanders of his forces
: Joab and Benaiah
Officer in charge of forced labor
: Adoniram
Recorder: Jehoshaphat
Priest: Zadok and Abiathar(son Ahimelech)
Secretary: Seraiah (Sheva)
Royal adviser
: David's sons and Ira

Tong Point

	Adversary	King	Battlefield	Scriptures
Wars of David's Kingdom	Philistines		Rephaim Valley	II Sa.5:17-25
	Jebusites		Jerusalem	I Ch. 11:4-7
	Moab			II Sa.8:2
	Soba, Damascus Aram	Hadadezer	Near the Euphrates	II Sa.8:3-6
	Edom		The Valley of Salt	I Ch.18:12
	Ammon, Aram, others	Hanun,Hadadezer	Helam	II Sa.10:1-19
	Ammon		Rabbah	II Sa.12:26-31
	Absalom's revolt	Absalom	Ephraim forest	II Sa.18:1-15
	Sheba's revolt	Sheba(leader)	Abel Beth Maakah	II Sa.20:1-22
	Philistines		Gob	II Sa.21:18-22

Tong Point

Hyssop Purification
Hyssop was a plant in the mint family that can be seen in Egypt, Palestine and elsewhere. It is said to have bitter taste. David prayed that his sin be cleansed with hyssop. Let's remember David having confessed that his first priority was to restore his relationship with God although bitter taste might come upon his life.

4. David's humanly side

II Sa. chap.11-24/(I Ch. chap.20-29)

The reason census was a mistake
God once ordered Moses to take census (Exo.30:12, Num.1:2). Therefore, census itself is not a sin. The reason God considered David's census evil was because of his condition of heart. Briefly forgetting that his strong military was the result of God's blessing, he intended to boast his power and great accomplishments. This kind of temptation whose prey anyone can easily become often comes out of pride.

David we have observed so far was indeed great. However, since he was human as well, he was unable to avoid mistakes and errors. One day David committed adultery with Bathsheba (the wife of general Uriah) and heard that she became pregnant. He sent Uriah into a most fierce battlefield and had him killed. In order to meet his lust, he used his power to hide his sin and killed innocent Uriah. What David did was very wicked in the sight of God.

God sent prophet Nathan to point out David's sin. Immediately admitting his sin, David came before God and repented greatly with tears in his eyes(at this time, he wrote Psalm 51). However, the first child Bathsheba gave birth to died as the penalty for the sin.

In the remaining part of II Samuel are described the pains David went through as punishment for his sin. Amnon the first son of David raped Tamar who was his step sister, and Absalom his third son revenged himself on Amnon. Absalom who became distant from David because of his killing Amnon pretended to be reconciled with his father. But soon he rebelled against David to become king and David had to run away from Jerusalem to avoid his son's coup d'etat.(Psa.3, 7) However, Absalom was killed and David was able to return to Jerusalem (II Sa. chap.22 and Psa.18).

In the last days of his life David commited another sin. He forcefully took census as he felt like showing off his accomplishments. Only when David was given the report of the census, he realized his mistake and regreted. Repenting of his sin, David built an altar and sacrifices to God at the threshing floor of Araunah as instructed by Prophet Gad. Later his son Solomon built the temple at this place. That is also Mt. Moriah where Abraham intended to offer Isaac to God long ago.

5. David's Will I Ki. chap.1-2

David who used to be a shepherd in Bethlehem and then lived as king of Israel left his two important wills with Solomon as he approached death. First, he told him his religious will that Solomon should obey the commandment of God and do according to that way. He taught him that it was the secret to living a blessed life. Then he told him his political will. He advised Solomon (using high-level political language) concerning the urgent assignments he should politically solve when he who was still young and inexperienced, became king. This way David died and Solomon succeeded him as king of Israel.

What David left behind
David closed an extremely eventful life. By showing people an example, David left behind a community who gave its possession gladly to God. (ICh.29:9,14) He left behind a lot of fund for building temple as well.(I Ch.29:3) Then he died while praying for the dream of God to remain in the heart of Solomon(I Ch.29:19) Since he lived such a beautiful life, his name came to remain in our hearts as well.

6. David's Psalms Psalms

David who wrote extremely beautiful Psalms was a poet. Even when he narrowly survived avoiding and running away from Saul, his songs were full of gratitude and praise for God. His earnest pleading and appealing to seek God eventually used to end with the songs of joy for Him. Living in the twenty first century, we are very grateful that we also can read and sing the beautiful Psalms of David who did not live complaining and unsatisfied but lived for the glory of God and offered praises to Him.

Write down the contents of this lesson in the form of Tong Story

Let's pray in a loud voice so that we may be able to teach the contents of this lesson to our children

- Teach them to your children, talking about them when you sit at home and when you walk along the road, when you lie down and when you get up……so that your days and the days of your children may be many……as many as the days that the heavens are above the earth (Deuteronomy 11:19-21).
- you know those from whom you learned it, and how from infancy you have known the holy Scriptures(II Timothy 3:14-15).

Session 6

Mind and Wisdom

Tong Map

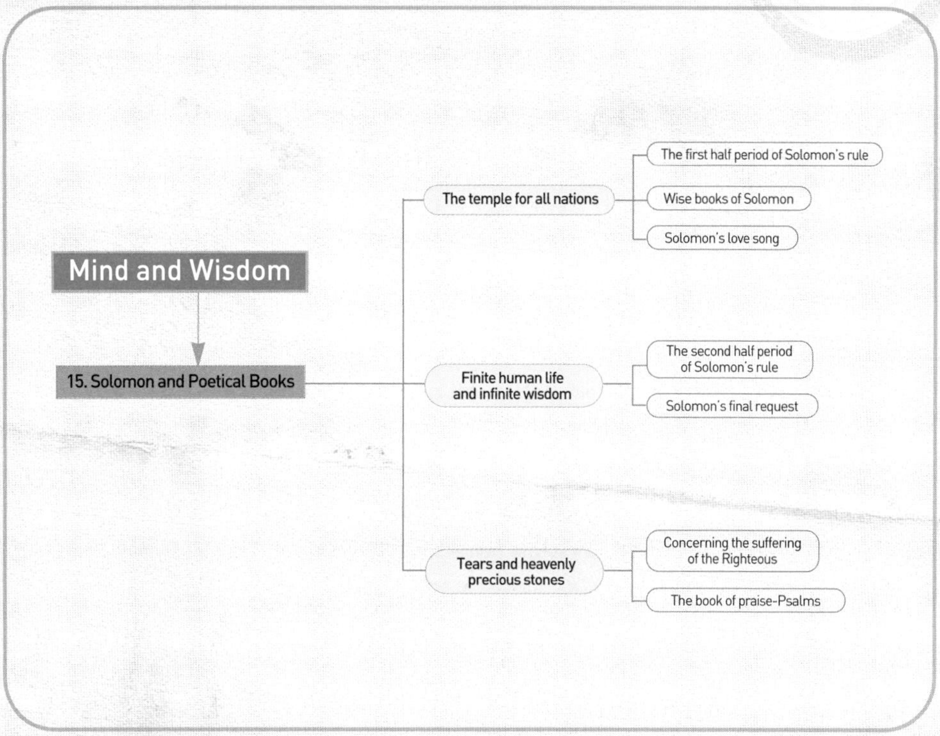

Tong Concept

- **We observe Solomon with 'mind and wisdom.'**

Let's observe Solomon's 40 year rule with the viewpoint of 'mind and wisdom' by dividing it into the first half of 23 years and the second half of 17 years.

- **The temple for all nations**

Solomon who inherited David's kingdom, stared building the temple. Let's remember that the temple was not only for the nation of Israel but also for all the nations.

Tong At a glance

* Looking around the forest

Solomon who asked for wisdom from God came to enjoy the most prosperous era of Israel. His knowledge and wisdom are famous to this day. Literature containing wisdom such as; Song of Songs, Proverbs and Ecclesiastes began with him. However, the era of Solomon began to break down along with his bad choices. Only belatedly Solomon realized how meager human life is in the great sovereign administration of God and as a result left behind Ecclesiastes which powerfully preaches that fearing God is wisdom. Job is located here in the extension line of wisdom literature so that we may read it with other poetical books although its chronological background is the era of Patriarchs which was much earlier than the times of Solomon. Job is the book which deeply explores human suffering. Its theme is 'human tears and heavenly precious stones.' It proclaims that true wisdom is trusting God in all situation.

* Land and annual ring

Solomon who succeeded David spent the first three years aligning the ruling system and started building the temple four years and two months after his enthronement. It took seven years to build. The Jerusalem temple was not only for Israel but for all nations. This purpose is revealed in the prayer Solomon prayed in the ceremony of dedication in the sight of all people. Solomon was a genius in commerce. Palestine was located in an area favorable for trade strategically(I Ki.10:28-29). Solomon traded with ship between Ezion Geber located at the northeastern end of the Coast of Eden and Ophir located at the southwestern side of Arabia while being helped by Hiram king of Tyre.(I Ki.9:26-28, 10:11-12,22)

* Wind and Climate

Solomon established 12 administrative districts, dispatched ministers to each district and entrusted them with tax and public labor. Militarily he imported horses and chariots from Egypt, organized permanent army not for real battle but for display of national power. Economically, he possessed the important places of trade of the world and imposed passage tax. He traded with Egypt, Arabia and the like vibrantly. He also built ship-building plants, and bronze smelting works. However, as time went by, he had to hear people complaining about his military conscription and forced labor that made them tired, which became one of the reasons for the nation being divided after his death. So many pagan princesses came into Jerusalem whom he married politically for the purpose of keeping stable relations with surrounding countries. They caused Solomon's heart to depart from God gradually and idol-worship culture of the Gentiles began to spread in Israel.

Tong Seeing the forest

Proverbs If we summarize the overall theme of proverbs in a word, it is 'wisdom'. Solomon explains wisdom in proverbs in a variety of ways. In Proverbs wisdom gives feast like humans do, invites us and explains by comparing the wise with the unwise and showing the difference. Proverbs stresses that wisdom is never attained through the teachings of the wise or artificial efforts but it comes through only 'the mind that fears the LORD.

Song of Songs Song of Songs implies the most beautiful song. Song of Solomon shows the pure and beautiful love between Solomon and the Shulammite woman. This book praises God's goodness and holy plan through the love of human beings who are creatures of God. The love described in this book has no barrier and contains truthfulness, care, devotion and responsibility for each other. This love was made perfect by the love of the cross of Jesus Christ who made us His bride.

Ecclesiastes "Meaningless, meaningless, everything is meaningless." This first declaration of the preacher is the theme of the whole Ecclesiastes. While living this world, many people seek wealth and comfort by using tricks and conjurings and shout to people as if it were the wisdom to live well in this world. But, Solomon who enjoyed various luxuries more than anybody else firmly claimed, everything apart from God is meaningless. Solomon taught through this book that fearing God and doing righteousness and justice is true wisdom to valuably live this life which is given to us only once.

Job Job is the book which teaches us that the problem of affliction is not useless for man but it is a process of making a jewel in us. One day a great disaster came upon Job who was praised by God and people for living honestly, righteously and piously. Losing lots of wealth and children in a moment and groaning due to a terrible sickness, Job still did not lose faith in God in spite of that. His three friends who visited him condemned him with the logic that all suffering is God's punishment against sins. Job claimed his innocence and sought God's answer. After the dialogue between him and his friends which did not seem to have any solution but just was repeated, God talked about His might and wisdom that human beings can not dare to figure out. God rewarded a greater blessing to Job who knelt down before Him humbly.

Psalms Psalms is the book of prayer and praise of Israel which was written for the purpose of praising and worshipping God. Though this book is not classified as one kind, generally it is classified as follows: Psalms of entreaty by which we ask God for help, Psalms of praises which contain praise sung by communities or individuals, imperial Psalms by which people praise God's royal authority or kings of Israel, Psalms of wisdom which teach lessons and wisdom and Psalms of worship whose background was the worship carried out at the temple.

15 Lesson Solomon and Poetical Books

I kings chap.3-11, Proverbs, Song of songs, Ecclesiastes, Job, Psalms

Accumulative reading amount 41.33% 1189

The One Year Tongdok Bible Days 113-158 | Reading time 330 minutes

TongBible Story Overview

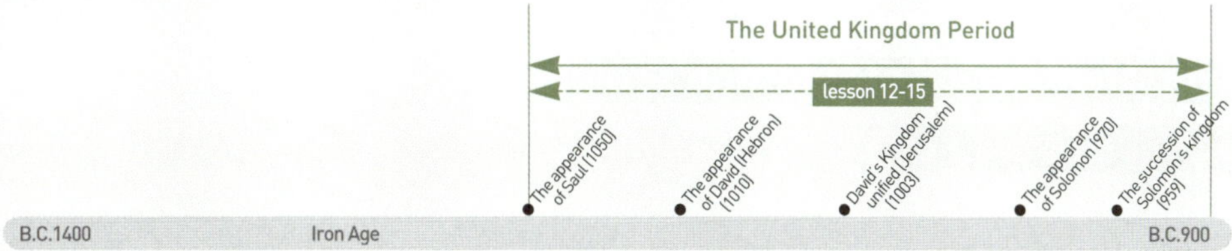

Reading the Old Testament in detail in the order of history (15)

Now comes the story of Solomon the son of David. I Kings chapters 3 to 10 records the first half period of Solomon. It would be beneficial to read also Psalms 72, 127, Proverbs and Song of Songs which were written by Solomon. Then we read I Kings chapter 11 was the second half of Solomon's rule together with Ecclesiastes which he wrote towards the end of his life. After that, we read through Job and Psalms. Job was nearly a contemporary of Abraham. Therefore it might make more sense to read it together with Genesis. Despite so, it is also beneficial to read Job and Psalms together after Ecclesiastes in the context of flow, because it is classified as a poetical book along with Psalms, Proverbs and Song of Songs.

SENSE! How to read Solomon and poetical books

Solomon ruled Israel for forty years from around B.C.970 to around B.C.930, spent about three years after enthronement putting the governing system in place, started building the temple on the second month of the fourth year and finished it in seven years. Then he built the palace for 13 years. However, Solomon who enjoyed such a luxurious life had to hear complaints from the people who were getting tired of compulsory military service and forced labor. Furthermore, due to his political marriage aimed at maintaining a stable relationship with surrounding foreign countries, lots of foreign princesses came into Jerusalem. Solomon's heart gradually drifted away from God because of them. Ecclesiastes is the book he wrote after he belatedly realized how vain the human life is when apart from God.

The chronological background of Job is the period of patriarchs which was much earlier than the days of Solomon, but it has been placed here for the purpose of reading it with other poetical books on the extension line of wisdom literature. In addition, we are going to read through most Psalms besides the Psalms which were read along with the period of David.

Tong Point

The temple for all nations
We can put in order Solomon's first half of rule as a total of 23 years; the first three years to align his cabinet + 7 years to build the temple + 13 years to build the palace. Israel established the foundation of nation as the 'kingdom of priest and holy nation', which takes us back to the days of Moses which also dreamt of itself becoming the channel of blessing.

1. The first half period of Solomon's rule

I Ki. chap.3-10/ (II Ch. chap.1-9)

● Solomon who asked for wisdom

After David died, Solomon succeeded him as king of Israel. King Solomon sacrificed to God one thousand burnt-offerings in Gibeon. Pleased with this, God appeared to Solomon in his dream and asked what he wanted. He asked God for wisdom with which he can judge so that he may rule the people wisely. God promised him that He would give him wealth and glory in addition to wisdom he asked for. There is a famous story about Solomon's trial. The case is about two women who quarreled each other claiming each was the true mother of a baby. Solomon who solved this issue brilliantly with the wisdom God gave him came to be trusted and loved by the people greatly. He finally started building the temple on the foundation of political and material legacy he was handed down from David.

● Temple oriented toward nations

Mobilizing 183,300 people, Solomon started building the temple. This temple was completed after seven years long

Solomon's temple

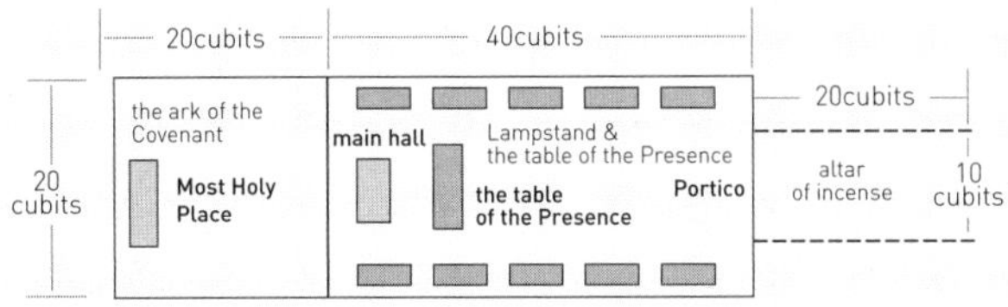

-Started building the temple: the month of Ziv(second month), 480 years after Exodus, fourth year of King Solomon
-Duration of building the temple: seven years
-Completion of the temple: the month of Bul(eighth month), 11th year of King Solomon
-Temple outskirts: length 60: width 20: height 30(cubits)
Most Holy Place: length 20: width 20: height 20(cubits)

construction and Jerusalem became the center of all people as political capital and as the religious holy land. On the day of temple dedication, Solomon (as representative of all the people) confessed God as the LORD of all Israel and declared that they would observe the LORD's ordinances and laws. He offered the prayer that this temple would be used so that all the nations of the world would know the will of God and the people of Israel would be aware of it as responsibility and mission.

Solomon ruled aware of the mission for the nations.

Temples recorded in the Bible

- Temple by Solomon: destroyed by Babylon in B.C.586(II Ki.25:8,9)
- Temple by Zerubbabel: could not amount to the temple by Solomon in massiveness and elegance (Ezr.5:2, 6:15-18)
- Temple by Herod: was started on the vast lot in B.C.20 and completed in A.D.64. It was destroyed by Roman general Titus in A.D.70 and now a rocky dome is on the site.

2. Wise books of Solomon Pro. chap.1-31

Proverbs is the book about wisdom, written by Solomon. He defined in detail what wisdom is. True wisdom is gained from the attitude of mind to rely on and trust God rather than from the result of deep study and effort.

Solomon was the one who got wisdom from God. Therefore, the core of wisdom told by Solomon was none other than 'God.' It meant that God is the root of wisdom. Wisdom came from the mind of fearing God.

- **Wisdom as said by Proverbs - what is wisdom?**

1) To fear and trust the LORD - Pro.1:7; 15:33, 16:3; 19:23
2) To know man's lack and weakness - Pro.30:2-4
3) To speak truth with an honest mind - Pro.11:6, 20:23
4) To care for poor neighbors - Pro.3:27-28, 11:25, 14:31
5) To love to be admonished and disciplined
   - Pro.3:12, 12:1, 13:1
6) To watch out for what the lips speak
   - Pro.10:11, 10:19, 20:15, 21:23
7) To have the attitude of diligent life - Pro.6:6-11, 10:4-5
8) To make good friends - Pro.13:20, 22:24-25, 27:1
9) To not envy prosperity of the wicked
   - Pro.24:1-2, 24:19-20
10) To turn down foolish temptations - Pro.4:23-27, 5:7-8
11) To be slow in anger - Pro.16:32, 25:15, 29:11

Wisdom any one can gain
Solomon was sure that wisdom was given to all who fear God and earnestly asked Him for wisdom. The reason was that God who was the root of wisdom was pleased to give wisdom to people.

Jesus the very body of true wisdom
Meeting with wisdom personally is loving to receive the request of God who tells people to return to the state prior to man's fall, that is, the state that God made man good. If we see this from the overview of the whole Bible, later the way is opened that we can meet true wisdom through Jesus Christ.

3. Solomon's love song Son. chap.1-8

Song of Songs is a pure and beautiful love story between Solomon and the Shulammite woman. Through beautiful and sorrowful love songs we can know how abundant the heart of love for each other was.

The love of Song of Songs
Song of Songs compares the love of God for the people of Israel to the love of Christ for the church his bride.

- **The love that Song of Songs teaches - What is love?**

1) Love is beyond limit - Son.1:5-6
2) Love is to focus on each other - Son.2:2-3
3) Love is detailed concern and caring - Son.2:6-7
4) Love is walking together - Son.2:10-13

5) Love is to cover each other's flaws - Son.4:7

6) Love is belonging to each other - Son.2:16, 6:3

7) Love is overcoming even death - Son.8:6-7

Tong Point

Finite human life and infinite wisdom

Solomon's second half of rule of 17 years was a very regrettable time when all the foundation stored up during his first half of rule, (proverbs, philosophy, knowledge, wisdom and all the foundation of Jerusalem) was destroyed. He lost the center of his heart to the point of having his country divided into South and North. The final precious stone Solomon found in the last days of his life was 'vain.'The book which contains that realization is Ecclesiastes. Meanwhile, although all the 12 tribes looked like one nation outwardly until the days of Solomon, let's remember that inwardly, divisive elements were budding like bruised apples.

4. The second half period of Solomon's rule I Ki. chap.11

The forty years when Solomon ruled Israel are largely divided into two periods. The first period was twenty three years Solomon spent after he became king putting in place his cabinet (three years), building the temple (seven years) and building his palace (thirteen years). One important characteristic of his rule during this period was that he loved God. However, during the second half period of his rule, Solomon's heart drifted away from his love for God. In those days Solomon had over 1,000 concubines he brought through political marriage. He built luxurious palaces for Gentile princesses of many countries. Lots of temples of idols such as Chemosh, Molek, Ashtoreth which the Gentile women served were built. God told Solomon to return to Him as often as twice but he did not decide to turn to God.

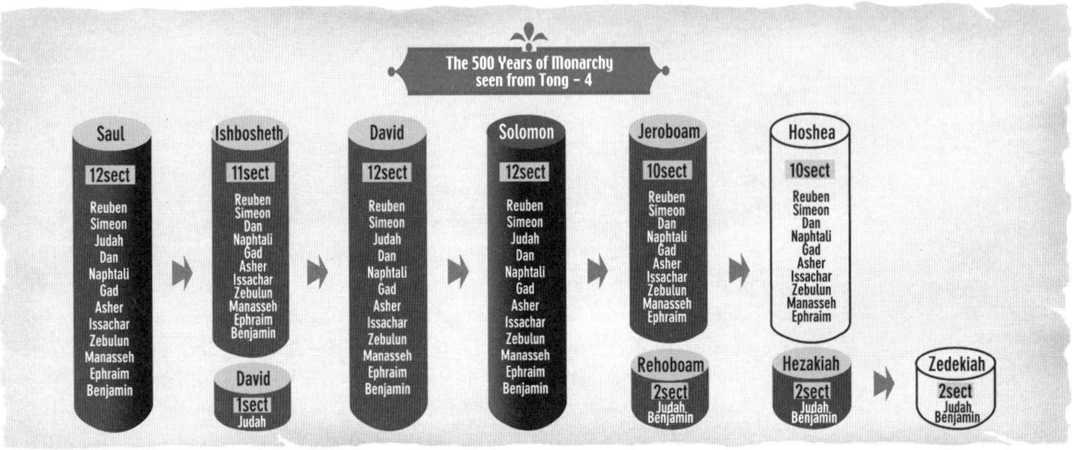

5. Solomon's final request Ecc. chap.1-12

Solomon was the person who had and enjoyed more wealth than anybody else without lack in human history. He also enjoyed all kinds of pleasure and entertainment to his full satisfaction. However, when he faced the end of his life, he realized that all he enjoyed in the past was vain. 'Ecclesiastes' is the book which contains this realization.

● The preacher's confession about life

1) The labor of man is vain - Ecc.1:14

2) There is nothing new under the sun - Ecc.1:10

3) Pleasure is vain - Ecc.2:1

There is a time (Ecc. chap.3)

"There is a time for everything, and a season for every activity under heaven"

a time to be born	a time to die
a time to plant	a time to uproot
a time to kill	a time to heal
a time to tear down	a time to build
a time to weep	a time to laugh
a time to mourn	a time to dance
a time to scatter stones	a time to gather them
a time to embrace	a time to refrain
a time to search	a time to give up
a time to keep	a time to throw away
a time to tear	a time to mend
a time to be silent	a time to speak
a time to love	a time to hate
a time for war	a time for peace

"He has made everything beautiful in its time. He has also set eternity in the hearts of men; yet they cannot fathom what God has done from beginning to end" (Ecc. 3:11)

4) Human wisdom has limit - Ecc.2:14-16

5) There is a time for everything - Ecc.3:1-8

6) All people return to dust - Ecc.3:20

7) We can't be satisfied with wealth - Ecc.5:10

● The preacher's exhortation - if we want to live happily

1) The man who does good is happy - Ecc.3:12

2) Those who help one another are happy - Ecc.4:12

3) The man who watches his lips is happy - Ecc.5:2

4) Those who remember death are happy - Ecc.7:2

5) The man who is not biased is happy - Ecc.7:16-18

● Preacher's Request- Remember

1) Remember that all belong to God - Ecc.9:1

2) Remember all people are sinners - Ecc.9:3

3) Remember God's judgment - Ecc.11:9; 12:14

4) Remember that you will become old - Ecc.12:1-7

5) Remember your Creator when you are young - Ecc.12:1,13

Although Ecclesiastes declared uncertainty and passing of life, it is not the theme of the whole book. "In the preacher's strong declaration, "All is vain" is contained an alternative of how to be able to overcome that vanity. The alternative that the preacher suggests was that you should remember God the Creator as soon as possible while you are young.

Tong Point

Tears and heavenly precious stones
What meaning does human hardship have? Hardship is not something that is useless to people but a process which makes precious stone within. Let's discover in Job the fact that our life keeps becoming heavenly stones in God. We should trust, praise and glorify God in the middle of any hardship or difficulty.

6. Concerning the suffering of the Righteous

Job chap. 1-42

Job was the person who was evaluated, "This man was blameless and upright; he feared God and shunned evil"(Job 1:1). He lived a model life without any blame.

However, all his wealth was taken away in a moment and even his children were killed on the same time and on the same day. All of Job's body, from the top of his head to the soles of his feet came to have painful sores. Yet, thinking that a man blessed by God can also receive trouble, he did not complain to God but accepted his miserable reality as it was.

Meanwhile, Job's friends, Eliphaz, Bildad, Zophar came to Job. When they saw his terrible situation, they mourned together. However, they increasingly condemned and blamed Job. This suffering was all the result of sin, according to their thoughts. They condemed Job with rough and piercing words. Of course, his friends' argument was not groundless or wrong at all, but they were unable to understand that sometimes the righteous can suffer in the midst of the will of God.

In this situation, Job came to see that his suffering was the will of God. He realized that this suffering was never meaningless but there was a clear purpose of God who intended to refine Job and make him pure.

"But He knows the way that I take; when He has tested me, I will come forth as gold"(Job 23:10).

Finally God intervened in the seemingly endless argument between Job and his friends. God proclaimed the providence of nature that was operated according to His will and how limited and prejudiced people's wisdom was. Both Job's suffering and restoration were in the hands of God. Job confessed, "Now my eyes have seen you"(Job 42:5). This way the deep encounter between Job and God was made and then the book of Job came to an end.

Suffering also is blessing because suffering refines us in the hand of God and helps us grow into the children of God. Suffering is not something useless to human beings but the process of making a precious stone within me. In the God who sheds tears along with man's pain and makes people understand many things, our life becomes a heavenly precious stone.

7. The book of praise - Psalms Psalms

Psalms is the book of prayer and praise of Israel in order to praise and worship God and contains the contents of hope and passion of Israel.

Generally, Psalms can be divided into Psalms of petition asking God for help, Psalms of praise containing the praise communities or individuals sing, imperial Psalms praising

God's royal authority or kings of Israel, wisdom Psalms teaching instruction or wisdom, worship Psalms with worship in the temple as background and the like. The majority of Psalms(73 out of 150) were written by David. We can see David as a politician in the books of Samuel whereas in Psalms we can see him as a man of faith who had a deep and close encounter with God with prayer and praise. We can know that the strength of David who was able to read the dark flow of the times of Saul's rule into the God-centered flow was contained in his confession of faith.

Authors of Psalms

Volume	Chapter	Author
First	1-41	David, unanimous
Second	42-72	David, sons of Korah, Asaph, Solomon, unanimous
Third	73-89	David, sons of Korah, Asaph, Heman, Ethan
Fourth	90-106	Moses, David, unanimous
Fifth	107-150	David, Solomon, unanimous

We can praise God with all our heart and sincerity through Psalms of various Psalmists other than those of David. Thus Psalms is a beautiful book where we can take a look at life philosophy of David and other psalmists through their language of heaven used by them for God.

- Psalms and praise

1) Who is blessed? - Psa.1-9

2) Since there is faith in God - Psa.10-18

3) Even amid deep sigh - Psa.19-27

4) God who is a true protector and refuge - Psa.28-34

5) God's just judgment - Psa.35-41

6) God is our strength and help - Psa.42-53

7) God who listens to the prayer of the righteous - Psa.54-66

8) God who is the source of all blessings - Psa.67-72

9) Great and wonderful things God has done - Psa.73-78

10) In the tent where God dwells - Psa.79-85

11) The one who gives strength to those who follow the way of the LORD - Psa.86-89

12) To God who is full of power and beauty - Psa.90-102

13) The wonderful love God extends - Psa.103-106

14) God who knows our condition - Psa.107-108

15) Longing for the LORD's statutes and commandments - Psa.119

16) Praise of the joy of going up to the temple of God - Psa.120-134

17) The one who watches over all people's hearts - Psa.135-142

18) God whose kindness is eternal and infinite - Psa.143-150

Write down the contents of this lesson in the form of Tong Story

....

....

....

....

....

Let's pray in a loud voice so that we may be able to teach the contents of this lesson to our children

- Teach them to your children, talking about them when you sit at home and when you walk along the road, when you lie down and when you get up……so that your days and the days of your children may be many……as many as the days that the heavens are above the earth (Deuteronomy 11:19-21).
- you know those from whom you learned it, and how from infancy you have known the holy Scriptures(II Timothy 3:14-15).

7 Session

Line of Love, Line of Mission

Tong Map

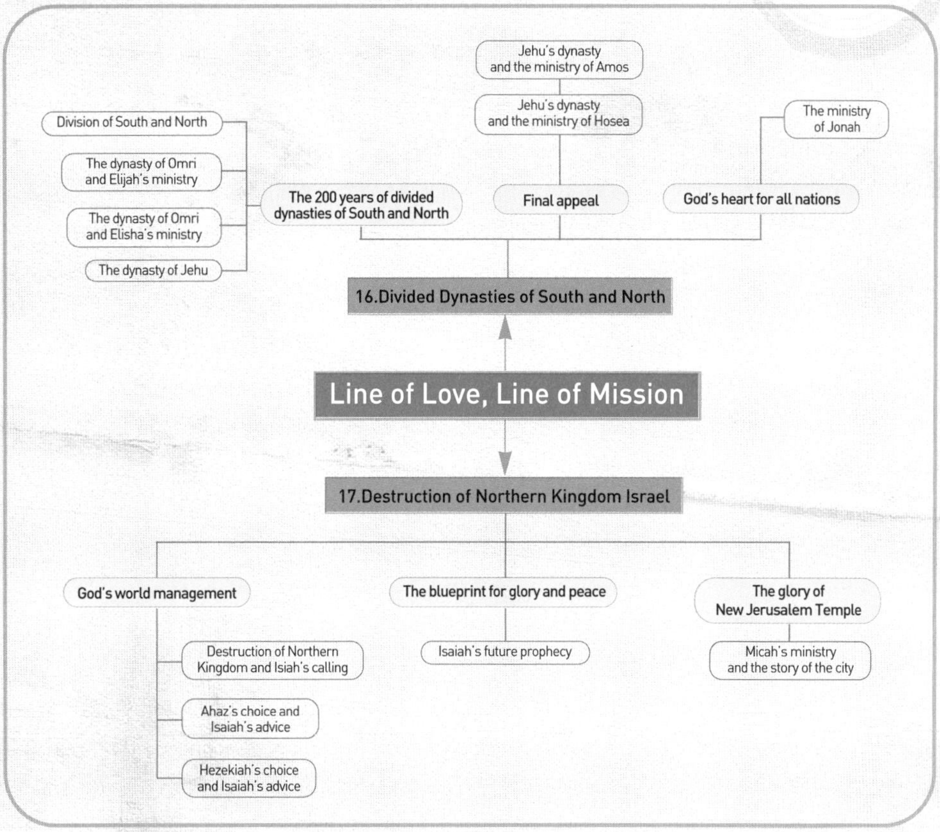

Tong Concept

- **Divided dynasties of South and North in Tong!**

It is important to observe I Kings and II Kings and prophetical books by connecting them. By putting into order prophets who were respectively active in Northern Israel and Southern Judah, we should be able to observe the situations of those days; international situations and prophets' messages.

Tong At a glance

* Looking around the forest

Now is unfolded the history of divided kingdoms of South and North in Israel. The era of Israel's royal rule was geared with the age of prophets. So, only when we read the books of Kings and Chronicles with prophetical books, we can go after the heart of God within those times more closely. During this period, in Northern Israel ministered Elijah, Elisha, Amos, Hosea, Jonah and the like whereas in Southern Judah ministered Isaiah, Micah and the like. God's world management is revealed more prominently in this part.

* Land and annual ring

The general view regarding the year of Israel's division is B.C.931 while another view is B.C.922. There is not much difference. The tribes of Judah and Benjamin were made to belong to South and ten remaining tribes to North. Regrettably, Jeroboam (the first king of North) built the idol of gold calf in Dan the northernmost city of Northern Kingdom and in Bethel the southernmost city and even changed feasts and priests as he willed. Particularly, the days of Ahab were the dark days when the whole Northern Israel was saturated with idolatry. During this period, Elijah and Elisha ministered. Later the country became prosperous during the rule of Jeroboam II of Jehu dynasty which destroyed Omri dynasty. But there were extreme religious depravity and severe economic inequality. Northern Israel who did not give their heart to God in spite of the earnest appeals of prophets Amos and Hosea who tried to change such situation was eventually destroyed by the Assyrian Empire in B.C.722.

* Wind and Climate

The military power of Northern Israel during the rule of Jeroboam II was strong enough to restore the boundaries from the mouth of Hamath to the sea of Arabah. They enjoyed economic prosperity through vibrant commerce. However, such prosperity and stability did not lead to mature life but was revealed as license and corruption. Thus, Amos and Hosea began to prophesise judgment.

Meanwhile, Micah who was from a small agricultural village called Moresheth was a prophet who ministered in Southern Judah during the rule of Jotham, Ahaz and Hezekiah of Southern Judah. He also shouted telling the corrupt social and religious leaders to establish justice correctly.

Tong Seeing the forest

II Kings Both Judah and Israel ignored God and served the idols and running to destruction. God did not give up and sent Elijah and Elisha and then He both rebuked and appeased them by sending lots of prophets again. However, Northern Israel who kept on rejecting God's plea for their return was finally destroyed by the Assyrian Empire from the North in B.C.722. Southern Judah was also destroyed by Babylonian Empire in B.C. 586 and taken captive.

Amos Amos was a prophet who was from Tekoa, a small town in Southern Judah and went to Northern Israel and preached the word of God there. The first part of Amos begins with the message of judging such different nations as Syria, Philistine, Tyre, Edom, Ammon and Moab. The people of Northern Israel who heard this prophesy of Amos might have welcomed his prophecy because the nations Amos prophesised judgment against were the nations Israel despised.

However, immediately, his prophecy of judgment was continued to be aimed at Northern Israel. Amos strongly pointed out the sins of the rich, the national officials and priests (who were the established class of society) for having failed to lead the society justly as well as oppressing and exploiting the poor and the weak. He clearly declared the fact that however many gifts and however much tithe they offered, if they did not care for the poor, God would not be pleased with their worship.

Hosea Prophet Hosea worked in Northern Israel in the similar period as prophet Amos or a little later. His life was not an easy one. He married an adulterous woman Gomel according to the commandment of God. He came to bear adulterous children through her. Through this experience he came to understand the Heart of God for Northern Israel of that age. He came to realize deeply the Heart of God who could not give up his love toward Israel to the end even while striking unappreciative Israel with lashes. That way Hosea was able to become the prophet of love who pleaded with the people with tears to return to God.

Jonah God called Jonah as prophet and commanded him to go to Nineveh, the capital of Assyria and shout the imminent judgment of God against them. However, Jonah disobeyed the word of God and ran away to Tarshish which was on the opposite side of Nineveh. Eventually, he experienced going into and out of the belly of a big fish due to a storm God sent. He did not feel the deep sincerity of God in spite of that.

When the people of Nineveh came to repent and God on hearing this message granted mercy, the innermost feelings of Jonah who wished Nineveh to perish can be seen. Then God persuaded Jonah so that he may be able to realize the Heart of God who spared and loved not only the people of Israel but also all the nations of the world.

Isaiah

In the midst of the expansion of the Assyria Empire, its power to the south, (King Ahaz of Southern Judah) tried to find ways to be able to avoid this crisis from a wrong diplomatic policy. Stressing that God was the one who managed the world, prophet Isaiah told king Ahaz to believe that if he trusts in God, then He would keep and protect him. But king Ahaz did not obey to the end.
Hezekiah (the next king) faced the most dangerous moment when Assyria was surrounded by the wall of Jerusalem. He fortunately saved the country by kneeling down before God. However, the shout of prophet Isaiah was not accepted by the whole Israel. Isaiah prophesied that Southern Judah would be taken captive by Babylon. The book of Isaiah is the book which is famous for containing the most prophecy about Jesus Christ who was the Messiah to come.

Micah

The message of Micah who was a contemporary in the similar period to that of Isaiah was proclaimed toward Samaria and Jerusalem, capitals of two divided kingdoms in the south and north. Amos proclaimed social justice in Northern Israel whereas Micah preached the similar message to Southern Judah and Northern Israel, with focus on Judah particularly.
He sharply criticized corrupt social and religious leaders who oppressed the poor and gave bribe to judges and urged the people of Samaria and Jerusalem to repent. In spite of that, Micah preached God's salvation and forgiveness which were to come and also prophesied that Jesus would be born in Bethlehem.

16 Lesson

Divided Dynasties of South and North

I Kings chap.12-22, II Kings chap.1-14, Amos, Hosea, Jonah

Accumulative reading amount 45.5% 1189

The One Year Tongdok Bible Days 159-174 | Reading time 120 minutes

TongBible Story Overview

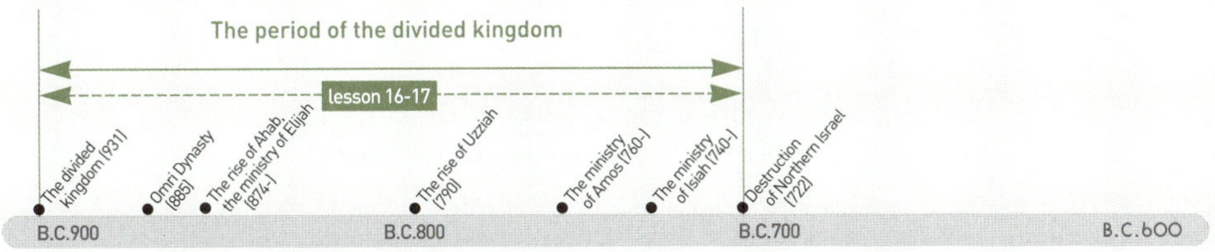

Reading the Old Testament in detail in the order of history (16)

Israel was a united nation from Saul to David to Solomon. We now begin to study the era of divided kingdoms. The nation was divided into two during the rule of Rehoboam, Solomon's son. It would be easy for you to remember that the books of Kings deal with the stories of Northern Israel and Southern Judah together whereas the books of Chronicles deal with only the history of Southern Judah. First we read I Kings chapters 12 to 22 and up to II Kings 1 to 14. Here are contained the stories from the division of the nation in B.C.931 to the era of Jeroboam II of the middle of B.C. 8th century. In those days, Elijah and Elisha ministered in Northern Israel. During the rule of Jeroboam II of Northern Israel, Amos and Hosea ministered. In the same period, Jonah ministered in Nineveh. As their ministry was over, Northern Israel came to decline.

How to read divided dynasties of South and North

Regrettably, all the 19 kings of the Northern kingdom ended up following the evil way of Jeroboam. In Northern Israel various coup d'etats took place which resulted in various dynasties being established. Especially, in Omri dynasty, king Ahab the son of Omri was notorious for (along with queen Jezebel) unhesitatingly committing the evil of making the whole country of Israel an idolatrous country serving Baal and Asherah. During this period ministered prophets Elijah and Elisha. After this, in Jehu dynasty which destroyed the Omri dynasty, the country was very strong when Jeroboam II was king. At this time, such prophets as Amos, Hosea and Jonah ministered. However, despite the earnest appealing of these prophets, Northern Israel did not turn to God. Eventually, the kingdom was destroyed by the Assyrian empire in B.C.722. This way the period of Israel's king's rule went in gear with the period of prophets' ministry.

Tong Point

The 200 years of divided dynasties of South and North

Israel was a united kingdom during the rule of Saul, David and Solomon. After that, divided kingdoms began. Things got complicated, which also meant it became more abundant. The whole country of Northern Kingdom was in an age totally apart from the mission of 'kingdom of priests and holy nation'. Important points to note;

- The characteristic of 200 year Southern Judah : went back and forth from the way of David to that of Jeroboam.
- The 200 year Northern Israel can be explained in four ways as follows;

- First, it went straight in the way of Jeroboam 200 years.
- Second, it began with Jeroboam and ended with Hosea. Dynasties of Omri and Jehu rose and fell.
- Third, prophets Elijah and Elisha during the dynasty of Omri, and Amos and Hosea during the dynasty of Jehu attempted to make U-turn into the way of David.
- Fourth, eventually, Assyria appeared in B.C. 8th century and turned Samaria into Samaritans (mixed blood).

1. Division into South and North

I Ki. chap.12-16:14/(II Ch. chap.10-17)

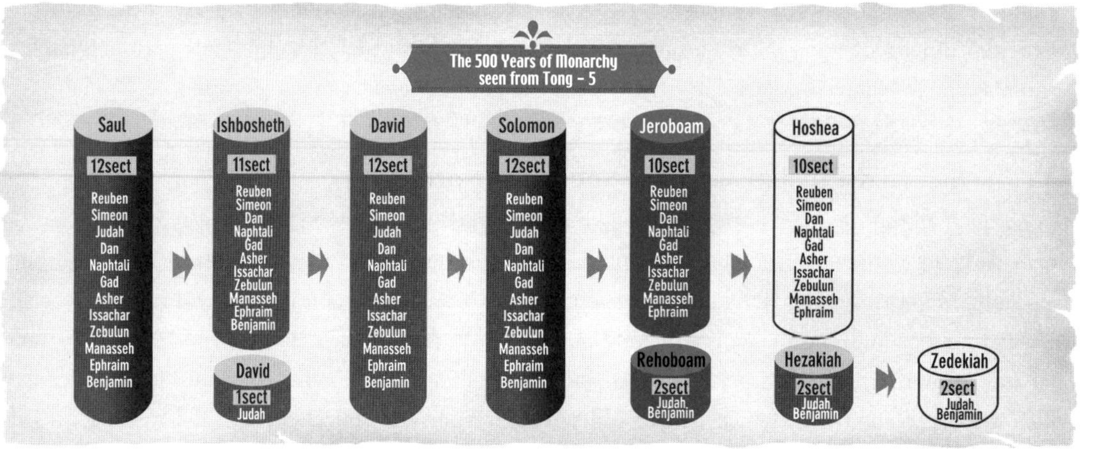

Jeroboam
Originally Jeroboam was a leader in construction. Soldiers were important elites in times of war while those in charge of construction were elites in times of peace. During the era of Solomon, construction was a major state policy project.

● The condition of division

Solomon died and Rehoboam his son succeeded him as king. However, he also repeated his father's religious and political evils exactly and drove the political situation further into division. At last, God harbored the plan of dividing the country into North and South and entrusted Jeroboam with Northern Israel.

Although God divided Israel into the south and north, He wanted the two countries to cooperate each other with Jerusalem as their religious as center. Therefore, He commanded all the male adults living in the Northern Israel to come down to the southern Judah(where Jerusalem was located) three times a year. **It was because their faith in God was to be maintained in the same way although the country was divided politically.**

Subjecting Faith to Politics
Jeroboam ideologized faith for politics. It was the beginning of the evil of abusing God's love and mission and world missions for his own political purpose. This was the way of Jeroboam. The kings after Jeroboam repeated this evil. That evil was on its climax during the dynasty of Omri

● The way of David vs. the way of Jeroboam

However, king Jeroboam of Northern Israel was afraid that if he sent male adults to Jerusalem in the south three times a year, their hearts may incline toward the South. Eventually Jeroboam built golden calf idols in Dan and Bethel and appointed ordinary people as priests, instead of Levites. He ignored the feasts commanded by God to observe and then even changed the dates of the feasts as he pleased.

God evaluated the ways of the kings of Israel in two ways. They was **the way of David and the way of Jeroboam**. In Northern Israel, a regrettable history continued that all 19 kings after Jeroboam followed the way of Jeroboam and served idols.

The 200 years of Northern Kingdom

Year(B.C.)	Northern Kingdom(years ruled)	dynasty	prophets	major events
931	1) I Jeroboam(22)		Ahijah, Iddo, etc	
910	2) Nadab(2)			
909	3) Baasha(24)		Jehu	
886	4) Ela(2)			
885	5) Zimri(7days)			
885	6) Omri(12)			'Samaria' became Capital.
874	7) Ahab(22)	Omri	Elijah	Mt. Carmel contest/ incident of Nabot's vineyard/ war with Aram by allying with Southern Judah (Ahab got killed)
853	8) Ahaziah(2)		Elijah, Elisha	Elijah to heaven/stories of Elisha's miracles
852	9) Johoram(Joram)(12)		Elisha	
841	10) Jehu(28)		Elisha	
814	11) Jehoahaz(17)		Elisha	
798	12) Jehoash(16)	Jehu		
793	13) II Jeroboam(41)		Amos, Hosea, Jonah	
753	14) Zechariah(6months)		Hosea	Amos' ministry
752	15) Shallum(1month)			Hosea's ministry
752	16) Menahem(10)		Hosea	Jonah's ministry
742	17) Pekahiah(2)			
740	18) Pekah(20)		Hosea, Othet	
732	19) Hoshea(9)		Hosea	
722	Northern Kingdom destroyed (about 210 years)			

2. The dynasty of Omri and Elijah's ministry

I Ki. 16:15-chap.22/ II Ki. chap.1/(II Ch. chap.18-20)

In the Northern kingdom, coup d'etats continued to take place. Omri's role to power was also through coup d'eta. He brought in Jezebel the princess of Sidon as his daughter-in-law. Sidon was a very prosperous country beside the sea in those days. The Northern Israel was saturated with the faith of Baal by this woman.

God sent prophet Elijah. In order to change the situation of the evil period, Elijah proposed 'confrontation' at Mt. Carmel by risking his own life. He proposed that each side sacrifice to their God and prove that the God or god who responses with

Omri and Ahab
When Zimri died, Omri defeated Tibni who competed with him for power and became king. He made Samaria capital, expanded the territory a lot and had Ahab his son marry Jezebel the Sidonite. Meanwhile, the marriage between Ahab and Jezebel was more than just international marriage. They were evil leaders who united their will in killing the LORD's prophets for the worship of Baal.

fire was the true God. No wonder the fire of God came down upon the altar of Elijah and all 450 prophets of Baal were killed. However, Queen Jezebel was not shocked at all but rather tried to kill Elijah.

'Vineyard incident of Naboth' in I Kings chapter 21 is a straightforward example which shows injustice of the period of Ahab. Ahab and Jezebel had the depraved stone innocent Naboth to death and took his vineyard unjustly just for the reason that they wanted to have his vineyard. Seeing that the level of the leader was this low, we can guess how miserable and desolate the atmosphere of every corner of the society was in those days.

Northern Israel and Southern Judah made a treaty and waged a war with a country called Aram. Ahab was killed in this battle. This way, the book of I Kings came to the end and the book of II Kings began with Ahaziah the son of Ahab.

3. The dynasty of Omri and Elisha's ministry

II Ki. chap.2-8/(II Ch. chap.21-22:6)

The ministry of Elisha who succeeded Elijah was focused on educating the prophet students. Many miracles happened in the ministry of Elisha. One prophet student died and his wife became a widow, who was so poor that her son was made to be sold as slave. Hearing this, Elisha performed the miracle of having the bottles she brought be filled with oil. There happened miracles such as the miracle that the axe which fell into waters was made to float back, the miracle that flour was scattered onto poisoned food and poison disappeared. Since they had to pick herbs from the field to make soup for their meager meals, the poison had to be eliminated. **If we seek only miracles as performed by Elijah and Elisha without understanding this kind of chronological background, it would be failing to figure out both the overview of the Bible and the Heart of God.**

Elisha's request
Elisha asked Elijah.(II Ki.2:9). This request of his was based on Deuteronomy 21:17. This meant that the first born received the double share of his father's inheritance, that is, twice more than other sons.

4. The dynasty of Jehu II Ki. chap.9-14/(II Ch. 22:7-chap.25)

God planned to abolish the dynasty of Omri and establish a new dynasty through a general called Jehu. Jehu showed decisiveness and courage in destroying the household of Ahab of Northern Israel and killed all the prophets of Baal in Northern Israel. However, pitiably he did not remove golden calf idols in Dan and Bethel.

Meanwhile, king Jehoram (Joram) the fifth king of Southern Judah married Athaliah Ahab's daughter of Northern Israel, which became a chance that the evil of Northern Israel which was saturated with idolatry was expanded to Southern Judah. Athaliah controlled her husband Jehoram and her son Ahaziah who became king as she pleased and spreaded the worship of Baal in Judah. Even worse, when her son Ahaziah died, she herself became king of Judah and tried to destroy the king's seeds, who was David's descendants.

However, in the midst of the situation that Athaliah tried to kill all the princes, Jehosheba (the wife of priest Jehoiada)secretly hid prince Joash and raised him up for six years

Joash and Jehosheba
Since Jehosheba who rescued Joash was the sister of Ahaziah, she was the aunt of Joash. The name of Jehoram the husband of Athaliah can be changed to 'Joram' for use

The era of II Jeroboam
Before II Jeroboam became king, the international situation was that Aram who bothered Northern Israel was less powerful than Assyria in the north, who became weaker due to war with Aram. Taking advantage of this, II Jeroboam restored the territory from 'the mouth of Hamath to the Sea of Arabah'(II Ki.14:25). For 50 years from then on Northern Israel got out of foreign threats and enjoyed the time of economic prosperity.

without Athaliah knowing. Eventually under the leadership of priest Jehoiada, Athaliah was dethroned and Prince Joash who was seven years old was enthroned. During the first half period of Joash's rule, Judah was able to renew their covenant with God because of priest Jehoiada and repair the temple. However, after Jehoiada died, Southern Judah came to go the way of dilapidation again.

Meanwhile, the dynasty of Jehu of Northern Israel from Jehu, Jehoahaz, Joash and Jeroboam II followed the evil way of Jeroboam I, not the way of David. The period of Jeroboam II (the 13th king of Northern Israel and the fourth king of the dynasty of Jehu) was a very prosperous period in the history of Israel but in those days God's justice was not realized. **God sent such prophets as Amos, Hosea, Jonah with a pitiable mind.**

Tong Point

Final appeal
After studying up to these contents, we study prophets Amos and Hosea who eagerly appealed with all their life to Northern Israel who were running towards destruction. 'Appeal' is not requesting properly or persuading appropriately. Appeal is bodily struggling. In spite of the appeals of prophets Amos and Hosea, Northern Israel did not listen to them til the end. Their shouting was indeed a 'final appeal.'

5. Jehu's dynasty and the ministry of Amos Amo. chap.1-9

During the rule of Jeroboam II idolatry was prevalent in Northern Israel and the rich perpetrating against the poor became extremely serious. In this situation prophet Amos began to declare the judgment of God in Samaria the capital of the Northern Israel.

In Israel it was very cold at night. So the homeless who were poor and had no quilt had to sleep with their only cloak covering them. Long ago when God gave the law through Moses, He made it clear that the cloak of the needy which was taken as a pledge should be returned to the owner before sunset(Exo.22:26-27). However, during the period of the rule of Jeroboam II, this word of God was not practiced at all which meant the poor had to suffer from cold after sunset. Yet the rich built palaces for summer and winter respectively, lay on ivory beds, killed and cooked fat sheep, drank wine in bowls and played lyres and harps.

God ordered through Amos, "Let justice roll on like a river, righteousness like a never-failing stream"(Amo.5:24). However, the people of Northern Israel did not listen to the word of God.

Prophetic foreshortening
Prophetic books are different from historical ones. Historical books record historical facts of the past while prophetic books contain even the time of past and future prophecy. They use synchrony and diachrony at the same time. Therefore, writers of prophetical books were the ones who had intellectual and spiritual power with which they were able to see through those days.

6. Jehu dynasty and the ministry of Hosea Hos. chap.1-14

God intended to convey His love through the marriage life of prophet Hosea. He commanded Hosea to marry an adulteress (Gomel) and have adulterous children.

In those days the people of Northern Israel worshipped Baal and Ashtoreth, whose faith was that if Baal and Ashtoreth had a happy married life, it would rain sufficiently and farming would become abundant and prosperous. Therefore, in order to excite Baal and Ashtoreth, there were many female priests, and

Comparison between the books of Amos and Hosea	
Amos	Hosea
Economical social corruption	Religious corruption
Warning against wrong relation with neighbors	Warning against wrong relation with God

their life of faith was that they and male believers did adulterous acts in the temple where there was no roof. Perhaps Gomel was a female priest of such Baal temple.

While Hosea lived a married life with this Gomel, he poured a purest love on her. However, never recognizing such love of her husband, Gomel did not stop the adultery. Such act of Gomel was like the shape of Northern Israel who could not appreciate the love of God.

While Hosea harbored the Heart of God whose heart was burning, he shouted, "return to God". However, the people of Israel did not repent.

Tong Point

God's heart for all nations
Jonah was a prophet who ministered with Amos and Hosea. Long ago God chose Israel as 'kingdom of priests and holy nation.' His intention to save all nations through them was God's plan begun from the times of Abraham. Let's remember that God wanted to let Jonah know this Heart of His.

7. The ministry of Jonah Jon. chap.1-4

While Amos and Hosea ministered in Northern Israel, God sent Jonah to the city of Nineveh, the capital of Assyria. However, Jonah got on board of a ship going to Tashish to the opposite direction rather than obeying the word of God. Northern Israel ruled by Jeroboam II was in a delusion that only they were the objects of salvation. Therefore, they avoided the effort, if possible, to go and save their enemy Assyria who harassed them.

However, Jonah was thrown into sea amid the storm God sent and then into the belly of a big fish. He spent three days inside the belly of a fish which made him decide to go to Nineveh. Even after he arrived in Nineveh, he was not so passionate about proclaiming the word of God. He only traveled a day in the city despite the large capacity of the city. It would have normally have taken him three days to travel the whole city.

In spite of Jonah's insincere shout, the people of Nineveh attentively listened to his message and all began to repent. Seeing such people of Nineveh, God extended mercy by changing His will to judge. At that, Jonah who hoped Nineveh would perish got angry with God. In Jonah's v.iew he could not understand why God would not destroy Israel's enemy. Then God helped Jonah understand through a vine and said;

"You have been concerned about this vine, though you didn't tend it or make it grow. It sprang up overnight and died overnight. But Nineveh has more than a hundred and twenty thousand people who cannot tell their right hand from their left, and many cattle as well. Should I not be concerned about that great city?"(Jon.4:10-11).

Jonah's prayer

The prayer of Jonah in Jonah 4:2 seemingly praises God's graciousness and patience. However, the tone of his word reveals his grudging spirit about God who did not punish the Gentiles. In Jonah's standing he could not understand why God would forgive the enemy nation who threatened his nation . Here we can see the perverted consciousness of being elected and the wrong nationalism of Israel.

Write down the contents of this lesson in the form of Tong Story

Let's pray in a loud voice so that we may be able to teach the contents of this lesson to our children

- Teach them to your children, talking about them when you sit at home and when you walk along the road, when you lie down and when you get up……so that your days and the days of your children may be many……as many as the days that the heavens are above the earth (Deuteronomy 11:19-21).
- you know those from whom you learned it, and how from infancy you have known the holy Scriptures(II Timothy 3:14-15).

17 Lesson

Destruction of Northern Kingdom Israel

II Kings chap.15-20, Isaiah, Micah

Accumulative reading amount 51.75% 1189

The One Year Tongdok Bible Days 175-196 | Reading time 180 minutes

TongBible Story Overview

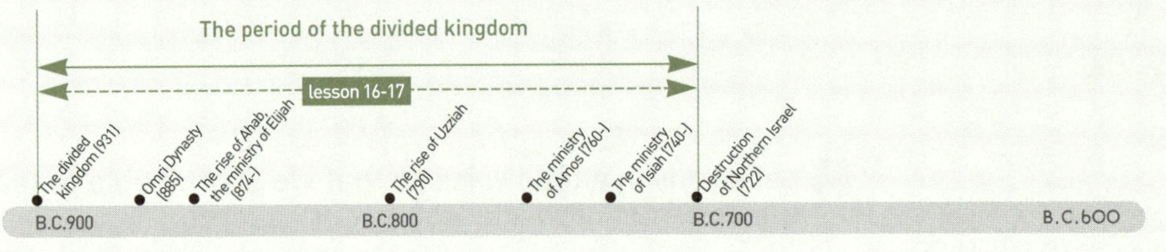

Reading the Old Testament in detail in the order of history (17)

II Kings chapter 15 depicts the last of Northern Israel whose national fate was gradually coming to an end. It contains the scene in which Hoshea (who was to become the last king) became enthroned through coup d'etat. At that time the king of Southern Judah was Ahaz. Micah and Isaiah began their ministry in Southern Judah. We read Isaiah and Micah along with II Kings chapters 15 to 20.

How to read the period of destruction of Northern Israel, Isaiah and Micah

The prophets who ministered in B.C. 8th century when the Assyrian empire was expanding its power were Amos, Hosea, Isaiah and Micah. In those days, the situation was so severe that even Egypt in the south became invaded by Assyria which expanded its power in the north. In times like this the secret for the Southern and Northern Israel for survival was not to get support from Assyria, Babylon or Egypt but only to seek the help of God who managed the world.

However, seeing that they would not return to God despite the shout of Amos and Hosea, God closed the gate of Northern Israel in B.C.722. Around these times, Isaiah and Micah ministered in Jerusalem the capital of Southern Judah. The two prophets proclaimed the earnest hope of God who wanted to restore Southern Judah.

While warning that Judah would be taken captive by Babylon, Isaiah prophesied that God would extend His grace so that sincere people among the people of Judah would not be punished. He also proclaimed that the Messiah would come from the descendants of king David, give the whole world peace and restore His kingdom.

Tong Point

God's world management

We have studied the dynasties of Northern Israel. Now let's move on to observe the dynasty of Southern Judah. Starting from Lesson 17, we will focus on the contents after Uzziah died. Here we study Isaiah and Micah (prophetical books) and II Kings (historical book) together. To understand the background of this scene, it is necessary to study the international affairs around B.C. 8th Century.

B.C.	Southern Kingdom(years of rule)	Dynasty	Prophets	Major events
931	1) Rehoboam(17)		Smaiah, Iddo	
913	2) Abijah(3)		Iddo	
910	3) Asa(41)		Azariah, Hanani	
872	4) Jehoshaphat(25)		Jehu,Jahaziel,Eliezer	War with Aram By allying with Northern Israel
848	5) Jehoram(Joram)(8)			Married Athaliah Ahab's daughter
841	6) Ahaziah(1)			
841	7) Athaliah(6)	Ahab's daughter Jehoram's wife Ahazia's mother		Priest Jehoiada's reform
835	8) Joash(40)	Jehoram's son		
796	9) Amaziah(29)			
790	10) Uzziah(Azariah)(52)		Isaiah	
751	11) Jotham(16)		Isaiah, Micah	
742	12) Ahaz(16)		Isaiah, Micah	Assyria friendly, anti-Northern Israel Anti-Aram
725	13) Hezekiah(29)		Isaiah, Micah	Anti-Assyria, Egypt friendly
697	14) Manasseh(55)			
642	15) Amon(2)			
640	16) Josiah(31)		Jeremiah, Nahum, Zephaniah	
609	17) Jehoahaz(3 months)		Jeremiah	
609	18) Jehoiakim(11)		Jeremiah, Habakkuk	
598	19) Jehoiachin(3 months)		Jeremiah, Daniel	
598	20) Zedekiah(11)		Jeremiah, Daniel, Ezekiel	
586	Southern Judah destroyed (around 345 years)		Obadiah	

1. Destruction of Northern Kingdom and Isaiah's calling

II Ki. chap.15/ (II Ch. chap.26-27)/ Isa. chap.1-6

During the first half of B.C. 8th century, Assyria in the north and Egypt in the south maintained balance in power. However, as the power of Assyria increased, there was an increased danger of war. It was a situation that Israel would become the battlefield if a war was to break out. At this time the prophets of God who saw the big flow of the world, pointed out their folly and evils and preached the Heart of God, but the people of Israel ended up rejecting them.

When the period of Jeroboam II was over, and the prophets Amos and Hosea ministered, northern Israel fell into a great confusion. King Zechariah after Jeroboam II was assassinated by Shallum six months after enthronement. After Shallum, Menahem became king. During the rule of king Menahem, king Pul (Tiglath-Pileser the third) of Assyria attacked Israel and king Menahem had to give 1,000 silver talents to the king of Assyria. Pekahiah, Pekah and Hoshea became kings after Menahem and the last king was Hoshea.

Meanwhile, Uzziah died in Southern Judah and his son Jotham succeeded him as king. Though Jotham lived rightly before God, it was pitiable that the people of those days did not. After Southern Judah spent the period of Jotham, the worst period called 'period of Ahaz' came. In such sensitive times, prophet Isaiah was called by God.

Isaiah

Isaiah was a great scholar in his days. He was well versed in the law and could see the international situation as easily as he saw his palm. Having passion for God and insight for those times, Isaiah devoted himself to introducing God to the people of Judah and earnestly persuading them to return to Him. Though he showed how brilliant the glory of God's salvation is and had them be able to have hope, the response of the people of Judah was 'rejection' at the end.

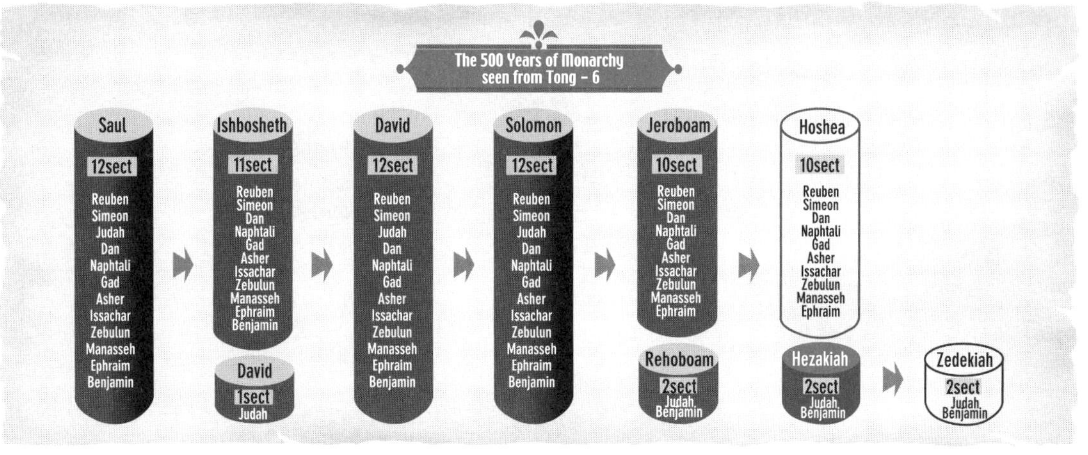

2.Ahaz's choice and Isaiah's advice

II Ki. chap.16-17/ (II Ch. chap.28)/ Isa. chap.7-14

In order to understand the ministry of all prophets (especially, **Isaiah and Jeremiah who was to come later) we should review the international affairs during those times.**

- Situation surrounding Judah in those days

Now, the international situation surrounding Southern Judah was in confusion. In those days Assyria was the most powerful. Assyria had a plot in mind to conquer Aram and next, Northern Israel, then Southern Judah and even Egypt. Seeing the map, we can guess the route of their invasion.

- Ahaz's plan and Isaiah's advice

Knowing this fact, Northern Israel and Aram made a treaty and showed the sign of attacking Southern Judah. Naturally, king Ahaz of Southern Judah was gripped with great fear. At this time, Isaiah went to Ahaz and said that even if the two countries attack Southern Judah, their attack would not be successful and told the king not to worry but to trust and rely on God since it was God who managed the world.

The world map in the days of Isaiah

● Ahaz's choice and the result of his choice

However, Ahaz ignored the advice of Isaiah and sent an envoy to Assyria to ask for help. Assyria came down and conquered Northern Israel and Aram as if they had been waited for it. Demanding Southern Judah to pay a huge amount of tribute, Assyria picked quarrel with Judah to arrange some pretext for invasion. Amid this situation, Ahaz died and his son Hezekiah became king.

● The destruction of Northern Israel(B.C.722)

Meanwhile, in II Kings chapter seventeen is the story of Hoshea (the last king of northern Israel). There is an explanation for the reason for the destruction of northern Israel. Although God expected Israel to live as the people of God, they never gave up the habit of idolatry to the end. Eventually they were destroyed by Assyria and made to live scattered all over the Gentile land according to Assyria's colonial policy.

3. Hezekiah' choice and Isaiah's advice

II Ki. chap.18-20/ (II Ch. chap.29-32)/ Isa. chap.15-39

God's world management
Babylon (Isa.13:1-14:23)
Assyria (Isa.14:24-27)
Philistines (Isa.14:28-32)
Moab (Isa.15:1-16:14)
Damascus (Isa.17:1-14)
Cush (Isa.18:1-7)
Egypt (Isa.19:1-20:6)
Dumah (Edom) (Isa.21:11-12)
Arabia (Isa.21:13-17)
Jerusalem (Isa.22:1-25)
Tyre (Tarshish) (Isa.23:1-18)

● Hezekiah's reform

Becoming king at the age of 25, Hezekiah surprisingly attempted to restore relationship with God by removing idols that filled the whole land of Judah. The people crushed all kinds of idols and Asherah poles in their towns, and Hezekiah restored the systemic apparatus by restoring the positions of priests and Levites so that they could devote themselves to their service in the temple.

● Hezekiah's plan and Isaiah's advice

However, the work of transforming the people of Judah who had run the evil way for so long was not at all easy. Furthermore, Hezekiah felt that the tribute to Assyria, which had been paid since the time of his father, was getting burdensome so he planed to prevent Assyria from invading Judah by making a treaty with Egypt in the south.

Although Isaiah dissuaded him, Hezekiah made a treaty with Egypt. Then, Assyria invaded Southern Judah on the pretext of this treaty and soon the whole country except Jerusalem became occupied by Assyria. Fortunately, since the city of Jerusalem was originally an impregnable castle city by nature, it was not easily occupied but was able to stand their attack for a while.

Various titles of God revealed in Isaiah
The LORD Almighty(Isa.1:9)
The Mighty One of Israel (Isa.1:24)
The God of Jacob(Isa.2:3)
Potter(Isa.29:16)
Redeemer(Isa.41:14)
Israel's Creator(Isa.43:15)
Savior(Isa.49:26)
The God of all the Earth (Isa.54:5)
Our Father(Isa.63:16)

● Hezekiah's choice

Within this critical situation, finally Hezekiah chose God.

God who heard Hezekiah's prayer totally destroyed 185,000 troops in one morning which were the major forces of the king of Assyria. As prophesied by Isaiah, Assyria was judged by God and after this event the great empire of Assyria disappeared from the stage of history.

● Hezekiah's Prayer

Meanwhile, after driving out Assyria, Hezekiah got extremely ill to such an extent that his life was in danger. His sorrow deepened due to the fact that he had no heir to pass on his throne. Hezekiah knelt down before God and prayed for his life. He prayed so earnestly that God granted his prayer. God healed Hezekiah and further extended his life. Hezekiah received an extra 15 years to live in which he was able to govern Southern Judah.

Tong Point

With Isaiah chapter 40 as dividing point, Isaiah's prophecy of judgment against Southern Judah was followed by the promise of salvation. We should be able to see the picture of strong and powerful Jesus of Isaiah chapter 9 and that of Jesus like tender shoot in chapter 53.

4. Isaiah's future prophecy Isa. chap.40-66

Prophet Isaiah prophesied what Jesus would be like who was to come 800 years later from those days. Isaiah chapter 9 said that He was the almighty God, the wonderful, the counselor and the root of Jesse. It described a powerful Messiah

Peace ministry

Messiah's mission	Declaring Jesus' mission
Isaiah chapter 61	Luke's Gospel chapter 4

Will preach the good news to the poor, bind up the brokenhearted, proclaim freedom for the captives, release the captives, give comfort to all who mourn, provide the joy of gladness instead of mourning, bestow a garment of praise instead of a spirit of despair, restore the ancient ruins, restore the places long devastated and renew the ruined cities that have been devastated for generations.

and the almighty Jesus. **We should be able to see the two sides of Jesus at the same time; what Jesus was like who was strong and powerful as described in Isaiah chapter 9 and what Jesus was like who looks as weak as a tender shoot as described in Isaiah chapter 53.**

The prophecy of Isaiah also came to an end. The promise for God's salvation and new creation were prophesied.

"Behold, I will create new heavens and a new earth. The former things will not be remembered, nor will they come to mind. But be glad and rejoice forever in what I will create" (Isa.65:17-18).

Tong Point

Micah was a contemporary prophet of Isaiah and specifically pointed out the sinfulness of Jerusalem and Samaria. Along with rebuking cities like this, he prophesied that the great one to rule Israel would come out of a small town called Bethlehem.

5. Micah's ministry and the story of the city Mic. chap.1-7

Micah made a complaint against idolatry of Jerusalem and Samaria who were far from the word of God and then immediately talked about the sins the powerful committed against the poor public. He also pointed out specifically the sin and evils of leaders such as heads who judged for bribe, priests who instructed for wages and prophets who told fortunes for money.

However, prophet Micah began to proclaim the future of Jerusalem with hope after pointing out the sinful shape of Jerusalem. This was to prophesies that the people of God who were to be taken captive to Babylon and spend the time of suffering would return and make a strong country.

Prophet Micah prophesied that a great man would come out of a small town called Bethlehem. This prophecy became the word that prophesied the place of Jesus' birth.

Write down the contents of this lesson in the form of Tong Story

Let's pray in a loud voice so that we may be able to teach the contents of this lesson to our children

- Teach them to your children, talking about them when you sit at home and when you walk along the road, when you lie down and when you get up……so that your days and the days of your children may be many……as many as the days that the heavens are above the earth (Deuteronomy 11:19-21).
- you know those from whom you learned it, and how from infancy you have known the holy Scriptures(II Timothy 3:14-15).

8 Session

Hope Standing before Despair

Tong Map

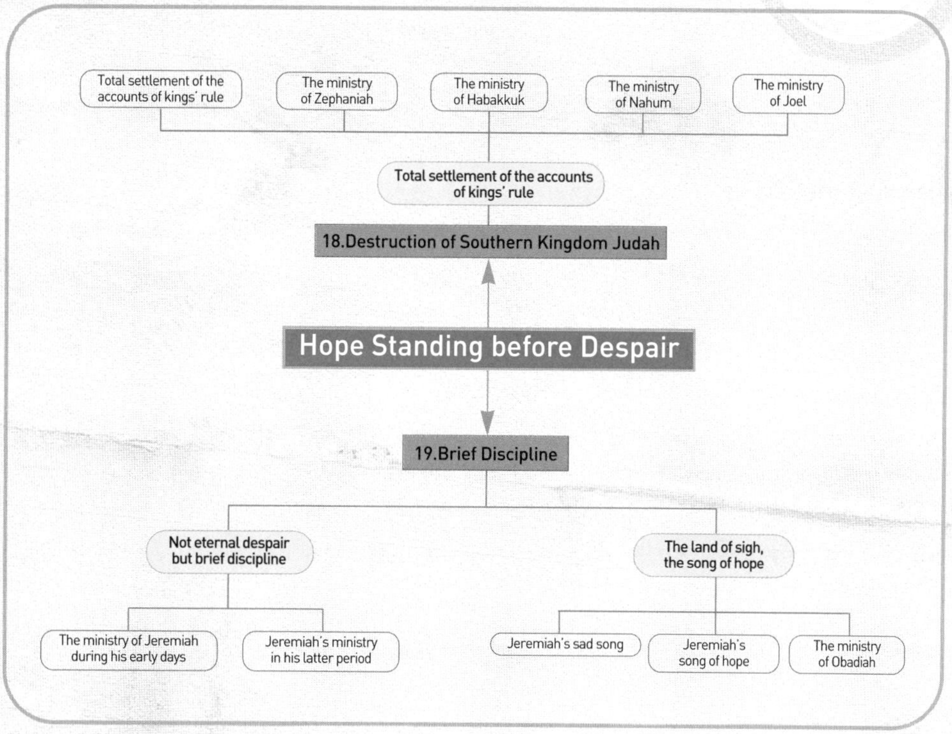

Tong Concept

- **Why 'Wrap up of kings' rule'?**

Now we come to focus on Manasseh's life and the impact he exerted on Israel. Along with this we will observe the beginning background and process of two religious reforms of king Josiah.

- **The situation of those days and messages of prophets!**

We observe the ministry and messages of Zephaniah, Habakkuk and Nahum who worked in Southern Judah

- **Brief discipline**

We observe the last days of Southern Judah and the ministry of prophet Jeremiah. Let's carefully study the message of Jeremiah while remembering that the destruction of Southern Judah was not eternal destruction but a brief discipline.

Tong At a glance

✱ Looking around the forest

After King Josiah was killed in the battle of Megiddo, Southern Judah began to get weakened rapidly. During this era prophets Zephaniah, Nahum, Habakkuk, Jeremiah and prophetess Hulda(II Ki.22:14) worked together. It was such a desperate time that during no other era this many prophets ministered at the same time.

The message of Jeremiah right before the destruction of Southern Judah was to tell them to let down its banners and yield to Babylon. However, King Zedekiah did not accept the persuasion of Jeremiah and miserably faced his last moment.

✱ Land and annual ring

The Babylonians became powerful during the rule of King Nabopolassar and then soon destroyed Nineveh the capital of Assyria. Afterward, Nebuchadnezzar who became king in B.C.605 carried out military conquest successfully as he attacked Palestine and Egypt. In the first year of Nebuchadnezzar happened his first attack on Judah and at this time people such as Daniel, Shadrach, Meshach and Abednego were taken captive to Babylon.

Jehoiakim died and in B.C.598 Jehoiachin the son of Jehoiakim became king at the age of 18. But he had many administrative officials and more than 10,000 talented workers taken captive to Babylon three months after he became king. Nebuchadnezzar appointed Mataniah as king, who was an uncle of Jehoiachin and the youngest son of Josiah, and changed his name into 'Zedekiah.' He was the last king of Southern Judah.

✱ Wind and Climate

During the rule of King Josiah, high priest Hilkiah discovered the Book of the Law and gave it to King Josiah through Shaphan, the king's secretary. Hearing all the contents of the book, King Josiah tore his robes and agonized. Among the religious reforms of Josiah were driving idol-worshipping priests out of the temple, destroying the houses where religious prostitution was done, having worship concentrated in Jerusalem, abolishing the sacrifice of offering children, breaking down the shrine and altar in Bethel, having priests work in the sanctuary, restoring the feast of Passover and the like. Southern Judah was destroyed in B.C.586, 135 years after Northern Israel was destroyed.

Tong Seeing the forest

Zephaniah It is presumable that Zephaniah who worked in the days of King Josiah of Southern Judah was a man of considerable power in the society of Judah. While King Josiah boldly carried out religious reform, it was very likely that he participated in it. His prophecy began with declaring judgment against Jerusalem and then continued to declare judgment against countries around Israel gradually. Even though they were the chosen people of God, they were unable to escape His judgment. Zephaniah shouted that only humble people who kept God's statutes would be able to avoid the day of God's wrath.

Habakkuk Prophet Habakkuk ministered around the end of B.C. 7th century when Babylon ruled surrounding countries as a superpower. Seeing ruthless Babylon getting stronger and stronger, Habakkuk asked God, 'Why are the evil more prosperous?' 'Why are the righteous troubled by the evil?'
God answered that the evil will eventually be judged. It meant that the prosperity of the evil and suffering of the righteous would be over after an appointed time. The righteous should look up to the day of God patiently enduring. Finding the answer to the question, Habakkuk praised God confessing that he will rejoice and be glad because of God.

Nahum Nahum's flow was proclamation of judgment against Nineveh from the beginning to the end. The people of Nineveh who had repented upon hearing Jonah's proclamation of destruction on them 150 years earlier soon returned to their old shape of cruelty and arrogance. Even when the people of Nineveh heard Nahum's fearful prophecy of judgment upon them, they were insensitive and as good as storing up God's wrath against them. Nahum contains the justice of God who judged the evil, and also the love of God who saved His people who were suffering amid their oppression

Joel We do not know exactly which king ruled when Joel was a prophet. Joel urged people to repent due to an imminent tribulation. That was the word of God who asked Israel to repent, who invited disaster upon themselves by sinning against God. However, Joel was also prophesied that those who turned away from sins would be given the promise of salvation and come to live under God's just rule. Seeing the contents of the prophecy, we can guess that he worked as prophet before Southern Judah was destroyed.

Jeremiah Jeremiah was called by God at the age of about twenty. When the destruction of Southern Judah was imminent, the core of Jeremiah's prophecy was that Judah should put down the country's banners and give in to Babylon. The will of God that Judah should go to Babylon to be trained and come back was an imminent irrevocable event. Accordingly, in order to minimize a terrible situation to come upon the weak, Jeremiah tried very hard to persuade leaders. However, King Zedekiah of Southern Judah refused Jeremiah's prophecy and brought in a terrible end to Jerusalem and Southern Judah ended up being destroyed by the Babylonian army.

Lamentations Seeing the city of Jerusalem destroyed by Babylon in B.C.586 with lots of people being taken captive to Babylon, Jeremiah felt the agony of his liver being poured out. However, when he wept all night to the point of his eyes wounded by tears and faced the morning, God's goodness and mercy came to him as new hope. Even though he was situated in an extreme hopelessness, he earnestly prayed for the restoration of Jerusalem with hope of salvation based on God's mercy.

Obadiah Although this is the shortest book of the Old Testament and made up of only one chapter, the message is crystal clear. Edom committed the sin of allying with Babylon for their interest and mocked the suffering of their brothers rather than regrettably thinking while seeing Judah (their brother nation) perishing. For this reason the nation of Edom was judged to be the arrogant one, bystander and persecutor. The prophet declared that Edom was to be judged with God's just judgment.

18 Lesson

Destruction of Southern Kingdom Judah

II Kings chap.21-23, Zephaniah, Habakkuk, Nahum, Joel

Accumulative reading amount 52.96% 1189

The One Year Tongdok Bible Days 197-201 | Reading time 35 minutes

TongBible Story Overview

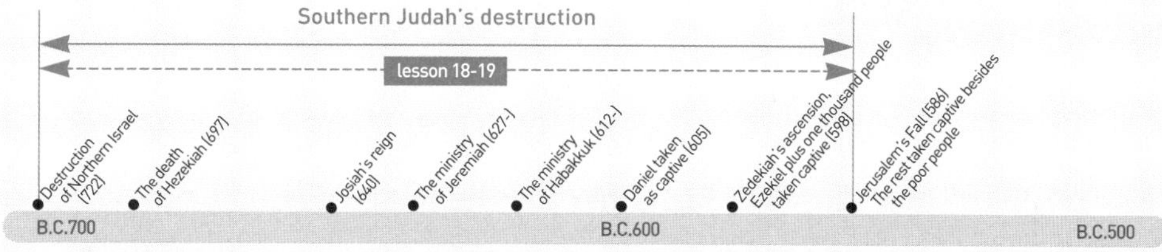

Reading the Old Testament in detail in the order of history (18)

We go on to read II Kings chapters 21 to 23. King Hezekiah (who rescued the nation out of crisis by obeying the word of God given through Isaiah died). Then Manasseh became king. He committed such terrible sins that he provided the causes for the destruction of Southern Judah. Amon became king after Mannasseh. When Josiah became king after Amon, Southern Judah inclined towards destruction. At this time God sent Zephaniah and Nahum. A little later, Habakkuk ministered.

How to read the last days of Southern Judah

After the destruction of Northern Israel, Hezekiah of Southern Judah changed the situation of himself and the country by praying to God with full reliance on Him after he belatedly realized God's world management. However, Manasseh his son (unlike his father) made it a rule to do evil as long as 55 years as king. As a result, in spite of reform of Josiah (his grandson) and the effort of various prophets, Southern Judah came to face a terrible end.

Zephaniah worked as prophet during the period of king Josiah's ministry. During this period prophets Nahum, Habakkuk and Jeremiah and prophetess Hulda(II Ki.22:14), ministered. That was the most number of prophets in the history of Israel working in the same period. In the history of Israel, there were no other period when these many prophets were active at the same time. This indicates that this period was in such a desperate crisis. Although Joel did not mention the exact period of his time, we can judge that it was written before Babylonian captivity. Joel urged the people of Israel to repent, telling them that the day of the LORD (which has been known only as the day of salvation of great joy to them so far) could not help become the day of judgment unless they were to repent and turn away from their sins.

Tong Point

Total settlement of the accounts of kings' rule
The calculations for Southern Judah's judgment came to a conclusion. The conclusion was that the kings' rule of Southern Judah would come to a close.

1. Total settlement of the accounts of kings' rule

II Ki. chap.21-23/ (II Ch. chap.33-35)

After Hezekiah, Manasseh became king at age 12. Yet, doing what was totally contrary to what his father did, he built idols all over the country and served Gentile gods. After Manasseh died, Amon his son became king and carried out the way of his father. His subjects rebelled against him and killed him. The people drove out the rebelling ones and made Josiah (Amon's son) king.

Josiah became king at age 8 and ruled the country for 31 years. Though he became king at the young age, he was a great king who intended to rule the nation according to God's will. Josiah's first religious reformation took place in the 12th year of his rule. Then he did a great cleaning of idols with priest Hilkiah. 6 years later, when priest Hilkiah found the Book of the Law in the temple in the 18th year of Josiah's rule, the second reformation took place. Josiah read the Book of the Law to many people and gathered their mind together with the determination to keep all the commands and laws and decrees. **Josiah was evaluated as a king who tried to keep the law most faithfully among the total 40 kings of Israel.**

However, pitiably, Josiah was killed when he went for a war

Succession of Passover
Hezekiah's reform began with removing idols and continued the resurrection of Passover. However, the Passover he observed was observed a month late for the reason that there were not enough priests who completed holiness ceremony and all the people could not gather. Thus it was remembered that the Passover which was observed properly first after the times of Samuel was not when Hezekiah ruled but when Josiah (his great grandson) ruled(II Ch.35:18).

aimed at preventing Egyptians from passing the land of Judah in their endeavor to wage war with Assyria. Upon Josiah's death, the people soon went back to idolatry. We can know how deeply idolatry was rooted in their life.

Following Josiah, his son Jehoahaz reigned. But he was taken captive to Egypt and another son of Josiah, Eliakim (Jehoiakim) took charge of the nation. Eliakim had to impose heavy tax on the people to offer much tribute to Egypt.

2. The ministry of Zephaniah Zep. chap.1-3

Zephaniah
Zephaniah whose name had the meaning"the one the LORD protects" was a descendant of King Hezekiah of Southern Judah(Zep.1:1). We can guess that his social standing was high. His preaching was carried out during the rule of King Josiah and he ministered earlier than Jeremiah. Zephaniah declared 'the day of the LORD' which was both the day of Judgment and that of blessing as Joel and Amos did.

Zephaniah was a prophet who ministered during the rule of king Josiah. Zephaniah spoke about the LORD's great day; the day of judgment which would come due to people's sin. He proclaimed the discipline of God against Judah. Only those who kept the ordinances of the LORD and seeked justice and humility were to be kept away from the wrath of God.

After declaring punishment against neighboring countries like Moab, Amon, Cush and Assyria, he again declared God's discipline with focus on Jerusalem. However, after declaring this judgment, Zephaniah exhorted those who suffered all kinds of affliction, because they followed the LORD's command, which was to be patient to the end. God expected a beautiful relationship in which God again became their God and they become His people.

3. The ministry of Habakkuk Hab. chap.1-3

Habakkuk asked why God kept silent about the wicked. Habakkuk thought the suffering of the righteous and the prosperity of the wicked were unfair. God proclaimed that He prepared Babylon to solve and correct Judah's wickedness. But, in the view of Habakkuk, Babylon to be used as a tool of judgment was more evil than Judah. Therefore, judgment on Judah through the tool of Babylon seemed irrational.

God told such Habakkuk that there was an "appointed time." It meant that though it may look belated, the righteous could wait because they lived by faith and they lived because of that faith.(Hab.2:4) The suffering of the righteous was not long. Neither was the prosperity of the evil.

Listening to this reply of God, the song of praise came out of Habakkuk's lips; "Though the fig tree does not bud and there are no grapes on the vines, though the olive crop fails and the fields produce no food, though there are no sheep in the pen and no cattle in the stalls, yet I will rejoice in the LORD, I will be joyful in God my Savior"(Hab.3:17-18).

Habakkuk
Habakkuk moved from warning to blessing, from wandering to worship, from anxiety to rest and from complaint to comfort.

4. The ministry of Nahum Nah. chap.1-3

When the men of Nineveh heard the preaching of Jonah about one hundred years ago, they repented. So God forgave them and did not destroy them. They now become arrogant and thought that they conquered other countries because their god overcame the gods of those conquered countries. At this,

The book of Jonah & the book of Nahum

The book of Jonah	The book of Nahum
The mercy of our God	God's judgment
The Repentance of Nineveh	The rebellion of Nineveh
The prophet who disobeyed	The prophet who obeyed
The nation which obeyed	The nation which disobeyed
The salvation from water	The destruction by water

prophet Nahum declared destruction upon Nineveh the capital of Assyria.

Perhaps Assyria dreamed of becoming an eternal empire while destroying many nations. But after it was defeated in Jerusalem, it was destroyed by Babylon's rule under Nebuchadnezzar.

5. The ministry of Joel Joe. chap.1-3

The New Testament and Joel

In his Mt. Olive lecture (Mat.24:29) Jesus connected the events mentioned in Joel chapter 2 verses 10, 31, and chapter 3 verse 15 with the signs of his second-coming. Peter quoted the book of Joel (2:28-32) in his preaching on the day of Passover (Act.2:16-21). Apostle Paul applied Joel 2:32 to the salvation of the Jews and Gentiles who believe in Jesus (Rom.10:12-13).

The contents of prophecy of Joel, son of Pethuel was the imminent crisis and the urging of repentance. Joel proclaimed that God would send a terrible disaster due to Israel's sin. But immediately following was the word that if Israel were to weep, fast and repent even now, God would cancel the plague.

Israel blemished herself with sin. But God wanted them to return to Him by renewing their mind. God would become "the refuge of his people and stronghold of the descendants of Israel" and fulfill the word of promise, "Judah will be forever and Jerusalem from generation to generation"(Joe.3:16, 20).

Write down the contents of this lesson in the form of Tong Story

Let's pray in a loud voice so that we may be able to teach the contents of this lesson to our children

- Teach them to your children, talking about them when you sit at home and when you walk along the road, when you lie down and when you get up……so that your days and the days of your children may be many……as many as the days that the heavens are above the earth (Deuteronomy 11:19-21).
- you know those from whom you learned it, and how from infancy you have known the holy Scriptures(II Timothy 3:14-15).

19 Lesson — Brief Discipline

II Kings chap.24-25, Jeremiah, Lamentations, Obadiah, I & II Chronicles

Accumulative reading amount 65.11% 1189

The One Year Tongdok Bible Days 202-242 | Reading time 350 minutes

TongBible Story Overview

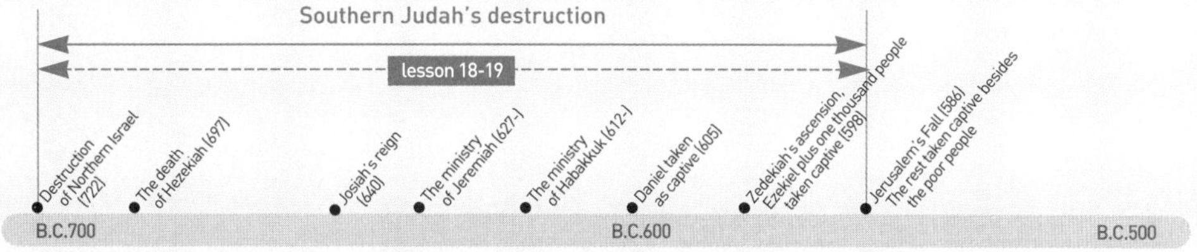

Reading the Old Testament in detail in the order of history (19)

We come to the last days of Judah. The royal rule that lasted about 500 years came to the end as described in II Kings chapters 24 to 25. Here we read also the book of Jeremiah who ministered from the days of Josiah to those of Zedekiah the last king of Southern Judah. Meanwhile, ministered also Obadiah who proclaimed the word of prophecy toward the nation of Edom. When Jerusalem had been totally destroyed by Babylonian soldiers, Jeremiah witnessed the sad scences, wrote Lamentations and recited them. After this, we again put in order the erstwhile history of Israel by reading through Chronicles.

How to read the period of Southern Judah's destruction, Jeremiah and Obadiah

King Josiah was killed in Megiddo in B.C.609 while fighting Egyptian troops. Then his son Shallum(Jehoahaz) became king. However, three months later he was killed by Necho king of Egypt. Then Josiah's son, Jehoiakim became king. Jehoiakim served Egypt first. But he served Babylon which became stronger. However, that did not last long. When he showed the sign of betraying Babylon, Nebuchadnezzar attacked Egypt and Southern Judah. At this time Babylonian troops took the first captives of Judah to Babylon. One of the representatives of the captives was Daniel. After this, Jehoiakim was killed and Jehoiachin his son became king in B.C.598.

Nebuchadnezzar took captives but also the powerful of the country, with 10,000 able-engineers to Babylon. This was the second captivity. Then Nebuchadnezzar appointed Zedekiah the youngest son of Josiah as king. He was the last king of Southern Judah.

Tong Point

Not eternal despair but brief discipline

We come to the final days of Southern Judah. The 500 year royal rule ended with II Kings chapters 24-25 and II Chronicles chapter 36. However, the destruction of Southern Judah was not eternal despair. It was a brief discipline, which gave a new opportunity for people to rise up again.

Here we come to face with Jeremiah who ministered all his life from the era of King Josiah to the days of Zedekiah who was the last king of Southern Judah. We'll review Jeremiah's ministry by dividing it into his early ministry before Southern Judah's destruction and his latter ministry after the destruction.

1. The ministry of Jeremiah during his early days

II Ki. chap.24/ (II Ch. 36:1-10)/ Jer. chap.1-38

When Jeremiah was called as prophet, it was when the reform of King Josiah of Judah was at its height. However, after King Josiah died, Judah returned to the way of idol worship right away. Now Jeremiah declared the judgment of God. Squarely looking at the fate of Southern Judah to come, he shouted to the people to surrender to Babylon. In other words, he meant that they were to move to Babylon and get a chance to start again while spending some time there. However, the leaders and people in those days did not listen to him.

Then one day Nebuchadnezzar (the king of Babylon) began to attack Judah. King Zedekiah sent word to Jeremiah urgently to ask him for prayer. However, knowing that Judah's admitting and accepting God's judgment was the only way of salvation, Jeremiah strongly urged the king to surrender to Babylon.

However, Zedekiah did not accept Jeremiah's urging to the

Jeremiah

Jeremiah, a prophet who carried out the labor of declaring the message of judgment to the stiff-necked people of Judah over 40 years, was a son of priest Hilkiah and lived in Anathoth, about 3km North of Jerusalem. He received God's command not to marry as a means of an object teaching about Judah(Jer.16:2). He was a contemporary of Zephaniah, Habakkuk, Daniel and Ezekiel. His ministry was approximately from B.C.627 to B.C.580.

end and he refused to surrender with a foolish reason that he was afraid that if was to surrenders, those who had been taken captive to Babylon first and second times might mock him. Eventually he saw his two sons killed in his sight and himself being taken captive to Babylon with his eyes plucked out to face his miserable last minute.

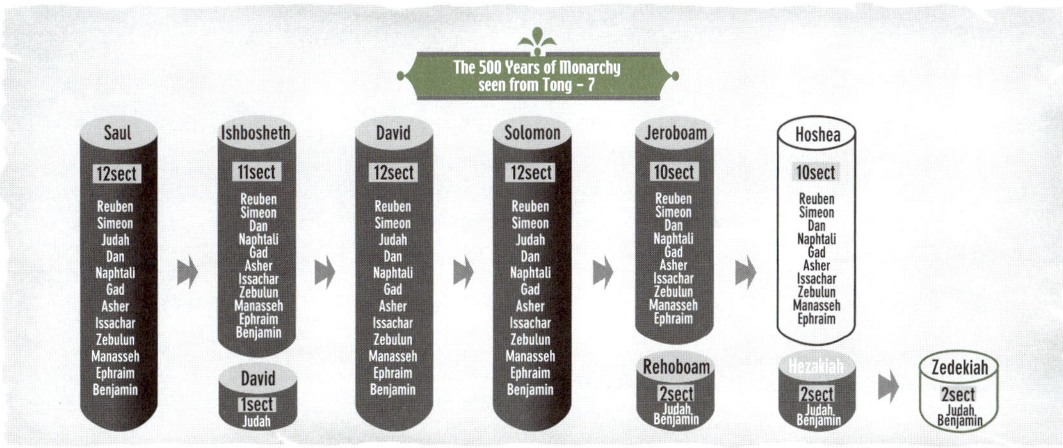

2. Jeremiah's ministry in his latter period

II Ki. chap.25/ (II Ch. 36:11-23)/ Jer. chap.39-52

Having occupied Jerusalem, the king of Babylon appointed Gedaliah as governor to rule the remaining people. He told the people of Judah to conform to the will of God who was working through Babylon. However, Judah was thrown into a crisis again because the governor was assassinated by anti-Babylonists who did not understand the will of God.

Meanwhile, Jeremiah sent a letter to his fellow countrymen, who had been taken captive to Babylon and lived everyday with despair and frustration, and persuaded them to give up the thought of returning home temporarily, live there rooted and discover the will of God. Fortunately, his letter was read by such people as Daniel. This brought the result of them being trained in Babylon willingly with the faith that they would be able to return home in the decided time.

Tong Point

The land of sigh, the song of hope
Destroyed, Jerusalem became the land of destruction. However, those who had been taken captive earlier had hope in what God had left behind. Jeremiah who found this sang the song of true hope.

3. Jeremiah's sad song Lam. chap.1-2

Lamentations is a sad song of Jeremiah who witnessed Jerusalem being burned to the ground by Nebuchadnezzar's troops in B.C.586.

Once Babylonian troops conquered the city of Jerusalem, they set the temple of the LORD and the palace on fire, burned all houses in Jerusalem and broke down all walls. They either broke down the instruments which were in the temple of the LORD or took all vessels of gold, silver and bronze to Babylon.

The king and many people were taken captive, the people who were left were killed miserably and the streets were filled with dead bodies. Seeing this, Jeremiah sheds constant tears. Had they surrendered a little earlier, not so many would have lost their lives. Jeremiah tried so hard to reduce harm to come

Type of Christ
Jeremiah (the prophet of tears) was a type of Jesus Christ in that he was the true prophet who wept seeing the city of Jerusalem about 600 years later(Mat.23:37-39, Luk.19:41-44).

upon the weak people by having the king and the powerful surrender in advance.

Jeremiah could not find any other words to describe the sadness and said that he felt as though his intestines were cut and his liver spilt to the ground. The whole city of Jerusalem was filled with the smell of burning bodies, sounds of weeping children and sighing old people. He could not help weeping continually. **Through these tears of Jeremiah, we come to learn that it was God who suffered the most in this scene.**

The subject and form of Lamentations
The Hebrew subject of Lamentations came from Ekah, "Oh, why!" which was the first word of chapters 1, 2 and 4. Lamentations use "irregular rhythm" which was usually used in funeral dirges.

4. Jeremiah's song of hope Lam. chap.3-5

We are aware that around the time before sunrise it is the darkest. Jeremiah found hope in the midst of despair caused by affliction and plagues.

"Though he brings grief, He will show compassion, so great is His unfailing love. For He does not willingly bring affliction or grief to the children of men"(Lam.3:32-33).

Jeremiah pinned hope on the mercy and love of the LORD. The destruction of Jerusalem did not mean God's failure. Not all were destroyed, and there were remnants; those who were taken captive to Babylon twice before the fall of Jerusalem. They were people like Daniel and Ezekiel. This was hope Jeremiah looked forward to while facing despair.

The book they read aloud every year
The Jews officially read aloud Lamentations every year to commemorate the destruction of Jerusalem that took place in B.C.586 and A.D.70

Tong Point

The day when tribulation came upon brothers
God's judgment was declared against the Edomites who did not mourn over their brother's tribulation on the day Israel was suffering, but rather rejoiced.

5. The ministry of Obadiah Oba. chap.1

Jacob and Esau were twin sons of Isaac who started fighting each other in the womb. While they were growing, they were not on good terms and eventually came to live like different nations to one other. The descendants of Jacob lived as Israel and those of Esau as Edomites. Yet, their root was one.

God declared Edom's destruction through prophet Obadiah because Edom helped Babylon when Jerusalem was destroyed by Babylon. Although for a long time Edom and Israel had lived as separate nations, in the sight of God, these two nations were brothers. Accordingly, God's wrath broke out when Edom rejoiced over Israel (their brother nation) being destroyed and helped Babylon. We should remember that considering brothers precious and caring for them is God's command.

Conflict between Edom and Israel
Israel went through conflict as they passed through the land of Edom during Exodus (Num.20:14-21). Hadad the Edomite resisted Solomon (I Ki.11:4). When Jerusalem was destroyed by Babylon in B.C.586, Edom helped Babylon which destroyed Israel. Obadiah declared God's judgment to come upon such Edom (Oba.1:10-12).

Write down the contents of this lesson in the form of Tong Story

Let's pray in a loud voice so that we may be able to teach the contents of this lesson to our children

- Teach them to your children, talking about them when you sit at home and when you walk along the road, when you lie down and when you get up……so that your days and the days of your children may be many……as many as the days that the heavens are above the earth (Deuteronomy 11:19-21).
- you know those from whom you learned it, and how from infancy you have known the holy Scriptures(II Timothy 3:14-15).

Concerning the Chronicles

The One Year Tongdok Bible Days 223 - 242

Seeing that the end of the II Chronicles (II Ch.36:22-23) and the beginning of Ezra (Ezr.1:1-3) are connected to each other with similar contents, it is easy to think that the Chronicles was written by Ezra. Chronicles is the story of events from the first king Saul to Zedekiah the last king of Southern Judah and especially records the events centering around the history of Judah, Southern kingdom. They deal with Hezekiah and Josiah together with David and Solomon whose period was the most abundant and stable in the history of Israel. We can guess that the purpose was to preach the message of comfort and hope to the people of Israel whose self-esteem fell to the ground because of the seventy year Babylonian captivity. The writer of the Chronicles stresses that when the role of priests and the Levites was played right with the temple as center, Israel received great blessing. Here is contained the meaning that the writer hopes that Israel may be reestablished with the word of God.

Tong Point

After reading through the books of prophecy along with I Kings, we read through the books of Chronicles where are recorded the events and incidents of the period same as the books of Samuel and Kings. Since the books of Chronicles record the history and events according to the dynasty, like the books of Kings, it would be effective if we read through it as if we once again put in order the events from the first king Saul of Israel until the city of Jerusalem fell, which we have already read through.

Tong Point

Books of Samuel/I Kings vs. Chronicles

Books of Samuel / Kings	Chronicles
Prophetic viewpoint	Priestly viewpoint
History of political revolutions	History on religion & temple
Wrote both Southern/Northern Kingdoms	Wrote with Southern Judah as center
Stressed continuity of history	Stressed continuity of descent
Wrote both success & failure	Wrote positive incidents mostly
Stressed the thought of retributive justice	Stressed grace coming from covenant
Ends with nation's destruction	Ends with return and restoration

Tong Seeing the forest

I Chronicles History has the power of establishing tomorrow's hope and dream through the past events. The first part of I Chronicles, chapters 1-9 is the genealogy from Adam to the return of Babylonian captivity. I Chronicles specially emphasizes the genealogy of the tribes of Judah, Levite and Benjamin. It reveals the legitimacy of David's dynasty while dealing with the stories that happened during his rule.

In the second half are recorded very emphatically the stories of the ark of testimony, the tribe of Levi and choir. This contains the intention of preserving priesthood and sacrifice while writing this book for the returnees from captivity and at the same time putting into order the seventy year captivity and having the returnees have a new start.

II Chronicles II Chronicles begins with the story of Solomon's rule in B.C. 10th century. The scene where Solomon built and dedicated the temple in a ceremony is described in detail. It also records how his wealth, splendor and fame were. Although II Chronicles records events from Solomon to Zedekiah the last king of Judah in the South and only stories about kings of Judah excluding kings of Israel in the North, we can say that the period dealt with here is the same as the books of Kings.

Particularly, it records the achievements of kings with focus on the temple and sacrifice. The last part of this book, which was written with the intention of stressing that all the people of Israel should live rightly as God's people, ends with the decree of king Cyrus of Persia who permitted the Jews, who had been taken captive to Babylon, to return home and the temple to be rebuilt.

Track 3

7 Books during the Persian Empire

Tong Track 3 - The atmosphere of the 7 books during the Persian Empire

The atmosphere of the 7 books during the Persian Empire (Daniel, Ezra, Haggai, Zechariah, Esther, Nehemiah, and Malachi) is that of high expectations of the re-founding of the A kingdom of Priests. The 7 books during the Persian Empire are about the Israelites' complete destruction from Babylon and their lives as continued under Persian rule. Due to the sacking of Jerusalem's temple and palaces by Babylon, the roads were full of corpses. Witnessing this horrifying annihilation, Jeremiah cried from so much pain. But at dawn, the tearful Jeremiah understood God's compassion.

"I remember my affliction and my wandering, the bitterness and the gall. I well remember them, and my soul is downcast within me. Yet this I call to mind and therefore I have hope: Because of the LORD'S great love we are not consumed, for his compassions never fail. They are new every morning; great is your faithfulness"(Lam.3:19-23).

At this point, Jeremiah realised that the captives who were taken to Babylon were their hope. It was because they were not all destroyed that they could hope to build A kingdom of Priests once more. This hope of Jeremiah's became reality through people like Ezra and Nehemiah under the Persian rule.

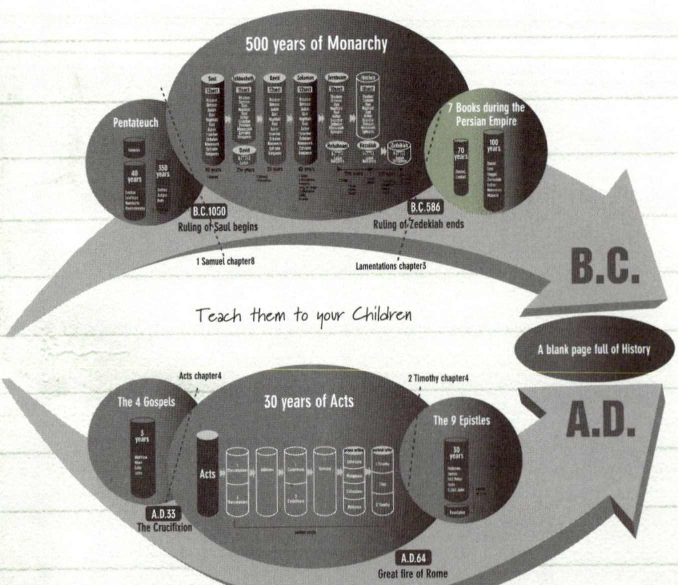

9 Session

Punishment, a Stepping Stone of Hope

Tong Map

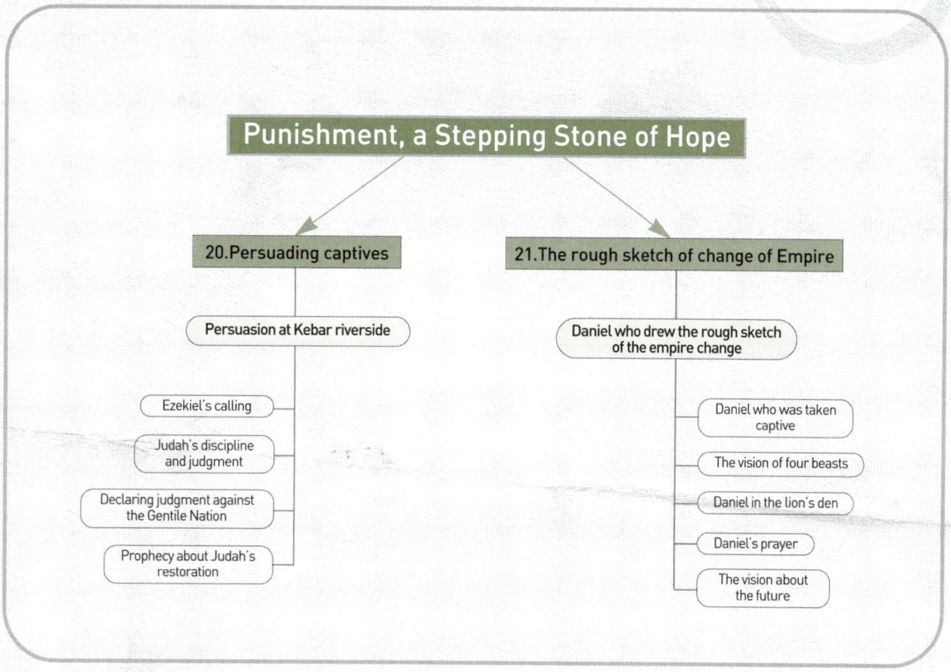

Tong Concept

- **First, second and third Babylonian Captivity**

Let's put in order the first, second and third Babylonian Captivity and study before observing Ezekiel

Captivity	Classification	Invaders	Jewish King	Number	Scripture
Three Babylon Captivities	First (B.C.605)	King Nebuchadnezzar	Jehoiakim	Daniel & others	II Ch.36:6-7
	Second(B.C.598)	King Nebuchadnezzar	Jehoiachin	About 10,000 of Ezekiel & others	II Ki.24:14-17
	Third(B.C.586)	Nebuzaradan (Captain Guard for Nebuchadnezzar)	Zedekiah	All but the poor	II Ki.25:1-21

- **What happened during the 70 years Babylonian Captivity?**

Let's observe and study with focus on the ministry of Ezekiel and Daniel.

Tong At a glance

✱ Looking around the forest

Seeing the short-lived fate of his fatherland, Ezekiel (who was taken captive in Babylon before Jerusalem was totally destroyed) prophesied judgment(Eze. chap.1-24). He declared the word of judgment against the Gentile nations as well(Eze. chap.25-32). Then he declared the restoration of Israel after the fall of Jerusalem(Eze. chap.33-48).

During the rule of Jehoiakim, the first attack by Babylon took place on Judah. The utensils of the temple of God were taken away and people also were taken captive. There was Daniel among them. God made Daniel equipped with both spirituality and sociality the instrument to fulfill the will of God in the center of history.

✱ Land and annual ring

The age of Daniel and Ezekiel was about the same. They were about 20 years younger than Jeremiah who ministered in Jerusalem. Afterwards, Nebuchadnezzar's third attack on Jerusalem took place in B.C.586 and he destroyed it after a long siege. He made the whole land of Judah desolate.

Ezekiel began his ministry as prophet beside Kebar River in Babylon. It was guessed that Kebar River was one of Canals dug by the empire of Babylon. It was a famous place in the East and a canal for passage of ships which formed a branch of Euphrates River in the upper region of the city of Babylon. As it was about 80km from Ezekiel's residence to the city of Babylon, it was thought that he often visited Daniel in the palace.

✱ Wind and Climate

Daniel and his three friends were nobles of Judah and were "young men without any physical defect, handsome, showing aptitude for every kind of learning, well informed, quick to understand, and qualified to serve in the king's palace"(Dan.1:4). Daniel received the highest education of Babylon and was given a new name 'Belteshazzar' aimed to praise one of Babylon's gods as a part of the course of changing his position.

Daniel used prophecies, parables, signs and symbols to dramatically convey God's message to his people, who became captives. Next to the first chapter written in Hebrew which was as good as a prologue, Daniel wrote in Aramaic starting from the second half of 2:4 to chapter 7 to describe the future course of Gentile powers. Then he used his mother tongue to write chapters 8-12 and outlined the future of Jewish nation under the rule of the Gentiles.

Tong Seeing the forest

Ezekiel Young priest Ezekiel was called by God as prophet five years after he was taken captive to Babylon with various engineers of Jerusalem. God came to him and comforted him who was in the mire of hopelessness as all other prisoners were and gave him a vision about new restoration. chapters 1-24, (the first half of the book) contain mainly the word of God who pointed out Judah's sins and judged them, with the condition of Jerusalem prior to its destruction as background. On the other hand, chapters 25-48, (the second half of the book) which was declared after the destruction of Jerusalem preached judgment against surrounding Gentile nations and God's promise of restoration for Southern Judah. Since Ezekiel was written with the methods of so many trances, visions, proverbs and metaphors, it is one of the more diverse books.

Daniel Daniel and his friends were taken captive to Babylon in B.C.605 earlier than Ezekiel. Daniel, who constantly kept faith in God even in a strange Gentile country, was highly exalted after interpreting dreams of kings Nebuchadnezzar and Belshazzar and the omen of dreams.
Although Daniel was of a minority nation and a prisoner, he was made the highest administrator in the empires of Babylon and Persia with his excellent wisdom and ability. At the same time Daniel saw visions while praying and was a man of deep spirituality who prophesied the events to happen in the future.

20 Lesson Persuading captives

Ezekiel

Accumulative reading amount 69.62% 1189

The One Year Tongdok Bible Days 243-259 | Reading time 130 minutes

TongBible Story Overview

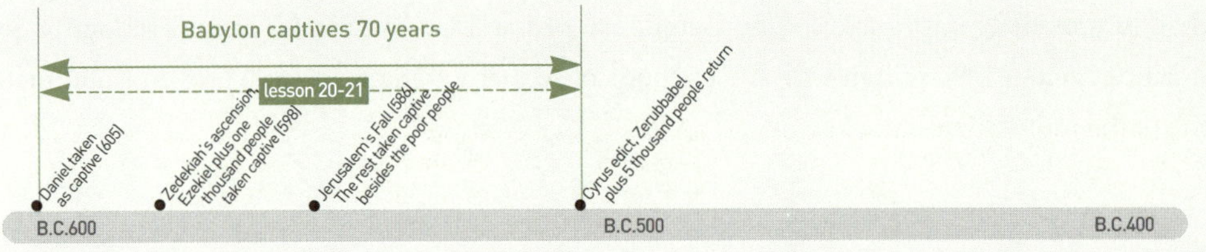

Reading the Old Testament in detail in the order of history (20)

Wonderful was the ministry of Daniel and Ezekiel who had been taken captive to Babylon the first and second times before Southern Judah was completely destroyed. They were the ones who revealed that God's working was done not only in Canaan but also everywhere. Here we first read Ezekiel.

How to read Ezekiel

Nebuchadnezzar took about 10,000 captives including King Jehoiachin and Ezekiel to Babylon. In the land of Judah, Jeremiah ministered as prophet and Ezekiel and Daniel stayed in Babylon together from this time on.

Ezekiel, who had already been in Babylon as a prisoner before the complete destruction of Jerusalem, prophesied judgment seeing the fate of his fatherland which was to exist just briefly. He said that God's discipline came upon the people of Israel due to their sin.

In the book of Ezekiel we can know the importance of "power of persuasion" among the virtues of a leader. The most difficult object to persuade was the one who was discouraged, weary and had given up. During the ministry of Ezekiel, the people of southern Judah had been taken captive to another country and lived as slaves because their country had been destroyed. It was never an easy thing to do to tell them of hope and vision. Despite so, it was Ezekiel who managed this.

Tong Point

Persuasion at Kebar riverside

The stage changed to Babylon. From now on let's look at what happened during the 70 year captivity in Babylon. First the mission given to Ezekiel was to explain to the elite captives of Judah in Babylon why they had to be taken captive as well as to comfort and encourage them.

Ezekiel can be divided into two parts largely with chapter 33 as turning point where the news of Jerusalem's fall was conveyed to the captives.

1. Ezekiel's calling Eze. chap.1-3

The thought of those captives from southern Judah lived in Babylon was that they would return to Jerusalem if the opportunity was given to them. Right this time God came to Ezekiel who had been in Babylon as prisoner for five years and began to speak to him who was in despair. He proclaimed that they could not return home to Jerusalem soon. In those days many captives from many nations lived in Babylon. God said that the Jews in Babylon should have hope and become able among those many nations and make the effort to become the best nation. **Ezekiel's calling was to explain to those taken captive first or second time to Babylon why they had to be brought there as captives and to comfort and encourage them.** "Son of man, I have made you a watchman for the house of Israel; so hear the word I speak and give them warning from me"(Eze.3:17).

Ezekiel and Jeremiah
In Jerusalem Jeremiah announced the end of the country and in Babylon Ezekiel declared the last minute of Kingdom Judah. Ezekiel saw the vision of the glory of God leaving the temple. Now the mind of Ezekiel who saw the scene was no different from the sorrow of Jeremiah who mourned before the city of Jerusalem from which the glory of God disappeared.

2. Judah's discipline and judgment Eze. chap.4-24

While in vision Ezekiel came to see the evil sin of the people of Israel and their sins that desecrated the temple. Seeing that there was no hope in Jerusalem through the visions God gave him, Ezekiel conveyed this fact to the people in Babylon. He said that it was because of the sin of the people of Israel that the country was destroyed and many people had been taken captive. However, the captives did not accept this. Instead, they refused to repent of their sins and rather complained to God by saying that what they were experiencing was unfair. However, God clearly said that each person was punished by God because of the sin they themselves as individuals had committed.

God wanted those who were taken captive to be used in building new Jerusalem later. God set seventy years as training period for building new Jerusalem. Jeremiah kept persuading them to believe this fact by letter whereas Ezekiel did so verbally.

Journal of Revelation
The part where Ezekiel wrote the visions he saw is called the form of 'Journal of Revelation.' He saw a lot of visions. After he saw by vision what happened in Jerusalem, he returned to reality and explained what he saw to those who were captives of Judah in Babylon and persuaded them to believe the will of God. This way he conveyed the will of God.

3. Declaring judgment against the Gentile Nation

Eze. chap.25-32

Judgment against Israel was wrapped up in Ezekiel chapter 24. Then God declared judgment against Gentile countries. Ammon, Moab, Edom and Philistines and even Tyre were unable to avoid God's judgment. Against Egypt who seemed to be a powerful country forever, was prophesied the judgment of

God for as long as in four chapters. It was the warning of God to Southern Judah who instead of depending on God tried to get out of Babylon's threat by depending on Egypt.

4. Prophecy about Judah's restoration Eze. chap.33-48

In B.C.586 the news of destruction of Jerusalem was conveyed to the captives in Babylon. They could no longer harbor any particular hope for Jerusalem. Only those who were captives in Babylon had hope for future.

Ezekiel who declared judgment before the destruction of Jerusalem now began to proclaim a wonderful hope. The 'vision of dry bones' in Ezekiel chapter 37; the vision in which when the breath of God turned into dry bones, tendons and flesh appeared on them and became a vast army stands for that will of God. Israel would not be divided again but would become a kingdom of God that was ruled by the one after God's Heart like David the servant of God. This was the dream of God who saw Israel; the dry bone.

Those who were taken captive were persuaded by Ezekiel to live with their best hope in mind unlike the captives of other nations. They competd with other nations in the Gentile land and became successful. The descendants of those who stayed now in Babylon would return home and comfort their fellow Jews who were gripped with despair.

God who previously took Ezekiel to Jerusalem which was full of sin and evil took him again to Jerusalem and the Jerusalem He showed him this time was what it would look like after it had been luxuriously rebuilt in future. Telling the people about the temple he saw, Ezekiel shouted the restoration of salvation to the people living as captives in despair. Particularly in chapter 48 which adorns the end of the book of Ezekiel is contained the expectation about the history which was to unfold in the future.

Write down the contents of this lesson in the form of Tong Story

Let's pray in a loud voice so that we may be able to teach the contents of this lesson to our children

- Teach them to your children, talking about them when you sit at home and when you walk along the road, when you lie down and when you get up……so that your days and the days of your children may be many……as many as the days that the heavens are above the earth (Deuteronomy 11:19-21).
- you know those from whom you learned it, and how from infancy you have known the holy Scriptures(II Timothy 3:14-15).

21 Lesson

The rough sketch of change of Empire

Daniel

Accumulative reading amount 71.01% 1189

The One Year Tongdok Bible Days 260-264 | Reading time 40 minutes

TongBible Story Overview

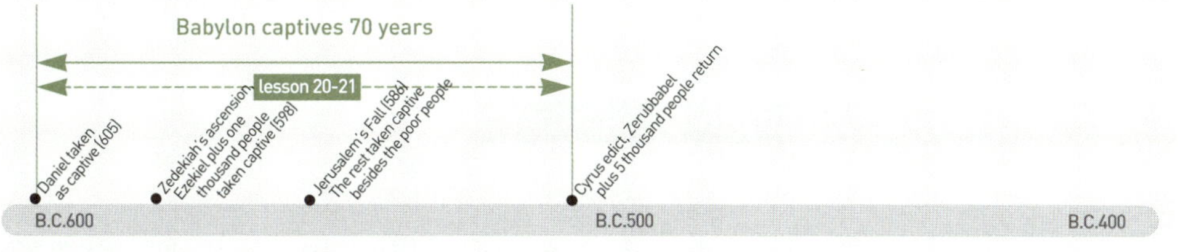

Reading the Old Testament in detail in the order of history (21)

The ministry of Daniel and Ezekiel who had been taken captive to Babylon the first and second times before Southern Judah was completely destroyed, revealed that God's working was done not only in Canaan but also everywhere. Here we read Daniel.

How to read Daniel

Daniel made up his mind to live serving God. God made such Daniel a tool who would fulfill the will of God in such times of hardship.

Originally, the country Daniel was taken captive to was Babylon. Then, Babylon was destroyed by Persia and suddenly Daniel was made to serve Persia. In those days although Daniel was a Jew, he held a high position as a public servant in the government of Babylon. More surprising was that the king of Persia had Daniel serve his government in a higher position than the days of Babylon. There was only one reason. He was not only excellent in the administrative power but also was faithful so that kings of any country wanted to scout Daniel.

The reason Daniel (who was once taken as captive) was used excellently like this was that when he was a in his teen, he made up his mind to live as a man of faith honoring the name of God while making the effort to be equipped with ability. Another reason was that a wonderful outcome example of Jeremiah's letter was none other than Daniel.

Tong Point

Daniel who drew the rough sketch of the empire change
It was under the Assyrian empire when Daniel was born. However, the country where Daniel was taken captive to was Babylon. Later Babylon was destroyed by Persia, which meant Daniel came to experience the change of empire head fist. On the basis of this experience, Daniel came to prophesize the rough sketch of empire change that would happen afterwards. Even while he was a high official of empires of Babylon and Persia, it was because of his high spirituality and sociality that he was able to serve as a prophet of God.

1. Daniel who was taken captive Dan. chap.1-5

Having destroyed southern Judah, Babylon took skillful and intelligent people from Judah to their country as captives. It was a plan of Nebuchadnezzar.

Along with other young men Daniel also was taken captive and received Babylon-style education at the palace of Nebuchadnezzar. In Babylon, they were made to change their names and eating style in the Babylonian way.

However, Daniel and his friends made up their mind to focus on God and refused to take the king's food and wine. God's grace was with them so that their faces were made to look better than those who ate the king's food.

Giving them wisdom and knowledge, God especially gave Daniel the wisdom to understand visions and dreams. It was a plan of God through Jeremiah.

One day king Nebuchadnezzar dreamed a strange dream and told the interpreters to interpret the dream without telling them the dream. If they were not able to interpret, he threatened to kill all wise men of Babylon. Daniel who was able

The men of God who greatly contended for victory in his teens

David
Contest in which he risked his life in front of Goliath (I Sa. chap.17).

Daniel
Contest in which he risked his life in front of Nebuchadnezzar (Dan. chap.1-2).

to interpret the king's dream with God's answer came to reveal the glory of God in the Gentile nation.

2. The vision of four beasts Dan. chap.7-8

Daniel had the insight to read the times through the wisdom and revelation given by God. God allowed him get into a deep vision and understand the will of God. In that vision, he saw four beasts which stood for the empires of Babylon, Persia, Greece and Rome which were to appear as great empires of the world in the future.

Two years after the first vision of four beasts, Daniel saw the vision of a ram and a goat. Here a surprising thing was the attitude of Daniel shown after he saw God's visions for a few days. "I, Daniel, was exhausted and lay ill for several days. Then I got up and went about the king's business"(Dan.8:27). Daniel was both a politician and an administrator. After he came out of the world of deep vision, he worked on 'the king's affair,' specifically, the duty of premier. Daniel was a man who could spiritually experience the deep encounter with God and at the same time carry out social duty such as administration in his daily life. **The ability to work, the mind to desire the LORD's grace, namely, the harmony of spirituality and sociality are common characteristics of the people of God that we come across while reading through the Bible.**

3. Daniel in the lion's den Dan. chap.6

In the process of the empire of Babylon being destroyed and a change of empire under way, Darius a Mede became king and appointed 120 high officials (and three premiers) to govern the whole empire. One of the premiers was Daniel. Furthermore, the king intended to appoint Daniel as the premier of the whole country among the three premiers because he exceeded in excellence in ability and loyalty. So Daniel's adversaries tried to find an opportunity to obstruct him.

However, no matter how much they investigated about Daniel, they were not able to find Daniel's flaws. So his adversaries ploted to obstruct him with other methods. Knowing that Daniel prayed to God towards Jerusalem three times every day, they proposed to the king, "If during the next thirty days anyone prays to any god or man except to the king, he shall be thrown into the lions' den". Not knowing what was going on, the king put his seal on the decree.

Yet, even though Daniel knew all this, he prayed toward Jerusalem as usual. He was the man who prayed with firm determination from the days of his teens. Turning 70 now, he still prayed towards Jerusalem three times everyday.

Throwing Daniel into the den of lions, the king was unable to eat nor sleep. Early the next morning, the king ran to Daniel and asked him how he was. Daniel answered that he was fine and alive. The king was so pleased and exalted the name of God by issuing a decree to all the land.

Daniel and rulers of the empires

Babylon	Nebuchadnezzar	Three friends of Daniel were thrown into a blazing furnace (Dan. chap.1-4).
	Belshazzar	Daniel interpreted the words written on the wall (Dan. chap.5, 7, 8).
Mede-Persia	Darius	Daniel was thrown into the den of lions (Dan. chap.6, 9)
	Cyrus	Implemented the measure of sending back captives (Dan. chap.10-12).

4. Daniel's prayer Dan. chap.9

Daniel

Daniel was a loyal man. It was the king who noticed this fact better than anyone else. The major work of the most powerful man of the country was to closely check the loyalty of his subjects. In the sight of the king, Daniel was not greedy for power but rather was most loyal. Daniel determined his will for God while he was in his teens. He was loyal to God for all his life time. He followed the laws of God beginning with discerning food to eat, which meant he was filled with the knowledge of God. It was on the basis of this knowledge that he was loyal to the God of heaven and also to the fellow workers and bosses of his office while working. Daniel believed that great and beautiful things came from heaven, his faith in God and his loyalty to the king did not collide into each other.

Daniel lived faithfully doing his best without losing hope even while he was a prisoner thanks to the letter Jeremiah wrote. Long ago Jeremiah sent a letter to those who had been taken captive, "This is what the LORD says: "When seventy years are completed for Babylon, I will come to you and fulfill my gracious promise to bring you back to this place"(Jer.29:10). Reading this letter, Daniel came to understand the number of years God promised(Dan.9:1-2).

Daniel first repented and earnestly prayed hoping that the prophecy would be fulfilled and he would be able to return to Jerusalem, "Give ear, O God, and hear; open your eyes and see the desolation of the city that bears your Name. We do not make requests of you because we are righteous, but because of your great mercy"(Dan.9:18).

5. The vision about the future Dan. chap.10-12

Three years passed after the first returnees of Israel arrived. However, when Daniel heard the news about rebuilding the temple which was not so smoothly carried out and saw visions about wars, he prayed to God in a great anxiety. God comforted Daniel saying, "Do not be afraid, O man highly esteemed," "Peace! Be strong now; be strong"(Dan.10:19).

The man who had hope and expectation was to be patient. The word of God that was given through the last message of Daniel was also 'wait'. Through the promise of restoration that God would save His people, he gave the message of hope to Israel who had gone through suffering amid tribulation.

The prayers of the men of God

- **David's prayer** - when God promised that He would make his throne firm forever, he humbled himself as a "servant" and prayed a thankful prayer (II Sa. chap 7).
- **Daniel's prayer** - realizing that the time to restore Jerusalem had come near; he prayed asking for God's mercy and forgiveness for his nation (Dan. chap 9).
- **Nehemiah's prayer** - he prayed for the restoration of the desolate city determining his devotion (Neh. chap 1).

Write down the contents of this lesson in the form of Tong Story

....

....

....

....

....

....

Let's pray in a loud voice so that we may be able to teach the contents of this lesson to our children

- Teach them to your children, talking about them when you sit at home and when you walk along the road, when you lie down and when you get up……so that your days and the days of your children may be many……as many as the days that the heavens are above the earth (Deuteronomy 11:19-21).
- you know those from whom you learned it, and how from infancy you have known the holy Scriptures(II Timothy 3:14-15).

10 Session

A Community of Reconstruction

Tong Map

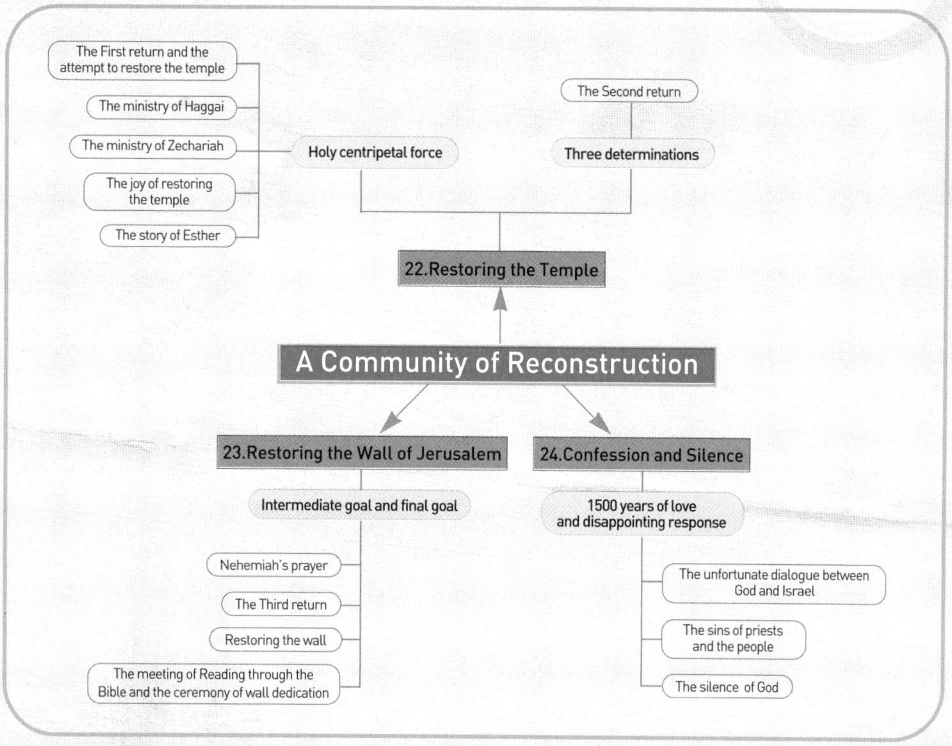

Tong Concept

- **Understanding the incident of 'Out of Persia.'**

We should put in order the three time return of captives, major incidents of each period and related characters and remember them. Let's put in order the three time return of captives of Persian times as follows in a big frame and study them.

Return	Classification	Leaders	Major ministry	Number	Scripture
Three time Return Under Persia	First(B.C.537)	Gov. Zerubbabel/Priest Joshua	Restoring the Temple	49,897	Ezr.chap.1-4
	Haggai, Zechariah ministered				Hag., Zec.
	Joy of restoring the temple				Ezr.chap.5-6
	The story of Esther				Est.
	Second(B.C.458)	Priest Ezra	Teaching law	1,754	Ezr.7:7-chap.9
	Third(B.C.445)	Gov. Nehemiah	Restoring the Wall of Jerusalem	A lot	Neh.chap.2

Tong At a glance

* Looking around the forest

As prophesied by Jeremiah, the return of captives began in B.C.537 according to the decree of King Cyrus of Persia. Restoring the temple started after the first return led by Zerubbabel. At this time Haggai and Zechariah came on stage. Revival movement of Israel the worship community and purification work of the community took place under the leadership of both scholars and priest Ezra who returned to Jerusalem on their second return of captives.

After that, Nehemiah returned on their third return with the goal of restoring the wall of Jerusalem. The contents of the book of Nehemiah in which the movement of wall restoring was followed by that of reading through the Bible followed by that of faith renewal shows us how God struggled and worked to restore Jerusalem which was made desolate.

* Land and annual ring

The ministry and restoring the temple of Haggai and Zechariah took place during the rule of I Darius and the incident of Esther during the rule of Xerxes. The second return of captives was carried out under the leadership of priest Ezra in B.C.458 during the rule of I Artaxerxes and the third return was in B.C.445 under the leadership of governor Nehemiah.

The project of restoring the wall by Nehemiah began from the northern half point of Jerusalem and was done counter-clock wise. Its length was about 2.4km. The distance crossing the castle south to north was about 1.1km. The wall was restored higher than before captivity happened.

* Wind and Climate

Babylon which destroyed Assyria did not follow the way of rule of Assyria but unfolded the policy of educating the talented of the conquered land in their own Babylonian way so that they could rule the conquered land through them. Although Babylon dreamt their empire would be eternal, they had to let down their banners in 70 years as prophesied by Jeremiah. Persia (Mede-Persia of the Bible) which became the new owner in place of Babylon in ancient Near East came to form a huge empire including not only the Mesopotamian region but also the Nile. Persia had been the most powerful empire until in B.C.333 when Alexander the Great became king of the Greek empire and spread its influence.

Tong Seeing the forest

Ezra Ezra who was the 16th generation descendant of high priest Aaron was both an erudite scholar and a priest. He returned to Jerusalem on the second return having in mind the mission of researching, carrying out and teaching God's law. Chapters 1-6 contain the story of restoring the temple spoken with the first returnees before his return. Chapters 7-10 contain the contents about his own return and reform movement.

Haggai Perhaps Haggai was one of the first returnees who returned under the leadership of high priest Joshua and governor Zerubbabel. Even though the community who returned started restoring the temple aggressively, soon they gave it up, and faced a lot of difficulties.
Eventually restoring the temple was on hold as long as 16 years. At this time prophet Haggai stood up and persuaded people to start restoring the temple.

Zechariah Prophet Zechariah ministered in the same period as Haggai and also played the role of urging the people who were neglecting restoring the temple. However, Zechariah moved one step further and showed the future image of Jerusalem; the shape of new Jerusalem filled with the glory of God. Surprisingly, in that shape was embroidered the coming of Jesus Christ. The people who were moved with the words of prophets Haggai and Zechariah started restoring the temple again and two months later came to complete the foundation.

Esther Esther, who lived in Persia with cousin Mordecai, was a beautiful and wise woman and became the queen of King Xerxes. Then a high noble in Persia called Hamman expanded his personal hatred against Mordecai and plotted an evil plan to kill all the Jews.
In order to overcome this crisis, Esther went to the king with the determination, 'If I perish, I perish' and the Jews were made to be delivered with God's excellent leading. Esther which is a story of God's deep love for a nation gave hope and courage to those who were in the mire of hopelessness and frustration.

Nehemiah Although over 90 years passed since the first returnees had returned to Jerusalem, the wall of Jerusalem which had been broken down was still left desolate and the weak people trembled with the threats of bandits and beasts. Hearing this and praying tearfully, Nehemiah heard his calling. He became a cupbearer of Persian king and was eventually dispatched to Jerusalem as governor with the permission of King Artaxerxes. Wisely overcoming lots of hindering power groups and internal problems, he successfully carried out the enormous mission of restoring the wall of Jerusalem in just 52 days. He also held Reading through the Bible Meeting during the feast of tabernacle, a Jewish feast by cooperating with Priest Ezra. On the day of Wall dedication, the sound of laughter of women and children which resounded everywhere around Jerusalem was the joy of weak neighbors and that of our God also.

Malachi When restoring the temple had been completed and Nehemiah returned to Persia, the Jews did not observe the statutes about tithe and Sabbath. Priests were also corrupted. As the last prophet of the Old Testament, Malachi pointed out these sins which were prevalent in the community who returned.

The sin of Israel Malachi pointed out more fundamentally was their unfortunate mind that rejected the love of God who did not spare affection and tears for them. In front of the people of Israel who sarcastically asked back, "How have you loved us?" in response to the word of God, "I have loved you," our God began a tough silence.

22 Lesson : Restoring the Temple

Ezra, Haggai, Zechariah, Esther

Accumulative reading amount 73.44% 1189

The One Year Tongdok Bible Days 265-275 | Reading time 70 minutes

TongBible Story Overview

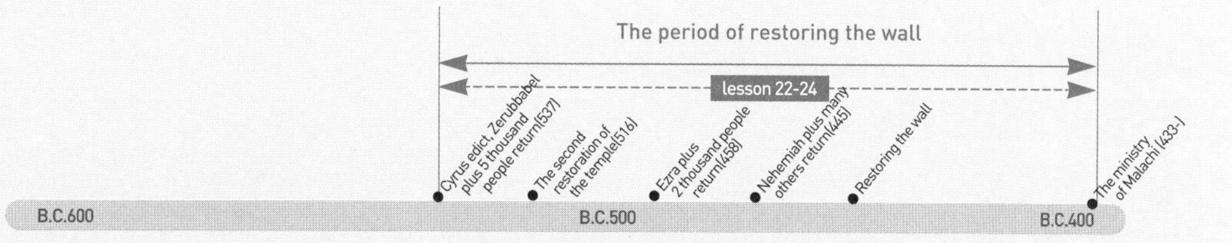

Reading the Old Testament in detail in the order of history (22)

The empire of Babylon became destroyed and the Persian Empire came into power. King Cyrus of Persia sent back captives to their home country who had been taken captive by Babylon. The story of the people who returned the first time was recorded in Ezra chapters 1 to 4. However, as they spent about 16 years not restoring the temple, God sent prophets Haggai and Zechariah to stress loudly the importance of temple building. The story that the temple was being restored with the help of Haggai and Zechariah appears in Ezra chapters 5 and 6. Forty years after, the incident described in Esther took place in Persia. Afterward, Ezra led the second group of returnees to Jerusalem. We read Ezra chapters 7 to 10 which contain that story. It would be useful to read Psalm 119 alongside this which is assumed to have been written by Ezra.

How to read the returnee community

Those who returned to Jerusalem first restored desolate Jerusalem and began the foundational construction of the temple. The book of Esther belongs between the first return and second return. Also, it is the book of Esther that identifies the origin of the feast of Purim the Jews observe in the month of Adar every year.

Ezra who returned on their second return traveled about 1,500km from Babylon to Jerusalem along with many Jews. Scholar and priest Ezra caused the revival movement and purification work of the community of Israel to happen.

Tong Point

First and second return of captives

The Jews were made to return to Jerusalem over three times because of the announcement of the decree of king Cyrus of Persia in B.C.537. Let's study in the order of history while observing that the related stories are centered around Ezra.

Ezra chap.1-4 — (Haggai, Zechariah) — Ezra chap.5-6 — (Esther) — Ezra chap.7-10

1. The First return and the attempt to restore the temple Ezr. chap.1-4

King Cyrus of Persia implemented the policy of having the captives taken by Babylon return home. This meant that the training period of 70 years God proclaimed was over. King Cyrus sent back the Jews to their country and permitted the temple of God to be restored.

The leaders of the people returning from every part of Persia according to the decree of Cyrus were governor Zerubbabel and priest Joshua (Jeshua). The steps they took to return home were full of hope. **We can call the new community the 'community of reconstruction.' They carried out the important task of restoring the Jerusalem temple which was burnt down to the ground and the faith community of Israel had therefore collapsed.**

After the community of reconstruction arrived in Jerusalem, they first restored the religious feast. Then, two years and two months after they returned, they started restoring the temple of the LORD.

The chronological background of the book of Ezra

The book of Ezra contains stories about the two returns from Babylon

The First return	Restore the temple under the leadership of Zerubbabel
The interval of 80 years	Queen Esther of Persia
The Second return	Awakening spiritual condition under the guidance of Ezra

Old people shed tears of joy remembering their past and many people rejoiced together.

However, the Gentile peoples who were made to live in Israel by Assyria began to obstruct the temple restoring of Israel. Even though the people of Israel built 'the temple,' their adversaries sent a letter to the king of Persia falsely saying that the people of Israel were restoring 'city and wall.'

Comparison between Haggai and Zechariah

Haggai	Zechariah
exhortation	encouragement
more specific	a little abstract
briefly	far-reaching
present matter of concern	future matter of concern
participate!	be courageous!
a little old	a little younger
behaviorist	man of vision

Their false letter made the king order them to stop restoring. Gradually losing their courage, the community of reconstruction eventually stopped restoring the temple. At this time, God sent prophets Haggai and Zechariah.

2. The ministry of Haggai Hag. chap.1-2

Restoring the temple had been on hold for sixteen years with the foundation only laid. While restoring the temple was on hold, they cultivated the land, did selling business but the result was not productive. They just sighed and complained. Prophet Haggai explained thc reason to them. It was that they were just blaming the circumstances surrounding them and making the mistake of not working on the temple restoring positively.

"You expected much, but see, it turned out to be little. What you brought home, I blew away. Why?" declares the LORD Almighty. "Because of my house, which remains a ruin, while each of you is busy with his own house"(Hag.1:9).

Telling the word of comfort to those who restore the temple,

Haggai also told them that although the Jerusalem temple was desolate, it would be full with the glory of God in the future. The people obeyed the word of God spoken by Haggai. God said, "I am with you."

3. The ministry of Zechariah Zec. chap.1-14

Along with Haggai prophet Zechariah also stood up to speak after hearing the word of God. Although restoring the temple was temporally delayed by the obstruction of outsiders, God encouraged and comforted the people of Israel so that they could start again. Particularly God encouraged Zerubbabel and Joshua by telling them He would clothe them with the power of the Holy Spirit.

Now the task of the people of Israel was to move ahead believing and obeying the promise of God that He would make Israel His people. The work of restoring the temple which was on hold for more than sixteen years was resumed.

The prophecy of Zechariah about Christ

- The angel of the LORD (Zec.3:1-2)
- Branch (Zec.3:8; 6:12)
- Stone with seven eyes (Zec.3:9)
- King, Priest (Zec.6:13)
- Humble king (Zec.9:9-10)
- Cornerstone, tent peg and battle bow (Zec.10:4)
- Being rejected, Good shepherd sold for 30 shekels of silver which was a servant's wage (Zec.11:4-13)
- The one they have pierced (Zec.12:10)
- A fountain that cleanses them from sin and impurity (Zec.13:1)
- Shepherd stricken by sword (Zec.13:7)
- Judge and King to come (Zec. chap.14)

4. The joy of restoring the temple Ezr. chap.5-6

The people of Israel were ready to resume restoring the temple after hearing Haggai and Zechariah. At that time, king Darius who found the document of king Cyrus gave orders to resume the temple construction speedily. Even those who were going to obstruct it came to help them upon receiving the order of the king.

Finally the exciting and joyful day came. The people of Israel enjoyed excitement and joy observing the Passover which had not been observed properly. Coming through all this process including much difficulty, hardship, obstruction and persecution of those people around them, the people of Israel rose up again and came to be able to stand before God as His holy people.

5. The story of Esther Est. chap.1-10

In the third year of king Xerxes of Persia, beautiful virgins from all the country gathered in the palace to be selected as new queen and Esther was among them. Though she was a captive from Judah and was raised by her cousin Mordecai without her parents, she became new queen in the providence of God.

Haman enters the scene, who was the man who held the highest position among the subjects of king Xerxes. He was very arrogant. When he knew that Mordecai, who did not bow down to him, was a man from Judah, he planned to kill all the people of Judah. Haman's plot made a decree of the king be issued that ordered all the people of Judah be killed at the same time on an appointed day.

Feast of Purim
The 13th day of the month of Adar which almost became the most tragic day turned into the day of joy and victory. The word Purim came from the Assyrian word puru which means 'lottery' This came from the fact that Haman cast lots to choose the day when he would kill the Jews.

Hearing this news and wearing thick sackcloth, Mordecai put ashes on his head and cried loudly at the gate of the palace. Conveying the whole story of the event to Esther, Mordecai asked Esther to "go to the king and earnestly plead with him for the Jewish nation." In those days, according to the Persian law, if somebody went to the king when they were not called by him could have been killed. Though she was queen, that matter required her to be prepared even to die. However, in spite of the danger that she may lose her life, she decided to go to the king, saying, "If I perish, I perish"(Est.4:16).

Esther fasted and prayed for three days for this matter and went to the king. Able to stand before the king safely by the protection of God, Esther wisely invited the king and Haman to her feast. At the second feast Esther prepared for the king, King Xerxes told Esther to tell him what she wanted since he was willing to give her even half of his kingdom. Right this time Esther disclosed Haman's conspiracy. Hearing this fact, the king became so angry that he ordered Haman to be hung on the gallows Haman made to hang Mordecai. The whole nation of Judah were made to live again thanks to such effort of Mordecai and Esther for which they risked their lives. Since then the Jews have observed this day as the feast of Purim.

Through this event that happened in Persia, the book of Esther shows us the deep and broad love of God. **Although it looked like an accident in the sight of man, it was indeed the greatest drama God unfolded.**

Tong Point

Three determinations
Priest Ezra who decided to study, keep and teach the law of God to the people returned to Jerusalem harboring that mission in mind.

6. The Second Return Ezr. chap.7-10

It was scholar and priest Ezra who about eighty years after the first return led the second return of Israel during the rule of I Artaxerxes.

Ezra was well versed in history and skilled in studying the law. He held a high social position which made him have a close relationship with the Persian king. Now he made up his mind to return to Jerusalem. He decided to go not alone but along with "Some of the Israelites, including priests, Levites, singers, gatekeepers and temple servants".

The reason Ezra decided to return was that he wanted to study the law of the LORD, observe it and teach the ordinances and regulations to the people of Israel (Ezr.7:10).

When Ezra returned home, he received lots of support from king Artaxerxes. He did so not to store up wealth for himself but to establish a community and to use the wealth to help the Levites make a living. Ezra appointed the Levites who would carry out his determinations and perform sacrificing at the temple and then held the meeting of Reading through the Bible with Nehemiah who returned on their third return. This was the beautiful ministry of Ezra.

Write down the contents of this lesson in the form of Tong Story

....

....

....

....

....

....

Let's pray in a loud voice so that we may be able to teach the contents of this lesson to our children

- Teach them to your children, talking about them when you sit at home and when you walk along the road, when you lie down and when you get up……so that your days and the days of your children may be many……as many as the days that the heavens are above the earth (Deuteronomy 11:19-21).
- you know those from whom you learned it, and how from infancy you have known the holy Scriptures(II Timothy 3:14-15).

23 Lesson Restoring the Wall of Jerusalem

Nehemiah

Accumulative reading amount 74.65% 1189

The One Year Tongdok Bible Days 276-279 | Reading time 35 minutes

TongBible Story Overview

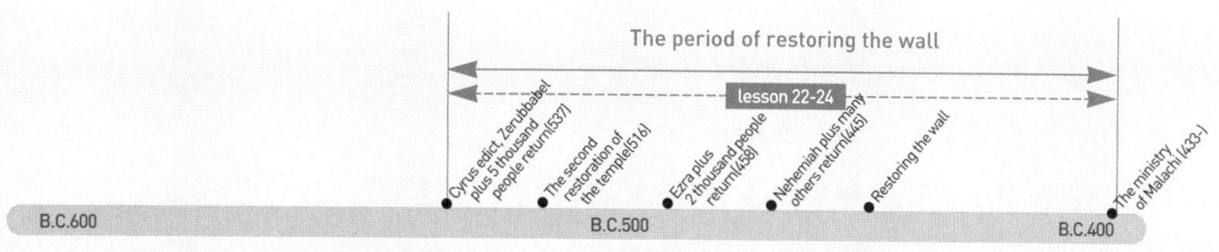

Reading the Old Testament in detail in the order of history (23)

About 13 years after Ezra returned, Nehemiah returned to Jerusalem on their third return. He came to Jerusalem as governor with the dream of restoring the temple. Here we read the book of Nehemiah.

How to read Nehemiah

The wall of Jerusalem was broken down by the soldiers of Babylon in B.C.586 and since then nothing was done for the wall for 140 years. Nobody dared restore the wall which contained political as well as religious significance. However, Nehemiah had the goal in mind to restore the temple.
With the permission of the king, Nehemiah fulfilled the dream of restoring the wall. Nehemiah was humble and honest as governor and was the role model of love, passion, godliness and sacrifice for the people.

Tong Point

Intermediate goal and final goal
That Nehemiah should become the king's cupbearer and restore the wall of Jerusalem was only his intermediate goal. Then, what was his final goal? It was the joy of God and of neighbors(Neh.12:43).

1. Nehemiah's prayer Neh. chap.1

The chronological relation of Ezra, Nehemiah and Esther

B.C.537-515	B.C.483-473	B.C.458	B.C.445-425
Zerubbabel	Esther	Ezra	Nehemiah
Ezra chap.1-6	The book of Esther	Ezra chap.7-10	The book of Nehemiah
First return		Second return	Third return

The people who returned on their first return under the leadership of Zerubbabel restore the temple. After that, on their second return the people returned under the leadership of Ezra. After their second return under Ezra, more than ten years passed. Nehemiah always wondered about the current affairs in his fatherland. Then one day he came to hear about the desolate situation of Jerusalem and the suffering his fellow Jews were going through.

Hearing this news, Nehemiah wept, fasted and prayed for many days. His prayer was based on the good understanding of the laws, commandments and statutes and on the word. In his prayer he asked God to remember his promise that if they, the descendants of their forefathers receive God's discipline willingly and turned to God and observed His commandments; "even if your exiled people are at the farthest horizon, I will gather them from there and bring them to the place I have chosen as a dwelling for my Name." And he asked God to use him as the man who was fit to fulfill that word. Nehemiah dreamt of returning to Jerusalem himself and restoring the wall.

2. The Third return Neh. chap. 2-3

The reason why it was difficult to restore the wall of Jerusalem
Restoring the wall of Jerusalem was never easy in the midst of the historical situation of those days. Let's refer to a historical record of Ezra 4:19-21 as follows; "Jerusalem has had powerful kings ruling over the whole of Trans-Euphrates, and taxes, tribute and duty were paid to them." Because of this record, the king of Persia once ordered the construction of the city and wall to be stopped. It meant that it was dangerous to restore the wall. However, Nehemiah challenged this difficult task and got the king's permission.

Nehemiah became a trusted servant to the king as he worked in the palace. In those days the position of 'officer in charge of the king's wine' was one of the closest ones to the king and so a very important position politically.

One morning, when Nehemiah was giving the king wine, his face showed much sadness unlike usual. Then, the king asked him the reason. At that, Nehemiah became very afraid. According to the Persian law, if a subject showed sadness in front of the king he was thought to have intentions to harm the king and as a result could have been killed themselves.

Nehemiah immediately answered, "Long live the king." He clearly expressed that he had no intention to harm the king. And then he said, "Why should my face not look sad when the city where my fathers are buried lies in ruins, and its gates have been destroyed by fire?" Hearing that, the king asked, "What is it you want?" Right away he prayed to God silently and then said, "Let him send me to the city in Judah where my fathers are buried so that I can restore it." In other words, he asked the king to send him as governor to Jerusalem and allow him to restore the wall. Based on his usual willing trust in Nehemiah, the king gladly granted the request. In addition to the position of governor to Jerusalem, the king gave Nehemiah the king's letters, construction material and furthermore a military commander and horses and soldiers that Nehemiah did not even ask for.

About six months after Nehemiah left for Jerusalem with many fellow Jews, he arrived in Jerusalem, had a preliminary on-site field investigation of desolate Jerusalem, established a specific plan of restoration and persuaded the people. The people who heard Nehemiah's proposal accepted it and agreed to start restoring the wall.

3. Restoring the wall Neh. chap.4-7

Restoring the wall faced obstacles. The first obstacle was the obstruction of outsiders who tried to get some profit by taking advantage of the desolate condition of Jerusalem. Yet, Nehemiah and the people did not yield to them but carried out their work by overcoming the crisis with tools in one hand and swords in another. Finding out even their plot to assassinate him in advance, Nehemiah solved problems wisely.

Nehemiah's leadership
1. Going together by persuasion
2. Getting cooperation
3. Defeating hinderers
4. Reforming basic order

The second obstacle against restoring the wall was within the community of Israel. Because of the difficult condition, the poor borrowed money from the rich on very high interests and could not pay the money back so that they even had to sell their children as slaves. So Nehemiah called nobles and officials, persuaded them to help the poor fellow Jews and eat with them so that they could solidify their internal bond. This excellent leadership of Nehemiah was a source power with which they were able to restore the broken wall of Jerusalem in just 52 days.

Obstacles (Neh. chap.4,6)
1. scornful laugh
2. Political trick and assassination plan
3. Shemaiah's false prophecy
4. Bribe

4. The meeting of Reading through the Bible and the ceremony of wall dedication Neh. chap.8-13

Nehemiah held the meeting of Reading through the Bible in

Social safety network

The wall in those days was first, a shield against outside enemies and second, a shield against beasts (Wild beasts even strode around during the daytime so that the poor who did not have gates at their house were exposed to danger). That a society was healthy meant that the relatively weak of the society could be comfortable. Nehemiah's restoring the wall of Jerusalem was to provide a basic safety apparatus in which the women and children living in Jerusalem could make a living safely.

commemoration of the ceremony of wall dedication(Neh.8:1-3).

In this meeting of Reading through the Bible of one week, priest Ezra taught while reading aloud the book of laws, and the people shed tears of repentance realizing the will of God in front of His word. As the people who heard the word began to realize their sins, a great movement of repentance took place in Jerusalem.

During the ceremony of wall dedication, women and children and all the people of Jerusalem rejoiced so loudly that their sound was heard from afar (Neh.12:43). **What Nehemiah intended to accomplish by laboring and making much effort was not simply the wall of stones. It was his intention to make a safety apparatus for the weakest and the poorest who could not survive without a strong shield of protection.** Due to restoring the wall with Nehemiah as center and the reform of faith with Ezra as center Jerusalem became the center of faith, where a great joy given by God came to overflow.

Write down the contents of this lesson in the form of Tong Story

Let's pray in a loud voice so that we may be able to teach the contents of this lesson to our children

- Teach them to your children, talking about them when you sit at home and when you walk along the road, when you lie down and when you get up……so that your days and the days of your children may be many……as many as the days that the heavens are above the earth (Deuteronomy 11:19-21).
- you know those from whom you learned it, and how from infancy you have known the holy Scriptures(II Timothy 3:14-15).

24 Lesson
Confession and Silence

Malachi

Accumulative reading amount 75% 1189

The One Year Tongdok Bible Days 280 | Reading time 10 minutes

TongBible Story Overview

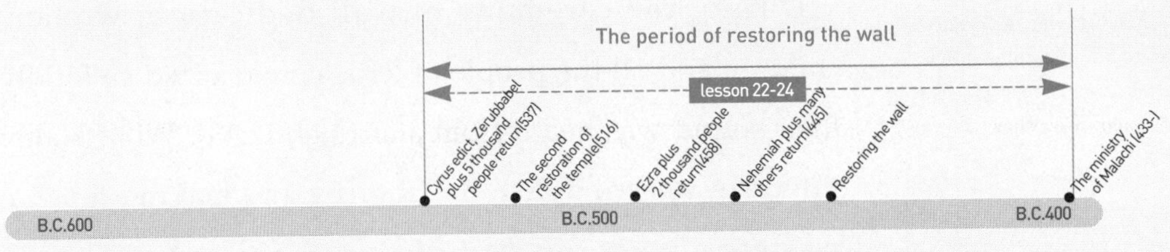

Reading the Old Testament in detail in the order of history (24)

Malachi ministered as the last prophet of the Old Testament as a contemporary of Nehemiah or presumably later than that.

How to read Malachi

After Nehemiah finished his governorship and returned to Persia, the Jews again fell into sin. Priests neglected their responsibility, often divorced their wives and remarried Gentile women so that there happened a serious problem of the common people falling into idolatry. And they even neglected tithe and offerings. In Malachi we see that in this situation God decided to keep silent. That silence continued for 400 years. After that God came to us with a greater love. God's silence was a period of preparing a more wonderful love.

Tong Point

1500 years of love and disappointing response
God kept silence for 400 years to the people of Israel who asked; "How have you loved us?"

1. The unfortunate dialogue between God and Israel

Mal. 1:1-5

Prophet Malachi
Prophet Malachi ministered during the same period as that of governor Nehemiah or a little later. For lots of evils Nehemiah faced, the people were specifically rebuked in the book of Malachi. The cold indifference of the people for God which was described in the books of Malachi and Nehemiah was the chronological atmosphere which was prevalent in Israel in those days.

The reconstruction community, who finished the training period of seventy years according to the word of God, returned and were expected to do well. Pitiably however, they turned cynical as time went by. Israel once again became arrogantly apathetic to the love of God who made them a great nation and a kingdom of priests.

God loved them one thousand years like one day whereas the people of Israel spent more time turning against God rather than loving Him. God said to them;

"I have loved you."

They responded; "How have you loved us?"(Mal.1:2).

This was a truly lonely and heart-aching dialogue between God and Israel.

2. The sins of priests and the people Mal. 1:6-chap.3

God pointed out the sins and evils of priests.

"By offering defiled food on my altar. "But you ask, 'How have we defiled you?' "By saying that the LORD's table is contemptible. When you offer blind animals for sacrifice, is that not wrong? When you sacrifice lame or diseased animals, is that not wrong? Try offering them to your governor! Would he be pleased with you? Would he accept you?"(Mal. 1:7-8).

The sins of the people also were disclosed one by one. Their sins could not be counted by fingers; perfunctory worship such as laying dirty bread on the altar of God, sacrificing the animals which were blind, lame and sick, idolatry, people divorcing their wives, doubt about God's justice, stealing tithe and offerings which were God's, not fearing God but resisting with stubborn words and so on.

God's unfortunate heart

Out of 55 verses of the book of Malachi, forty 7 verses were spoken by God. This ratio is the highest among all the prophetical books.

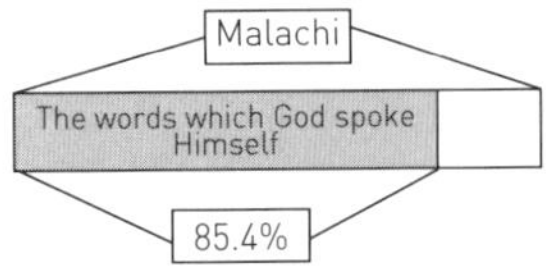

3. The silence of God Mal. chap. 4

God is the God of love. The God of love always loved to have dialogue with Israel His children. Every time they went the way of evil, he tantalizingly called them to come back by sending the men of God. He punished them and made them be taken captive to another nation and return. Now, God kept silent. Not just for one or two days, but four hundred years He kept silent. **He spent the silent period of preparation in order to show directly as said, "I have loved you like this" in response to Israel who ask, "How have you loved us?".**

Afterwards, until John the Baptist who was "A voice of one calling in the wilderness"(Mat.3:3). appeared, God kept silent for a long time. God could not help keeping silent because of the reality of Israel. However, God eventually prepared a message of love.

Finally God sent His only begotten Son to this world because He could not give up human beings. God is love. The silence of four hundred years of God who was the very body of love was the silence aimed at showing the substance of a deeper love.

Write down the contents of this lesson in the form of Tong Story

Let's pray in a loud voice so that we may be able to teach the contents of this lesson to our children

- Teach them to your children, talking about them when you sit at home and when you walk along the road, when you lie down and when you get up……so that your days and the days of your children may be many……as many as the days that the heavens are above the earth (Deuteronomy 11:19-21).
- you know those from whom you learned it, and how from infancy you have known the holy Scriptures(II Timothy 3:14-15).

Track 4

A Blank Page Full of History

Tong Track 4 - The atmosphere of the intertestamental period

The atmosphere of the intertestamental period(a blank page full of history) is that of the universalization of the Old Testament and the formation of the Jewish branches. This was the 400 years between Malachi, the last book of the Old Testament, and Matthew's Gospel, the first book of the New Testament.

During the 400 years, the Bible originally recorded in Hebrew was translated by the Ptolemy Dynasty (a branch of the Hellenistic Empire) into the universal language at the time: Ancient Greek.

During the time of under going pressure from the Seleucus Dynasty (another branch of the Hellenistic Empire), the Jewish branches such as the Sadducees and the Pharisees formed.

But the important point to notice here is that God used these years to prepare to send His only son Jesus Christ down to earth.

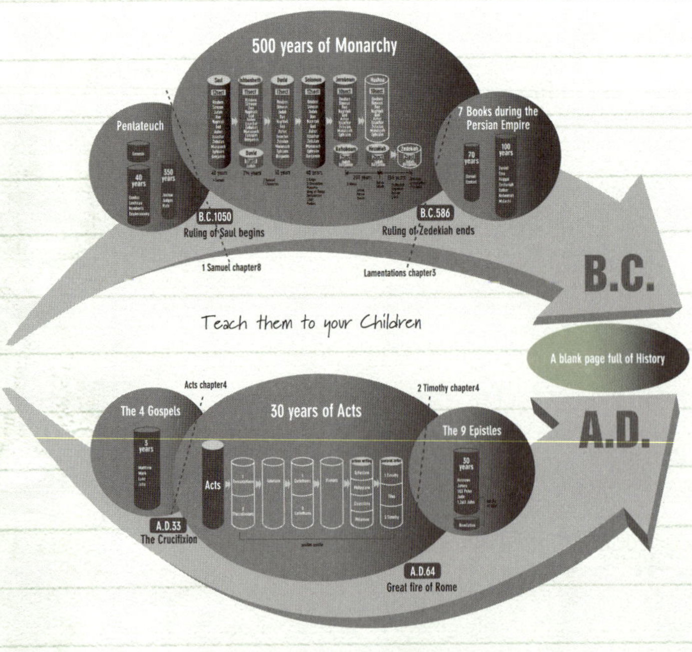

11 Session

A Blank Page Full of History

Tong Map

- **A Blank Page Full of History**
  - **25.The Hellenistic Empire and the Intermediate History**
    - Between 'how' and 'like this'
      - The Persian Empire
      - The Greek Civilization
      - The Hellenistic Empire
      - Ptolemy Dynasty
      - Seleucus Dynasty
      - Emerging Rome
      - Maccabean Revolt and Hasmonean Dynasty
  - **26.The Roman Empire and the Intermediate History**
    - Rome's rule
    - Jesus and Caesar
    - Roman governors of the New Testament times

Tong Concept

- **Happened during the intertestamental period?**

It takes only a second for us to move from Malachi the last book of the Old Testament to Matthew's Gospel the first book of the New Testament. However, there is a 400 years history between them. We can know that the last days of the Old Testament was during the Persian era while the beginning of the New Testament was during the Roman Era. Let's figure out the flows of change in world history between them.

- **What relationship was there between the New Testament and Roman times?**

All the events of the New Testament happened under the rule of the Roman Empire. All the 27 books from Matthew's Gospel to Revelation was during the Roman Empire. Let's observe with focus on the contents helpful for us to understand the New Testament.

Tong Seeing the forest

The intertestamental period Although there is only a thin sheet of paper between the Old and New Testament, the time of over 400 years was contained within that page. During this period of over 400 years, the hegemony of Palestine area was changed, and accordingly, many changes took place in all the fields of politics, economy, society and culture. The stories of the community who returned from Persia and restored Jerusalem adorn the last part of the Old Testament whereas in the New Testament we find ourselves amidst the Roman times.

25 Lesson The Hellenistic Empire and the Intermediate History

TongBible Story Overview

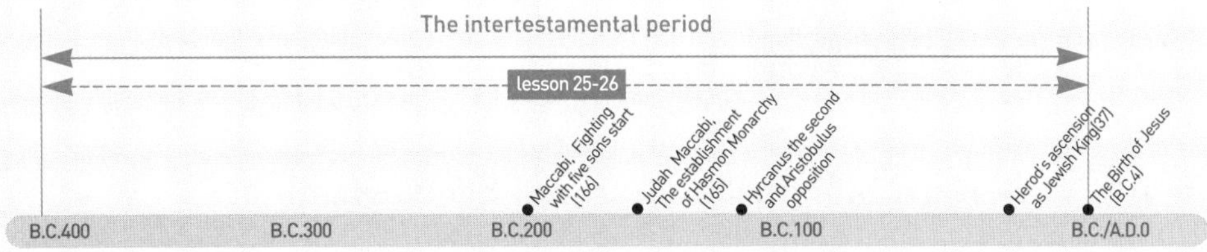

How to read the intertestamental period

The Jews who were scattered were called 'Diaspora'. They were the people who were taken captive to Babylon and had settled in Mesopotamia or chose to go down to Egypt to live there, or had moved to other areas to avoid wars and maltreatment, or had gathered to major cities as Roman rule began, or even moved from Palestine to other areas for this reason or that.

In this lesson let us review the international situation of the Inter-Testament period which exerted tremendous influence on the Jews who lived continually in Palestine and the Diaspora who lived scattered over the areas of the Mediterranean Sea, and finally review the Greek empire as well.

Tong Point

Between 'how' and 'like this'
Why do we say that the history between the Old and New Testament is between 'how' and 'like this'? We can say that the history between the Old and New Testament, as seen in Malachi, was the time God took to prepare to show 'I loved you like this' by sending Jesus Christ to this world who was the son whom He loved as said in John 3:16 for the people of Israel who retorted, 'How have you loved us?' in response to God's confession of love.

1. The Persian Empire (B.C.539-333)

Cyrus II (Cyrus of the Bible) who destroyed Babylonian Empire and established the Persian Empire used conciliation policy and the policy of generosity which allowed some freedom to the conquered rather than using the cruel and violent way of previous lmperial rulings. Thanks to this policy, the captives from Judah were able to return home from Babylon (Ezr.1:1-3).

After the Jews who were forced to live with the synagogue as their center instead of Jerusalem temple and scribes instead of priests during their captivity in Babylon for 70 years-returned, the co-existence of the temple, priests, synagogues and scribes began.

Following Cyrus II, Cambyses II ruled Persia and died not leaving a clear successor after him. So Darius I (Darius of the Bible) who was selected out of the seven representative nobles of Persia, became king. That time was the prime of Persian prosperity. Luxurious palaces and monuments were built and each region ruled was controlled systematically.

On the basis of the stability of a strong empire, Persia unfolded the policy of conquest constantly. They did their utmost to expand their territory and dominion as far as Macedonia, which was, Europe. However, Darius I went to invade the mainland of Greece only to return due to a strong typhoon. Then he attacked Greece again but was defeated in the battle of Marathon. Following Darius I, his son Xerxes (Queen Esther's husband in the Bible) invaded Greece again but again was defeated terribly in various battles including the marine battle of Salamis. Thus, the Persian plan to conquer Europe was not carried out. Eventually Persia was deprived of hegemony of the world by Alexander the Great of Macedonia during the rule of Darius III.

Tong Point

- **Cyrus II**

- Father of Persian empire
- Policies for the conquered : Conciliation, generosity, provincialization, sending back captives
- Related Bible characters : Zerubbabel, Joshua

- **Cambyses II**

- Did not leave an heir behind and died eight years after enthronement

- **Darius I**

- Was enthroned after seven leaders consulted one another
- Married Atosa the daughter of king Cyrus for legitimacy
- In the sixth year of his rule(B.C.516) : Construction of Jerusalem temple was completed(Ezr.6:15-18)
- Attempted to occupy Greece: failed the first time/failed the second time(Marathon Battle)

- **Xerxes**

- Esther's husband
- Attempted to occupy Greece the third time : failed(Marine Battle of Salamis)
- Related Bible character: Esther

2. The Greek Civilization

Greece was composed of a variety of polis developing a civilization on the basis of the thought and spirit of philosophers such as Socrates, Plato, and Aristotle.

In August B.C.480 when the Greek civilization grew into a full scale empire, polis states such as Athens and Sparta (who heard that Persian troops left for Greece) formed an alliance and faced the huge army of Persia. The fierce battle ended with the Greek victory, and Greece through this victory were able to develop their civilization all the more while strengthening their national power. This developed civilization of Greece became the basis of western civilization to come.

Meanwhile, at this time Philippos II (Father of Alexander the Great) became king of Macedonia around B.C.359 and began to expand his influence. They were called 'barbarians' by Greeks but their power increased as they began accepting the culture of Greece. As a result, they prepared to emerge as a threaten being amidst the Greek empire.

Greek philosophers
Around B,C.481, a sophist called Protagoras strongly stated a subjective truth called "Man is the measure of all things." At that, Socrates who was famous for the saying, "Know yourself" rejected such logic of sophists and stated that an objective truth existed. Plato called the being of truth 'Idea' and said, "Material things are nothing but shadow of 'Idea.'" Furthermore, his disciple Aristotle insisted that "eventually the substance is the same as image and it is only divided into image and matter." These Greek philosophers were laying down the foundation of thoughts about a variety of fields such as politics, economy, ethics and philosophy. At this time in Jerusalem, Nehemiah and Ezra ministered.

Tong Point

- **Delian League**
  - After Persia attacked Greece, Greek cities allied with one another to prepare for the next attack of Persia(Athens, Sparta, Corinth, Thebes, etc.).
- **Pericles**
  - Led Delian League and Greek prosperity
  - Abolished Delian League

- Pericles of Athens used the expense of the allied cities for the development of Athens
- Athens ruling Corinth became a problem
- **Peloponnensian War**
- Delian League with Athens as center vs Peloponnensian League with Sparta as center
- Sparta's victory, Sparta ruled Greece 30 years
- Later Thebes ruled Greece

3. The Hellenistic Empire (Macedonia, B.C.359-323)

King Philippos II of Macedonia found a gold mine in the area called Crenides (Philippi of the New Testament) and came to attain enormous wealth. Later the first place where Apostle Paul came to preach the gospel in Macedonia (Europe today) was this place (Act.16:11-12).

Not long afterward, Philippos II came to occupy the whole of Greece which used to despise him and his people. However, Philippos II who accomplished this much was suddenly assassinated, and after him prince Alexander became king at the young age of twenty (B.C.336-323). He had a strong spirit of ambition and an enormous dream and came to possess a vast empire in just ten years.

Becoming king, Alexander began to march on the basis of a strong military his father Philippos II established. In winter of B.C.334, Alexander occupied western and southern parts of Asia Minor, and the next year fought the Persian army led by Darius III in Issus and enjoyed a great victory. After that, Alexander turned around and went down to Egypt along the shores of the Mediterranean Sea rather than immediately invading the city of Susa the capital of Persia.

On his way down to Egypt Alexander planned to occupy Tyre, a marine city which was quite far from the Mediterranean shore. At the time Tyre (which had the power of the Mediterranean as a major city of Phoenicia) refused to yield to Alexander unlike other surrounding cities. Since their city was an extremely strong natural fortress, they were confident that they would not be defeated in the war.

It was not easy to occupy Tyre. Alexander attempted to occupy it many times for seven months only to fail every time. Thinking carefully, Alexander ordered the soldiers to go to the mountains and come back rolling huge rocks. Then they began to fill in the sea between the shore and Tyre with the rocks. That way the troops of Alexander made the bridge between the main land and the island and then smoothly occupied Tyre.

Before that time, prophets like Amos, Jeremiah and Ezekiel prophesied the destruction of Tyre. Likewise, Gaza of Philistines who refused to yield to Alexander was invaded and occupied as Tyre was, which was the fulfillment of the prophecy of prophet Zechariah(Zec.9:5). **The intertestamental period was also the period when the words of prophecy about other countries were fulfilled as such.**

Alexander conquered Egypt in B.C.332 and built a city named Alexandria after his own name. In the city the largest library in the world was built. Like this, every time Alexander went occupying a certain area, he took with him scholars and engineers of each field and attempted an exchange between the culture of the conquered land and Greek culture. This way he built many Alexandrias and enlightened the conquered with

The purpose of Alexander's conquest

Alexander ruled his conquered lands generously. The purpose of his conquest was not necessarily to expand the range of his control so that he could collect much tax and his absolute power could be exercised, but to expand his thoughts about the human world and unite the peoples of the world. He also treated the soldiers he brought from Macedonia and Persian soldiers who yielded to him on an equal basis. He held group weddings of Macedonian soldiers and Persian women. He had Macedonian scholars study together with Persian scholars so that the work of combining cultures may be continued.

Greek culture.

Ancient eastern civilization was called Orient civilization. During the period of Alexander this Orient civilization and Greek civilization met together and produced Hellenistic Civilization, otherwise known as Hellenism. Through the conquest of Alexander, these civilizations were combined.

Alexander marched again along the shores of the Mediterranean and occupied Susa, Babylon, Persepolis(Persia), Ecbatana(Hamedan) one by one. Alexander who established such a vast empire continued to march to the east in B.C.326 and arrived at the basin of the Indus River of India. There his soldiers who were tired of the long war refused to follow him and therefore was forced to return with the troops and died young in B.C.323 at the age of 32.

The sudden death of Alexander brought great change to the Greek empire. After he died, the great empire was divided into seven. After a power struggle among them, three were eliminated and the other four ruled.

For a moment, let's focus on Ptolemy Dynasty which had a lot to do with the Palestine(Canaan) region. There was a commander-in-chief called Seleucus in the dynasty of Ptolemy, which came to rule Egypt. Not satisfied with his position as commander-in-chief, Seleucus secured his own political power and finally established the Seleucus Dynasty while king Ptolemy went out to check Antigonus who insisted that he was to become successor to Alexander. From this time on, the Seleucus Dynasty came to rule Syrian region of the Mesopotamia valley. These two countries were the most powerful and as time went by, they competed with each other with the Palestine region between them.

Tong Point

- **Philippos II**
- Discovered a gold mine in Crenides, which held a huge amount of financial resource
- Changed the name of Crenides into 'Philippi' after his name : the first gateway city of Europe during Paul's second missionary journey
- Occupied Greece: with troops having concentrated long-spears
- **Alexander**
- A son of Philippos II
- Had Aristotle as tutor for about four years in his teens
- Planned to occupy Persia
  . Planned to not just defend himself from Persia but to occupy it.
  . Had the launching ceremony of militry march in Berea
  . Issus Battle: defeated Darius III of Persia
  . Instead of attacking the city of Susa the capital of Persia, he advanced along the Meditarranean Shore.
- Occupied Tyre
  . Tyre(the major city of Phoenicia) : took control of the Meditarranean Marine right, Natural fortress
  . Alexander mobilized 10,000 soldiers, who rolled rocks in, made a breakwater and occupied Tyre.
  . Fulfilled the prophecies of Amos, Ezekiel and Jeremiah
- Occupied Gaza of the Philistines and Jerusalem
- Occcupied Egypt: Built Alexandria
- Occupied the four capitals of Persia
- Expanded the territory of rule to the whole of Persian Empire and even to the border of India.
- Hellenistic Empire: Cosmopolitanism, Forced the conquered to become Hellenized

4. Ptolemy Dynasty (B.C.301-198)

In B.C.301, Palestine was merged into Egypt by Ptolemy I Therefore, the Jews living in the land of Canaan were ruled by Egypt which was ruled also by Ptolemy. **Particularly during** the period of Ptolemy II (Ptolemy Philadelphus) the work of translating the Old Testament recorded in Hebrew into Greek was done. This version was (Septuagint, LXX) which was the first translation mentioned previously 72(70). Various people were chosen by Ptolemy II to translate the book of law into Greek respectively. It was also reported that their respective versions were not different from each other to the last word. In Septuagint, LXX they started translating the Pentateuch, then all 39 books of the Old Testament and then even Apocrypha.

As for this insistence there was an aspect that their translation was by the work of the Holy Spirit but we should know that it was definitely the providence and working of God that this translation was able to be carried out in this particular period. Due to this translation, many Gentiles were able to read the Bible, and the foundation of missions was established toward all the Greek empire.

The kings of Ptolemy dynasty generally unfolded a generous policy about religious convictions and customs of the merged countries. However, due to continuing war between Ptolemy dynasty and Seleucus dynasty Palestine faced hardship as it was trampled under foot by horses' hooves of both troops.

Tong Point

- **Septuagint, LXX**
  - Ptolemy II: had the Hebrew Old Testament translated into Greek
  - Cleopatra: Had the country taken away by Octavianus the first emperor of Rome and closed the over 300 year old Ptolemy Dynasty.
- **The policy of generosity**
  - The Jewish religious customs were granted.

5. Seleucus Dynasty (B.C.198-165)

The atmosphere of the land of Judea which spent a relatively peaceful time under the rule of Ptolemy dynasty began to change around the early days of B.C. 2th century. This was because Antiochus III of Seleucus dynasty took Palestine away from Ptolemy dynasty in B.C.198 and merged it into Syria. Just because Seleucus dynasty was handled after Ptolemy dynasty it did not mean that Seleucus dynasty appeared after Ptolemy dynasty was destroyed. After Alexander died, four people competed for hegemony. Among them the two powerful dynasties were Ptolemy and Seleucus. Palestine was ruled by Ptolemy dynasty, which lost its control later to Seleucus dynasty.

Antiochus III who occupied Palestine cared for the Jews as much as he could as Ptolemy dynasty had done. However, this favor which extended to the Jews did not last long. Having terribly lost in the war with Rome in B.C.190, Antiogchus III imposed a huge penalty as much as fifteen thousand talents. So he began to confiscate the property of temples in the country to make this huge amount of penalty. Jerusalem temple was no exception. This caused the opposition of the people everywhere and finally he was assassinated.

Following him, Seleucus IV ruled and he was also pressed by Rome to pay much tribute. After some time he was assassinated by a general. Then Antiochus IV, who was a younger brother of Seleucus IV and called 'Epiphanes,' became king(B.C.175-163).

He forced people of his whole territory to accept Greek

Antiochus IV
He refused to be called number 'IV' but wanted to be called 'Epiphanes' which meant incarnation of deity. He was a cruel man and followed Alexander's thoughts most thoroughly. He began to educate all the people of the conquered land with Hellenism. Canaan was no exception.

culture and customs. With his emergence as ruler, a very hard time, which was incomparable with previous days, began for the Jews. By receiving money he sold 'priesthood' which was the most important for the Jews. In addition they were forced to accept lots of Greek thoughts. The Jewish community of returnees who had firmly kept monotheism since the return from captivity, strongly rejected Greek thoughts. These were the reason for the beginning of their hardship.

Antiochus IV made an expedition to Egypt twice with the dream of conquering it and almost subdued it on his second expedition. However, when Antiochus IV burned his will of conquering Egypt like this, already another country was reaching out its hand of dominion to it. It was none other than Rome.

Tong Point

- **Antiochus IV('Epiphanes' : incarnation of deity)**
  - Forced Hellenistic customs and culture to be practiced all over his territory
  - Almost overpowered Egypt by attacking it twice
  - Faced Rome which wanted to occupy Egypt, and gave up
  - Launched a severe oppression on the Jews: became a background of the birth of the Sadducees, the Pharisees, the Essenes and the Zealots

6. Emerging Rome

Rome of the Italian peninsular was established by twins called Romulus and Remus in B.C. 8th century. After that, the whole country was unified and a dynasty was formed. In that country important battles took place for about two hundred years. It was none other than the power struggle between common people and the nobles. After a thorough class struggle, ordinary people came to draw out the Twelve Tables which defined certain rights of common people by law.

Rome which solidified its internal foundation on the basis of this law came to fight against a country called Carthage which brought about the Punic Wars. In the war which was fought three times over a period of more than 120 years, Rome became victorious and consequently came to gain enormous wealth and marine power. Rome built a great empire including all the lands the Greek empire conquered.

Soon Rome departed to occupy Egypt, which was ruled by the Ptolemy dynasty, with lots of battleships. At this time Antiochos IV of Seleucus dynasty also came to occupy Egypt with troops. These two forces came to collide by necessity. Popillius Laenas the Roman general had one of his soldiers draw a circle around Antiochos IV. The general told him to decide whether he would fight or not before he came out of the circle. When he saw the Roman battleships in front of him, it was evident that he would lose. Then Antiochos IV quietly turned around and came out of the circle and this indeed damaged his self-esteem.

However, what mattered was that he thought he failed in this battle because of the Jews. He said that he lost in the battle because the Jews refused to accept Greek thoughts and consequently the whole country became separated. So he began to oppress the Jews severely. Knowing that the Jews were not doing anything including fighting on Sabbath, he invaded them on a Sabbath and cruelly massacred them. He robbed

Hannibal

Hannibal was a famous general of Carthage and distinguished himself in the second Punic Wars. They say that his strategy was so excellent that even today the military academies of the world teach it. So we can guess what a talented general he was. The story that he went over Mount Alps with droves of African elephants and great troops and then invaded the mainland of Rome is one of the most interesting war stories in history. As Hannibal was about to occupy Rome, a young Roman general called Scipio led Roman troops and totally destroyed the mainland of Carthage. He used Hannibal's tactics and fighting methods. Since his mainland was ruined by Rome, Hannibal could not help return right before occupying Rome. Eventually Rome became victorious in the second Punic Wars. As a result, Carthage was deprived of all of its foreign territory and was imposed the enormous war penalty of ten thousand gold talents. At this time Scipio came to be called 'Africanus' which meant 'the conqueror of Africa.'
However, Carthage did not withdraw easily. Carthage seemingly broke the treaty with Rome and rebelled. Eventually general Scipio (also called young Scipio) who was an adopted grandson of Scipio Africanus totally burnt Carthage to ashes in six days. This way Carthage was totally destroyed over seven hundred years after its establishment and disappeared into history.

cities and burned many buildings. They were ordered neither to keep the Sabbath, nor to circumcise, nor to read the law of Moses. Even if they sacrificed in the temple, they were killed. In the temple of Jerusalem the statue of a Gentile god was set up and Greek soldiers drove lots of pigs into Jerusalem temple, killed them there and then shed their blood. This way they committed the sin of blasphemy against the temple to the extreme.

Tong Point

- **The birth of Rome**
  - Was established by twins Romulus and Remus in B.C.8th century. Romulus seized power
  - Over 200 year royal rule: king, senate, citizens
  - Over 200 year republican rule: The point of agreement after class struggle of Senate, Citizens Council, nobles and general public: Law
- **Punic War (120 year war fought three times)**
  - War between Rome and Carthage over Sicilia
  - First: Rome became the victor
  - Second: Hannibal of Carthage vs Roman Scipio: Roman victory
  - Third: Roman victory, won huge wealth and all the Meditarranean Marine right, established the great Roman Empire

7. Maccabean Revolt and Hasmonean Dynasty (B.C.165-63)

As Antiochos IV unfolded this wicked policy, the Jews were troubled about whether they were to follow this policy or resist it. As already mentioned, there were some Jews who accepted Greek thoughts little by little. They were the Sadducees. Such were quick in adjusting to contemporary power and compromise.

Unlike Sadducees, however, there were people who made up their minds not to accept Hellenism at all, and they were the Hasidim. These rejected any compromise and struggled to preserve the tradition of faith centering around the law and Jerusalem temple. Out of this Hasidim came 'the Pharisees.'

Meanwhile, there were many people in Judea who were faithful in the law besides Hasidim. There was a small village called 'Modein' in the basin between Jerusalem and Joppa. An official of Seleucus Dynasty came as far as this village and forced them to give up Hebrew thoughts and follow Greek thoughts. At this time old priest Mattathias was demanded to sacrifice to a Gentile god but he refused it. When another Jew was forced by the official to such an extent that he was about to sacrifice on the Gentile altar in place of Mattathias, he killed that Jew, the king's official and the soldiers who were with them.

This incident forced Mattathias, his five sons and their followers to flee to the mountains, and this led to the guerrilla warfare. More and more people came to them and formed a strong army of resistance, and the Hasidim also allied with them. Mattathias led the crowd and made a surprise attack to nearby small cities and villages, broke down the idols and Gentile altars, circumcised children, rebuilt destroyed synagogues and helped people keep the laws of Moses.

About a year later, Mattathias died(B.C.166) and the leadership was handed over to his third son Judah(B.C.166-160). The crowds who were led by Judah Maccabeo (Maccabee, which means 'hammer') enjoyed victory after victory with energetic spirit and excellent guerrilla warfare and got to form

Temple and Scriptures

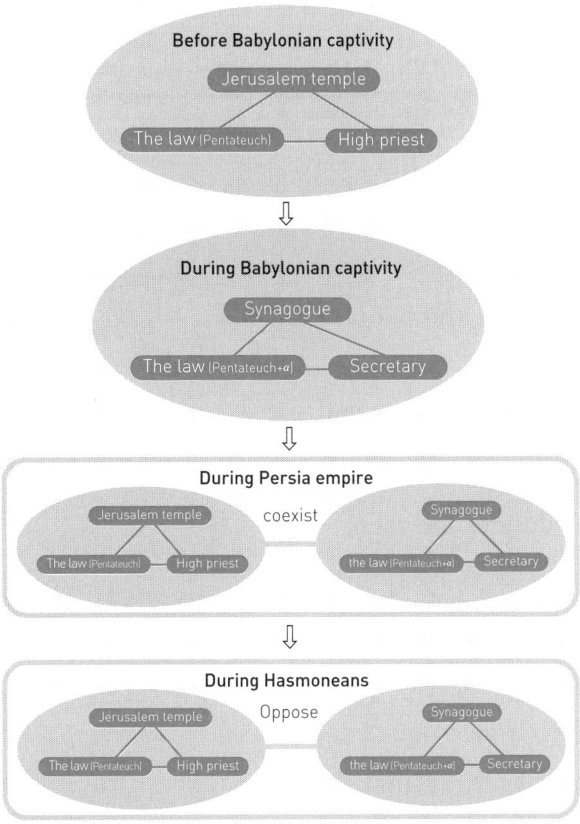

a greater army of troops.

Meanwhile, a general called Lysias of Seleucus (Syria) came with a great army. At that time, Antiochos IV was killed while waging war in another place. Therefore, general Lysias urgently made a treaty with Judah. The contents of the treaty was that Jerusalem temple would be cleansed and used for the original purpose and the Jews enjoy freedom of religion. The crowd of Maccabees who entered Jerusalem appointed that day when the temple was restored a festive day and commemorated it every year. This day was the feast of Dedication (Hanukkah).

This way, Judah Maccabee purified Jerusalem after armed struggles and many compromises. Judging their goal was realized, Hasidims left Judah Maccabee and returned to their original system in order to stop fighting. However, Judah Maccabee kept fighting for complete independence of Judea. The leadership of Judah Maccabee was handed over to John and then to Simon. Hasmonean dynasty was launched in the days of John Hilkanus the son of Simon.

However, more disagreements gradually emerged from within. While Alexander Jannaeus of Hasmonean dynasty was king (B.C.103-76), one incident took place in which the discord between the Sadducees and the Pharisees was at its height. Since Jannaeus was a ruthless and cruel king and Greek-friendly, he was supported by the Sadducees. As he became king, he married Salome Alexandra who was his elder brother's wife. He also had the position of high-priest. This was against the law. Therefore, when Jannaeus who was king and high priest appeared on the day of Tabernacle, the people of Judea threw on him the olive branches they brought to celebrate the feast of Tabernacle. Jannaeus immediately called for his soldiers and subdued the violent commotion so that hundreds of unprotected people were killed there and then.

Afterwards, civil wars broke out everywhere. Feeling that they could not stand the blasphemy and violent rule of Jannaeus any longer, the Pharisees eventually decided to ask the Syrian king for help. However, as the Syrian troops began to come down, the Pharisees, who began to think that they might be successful in driving out the Sadducees but their country may be occupied again, came to cooperate again with the Sadducees and drove out the Syrian army. However, Jannaeus and Sadducees (who had a grudge against the Pharisees) sorted out eight hundred leaders of the Pharisees and cruelly killed them by crucifixion. Due to this, the deeply rooted distrust between the Pharisees and Sadducees got so deep that further more compromise was possible.

Before his death in B.C.76 Alexander Jannaeus, regretting his life, handed over his authority to his wife Salome Alexandra and told her to reconcile with the Pharisees as his will. Salome Alexandra (B.C.75-67) established a friendly relation with the

Grecian Empire - appointed high priests by receiving money

Antiochus IV unfolded the evil policy of appointing high priests, which was a tradition of only the Jews, by receiving money. Since Judea was apart from Jerusalem temple during the Babylonian Captivity, the importance of the position of high priests was almost forgotten. However, as the temple was being reconstructed by the returned from Persia, high priests became important again. And Grecian Empire began to appoint high priests by receiving money.

High Priest

- It was a hereditary position from Aaron continually until then
- Antiochus IV of Seleucus Dynasty appointed 'Jason' as High Priest by receiving money.
- Menelaus became High Priest by giving Antiochus IV more money.

Pharisees according to her husband's will and successfully ruled the country. However, the Sadducees who were dissatisfied with the rise of the Pharisees cooperated with the queen's second son Aristobulus II(B.C.66-63) to attack the queen's successor and oldest son Hyrcan II(Hyrcanus). Rome came to Palestine to mediate the struggle for the throne between Hyrcan II and Aristobulus II that began this way. From this time on, Rome's intervention and control for Palestine began.

Tong Point

- **Mattathias**
  - Priest of a small countryside village called 'Modein.'
  - Rejected the request of Seleucus Dynasty asking him to offer sacrifice to Gentile gods
  - Led the army of resistance
- **Maccabee(Judah the third son of Mattathias)**
  - The oppression of Seleucus Dynasty was discontinued due to the death of Antiochus IV
  - Feast of Dedication (Hanukkah feast): restoring Jerusalem Temple
- **Hasmonean Dynasty**
  - During the days of Alexandes Jannaeus: Greece friendly, Supported by the Sadducees, Disharmony between the Sadducees and the Pharisees was at its height.
  - Salome Alexandra: in a friendly relation with the Pharisees
  - Hyrcanus II(supported by the Pharisees) vs. Aristobulus II(supported by the Sadducees)
  - Rome came to Judea to mediate these two's fight for throne.

26 Lesson The Roman Empire and the Intermediate History

TongBible Story Overview

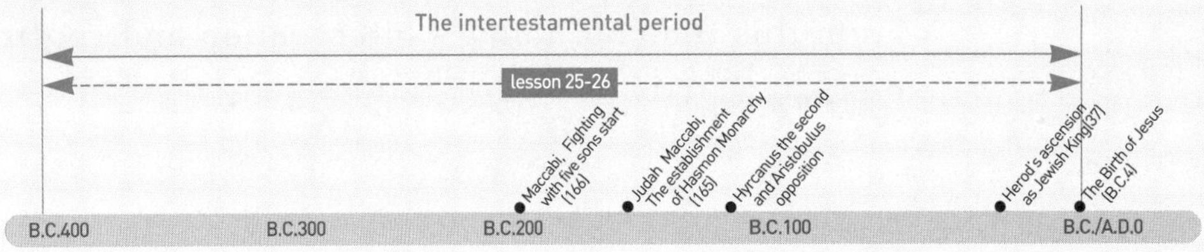

How to read Rome and the New Testament

All the events in the New Testament took place under the rule of the Roman empire. Romans unfolded a thorough policy of not mistaking even a penny of tax by precisely putting in order census in the countries they ruled. Therefore, while Octavianus (the first Roman emperor) ruled, Joseph and Mary had to register for census in their home town Bethlehem. In addition, Revelation (the last book of the New Testament) was written while John was in exile by Rome on the island of Patmos.

Tong Point

Give what belongs to Caesar to Caesar and what belongs to God to God

Zacchaeus and Matthe's employment in the New Testament and the fact that Joseph and Mary travelled a long way to register for census are all related to Roman 'tax.' Only when we know the story about this currency and tax, can we understand why the Pharisees tested Jesus.

- The question of the Pharisees: Is it right to pay tax to Romans or not?
  - · If Jesus said, Yes: The people who were suffering due to tax would turn their back on him.
  - · If Jesus said, Not right: was in danger of being named as a dissident by Rome.
- Jesus' answer: Give what belongs to Caesar to Caesar and what belongs to God to God.

1. Rome's rule (B.C. 63-)

Around B.C.63, Roman general Pompeius came to Jerusalem on the pretext of mediating internal fight within Judea. Pompeius decided to support Hyrcanus II As a result Aristobulus II was driven out of the fortress where he was stayed and was forced to flee. Finding the gates of Jerusalem closed, General Vavinus sent by Pompeius kept attacking it by surrounding the city. Eventually Roman troops occupied Jerusalem in three months by digging holes through the wall. This way the land of Canaan including Jerusalem came under the control of Rome the new empire.

Not only this, but Rome itself changed. About sixty years before Jesus came, a man called Julius Caesar emerged in Rome and began to shake Rome's Senate system. Caesar is thoughts were that Rome could not be maintained and developed with the present Senate system and that Rome should be ruled by an emperor. Caesar accomplished the first triumvirate by combining himself, Pompeius and Crassus. These three came to rule Rome together.

Julius Caesar conquered Gallia which was western Europe today and gained great wealth as well as a great reputation in the country. The Senate which was afraid of the increasing power of Caesar made him fight against Pompeius. But Caesar sensed this fact. When the Senate decided to ask Caesar to dismiss his army and return to Rome, he marched toward Rome by crossing the Rubicon River, the borderline in January B.C.49 along with his famous saying, "Dices are cast." After the two year civil war Caesar (who quieted down the internal struggle of Rome) came to seize power.

This way he became the sole ruler and promoted reform projects such as all kinds of social policies and relief work for the poor. However, since power was concentrated on him alone, it was no doubt that there was those who wish to covet the throne. In March B.C.44 he was assassinated by advocates of republicanism of the Senate at the meeting place of the Senate.

After Julius Caesar died, his adopted son Octavianus began the second triumvirate with Antonius and Lepidus who were his father's subjects. Afterwards, his struggle with Antonius grew intense. Octavianus got the hegemony after defeating the united forces of Antonius and the Egyptian queen Cleopatra at the Battle of Actium in B.C.31. This way Rome began its imperial rule whilst maintaining republicanism nominally.

Meanwhile, Edomites intervened and tried to get their share in the colony. Herod the son of Antipater (who was an Edomite) went to emperor Octavianus and received the title 'tetrarch' through excellent political tactics and flattery. Rome used the policy of ruling by sending Roman governors or setting up tetrarchs who were very loyal to the empire. Herod used this to his advantage and was given the position of the king of the Jews.

Herod did not fear God. He was indifferent about the law and killed many people so naturally, the Jews did not like him at all. Herod ruled for thirty four years and died in B.C.4. According to his will, his kingdom was divided to his three sons. Herod Archelaus was king of Judea (including Samaria and Idumea), Herod Antipas was tetrarch of Galilee and Berea and Herod Philip was tetrarch of the provincia located in the eastern part and south eastern part of the sea of Galilee.

Living under the oppression and dominion of strong countries like this continually, the Jews naturally had the desire 'For salvation.' As their ancestors lived in Egypt long ago as slaves more than four hundred years and pleaded with God to save them, so the Jews had the Messianic thought of believing and expecting that God would send a savior someday. They believed that if God blessed them, a strong savior like David would appear, defeat Rome and restore the glory of David's times again. Our LORD came among the Jews who were living with such a strong passion in mind.

Tong Point

- **Pompeius**
  - In B.C.63, he attacked Jerusalem on the pretext of pacifying the internal war of Judea. Occupied the Orient World.
- **Rome the great Empire**
  - Punic War: Africa/ Pompeius: Orient World/ Caesar: Western Europe
  - Opinion about how to run Rome the great empire
    : Centering around the Senate(senators with Cicero as representative) vs. imperial rule(Julius Caesar)
- **Julius Caesar**
  - Born in B.C.100 / became the core of Rome at age 40 / Occupied Gallia(Kelt)
  - First Triumvirate: Caesar, Pompeius, Crassus
  - The senate persuaded Pompeius to become the enemy of Caesar
  - "Dices are cast." : Caesar crossed Rubicon River and occupied Rome
  - Civil war over two years to see Caesar as victor: Dictator in perpetuity, was assassinated at age 56
  - What Caesar left behind: Heir Octavianus/Blueprint of how to run Rome/gave his property to Roman citizens as inheritance
- **Octavianus(honorific: Augustus)**
  - Made Roman citizens think that assassins of Caesar were 'those who killed father.'
  - Took advantage of this situation and secured his political standing
  - Second triumvirate : Octavianus, Antonius, Lepidus

- Battle of Actium : defeated the army of Antonius and Egyptian queen Cleopatra
- First Roman emperor
- Caesar Augustus of the New Testament(referring to Octavianus the first Roman emperor): ordered census(Luk.2:1)

- **Herod the Great**
  - An Edomite
  - Was given the title tetrarch by Rome thanks to his excellent political tricks and flattery
  - Built a new city called 'Caesarea.'
  - Built Jerusalem Temple(46 years)
  - Herod of Matthew chapter two
  - Divided kingdom into three for his three sons

*Caesarea means a city for Caesar, that is, a city devoted to Roman Emperor

Herod Archelaus	Herod Antipas	Herod Philip
· Judea (including Samaria & Idumea) · Luk.2:22-23	· Galilee & Berea · Most related to Jesus' 3-year public life · Killed John the Baptist · 'That fox'(Luk.13:31-32) · Luk.23:12	· Eastern & southeastern area of Galilee Lake · Built Philippi

2. Jesus and Caesar

When Jesus came to this world, Judea was under the rule of the Roman Empire which ruled the whole Europe including present day U.K., France, Spain, North Africa and even middle eastern region including Judea. Unlike previous empires, the Roman Empire unfolded the policy of authorizing self-rule of the country and particularly allowed much freedom for religion. This was because Rome was a country of polytheism where there were as many as 300,000 gods in the days of Jesus.

Therefore, even though Judea was under the rule of Rome, Judean religious leaders were not forced to undergo much change. However, due to heavy tax, the Jewish people had to live poorly and therefore their religious and political hope was to wait for the Messiah mentioned in the Old Testament. The Messiah the Jews were expecting was a strong powerful Messiah based on Isaiah chapter 9. However, as already explained in the book of Isaiah, the Messiah prophesied by Isaiah can be understood only when we see the strong Messiah of Isaiah chapter 9 and the Messiah of suffering of Isaiah chapter 53 together.

In those days the Jews expected that the Messiah would appear and they would be released from Rome and then be able to live enjoying the privilege as God's elected people. Therefore, when our LORD Jesus came to Bethlehem of Judea, nobody took note of him. Only the wise men from the east who came following the star and the shepherds who were tending the sheep in Bethlehem, rejoiced over the birth of our LORD Jesus.

Joseph and Mary who were parents of Jesus by flesh went to Bethlehem for registration because of the decree of emperor Octavianus (the first emperor of Rome). Rome continued the political system through the negotiation of the Senate for hundreds of years. Then Julius Caesar emerged in Roman history and then the empire's policy of ruling by emperor began to bud. Octavianus who was an adopted son and nephew of Julius Caesar became Augustus(which meant the majestic one, the honorific name given by the Senate) and the first Roman emperor. He was none other than Caesar Augustus who appears in the New Testament. After Julius Caesar, his name 'Caesar' became the title for all following emperors.

Caesar Augustus (the first Roman emperor) intended to collect more tax based on correct registration. Therefore, Joseph and Mary who was fully pregnant could not be excused from the Roman emperor's decree even with her imminent delivery. That was why Jesus was born in Bethlehem. Of course, this event was the fulfillment of the prophecy of Prophet Micah who said "But you, Bethlehem Ephrathah, though you are small among the clans of Judah, out of you will come for me one who will be ruler over Israel, whose origins are from of old, from ancient times"(Mic.5:2).

Today the bills of each country of the world bear faces of particular people. The bills of South Korea show Sejong the Great, Yulgok-Yi Yi and so on. The bills of United States bear the faces of president Lincoln or president Washington and British bills bear the face of queen Elizabeth. Inscribing the faces of people on the bills and coins was started by Julius Caesar.

He had his face inscribed on the coin for the first time in human history in order to let himself be known to the whole Roman empire. Long ago, more than two thousand years ago, a man called Julius Caesar knew the great power of money. Therefore, although all the people under the rule of Roman empire had never seen the face of Julius Caesar in person, all of them knew his face through coins.

In the days of Jesus the Pharisees once tested Jesus to put him in a difficult situation. As said already, the Jews in those days went through suffering due to heavy tax. In that situation the Pharisees asked Jesus, "Is it right to pay tax to the Romans or wrong?" In this case if Jesus said it was right to pay tax to the Romans, the people who suffered due to heavy tax would turn against Jesus. On the contrary if he said it was not right to pay tax to Rome, he would have been in danger of being arrested because he would be regarded by Rome as a dissident.

At this time our LORD Jesus said, "Show me a denarius. Whose image and inscription are on it?"(Luk.20:24). The people there responded, "Caesar's." Then Jesus gave them a clear answer. "Then give to Caesar what is Caesar's, and to God what is God's." It meant that the money which beared the face of Caesar should be paid to Caesar as tax and the gift to be given to God should be given to him accordingly.

3. Roman governors of the New Testament times

We should bear in mind the relationship between Judea and Rome also when Jesus was crucified. In those days the king who was given authority to rule Judea by Rome was Herod. However, Rome also sent their former law officials as governors to all the countries of the world they ruled. In the days of Jesus, the governor sent by Rome was Pilate. Planning to falsely entrap and kill Jesus, the religious leaders of Judea including the Pharisees and high priests charged Jesus to governor Pilate. Although Rome gave certain authority for each community to solve problems such as the ethnic group's internal religious problems or small civil matters as they were ruling each colony, Rome directly controlled political matters or criminal cases. Therefore, if those people in power like the high priest wanted to Jesus killed, it was required that the Roman governor gave the death sentence. Eventually Jesus was questioned first in the courts of the house of the high priest and stood trial by Pilate.

The charge they accused Jesus of was that he agitated the people without the permission of Rome and tried to become king of Judea. They knew that this was the case that made the Roman governor the most sensitive. However, after governor Pilate questioned Jesus, he was unable to not find any sin from Jesus legally. Yet the thing governor Pilate was afraid of the most was revolt. Therefore, the foolish Jewish people, who were masterminded by religious leaders including the Pharisees and the high priest, created an atmosphere serious enough to cause a revolt and made governor Pilate uncomfortable. Even though governor Pilate knew that our LORD Jesus was innocent, he unwillingly granted that Jesus be crucified. Like this, the event of Jesus' crucifixion is deeply connected with chronological and histrocial background of the Roman empire.

We also know through the New Testament that Paul had Roman citizenship. In those days the privilege of those who had Roman citizenship were able to enjoy was significant. Any citizen who was not proven to be guilty through trial could not be beaten by somebody or put into prison.

When apostle Paul visited Jerusalem after his third missionary journey, he was in danger of being killed in the temple of Jerusalem. At that time Paul was able to save his life by telling the chiliarch of Rome that he was a Roman citizen. In those days if a Roman citizen was killed unfairly without reason, the chiliarch had to take responsibility. That was why the chiliarch mobilized many soldiers and protected Paul who was a Roman citizen. Paul was able to appeal to the Roman emperor for trial in the capacity of Roman citizen.

Worrying news was conveyed to Paul who waited for trial in Rome. Regretably, the emperor who ruled the Roman empire at that time was the notorious emperor Nero we all know well. It was the time when Nero falsely accused Christians of being responsible for the great fire of Rome, and for this Paul was martyred. It was the Roman empire that also sent apostle John the author of revelation to the island of Patmos on exile.

● Reference material for reading through the New Testament

1. Herod

As we read the four gospels which are the stories of Jesus, we often come across a man called Herod. However, Herod was not one man's name but the name of a dynasty which ruled Palestine and its nearby region from the middle of B.C. first century to around A.D. first century. Therefore, understanding Herod and his family is very helpful for us to understand the New Testament.

(1) Herod the Great

He was a son of Antipater and the founder of Herod dynasty. As previously mentioned, he was appointed king of the Jews by Roman emperor Octavianus through his excellent lobbying skill. However, since he was an Edomite, he had in mind the popular mind of the Jews all the time and maintained relationship with Rome in a friendly way. He built 'Caesarea' which was the city that commemorated Caesar. In this city apostle Paul stayed for two years before going to Rome for trial. He also devoted himself to rebuilding the temple of Jerusalem in order to get in the good books of the Jews. The construction of the temple which started around B.C. 20 was still under way in the days of Jesus and finished as late as around A.D. 64 only to be destroyed by Rome six years later. Looking at this temple, Jesus said to his disciples, "Do you see all these great buildings?" "Not one stone here will be left on another; every one will be thrown down" (Mar.13:2).

Jerusalem Temple
1. By David and Solomon: Centering around Holy of Holies.
2. After Babylonian Captivity: built in a small scale with Persian tax.
2-1. By Herod: enlarged the temple, built by reconstruction community, in a large scale. However, since the High Priest was politically perverted after Antiochus IV of Seleucus Dynasty, they built it while neglecting Holy of Holies and only making outside walls luxurious.

(2) Herod Archelaus

After Herod the Great died, he alloted Judea, Jerusalem, Samaria and Edom. The Bible says that when Joseph and Mary went to Egypt with Baby Jesus to flee from Herod the Great and returned, they did not go to Judea but to Nazareth in Galilee to flee from the eyes of Archelaus (Mat.2:22). Like this, Archelaus was very oppressive and violent politically. So the nobles of Judea and Samaria who could not stand him any longer sent their delegation to the Roman emperor and asked him to remove Archelaus. Eventually Archelaus was dethroned in A.D.6. From then on the region of Judea was ruled by Roman governor.

(3) Herod Philip II

Strictly speaking, he was Herod Philip II The Bible says that Philip ruled 'Iturea and Traconitis'. This place was part of the upper regions of the Jordan River, which was the northeastern region of Galilee. In order to gain the favor of the Roman emperor, Philip rebuilt a region called Panion and then called it 'Caesarea Philippi' after the names of emperor and himself. Another purpose was to distinguish it from Caesarea built by his father Herod the Great. It was in this city that Jesus asked his disciple; "Who do people say I am?"(Mat.16:13). Among the sons of Herod he was the meekest and respected by people. That was why Jesus was able to move around this region relatively safely.

(4) Herod Antipas

When Jesus ministered, Herod Antipas was tetrarch of Galilee and the region of Berea. Therefore, king Herod shown in the recording of Jesus' three year public life was this Herod Antipas. His first marriage was to a princess of king Nabataeans. He divorced princess Nabataeans in order to marry Herodias the wife of his younger brother Herod Philip I(Herod Philip I was Herodias' first husband and was not a public official). Rebuking publicly this immorality of Herod Antipas, John the Baptist was beheaded. After Jesus was arrested, he was questioned by this Herod Antipas for the reason that he was a Galilean. Luke's Gospel records, "That day Herod and Pilate became friends -- before this they had been enemies" (Luk.23:12).

(5) Herod Agrippa

He was Herod Agrippa I and grand son of Herod the Great and a brother of Herodias and also a nephew of Herod Antipas. Since he was sent to Rome while he was young and grew up in the Roman palace, he had the opportunity to become a friend of Caligula who became the third emperor of Rome. Thanks to this he was able to replace Philip II when he died. When Herod Antipas was driven out, that land under Antipas' rule was merged to his territory. This Agrippa I was the Herod who appeared in Acts chapter twelve, who executed Apostle James. He also put Peter into prison and tormented various leaders of the early church. However, when the people passionately cheered, he did not give glory to God and died of worms (Act.12:21-23).

(6) Herod Agrippa II

When Herod Agrippa died, his son Herod Agrippa II became king at the young age of seventeen. He was so young that from this time on Judea came to be controlled by Roman governor almost 100%. This Agrippa II listened to the testimony of Apostle Paul, who was in custody in Caesarea, together with governor Festus and was asked by Paul "King Agrippa, do you believe the prophets?" Then he replied "Do you think that in such a short time you can persuade me to be a Christian?" Hearing all the story of Paul, he said, "This man could have been set free if he had not appealed to Caesar"(Act.26:24-32). He was the last king of Herod's family and died in Rome while living there after Jerusalem was destroyed around A.D.70.

2. Roman governor

Octavianus (the first emperor of Rome) possessed brilliant power of politics. He ruled the whole empire as follows: when he delegated the territories of Roman rule, every year he chose two consuls and sent them to each province as governor in the capacity of former consul. Particularly, Judea was the place of unique religious cultural background and so he carefully considered and sent able and excellent governors there. Originally he ruled Judea by setting up the people of king's family as 'Tetrarch' but when Herod Archelaus' violent rule was too much, he sent one of the most able politicians as governor to the region of Judea where Archelaus reigned. Therefore, when Jesus ministered, there were tetrarch and governor in the land of Judea during the same time.

Pontius Pilate was the fifth governor who ruled Judea, Samaria and the region of Idumea for ten years from A.D.26. According to the record of historians he was stubborn and cruel. He was a coward who let Jesus be crucified. It is said that about seven years after the Crucifixion of Jesus, in A.D.36 he was called back to Rome and discharged and killed himself while living in depression.

While Jesus was living in this world, the Jews payed such high taxes; much as 30-40% to Rome. The revolt caused by the common people who lived so poorly was the Judean and Roman war of A.D.66-70. At last Jerusalem was totally destroyed by the Roman troops in A.D. 70.

3. High priest

Priests were classified into classes of high priest, head of temple, senior priests, ordinary priests and Levites.

1. High priest : They had the privilege of being able to enter Holy of Holies once a year. Every year they were fully in charge of three events (Passover, Pentecost and Tabernacle).
2. Head of temple : They were the candidate for the next high priest. They were the second man next to the high priest. He was a member of Sanhedrin.
3. Senior priests : In the New Testament the word 'High priest' appears often in plural. It seems that they referred to high priest, former high priest, and priests who belonged to special families who were to become high priest.
4. Ordinary priests : There were many ordinary priests. Some people calculated the number of priests of Jesus days to be 18,000. These were divided into 24 priestly divisions and each division performed sacrifice in the temple twice a year a week each.
5. Levites : These were also divided into 24 divisions and they served in the temple in a variety of forms including temple music.

There were no more kings for the community of returnees to Jerusalem from Babylonian captivity. It was maintained as a country of priests. Since the kings of such empires as Persia and Greece were generally interested in collecting much tax from the Jews but did not intervene in the religious matters or cultural aspects of people themselves, high priests were able to carry out the role of leaders of the people.

4. Secretary(Teacher of the law, Rabbi)

The model of secretary was Ezra who was both priest and scholar during the period of the Persian empire. The major task of secretary was to interpret and teach the people the law, and sometimes to solve their court cases and judge them. Secretary were also called 'Rabbi(Teacher)' or 'Teacher of law' and were able to become members of the Sanhedrin.

Secretary interpreted law in the capacity of lawyers and teachers of morality and were the leading the people in practicing the laws interpreted by them. They established schools and lived together with disciples. Among them there were some priests but most of them made a living by manual work and on relief fund. Since they were not paid at all for their teaching, they had to make money themselves for living.

5. Sanhedrin the Ruling Council

The nation of Judah who were taken captive to Babylon after Zedekiah the last king of Southern Judah no longer a the governing body. After Babylon was destroyed and the Persian Empire emerged, the Jewish governing body organized as Jews were made to return was Sanhedrin the ruling council, which was composed of 71 people including Judean governor, scholars of law and nobles and the like.

In the New Testament, Sanhedrin was called by many names such as ruling council, assembly of elders and the assembly. Sometimes the way of listing their members was "High priests and pharisees, high priests and elders and secretary".

It was the organization that advised the high priest. The high priests during the period of the Roman empire were chosen out of the rich Sadducees families and these families controlled the Sanhedrin. However, although the Pharisees were few, they exerted impact in and outside of the Sanhedrin on the foundation of the common people's support.

6. Sects in the New Testament

During Jesus' ministry the most hostile to him were the Pharisees and Sadducees. They often obstructed and criticized his ministry. Understanding what kind of people they were is very important for our understanding of the New Testament.

(1) Pharisees

As mentioned in lesson 25, when Antiochus Epiphanes of Seleucus dynasty prohibited the laws of Jews and persecuted those who kept the law in order to convert the Jews into Greek culture, those who kept fidelity to the end were called 'Hasidim.' From this Hasidim came the Pharisees. The word 'Pharisee' had the meaning of 'Separate.'

According to the record of historian Josephus, there were about six thousand Pharisees in A.D. first century. While the Sadducees were composed of some rich families and leading priest families, the Pharisees were the descendants of city merchants. They were very successful economically and commanded social and religious languages skillfully. Nicodemus who came to Jesus and Apostle Paul had been Pharisees.

(2) Sadducees

Sadducees were the descendants of those who among the descendants of priests maintained the religious power by accepting part of Greek thoughts. In other words, they were religious leaders with great power. They were called Sadducees because they were descendants of 'Zadok' who were high priest in the days of Solomon. They were in charge of all the duties of maintaining the temple.

On the one hand, they pretended to keep the law in order to maintain the life of religious nobles. On the other hand, they compromised with contemporary powers. Their life style was practical and, even by violating the law, compromised with Roman governor or king Herod.

Unlike the Pharisees, the Sadducees rejected tradition and accepted only the written law. They denied resurrection of the body or judgment after death or the existence of angels and the devil. In other words, they did not believe resurrection. Therefore, not the next life but present life was more important for them. After this, when Apostle Paul was arrested in Jerusalem and stood before the Sanhedrin, he saved himself by taking advantage of the different position between the Sadducees and Pharisees about resurrection(Act.23:6-11). Compared with the Pharisees, they were flexible in the law and life and overall had more, a worldly and liberal attitude.

(3) Zealot

These were characterized by performing guerrilla style terror or radically practicing their beliefs rather than accepting reality as it was. They were like the Pharisees in the great premise of trying to preserve Judaism. However, the Pharisees accepted the rule of the Gentiles and waited for God's time whereas the Zealots, like Mattathias who caused Maccabean Revolt, made it their goal to liberate Israel from Rome even by force. Although they were neither simple mob nor protestors who had systematic religious beliefs, they were no doubt patriotic Jews. If Essenes were world-evasive with a thorough separatist attitude, the Zealots could be said to be those who ran into the middle of the world to participate in current affairs.

There was a Zealot among the disciples of Jesus(Luk.6:15). Or it was guessed that the 'robbers' who were crucified beside Jesus or 'Barabbas' were also Zealots.

(4) Essenes

Essenes meant 'Silence' and 'Godliness.' It was a new sect that came into being after being excited by the Pharisees and Sadducees. Although they took strict position similarly as the Pharisees, they took the position of being reality-avoiding and reclusive. They lived together in the caves of the regions where there was almost no water or no trees. In one of those caves a copy of the Bible called Dead Sea Scrolls was discovered.

Tradition says that they were engaged in such work as agriculture and spent much time researching moral and religious problems including Scripture interpretation together. They shared all their property, had no slaves and paid careful attention to ceremonial purity. Some say that John the Baptist was from the sect of Essenes.

Track 5
The 4 Gospels

Tong Track 5 - The atmosphere of the 4 Gospels

The atmosphere of the 4 Gospels is that of the Kingdom of God being set-up. John the Baptist, who proclaimed the coming of the Messiah, introduced the Kingdom of God, and in the 4 gospels we can see Jesus telling the people about the Kingdom of Gd by performing miracles and using metaphors.

"After John was put in prison, Jesus went into Galilee, proclaiming the good news of God. "The time has come," he said. "The kingdom of God has come near. Repent and believe the good news!" (Mar.1:14-15).

Jesus used metaphors to suit each occupation to assist in their understanding - for example, he spoke of planting seeds to farmers, fishing nets to fishermen, yeast to housewives, and pearls to salesmen.

Every empire advocated the manifesto: "Long Live Imperialism!" But every empire saw its downfall. On the other hand, the Kingdom of God is forever, and our hopes should depend on the eternal Kingdom.

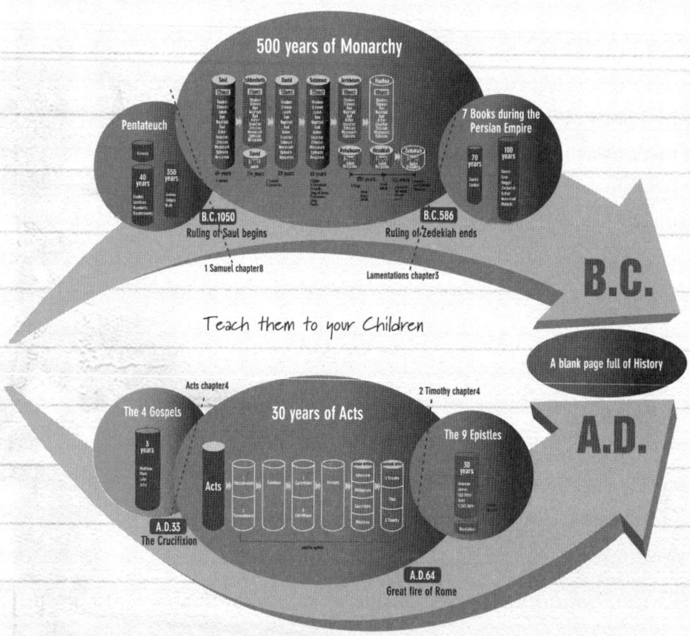

12 Session

A Joyful Birth

Tong Map

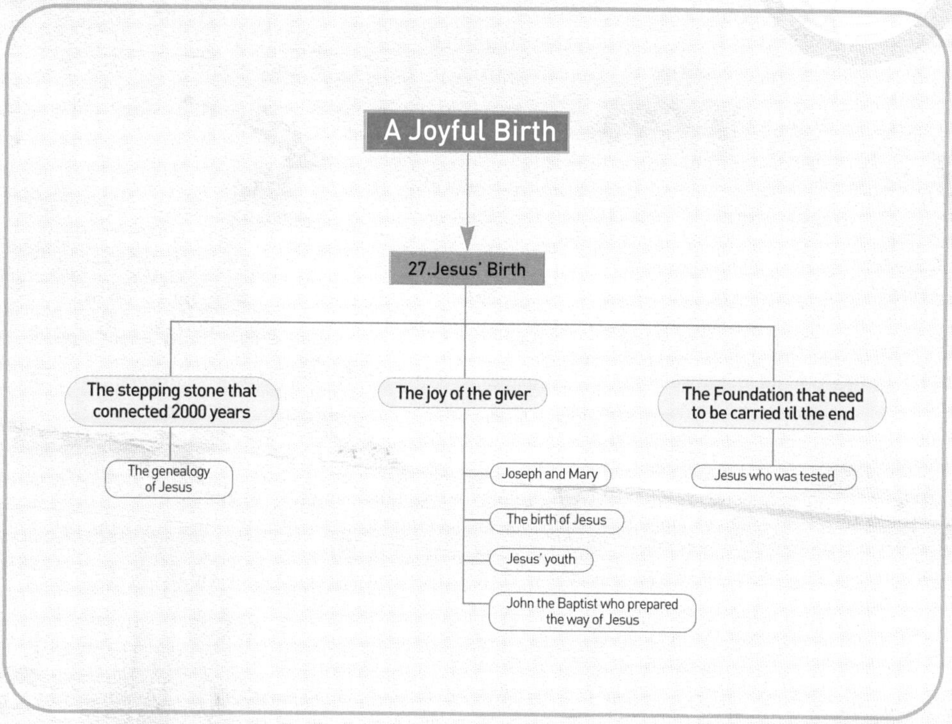

Tong Concept

- **Birth for Joy!**

As Jesus came into this world, the great light of God came to shine upon those who were sitting in the land and the shade of death and the kingdom of God came upon them. Let's study while remembering it was a birth for true joy.

- **Genealogy! Stepping stone which connected 2000 years!**

The history of God's salvation which started from the time of Abraham crossed the stepping stone of a thousand years to David and was fulfilled by Jesus. Let's remember the genealogy which played a very important role in introducing Jesus who came to the world on the basis of the 2,000 year Old Testament history.

- **The birth of Jesus. The joy of the giver!**

Let's review those who took pains and were loyal when Jesus came to the world.

Tong At a glance

* Looking around the forest

Among the 4 Gospels only Matthew and Luke record the birth of Jesus. Mark's Gospel begins with the story of John the Baptist appearing in the desert of Judea and starting his ministry. John began with the word, "In the beginning was the word"(Joh.1:1) and introduced Jesus by going back to the time before the world began.

The New Testament begins with "A record of the genealogy of Jesus Christ the son of David, the son of Abraham". This phrase is the core of Matthew's Gospel and the New Testament, and furthermore is the key word that summarizes the whole of the Old and New Testament.

* Land and annual ring

When Jesus came to this world, Palestine was ruled by the Roman Empire. In those days Palestine was largely divided into three regions. Way above was the Galileean region where the Sea of Galilee flowed. In the middle was Samaria where the Samaritans lived. Way down was where Jerusalem was. These regions included diverse landscapes such as desert, valleys and fields.

Nazareth (where Jesus lived before he began his public life) was the name of a village in Galilee. His ministry was carried out mainly in Galilee and Judea. Most of the people in Judea and Galilee made a living by working on the farm or fishing. But as Roman rule reached these regions, all kinds of road and harbors were built and Palestine began international trade.

The village of Bethlehem which was an another important place was in Judea. Micah (Old Testament prophet) prophesied that the Messiah who would deliver the people out of suffering, bondage and unrighteousness would be born there(Mic.5:2). This place was in a hilly district southwest of Jerusalem.

* Wind and Climate

There were wise men who saw a star in the east and came to celebrate the birth of Jesus. It seems that they came afar distance of Arabia, Babylon or Persia. Perhaps they were descendants of Daniel who had lived in Persia long before. Our LORD Jesus who came to this world receiving worship of eastern wise men and shepherds who tended sheep was the Son of God who came in human form.

Tong Seeing the forest

Matthew's Gospel Rome thoroughly collected tax through tax-collectors chosen by them among the people of Israel and took it to their country. That was why the people of Israel had hatred towards the tax-collectors chosen out of their fellow nationals. However, Jesus came to Matthew who was one of such collectors and made him his disciple.

Most likely Matthew thought that his three year life as his disciple could not have been any happier. He probably shed much tears of appreciation to the fact that someone like him became Jesus' disciple while living a meaningful and rewarding life each day. Matthew wrote 'Matthew's Gospel' because by writing in detail he wanted to tell his fellow Jews how good our LORD Jesus was and why he came to this world and died on the cross for us. Therefore, Matthew's Gospel begins with the story about the Jewish history. The writer explains Jesus through the knowledge and background of the Old Testament that the Jews were able to understand.

27
Lesson

Jesus' Birth

Matthew's Gospel

Accumulative reading amount 78.12% 1189

The One Year Tongdok Bible Days 281-289 | Reading time 90 minutes

TongBible Story Overview

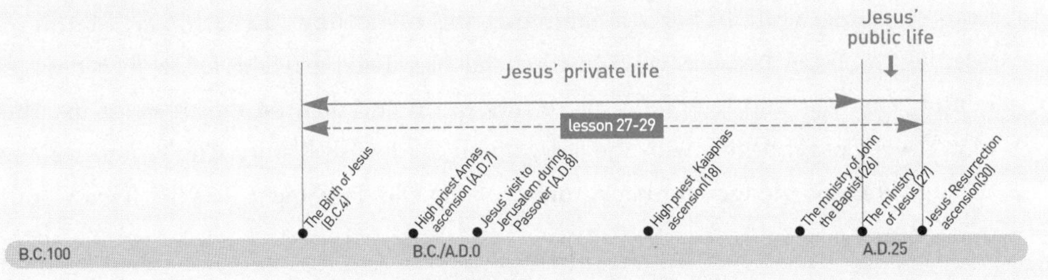

Reading the New Testament in detail in the order of history (1)

We read through Matthrew's Gospel with a particular observe the action of events prior to Jesus' public life, his birth, youth and the story of John the Baptist who prepared the way for Jesus to come.

How to read Matthew's Gospel and Jesus' birth

Although Herod(Herod the Great) threatened the life of Jesus because he felt a threat to his power, nobody was able to stand in the way of the birth of Jesus who came to give true joy and salvation to this world. He came to this world as God's fruit of love for the salvation of all human-kind.

Tong Point

The stepping stone that connected 2000 years.

"A record of the genealogy of Jesus Christ, the son of Abraham and the son of David"(Mat.1:1). Matthew puts in order the 2000 year history of the Old Testament within this sentence. Jesus' genealogy was the stepping stone that connected the 2000 years of the Old and New Testament.

1. The genealogy of Jesus

Mat.1:1-17/ Mar.1:1/ Luk.1:1-4; 3:23-38/ Joh. 1:1-18

The genealogy of Jesus
Matthew chapter 1:
Abraham-David-Solomon-Jesus'mother Mary.
Luke chapter 3:
God-Adam-David-Nathan-Jesus 'father Joseph.
Luke studied the history of Israel shown in the books of Chronicles in detail.

The New Testament begins with **"A record of the genealogy of Jesus Christ the son of David, the son of Abraham".** Abraham predated Jesus by 2000 years and David by 1000 years. Therefore we can say that the history of the Old Testament of 2000 years was put in order within this one sentence and the New Testament age opened at the same time. **This verse (Matthew chapter 1, verse 1) eloquently states the fact that the overview of the whole Bible centered around one person, Jesus Christ.**

Women in the geneology of Mathew's gospel chapter 1

Tamar	*The daughter-in-law of Judah the fourth son of Jacob *She disguised herself as a prostitute and slept with Judah, gave birth to twins	Gen. chap. 38
Rahab	*The woman who hid two spies of Israel in Jericho *The mother of Boaz and great-grandmother of David	Jos. chap. 2
Ruth	*Moabite woman, wife of Mahlon; son of Naomi *Remarried Boaz in Bethlehem	Book of Ruth
Uriah's wife (Bathsheba)	*David killed her husband Uriah and made her his wife *Solomon's mother	II Sa. chap.11
Mary	*Conceived Jesus as a virgin	Mat. chap.1

Another characteristic we can find in the genealogy of Jesus was the names of women. They are Tamar, Rahab, Ruth, Uraiah's wife and Mary. Four women's names are recorded but one woman's is not. Why was she referred as 'Uriah's wife' rather than her actual name, Bathsheba?

It is obvious that David was a

great king in history. However, even great David had one very shameful memory in his life, namely, he killed innocent Uriah to hide his sin. Pinpointing this matter, Matthew stated even David the great king, (respected and honored by the Jews) was also a sinner. This meant that he also was a sinner like us who needs to be forgiven by Jesus' blood shed on the cross. **That all people should bow down before his name and worship him was the point which Matthew wanted to make.**

Tong Point

The joy of the giver
Joseph and Mary who devoted themselves to the birth of Jesus, the wise men of the east, shepherds and John the Baptist who prepared the way of Jesus were all who enjoyed being a giver/helper. Let's review the birth of Jesus while remembering the joy of these people.

2. Joseph and Mary Mat.1:18-25/Luk.1:26-56

Through a woman called Mary, God opened the way for Jesus Christ to come into this world. When an angel came to Mary and told her the will of God, "You will be with child and give birth to a son, and you are to give him the name Jesus(Luk.1:31)", she obeyed saying, "I am the LORD's servant, may it be to me as you have said"(Luk.1:38).

Some time later, Joseph who was pledged to be married to Mary came to hear that she was pregnant. If things got worse and the rumor spread that a virgin became pregnant, Mary could have been stoned to death according to the law. Joseph who was righteous tried to protect Mary by cutting off their engagement quietly. Finally an angel came to Joseph and told him that she was with child through the Holy Spirit, saying "She will give birth to a son, and you are to give him the name Jesus because he will save his people from their sins"(Mat.1:21). Joseph took her home as commanded by the angel of the LORD and did not sleep with her until she gave birth to a son. Joseph and Mary played a truly beautiful role for our LORD at the main point of our LORD's coming to this world.

3. The birth of Jesus Mat.2:1-12/Luk.2:1-21

Rulers of Judea of Jesus' days

Roman Emperor	Tiberius	Luk.3:1
Governor	Pontius Pilate	Luk.3:1, Mat.27:2
Tetrarch	Herod Antipas - Galilee Herod Philip - Iturea, Traconit Lucinia - Abilene	Luk.3:1
High priest	Annas Caiaphas(Annas' son-in-law)	Luk.3:2 Joh.11:19

The Roman emperor issued a decree that everyone were to return to the place of his birth and register(Luk.2:1-2). It was to collect more tax by taking a census correctly. Joseph and Mary who was fully pregnant also had to travel a long way from Nazareth to Bethlehem.

They arrived in Bethlehem and the time came for Mary to give birth to a baby. However, all the Inns of Bethlehem were full with people. Joseph and Mary were not able to find a warm room and eventually had to give birth to a son in an animal stall. Our LORD came to this world through the devotion and loyalty of these people.

At last our LORD Jesus was born in this world. First, the shepherds who were tending sheep near Bethlehem heard the voice of angels and came running and worshipped the baby.

Next, the Magi from the east saw the star and came. When they saw the star stop over the place where the baby was, "They were overjoyed"(Mat.2:9-10). Reading through this portion of the Bible, let's also sing Hymn 122 "Oh come all you faithful" with the mind of celebrating the birth of Jesus by entering the stall of the Bethlehem village. "O come all ye faithful, joyful and triumphant, O come ye, O come ye to Bethlehem! Come and behold Him, born the King of angels! O come, let us adore Him, O come, let us adore him, O come, let us adore him Christ the LORD!"

4. Jesus' youth Mat.2:13-23/ Luk.2:22-52

Sometime later, hearing that a baby was born who would be 'king of the Jews', Herod gave orders to kill all boys in Bethlehem and its vicinity. Baby Jesus was able to avoid the crisis by going to Egypt away from Herod.

After Herod the Great died, the region of Judea was alloted to his son Herod Archelaus. The Bible records that when Joseph who knew this returned from Egypt, he went to Nazareth in Galilee to live, not the region of Judea(Mat.2:19-23). That was why Jesus was called 'Jesus of Nazareth'.

Regarding the youth of Jesus, only a brief record is left in Luke's Gospel. When Jesus was 12 years old, he went to Jerusalem for the feast of Passover. Then he heard the law from the teachers of law he met at the temple and also asked them questions. The Bible records that all those who heard him were amazed at his wise answers. The Bible records, "Jesus grew in

Nazareth
Jesus lived in Nazareth before he lived his public life. Since it was only a small countryside village which did not draw people's attention, Nathaniel retorted, "Can anything good come out of Nazareth?" when he heard from Philip that Jesus was from there(Joh.1:46). It was in this town Nazareth that Jesus prepared his future ministry while humbling himself.

wisdom and stature, and in favor with God and men" (Luk.2:52).

5. John the Baptist who prepared the way of Jesus

Mat. chap.3 (11:1-19; 14:1-12)/ Mar.1:2-11 (6:14-29)

Luk.1:5-25, 57-80; 3:1-22 (7:18-35)/ Joh.1:19-34 (3:22-36)

When Jesus was 30 years old, the land of Judea became very clamorous due to the emergence of a man called John the Baptist. The ministry of John the Baptist lasted only six months until Jesus emerged. He wore a garment made of camel's hair. His meal consisted of locusts and wild honey and he slept in the wilderness. If people came and said they wanted to be baptized, he immersed them in the flowing river. His preaching and baptism were very exceptional. His preaching was so bold and cutting that it was worthy to be called 'ax preaching'(Luk. 3:7-14).

When John the Baptist attracted all the attention on himself for six months, Jesus appeared. More and more people gathered around Jesus. Seeing this, the disciples of John complained, "All the people are going to him." Upon hearing this, John the Baptist calmly solved their misunderstanding;

"You yourselves can testify that I said, `I am not the Christ but am sent ahead of him'. The bride belongs to the bridegroom. The friend who attends the bridegroom waits and listens for him, and is full of joy when he

John the Baptist vs. Jesus

John the Baptist	Jesus
About 6 month ministry	About 3 year public life
"Repent because judgment is near."	"Repent and believe in me because God's rule is near."
The water baptism of repentance	The baptism of fire and the Holy Spirit
His ministry was prophesied by Isaiah and Malachi	Prophesied by Isaiah, Jeremiah, Zechariah and etc.

hears the bridegroom's voice. That joy is mine, and it is now complete. He must become greater; I must become less" (Joh.3:28-30).

John the Baptist knew where he stood and that he was to yield his place to Jesus when the time came.

Afterwards, boldly pointing out that it was not right for Herod(Herod Antipas) to marry Herodias the wife of his younger brother Philip, John the Baptist was killed by Herod(Mat.14:1-12). Later, Jesus made a very high evaluation of John, stating "more than a prophet"(Mat.11:9) and "among those born of women there has not risen anyone greater than John the Baptist"(Mat.11:11).

Tong Point

The Foundations that need to be carried til the end
Before preparing for a public life, Jesus laid down 'foundations to be carried til the end.' Let's remember that its core was none other than the Written Word.

6. Jesus who was tested Mat.4:1-11/ Mar.1:12-13/ Luk. 4:1-13

After Jesus was baptized by John, he went to the wilderness, fasted for forty days and prepared for his public life. By the time he finished fasting, he was tempted by Satan who blasphemed his ministry.

Satan tempted Jesus with three things; "If you are the Son of God, tell these stones to become bread", "if you are the Son of God, throw yourself down from this high top of the temple",

Temptations that came upon Jesus

-The first temptation

It was to become an **economical** Messiah.

-The second temptation

It was to become a **mystic** Messiah. Jesus was tempted to secure followers by performing great miracles. By throwing himself down from the top of Jerusalem temple, the center of Jewish life, Jesus could have started his ministry with great groups of supporters.

-The third temptation

It was to become a **political** Messiah. Jesus sharply felt that the hoof of Roman Empire was pressing down on the necks of his people. Being tempted to become like David was telling him to avoid the way of a suffering servant.

and "All in the world I will give you, if you will bow down and worship me". Jesus overcame Satan's temptation firmly and decisively. Particularly, he overcame Satan by answering, "It is written: 'Man does not live on bread alone, but on every word that comes from the mouth of God'". "It is also written: 'Do not put the LORD your God to the test'". "For it is written: 'Worship the LORD your God, and serve Him only'". He responded to Satan with the Pentateuch, the word of God. Jesus was the one who knew well that there was power in the Word.

Write down the contents of this lesson in the form of Tong Story

....

....

....

....

....

....

Let's pray in a loud voice so that we may be able to teach the contents of this lesson to our children

- Teach them to your children, talking about them when you sit at home and when you walk along the road, when you lie down and when you get up……so that your days and the days of your children may be many……as many as the days that the heavens are above the earth (Deuteronomy 11:19-21).
- you know those from whom you learned it, and how from infancy you have known the holy Scriptures(II Timothy 3:14-15).

13 Session

Love for One Soul

Tong Map

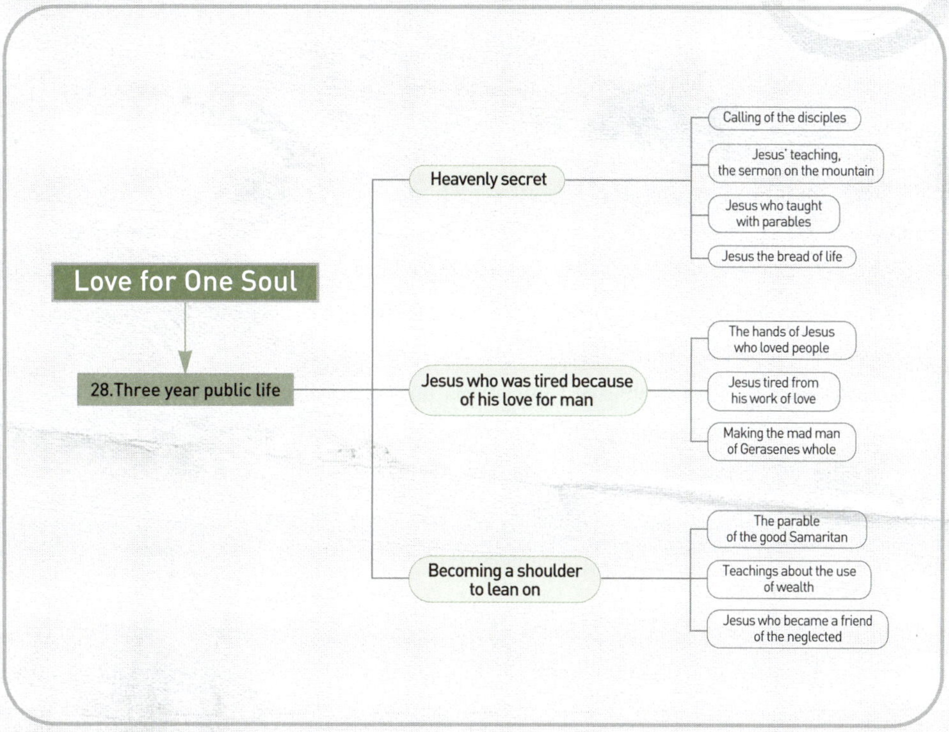

Tong Concept

- **The three year public life of love for one soul**

Although Jesus showed his power beyond time and space during his three year public life, he touched and healed people by using his own hands. Let's study with a particular focus on all the ministry Jesus did to 'love for one soul.'

Track 5 THE 4 GOSPELS

Tong At a glance

* Looking around the forest

The main point to note about Jesus' life was that he loved every soul. While enduring the fact that the Pharisees tried to argue with him, he healed the sick on countless occasions. His tiredness, hunger, going to low places himself, serving as servant and the like were the expressions of his heart. He great love was expressed most dramatically on the day he took up the cross.

* Land and annual ring

While going throughout Galilee and Judea, Jesus sometimes even went to the places where the Gentiles were living(Tyre, Syrophoenicia, the Decapolis and etc.). He taught the kingdom of God, served people, loved them and performed the miracle of healing many people. Galilee appeared in the gospels very often. Capernaum, Cana, Nazareth and the like were all in Galilee. Jesus' life and teachings were mainly carried out in Galilee.

Jerusalem was so important that we need not stress its importance any more. The reason Jerusalem was considered important was because of the temple. The Jerusalem Temple was the Jewish core and the high priests of the temple enjoyed the highest authority in those days.

* Wind and Climate

Jesus taught the kingdom of God by using various parables so that anyone could easily understand it and hope for it. So he explained the kingdom of God to people and made them long for it by telling the parable of sowing to farmers, the parable of net to fishers, that of talent to those who pursued business and that of yeast to housewives.

Tong Seeing the forest

Mark's Gospel There are 16 chapters in Mark. Among them 6 chapters(11 to 16) record the suffering, dying on the cross and the resurrection of Jesus. Because the Jews of those days had the misunderstanding that 'Messiah to come would be the king who would resolve the political liberation from Rome'. However, our LORD Jesus who was the true Messiah set us free from sin by dying on the cross on our behalf and was the Son of God. Mark wrote this gospel to help solve the misunderstanding of the Jews about Jesus and to let the saints in Rome know our LORD Jesus correctly.

In Mark's Gospel the power of Jesus who healed the sick and transformed people was most emphasised. It records a lot of miracles of Jesus such as healing the paralized man, making the mad man of Gerasenes whole, healing the man who had a shrivelled hand, healing the woman suffering from flow of blood and the like. In addition, Mark expressed Jesus' human aspect and deep love through many verbs Jesus carried out such as "touched the hand, healed, took him, grieved, sighed, loved and got angry" and so on.

28 Lesson Three year public life

Mark's Gospel

Accumulative reading amount 79.86% 1189

The One Year Tongdok Bible Days 290-295 | Reading time 50 minutes

TongBible Story Overview

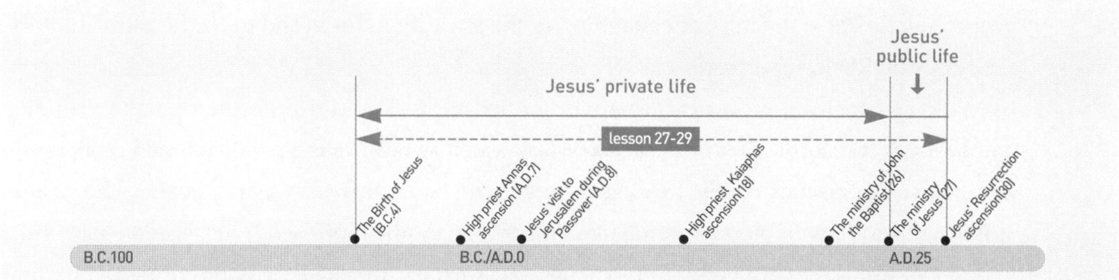

Reading the New Testament in detail in the order of history (2)

We go on to read through Mark Gospel. While reading through we observe the record that Jesus who came to the world as the Son of God preached the gospel of the kingdom of God for three years, touching the people and healing them by using his hands in person. Its focus is the period from the time when Jesus started his ministry until he went up to Jerusalem on Passover during his third year of public life to take up the cross.

How to read Mark's Gospel and "Three year public life."

Jesus who was baptized by John, fasted in the wilderness for forty days and prepared for the beginning of his public ministry. His ministry began with; "Repent, for the Kingdom of God is near." In those days the people of Israel were engaged in such basic activities of production for living as agriculture, tending livestock or fishing etc. Therefore, in the gospels are recorded his sayings as expression of parable in connection with such occupations.

The land of Israel was not fit for agriculture except for the region of shores of the Sea of Galilee. Therefore, the economy of the Israel was not high. Even worse, severely heavy tax was imposed on what little they had under the rule of Roman Empire. This was the suffering the common people of Israel had to go through. In this situation the word of Jesus and his miracles gave them wonderful joy that made them find the meaning of their life and look for a new purpose. At this time, Jesus came to this world to comfort and bless people.

Tong Point

Love for one soul 1) - Heavenly secret

Summarizing the three years of Jesus' public life in a word, we can say that it was the time when he practiced 'love for one soul' himself. The first contents of 'love for one soul' was that he taught people about 'heaven'. It was Jesus who introduced heaven the best.

1. Calling of the disciples Mat.4:12-25; chap.10; chap.16-17 / Mar.1:14-20; 2:13-17; 3:13-19; 8:27-chap.9 / Luk.4:14-6:19; chap.9-10:24 / Joh.1:35-2:12

Beginning his ministry, Jesus chose 12 disciples who was to work with him for three years. Jesus called Peter, Andrew, James, and John who were fishermen casting their nets at the shores of Sea of Galilee. They who responded to his calling became the disciples of Jesus. Eventually, on the basis of the precious memory of the time they were with Jesus, they became stepping stones of life who testified to people of Jesus' story of loving people and preached the gospel to them.

Jesus' twelve disciples
Peter, Andrew, James, John, Philip, Bartholomew, Thomas, Matthew, James son of Alphaeus, Thaddaeus, Simon, Judas Iscariot

The life of disciples
The life of the disciples who followed Jesus for three years was not easy or comfortable. They had to row oars in the Sea of Galilee, carry the loaves of bread in the fields of Bethsaida and help Jesus with jobs on the days Jesus healed the sick all night long. Jesus chose twelve as his close fellow workers. Those twelve people spent time with him loving people, listening to and learning the Word of Jesus for three years.

2. Jesus' teaching, the sermon on the mountain Mat.chap.5-7 / Luk.6:20-49; chap.11-12

Jesus preached the secrets of heaven. Particularly, Matthew collected the sermons Jesus preached on the mountain and put them together in chapters 5, 6, 7 of Matthew's Gospel. Now we can hear the Word of Jesus in person as if Jesus preached his Word to our ears directly.

The first sermon Jesus preached on the mountain was about 'blessing'(Mat.5:3-12.)

"Blessed are the poor in spirit, for theirs is the kingdom of heaven.
Blessed are those who mourn, for they will be comforted.
Blessed are the meek, for they will inherit the earth.
Blessed are those who hunger and thirst for righteousness,
for they will be filled.
Blessed are the merciful, for they will be shown mercy.
Blessed are the pure in heart, for they will see God.
Blessed are the peacemakers, for they will be called sons of God.
Blessed are those who are persecuted because of righteousness,
for theirs is the kingdom of heaven."

The 'blessing' Jesus preached was completely different from what the people of the world expected. To those who thought that being prosperous in everything in this world was blessing, Jesus taught that true blessing was to have in mind what belonged to heaven.

Jesus talked about how much God cared about people (Mat.6:25-26). He said, "See how the lilies of the field grow," and "Are you not much more valuable than they?" If we remember the providence of God who feeds the birds of the air and clothes the lilies of the field, there is no need to waste life with anxiety, complaints and resentment. **Therefore, we can say, "But seek first His kingdom and His righteousness, and all these things will be given to you as well"(Mat.6:33) is a summary and the core of the whole Bible.**

3. Jesus who taught with parables

Mat.chap.13/ Mar.4:1-34/ Luk.8:4-21; chap.13

Seven parables of heaven
1.Parable of sowing (Mat.13:3-8)
2.Parable of weeds (Mat.13:24-30)
3.Parable of mustard seed (Mat.13:31-32)
4.Parable of yeast (Mat.13:33)
5.Parable of hidden treasure (Mat.13:44)
6.Parable of a merchant looking for fine pearls (Mat.13:45-46)
7.Parable of net (Mat.13:47-50)

Jesus talked about heaven by taking illustrations from the common people of those days, who did not have much knowledge, in a way they were able to easily understand. He preached to the farmers with the parable of sowing, to housewives with the parable of yeast and to the fishermen with that of net. He explained so that the common people were able to understand easily.

Jesus also preached a variety of parables about the kingdom of God; the kingdom of heaven. He said "The kingdom of heaven is like a merchant looking for fine pearls"(Mat.13:45). When a man who deals in pearls comes across a good pearl, he attains it by selling all he has. It is so worthy as selling all one has to get it that the joy of heaven cannot be compared with any kind of joy of this world.

Tong Point

Parable
By using a teaching method called 'parable', Jesus explained precisely the circumstances hard to understand and helped people understand clearly.

4. Jesus the bread of life

Mat.14:13-36; 15:32-39/ Mar.6:30-56; 8:1-26/ Luk.9:1-17 / Joh. 3:1-21; 4:1-42; chap.6-7

Jesus taught the kingdom of God and performed many

miracles.

In Luke's Gospel chapter 9 verses 10-17(Mat.14-13:21; Mar.6:30-44; Joh.6:1-14) is recorded the event which Jesus fed 5,000 people in the field of Bethsaida. He preached the word all day long and it got dark.

Jesus could have had 5,000 people sit facing him, prayed and had bread and fish fall in front of them like drops of water one by one. However he did not do so but gave thanks for the two fish and five loaves of barley bread brought by the disciples and then had the disciples distribute with baskets in their hands. **This was because Jesus wanted his word rather than miracles themselves to be remembered by the people.** Therefore, the next day he said to the people who remembered the bread they ate the previous day and gathered there again, "I am the bread of life. He who comes to me will never go hungry, and he who believes in me will never be thirsty"(Joh.6:35).

One day a Pharisee and a public official of the Jews called Nicodemus came to Jesus. Jesus said to him, "No one can see the kingdom of God unless he is born again." However, not understanding what Jesus said, Nicodemus asked a ridiculous question, "Can he enter a second time into his mother's womb to be born?" Then Jesus explained that 'being born again' meant being born newly "with water and the Holy Spirit".

Jesus' self-introduction

1. I am the bread of life (Joh. 6:35, 41)
2. I am the light of the world (Joh. 8:12)
3. I am the gate for the sheep (Joh. 10:7, 9)
4. I am the good shepherd (Joh. 10:11, 14)
5. I am the resurrection and the life (Joh. 11:25)
6. I am the way and the truth and the life (Joh. 14:6)
7. I am the true vine (Joh. 15:1,5)

Tong Point

Love for one soul 2) - Jesus who was tired because of his love for man
The second contents of 'love for one soul' was that Jesus surrendered his body as an instrument for love. Let's discover Jesus who was physically tired touching and healing the people by using his hand in person, although he performed his power beyond time and space as well.

5. The hands of Jesus who loved people

Mat.8:1-17/ Mar.1:21-3:12; 3:20-35 / Luk.4:14-6:11; 7:1-17; 8:40-56 / Joh. 4:43-chap.5; chap.9

The miracles Jesus performed on Sabaths

- Healed the demon-possessed man in Capernaum (Mar.1:21-28)
- Healed the fever of Peter's mother-in-law(Mar.1:29-31)
- Healed a man who had a shrivelled hand(Mar.3:1-6)
- Healed a woman who was demon-possessed 18 years and bent over(Luk.13:10-17)
- Healed a man who had dropsy(Luk.14:1-6)
- Healed a man in Bethesda who had been ill for 38 years (Joh.5:1-15)
- Healed a man born blind (Joh.9:1-14)

Jesus considered every person precious. Particularly, he gave great comfort and joy of restoration to those who were poor and sick.

"When the sun was setting, the people brought to Jesus all who had various kinds of sickness, and laying his hands on each one, he healed them …… At daybreak Jesus went out to a solitary place"(Luk.4:40-42).

During the day time he taught the word of God. At night he healed the sick by laying his hands on each patient. Jesus loved people with all his life. Just as the garment of a priest was a uniform for serving God and people, so was the garment of Jesus stained with pus of the sick. **Jesus used his hand diligently.**

Tong Point

Seven miracles

John chose only seven among so many miracles Christ performed in order to express his divinity briefly and clearly.

Water becomes wine.	Religious rituals were replaced by actual grace(Joh.2:1-11)
Healed a high official's son	Gospel brought spiritual restoration (Joh. 4:46-54)
Healed a patient who suffered 38 years	Weakness turned into strength (Joh.5:1-9)
Fed many people	Met spiritual hunger(Joh.6:1-13)
Walked on water	Transformed fear into faith (Joh.6:16-21)

Man born blind could see	He overcame darkness and came as light (Joh.9:1-7)
Raised Lazarus who was dead	Gospel helps people move to life from death.(Joh.11:1-44)

6. Jesus tired from his work of love

Mat.8:18-27/ Mar.4:35-41/ Luk.8:22-25

On one occasion, Jesus taught people as usual and intended to go across the sea to the other side around sunset. However, as they crossed the Sea of Galilee, a storm rose and water ran over into their ship. The ship severely shook and was endangered of sinking.

During this hour, Jesus was fast asleep. How tired and how weary was he that he seemingly could not get up until his disciples woke him up even in the midst of the ship being shaken so much?

As the storm got stronger and stronger, the disciples woke Jesus up. Jesus rebuked the wind and the sea and it immediately calmed. The disciples were amazed, saying, "What kind of man is this? Even the winds and the waves obey him!" Of course, making the waves and the wind calm was a wonderful miracle. **However, we also should know the background hidden behind the miracle; Jesus who became tired loving people to the point of such tiredness.**

7. Making the mad man of Gerasene whole

Mat.8:28-34/ Mar.5:1-20/ Luk.8:26-39

Gerasenes
A city located in the east of the Sea of Galilee. It belonged to the Decapolis; the ten cities built by Alexander the Great and his generals in Palestine. In this area were many limestone caves, many of which were used as tombs where they laid bodies.

The place where Jesus and the disciples arrived through the storm was the region of the Gerasenes. The man they met upon getting out of the ship was a demon-possessed man. He was so violent that he was bound with chains and was abandoned by his family. In a word, he was a "ruined man." Jesus travelled such waves to heal this one man that night despite how he was extremely tired.

When Jesus asked the demon inside of the mad man what his name was, he replied, Legion. When the demon asked Jesus to permit them to enter pigs, he permitted. And the herds of 2,000 pigs rushed into the seas and drowned. When the 2,000 pigs and the life of the one man were considered, Jesus judged that the man was more precious. He paid 2,000 pigs as price to make whole the man who was abandoned by the family and friends. The love Jesus had for the mad man of Gerasenes is also for us.

Tong Point

Love for one soul 3) - Becoming a shoulder to lean on
Let's try to think the Jesus who became a true 'shoulder to lean on' for Samaritans, tax-collectors, prostitutes and helpless neighbors.

8. The parable of the good Samaritan

Mat.9; 11:20-12/ Mar.5:21-6:13; 10:1-16/ Luk.7:36-50; 10:25-42

A teacher of law who was one of the greatest scholars of the Jewish society and an intellectuals of those days came to Jesus and asked, "what must I do to inherit eternal life?"(Luk.10:25)

Jesus asked back, "What is written in the Law? and how do you read it?" To this question of Jesus he summarized the laws as many as 613 kinds of law like a great intellectual did and answered clearly "Love the LORD your God with all your heart and with all your soul and with all your strength and with all your mind and love your neighbor as yourself." At that, Jesus said, "You have answered correctly. Do this and you will live." Then the teacher of law asked once more, "And who is my neighbor?"

At this, Jesus gave the parable of a man who fell into the hands of robbers(the parable of a good Samaritan). "There were a priest and a Levite who saw a man who fell into the hands of robbers, was wounded and lay on the ground but they passed by pretending to have not seen him. On the other hand, a Samaritan saw him, bandaged his wounds and helped him with what he had. Which of these three do you think was a neighbor to the man who fell into the hands of robbers?" In those days a Samaritan was someone who was not treated equally by the Jews. However, it was obvious that the Samaritan, who helped the man was the true neighbor.

To the scholar of law who replied, "The one who had mercy on him," Jesus replied, "Go, and do likewise."

Jesus' narration

Asked by the scholar of law how he was to have eternal life, Jesus told him the parable of the good Samaritan and asked him, "Who do you think was a neighbor to the man who fell into the hands of robbers?" When Jesus was asked questions, he sometimes answered right away or other times asked back. He used this kind of narration in which he asked back and corrected their thoughts.

9. Teachings about the use of wealth

Mat.19:16-30/ Mar.7:1-23; 10:17-31/ Luk.12:13-21; chap.16; 18:18-43

Not 'how much' but 'how'
Seeing a poor widow put two very small copper coins into the temple treasury, Jesus evaluated that her offering was the greatest offering (Luk.21:1-4). The LORD sees 'how' rather than 'how much' in offering. His interest lies in the mind of the person who gives the gift, not the gift itself.

One day a public official came to Jesus and asked, "Good teacher, what must I do to inherit eternal life?" (Luk.18:18). At this, Jesus said, "Do not commit adultery, do not murder, do not steal, do not give false testimony, honor your father and mother."

That man said that he had kept all the commandments very well from youth. Then Jesus said, "You still lack one thing. Sell everything you have and give to the poor, and you will have treasure in heaven." However, this young official became very concerned, because he was a man of great wealth.

Already through the law God explained in detail the right thought about wealth and right way to use it while mentioning the spirit of the wage earner(steward)(Lev.25:55) and sharing with neighbors(Lev.19:9-10).

10. Jesus who became a friend of the neglected

Mat.15:1-31; chap.18-19:15/ Mar.7:24-37
/ Luk. chap.14-15; chap.17-18:17; 19:1-10/ Joh. chap.8,10-11

Jesus approved the devotion and faith shown by 'a woman who was a sinner' when she poured perfume on his feet. When he saw Zacchaeus who was a chief tax collector of Jericho having climbed on the sycamore-fig tree to see him, he called him in a soft voice and went to stay in his house. Like this, Jesus' concern about the weak is saturated throughout the Bible.

One day the Pharisees and Sadducees tested Jesus by bringing an adulterous woman to him and asked him what he would do about her (Joh.8:1-5). Writing something on the ground for a while and then lifting up his head silently, Jesus said, "If any one of you is without sin, let him be the first to throw a stone at her" (Joh.8:7). After a few moments of silence, those who had stones in their hands felt guilty in their conscience and dropped their stones one by one and left the place. Seeing all the people leave, Jesus told her, "Then neither do I condemn you, go now and leave your life of sin." **I admire our LORD Jesus who with all his life, became a shoulder for everyone to lean on.**

Write down the contents of this lesson in the form of Tong Story

Let's pray in a loud voice so that we may be able to teach the contents of this lesson to our children

- Teach them to your children, talking about them when you sit at home and when you walk along the road, when you lie down and when you get up……so that your days and the days of your children may be many……as many as the days that the heavens are above the earth (Deuteronomy 11:19-21).
- you know those from whom you learned it, and how from infancy you have known the holy Scriptures(II Timothy 3:14-15).

14 Session

Passion towards Forgiveness

Tong Map

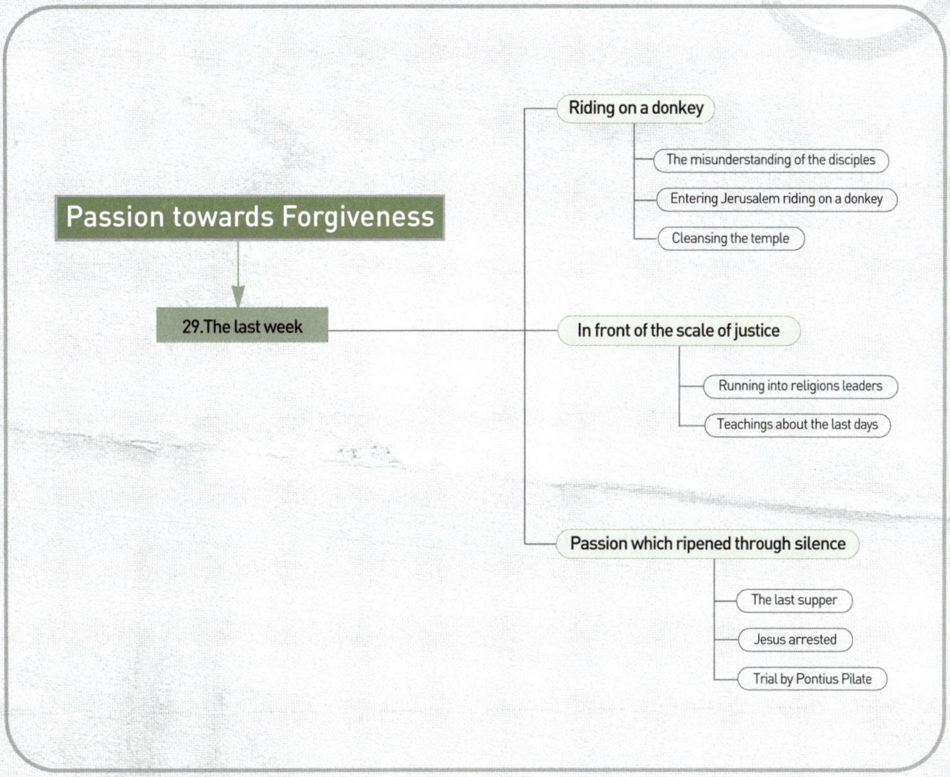

Tong Concept

- **The last week of passion towards forgiveness!**

Jesus' ministry of the cross was carried out in Jerusalem within a week centering around the Feast of Passover. It was the way Jesus himself chose to lead people who could not solve the problem of sin on their own into the way of salvation. It was a week when he poured out his passion toward the cross to forgive the sins of all people. Let's study while observing what Jesus did for a week in the order of time.

Tong At a glance

* Looking around the forest

The 4 Gospels are the books which all focus on Jesus' public life. Particularly, they focus on the time of the last week in which Jesus spent in Jerusalem. The one week of Passover, the last week, Jesus entered Jerusalem and finished his last day on the rugged tree cross built on the hill of Golgotha.

* Land and annual ring

There unfolds the story of the last week of the public life of Jesus who became the lamb of Passover himself to forgive the sins of people. We may say that this was the passion of God to forgive the sins of people. The God of justice, who punished His son for the sins of people, opened the way so the people who were now set free from their sins were able to come to God again. God's passion for forgiveness was revealed through the cross of Jesus.

* Wind and Climate

The Jewish funeral culture can be fully found from the stories of funerals of Jesus and Nazarus. The Jews washed the body clean, put spices on it and wrapped the whole body with fine linen before they buried it. We can guess this custom from the portion of the Bible where was said that Nazarus came out of the tomb with his hands and feet wrapped with strips of linen(Joh. 11:44). Since mourners usally mourned over the death in accordance with the sound of flute players, the Jews thought that he was 'going to the tomb to mourn' when he went to it (Joh. 11:31).

Usually bodies were buried under the ground, in caves or stone tombs. Nazarus was buried in a cave tomb. Jesus was buried in a man-made stone tomb. This kind was made by the rich to be used for themselves or their family. Jesus' tomb was prepared by the rich Joseph.

Tong Seeing the forest

Luke' Gospel Luke who wrote Luke's Gospel was a Greek physician as well as a historian. He had never seen Jesus face to face. However, after he heard about Jesus from Paul in Troas, he became an evangelist who devoted all his life to evangelism with Paul. He wrote The Acts of the Apostles in addition to Luke's Gospel.

We may say that Matthew's Gospel was written for the Jews and Mark's for the saints in Rome. Luke's Gospel and the Acts were the letters written to only one man called Theophilus.

He wrote Luke's Gospel about our LORD Jesus in detail from the beginning, as said in his prologue. Luke who was a Greek, a Gentile in those days also wrote much in his gospel about Samaritans and the neglected in society.

Particularly, he highlighted the picture of Jesus who took pains for the poor and neglected in society. He carefully collected lots of material in connection to Jesus about the two disciples going to Emmaus, Zacchaeus, the rich man and Nazarus, the story of Mary and Martha etc.

29 Lesson

The last week

Luke's Gospel

Accumulative reading amount 83.16% 1189

The One Year Tongdok Bible Days 296-306 | Reading time 95 minutes

TongBible Story Overview

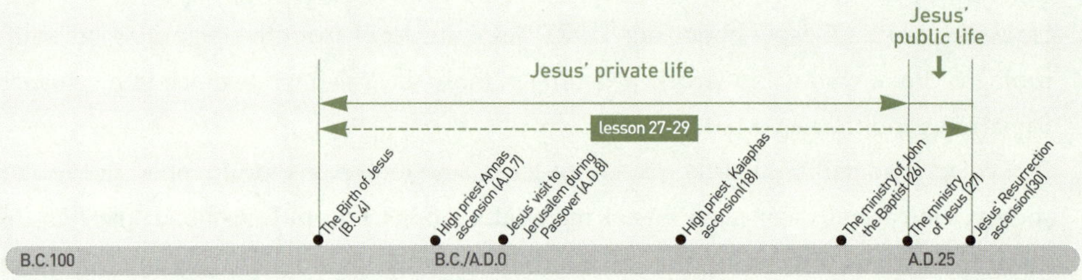

Reading the New Testament in detail in the order of history (3)

We go on to read through Luke's Gospel. While reading through Luke Gospel we can observe the story about Jesus entering Jerusalem for the event of the cross, which was his last and most important ministry. There, he was seized by Roman soldiers, flogged and sentenced to death.

How to read Luke's Gospel and 'the last week.'

A very significant part of Jesus' ministry was carried out within a week centering around the feast of Passover. Arriving in Jerusalem, he cleansed the temple on Monday, answered questions asked by the associates of high priests and elders on Tuesday who were the Jewish religious leaders then, argued with the Pharisees and Sadducees and the like and scolded their hypocrisy sharply.

He wept seeing Jerusalem from Mt.Olive and gave his 'Mt. Olive Lecture' in which he talked about the end of the world. Thursday was the day right before he was crucified. He spent the last day in this world with his disciples. In the upper room which was prepared in advance for the Passover he had the last supper and washed the feet of his disciples. Also, he had a last long dialogue with them and prayed for them. He was caught by the associates of the high priest that night, dragged around and was questioned. The next day he was sentenced to death by Pilate and crucified. In the midst of the imminent flow of time, Jesus carried out one by one the duties he came to fulfill.

Tong Point

Riding on a donkey
Jesus who talked about 'the love of God' and 'the value of man' began the journey of his last week as a humble king.

1. The misunderstanding of the disciples

Mat.chap.20/ Mar.10:32-52/ (Luk.9:46-48)

The rule for all gospel preachers
Jesus who gave power to cast out demons and heal sickness to the disciples who were going out to preach the gospel, spoke about important rules they were to keep. "Since you received freely, give freely" (Mat. 10:8).

We come to a week before the crucifixion, which was the most important ministry Jesus was given to carry out in this world. At this important moment, Zebedee's wife, the mother of John and James came to Jesus and asked him for a favor. She thought that Jesus would become king of Jerusalem and so asked him to make her two sons the two highest ministers of his cabinet.

In those days there was a strong faith among the people of Israel that a Messiah would come, defeat the rule of Rome and again establish a strong Israel as the days of David. Many people in those days expected Jesus to do so.

However, despite the incorrections, Jesus was neither angry with James and John nor scolded them. **Jesus waited for the future days when they would be able to abandon their greed and dream a dream worthy for the kingdom of God.**

As time went by, the disciples including James and John realized that the LORD was patient with their behavior. The disciples who realized this great love of the LORD became the apostles who devoted themselves to preaching and practicing his love with their lives after his death and resurrection.

2. Entering Jerusalem riding on a donkey

Mat.21:1-11/ Mar.11:1-11/ Luk.19:28-40/ Joh.12:1-19

Having preached the kingdom of God and the gospel centering around Galilee, Jesus entered Jerusalem (the center of of Jewish politics and religion) to accomplish his last and most important mission.

Jesus rode on a donkey. Riding on a donkey had already been prophesied by Prophet Zechariah more than 500 years before. Why then did Jesus enter riding on a donkey?

The reason Jesus prepared a donkey was to be approachable to every person, because the children or old people would not be able to go near a big horse. However, many people were able to come close to Jesus who rode on a colt and spread their clothes and cut palm branches on the ground.

Another important reason Jesus rode on a donkey was his humility. In preparing a colt, he came near to people with a humble and meek heart, comforting, encouraging and establishing them.

Those who were humble

Moses: Moses, who knew how to get on his knees before God and man, had greater meekness than any other on the earth.

David: Though David was king, he called himself 'servant' before God.

Jesus: As prophesied by Zechariah, Jesus rode on a colt when entering Jerusalem.

Apostle Paul: He considered himself, "less than the least of all saints."

Hosanna (Mar.11:9)

The Hebrew word of "O LORD, save us"(Psa.118:25) in Psalms is 'Hosia na'. When this word was translated into other languages in the era of the New Testament, they used 'Hosanna' by transliterating 'Hosia na.' 'Hosanna' was the word lots of people shouted while waving the branches of palm tree to welcome Jesus as he was entering Jerusalem with the ministry of the cross ahead around the last part of his public life.

3. Cleansing the temple

Mat.21:12-46/ Mar.11:12-12:12/ Luk.19:41-48/ Joh.12:20-43 (2:13-25)

Upon entering Jerusalem, Jesus became angry with those who sold things in the temple. Saying that they had made the temple where all people pray into a den of robbers, he drove out all who were buying and selling there and overturned the tables of money changers and the benches of those selling doves. At this the associates of the high priest, who controlled the temple and enjoyed the profit coming from there, ran to him and argued asking, "By what authority are you doing these things? And who gave you authority to do this?"(Mar.11:28).

Jesus responded to their question with a question. "I will ask you one question. Answer me, and I will tell you by what authority I am doing these things. John's baptism, was it from heaven, or from men? Tell me!" (Mar.11:29-30). They consulted one another but it was not a question they could easily answer. They said, "We don't know." Then Jesus also said, "Neither will I tell you by what authority I am doing these things."

Tong Point

In front of the scale of justice

If anyone or anything gets far from the will of God, be it the temple of Jerusalem, he or it becomes an object of judgment. We should always be ready to welcome Jesus who is to come without fail.

4. Running into religious leaders

Mat. chap.22-23/ Mar.12:13-44/ Luk. chap.20-21:4 (11:37-54)

There were people who were stored misunderstanding and prejudice about Jesus' ministry. They were the high priest, teacher of the law and the Pharisees. They were hostile to and obstructed Jesus who shook the frame they had shaped and kept. They plotted to crucify Jesus by using Rome and systematically implemented it.

Jesus said;

"Woe to you, teachers of the law and Pharisees, you hypocrites! You clean the outside of the cup and dish, but inside they are full of greed and self-indulgence. Blind Pharisee! First clean the inside of the cup and dish, and then the outside also will be clean. "Woe to you, teachers of the law and Pharisees, you hypocrites! You are like whitewashed tombs, which look beautiful on the outside but on the inside are full of dead men's bones and everything unclean. In the same way, on the outside you appear to people as righteous but on the inside you are full of hypocrisy and wickedness" (Mat.23:25-28).

Sharing with themselves

The Pharisees in the days of Jesus gave many parties. Though they looked generous, actually they were deceptive. Because they only invited those who had ability to pay back. The Pharisees in those days lived with a thought that the quantity of wealth was a part of methods of measuring the magnitude of piety. In accordance with the thought of retributive justice, the storing up of wealth was regarded as God's response to their pious life. So they gave many parties to reveal their piety. Today they ate in that house and tomorrow they invited friends to their house, living with the way of giving and receiving.

5. Teaching about the last days

Mat. chap.24-25/ Mar. chap.13/ Luk.19:11-27; 21:5-38/ Joh.12:44-50

As Jesus got out of the temple, one disciple asked him what would happen to it. Jesus said that not one stone would be left on another. He said that even Jerusalem temple would become an object of God's judgment if it got far away from the will of God.

As Jesus foretold the events of suffering that was to come in the future, he asked his disciples to be patient and victorious. Nobody could know when Jesus would come again. We should always be ready to welcome him who will come suddenly at a certain moment without fail.

Tong Point

Passion which ripened through silence
Was there 'truth' in the trial of Pilate? There exists only the truth of Jesus who kept silence to save sinners. We remember that there exists only the truth of Jesus full of passion toward the cross he had long harbored in that silence.

6. The last supper

Mat.26:1-35/ Mar.14:1-31/ Luk.22:1-38/ Joh. chap.13-17

The LORD's Supper
Jesus himself commanded his disciples to commemorate the LORD's Supper in which saints commemorate the blood he shed on the cross and his torn body. It became an important ceremony of Christianity along with 'Baptism.' While he was having the Passover Supper, he performed this ceremony and indicated that he would be sacrificed like the Passover Lamb (Joh.1:29,I Co.5:7,Rev.5:6). During the LORD's Supper saints ate bread and drank wine, remembering the grace of forgiveness given through Jesus' shedding of blood and confirmed the union of saints who became brothers and sisters in Christ.

As Jesus' public life came almost to the end, the fellowship between Jesus and the disciples got deeper beyond limit.

Jesus knew that Judas Iscariot would betray him soon and Peter would deny him. The evening when Jesus and the disciples observed the Passover together, he prophesied that all of them would leave him. **However, the sense of him being betrayed by Judas Iscariot and the sense of his disappointment about Peter did not stop his love towards his people.**

We call Jesus' last meal with his disciples on the night of the Passover before his crucifixion 'the last supper.' It was an important time that symbolized the death of Jesus. The bread and wine that Jesus said stood for his flesh and blood have been commemorated by the church as communion (Luk.22:19-20).

Also that night Jesus girded a towel around his waist, poured water into a basin and washed the feet of his disciples one by one. He showed them the example of serving. **Then he gave the disciples a new command, "Love one another" and called them his friends (Joh.15:13-15).**

7. Jesus arrested

Mat.26:36-56/ Mar.14:32-52/ Luk.22:39-53/ Joh.18:1-11

Having finished the last supper, Jesus climbed Mt. Olive at night. Leaving other disciples a little far, allowed only Peter, John and James follow him. After he asked the three disciples "to stay here and keep watch with me", he went away a little distance and prayed in anguish and sorrow.

"Father, if you are willing, take this cup from me; yet not my will, but yours be done" (Luk.22:42).

Although the cross was what he came on earth to fulfill, at the same time it was also an extremely great and deep anguish for him. However, praying "not as I will, but as you will," Jesus decided to obey the will of God.

Finally, Judas Iscariot came close to him with the people who had clubs and swords in their hands. Saying "Rabbi!", Judas came to him and kissed him. Peter who got agitated cut the ear of a servant of the high priest called Malchus with a sword but Jesus healed his ear even during the moment he was being dragged off. The love of Jesus was indeed infinite.

Four representative prayers of Jesus

1. Fasted and prayed for forty days before starting his public life (Mat.4:1-2).
2. Prayed all night before choosing 12 disciples (Luk.6:12-13).
3. Prayed for himself and the disciples after washing their feet(Joh.chap.17).
4. Deeply prayed in Gethsemane ahead of his cross ministry (Mat.26:36-46).

8. Trial by Pontius Pilate

Mat.26:57-27:31/ Mar.14:53-15:20/ Luk.22:54-23:25/ Joh.18:12-19:16

After Jesus was arrested, he was dragged off to the house of the high priest (Luk.22:54). He was flogged and mocked all night. When it was dawn, he was dragged off to the Sanhedrin (Luk.22:66). Then again he was dragged off to Pilate (Luk.23:1).

Pilate asked, "Are you the king of the Jews?" Jesus answered, "Yes, it is as you say." Jesus never protested but kept silent about false charges made against him by the high priest and elders. If he defended himself there, his will to bear the cross would not have been carried out.

Judging that Jesus was innocent, Pilate sent him to Herod(Herod Antipas). Though Herod asked him many questions, Jesus did not answer. Herod also did not find any charge to put him to death.

Eventually, the trial against Jesus was sent back to Pilate and began again. Pilate gave him the opportunity to defend himself but Jesus kept silent. Then Pilate pulled out the card of amnesty according to the custom of feast. However, the crowds objected to releasing Jesus and rather shouted, "Release Barabbas to us! and Crucify Jesus! Crucify Jesus!" Undergoing mental conflict between innocent Jesus and the increasing clamor of violent crowds, finally Pilate sentenced Jesus to death for fear of a revolt.

Though the death sentence was made by Pilate, actually Jesus chose the cross on his accord. **In order to fulfill the purpose he came to this world for, Jesus silently walked toward the cross.**

Pontius Pilate

Pilate was the fifth governor appointed by the Roman emperor Tiberius for the land of Judea. He ruled the regions of Judea, Samaria and Idumea for ten years from A.D.26. According to the record of history he was a stubborn and cruel man. Around A.D.36, seven years after Jesus' crucifixion he was called back to Rome and made to resign.

Write down the contents of this lesson in the form of Tong Story

Let's pray in a loud voice so that we may be able to teach the contents of this lesson to our children

- Teach them to your children, talking about them when you sit at home and when you walk along the road, when you lie down and when you get up……so that your days and the days of your children may be many……as many as the days that the heavens are above the earth (Deuteronomy 11:19-21).
- you know those from whom you learned it, and how from infancy you have known the holy Scriptures(II Timothy 3:14-15).

15 Session

Invitation to Glory and Peace

Tong Map

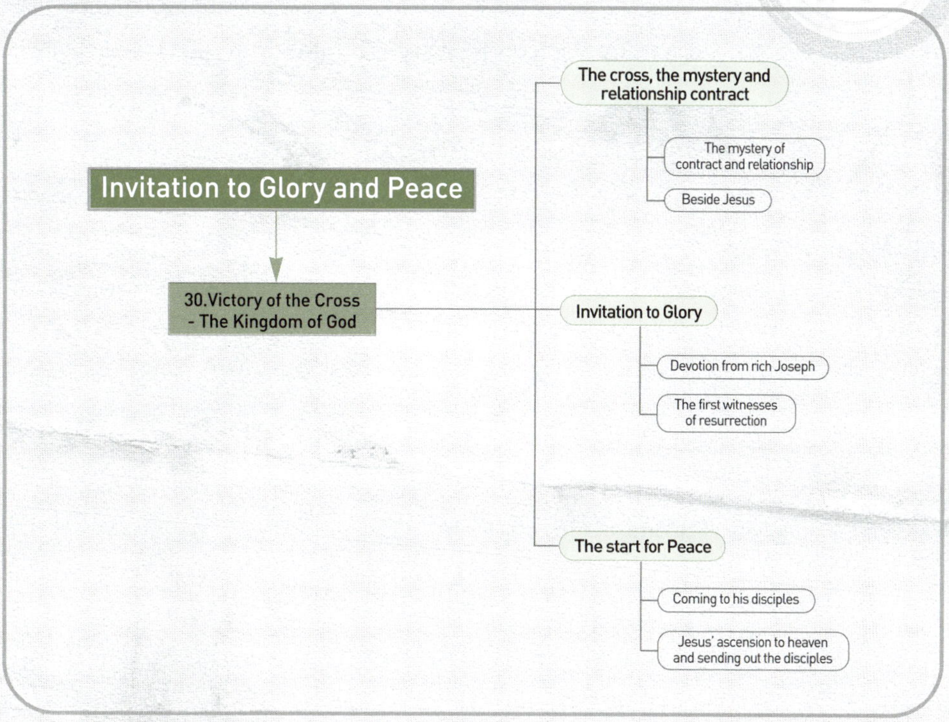

Tong Concept

- **The cross and resurrection**

The cross of Jesus was the place where the mysteries of God's justice, love, punishment, forgiveness, contract and relationship were harmonized. He, who willingly endured the suffering of the cross to pour down the grace, rose from the dead in three days by overcoming the power of death as he promised. Let's study with a focus on those contents.

- **Invitation to glory and peace**

He invited us to the world of glory and peace. Let's look at the course the disciples who experienced a new beginning of life.

Tong At a glance

* Looking around the forest

Jesus who rose from the dead first appeared to Mary Magdalene, other women and disciples in Jerusalem. As the two disciples of Jesus were on their way to Emmaus, they were stunned to see Jesus who rose from the dead. Jesus appeared to the disciples who went to the Sea of Tiberius to resume their old job after he died, as fisherman.

The disciples who went up to a mount in Galilee came to hear from Jesus about the duty of missions(Mat.28:16-20). Also, he took the disciples to Bethany, blessed them and ascended into heaven.

* Land and annual ring

After Jesus was seized, dragged around, interrogated and insulted, he eventually took up the cross to make the declaration, "It is finished."

Originally the chief priests had decided not to kill Jesus on this feast(Passover). However, Jesus decided to take up the cross on this feast. Incidentally, as Judas Iscariot betrayed Jesus, the decision of the chief priests was cancelled and they decided to kill him. It seems that they took the lead in the execution of the cross. Yet, the cross of Jesus was the plan of God from the beginning and the only way of saving us from sin.

* Wind and Climate

The people of the New Testament era had a deep interest in the world after death. Romans thought that souls were immortal and others who believed in mystical religions believed in gods who symbolised reincarnation. That was why there were people who thought that John the Baptist was the reincarnation of Elijah and Jesus.

His resurrection was an event in which he became the first fruit of the resurrection of all people. The resurrection of Jesus was the true victory we should sing.

Tong Seeing the forest

John's Gospel John wrote John's Gospel, I John, II John, III John and Revelation. He was asked by Jesus to take care of Mary (Jesus' mother) after he died on the cross. John carried out the duty very well to the end. He carried out the ministry the longest among Jesus' disciples. The conclusion he made after thinking over and over again was that 'God is love.'

This was because God could not give His only son to die for us unless He loved the world so much(Joh.3:16). John deeply realized this great love of God and wrote the John's Gospel.

John's Gospel has different characteristics in which other gospels do not have. Apostle John was the one who felt the humanliness of Jesus the most. Surprisingly, John's Gospel stressed the fact that Jesus was the Son of God. Just like Genesis, John's Gospel begins with the story of the beginning and introduces Jesus on the basis of deep spiritual knowledge.

30 Lesson Victory of the Cross - The Kingdom of God John's Gospel

Accumulative reading amount 86.28% 1189

The One Year Tongdok Bible Days 307-315 | Reading time 90 minutes

TongBible Story Overview

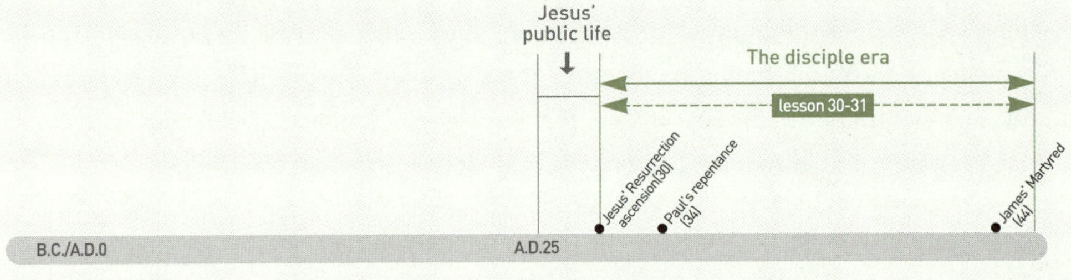

Reading the New Testament in detail in the order of history (4)

We read through John's Gospel which is the last 4 of the four gospels. After Jesus took up the cross on the hill of Golgotha and breathed his last, he rose from the dead on the third day after his burial. Then he came back to his disciples and restored them.

How to read John's Gospel and 'Victory of the Cross.'

The four gospels are divided into 'synoptic gospels' and John's Gospel separartely because the viewpoint of John's Gospel is different from that of the other three. The Sanhedrin which was the highest Jewish decision-making council was able to sentence the court cases of religious or civil matters of the Jews within their discretion of self-rule but were not able to sentence anybody to death. That was why Jesus was led to the courts of governor Pilate dispatched by Rome early on the morning of Friday. Before noon he was sentenced to death and crucified. Crucifixion was a Roman way of execution.

Six hours after Jesus was crucified(9A.M. to 3P.M.), he breathed his last and his body was buried before sunset; before Sabbath began. After Jesus was resurrected, the disciples began to get restored. The disciples who were scattered in despair began to gather in Jerusalem again. The death and resurrection of Jesus was not the end but indeed a new beginning.

Tong Point

The cross, the mystery and relationship contract

Seen as a contract, the cross was the place of punishment and judgment according to the contract that the price of sin was death(Rom.6:23). Since all the people had to die due to their sins, Jesus Christ the only begotten Son had to be crucified. However, the cross also contained the mystery of relationship. The cross was the place where contract, relationship, punishment, forgiveness, justice and love had been completed together. Therefore, let's remember that we should not see the cross from only one direction but from the two directions of contract and relationship through the method of Tong.

1. The mystery of contract and relationship

Mat.27:32-54/ Mar.15:21-39/ Luk.23:26-48/ Joh.19:17-37

The seven words of Jesus on the cross

1. Father, forgive them, for they do not know what they are doing (Luk.23:34).
2. I tell you the truth, today you will be with me in paradise (Luk.23:43).
3. Dear woman, here is your son. Behold. Here is your mother(Joh.19:26-27).
4. My God, my God, why have you forsaken me? (Mat.27:46; Mar.15:34).
5. I am thirsty(Joh.19:28).
6. It is finished(Joh.19:30).
7. Father, into your hands I commit my spirit (Luk.23:46).

Roman soldiers struck Jesus, put a crown of thorns on him, spat on him and struck his head with reeds. The chief priests, teacher of the law and the Jewish elders mocked Jesus who was hung on the cross, and said, "Come down now from the cross, and we will believe that you are the Son of God." The robbers who were also crucified beside him reviled Jesus. Jesus was hung on the cross for six hours enduring all the pain, anguish, being despised and mocked with his hands and feet nailed on the cross. The reason Romans nailed his hands and feet was to let the sinner die suffering most painfully since hands and feet were the farthest from the heart. Seeing Jesus suffering so much on the cross, someone tried to give him wine vinegar to reduce his pain but Jesus refused even that offer. Jesus' anguish was at its height. It was getting dark. Jesus loudly shouted, "Eloi, Eloi, lema sabachthani?"

"My God, my God, why have you forsaken me?" (Mat.27:46). When he had received the drink, Jesus said, "It is finished." With that, he bowed his head and gave up his spirit (Joh.19:30).

Jesus finished all. The life of him who loved poor souls, hungry souls and hurting souls came to an end like this.

We have been made children of God through the precious blood of the cross. The relationship that was cut off between God and man was perfectly connected by Jesus. The curtain of the tabernacle through which only priests came and went during the whole of the Old Testament had been torn from top to bottom. Now sacrifice through the blood of animals was not necessary any more. All the sin of mankind had been redeemed by the cross once and for all.

2. Beside Jesus

Mat.27:55-56/ Mar.15:40-41 Luk.23:49(8:1-3)/ Joh.19:25-27

Though all the disciples ran away while Jesus suffered on the cross, the women who followed him all the way from Galilee serving him watched him from afar to the end(Mat.27:55-56). Are there any other person more blessed than these women? In fact, these women were the ones who were able to watch the most beautiful moment in the world. They were the blessed ones who shared the moment when the love and justice of Jesus bloomed into red flowers.

Who is a Christian?

We are Christians. Who is a Christian? First, a Christian is someone who knows God's love and continues to know it. Second, a Christian is someone who knows the value of a life and continues to know it. Third, a Christian has received God's wonderful forgiveness and is practicing it. That we have become Christians is by the grace of God. The qualification of becoming a Christian can be obtained only through faith in Christ. On this foundation we can live dreaming true freedom, equality and justice.

3. Devotion from rich Joseph

Mat.27:57-66/ Mar.15:42-47/ Luk.23:50-56/ Joh.19:38-42

After Jesus did his best in preaching the kingdom of God for

The Joseph of Arimathea
The record about Joseph who buried the body of Jesus can be found in all four gospels (Mat.27:57-61, Mar.15:42-47, Luk.23:50-56, Joh.19:38-42). In Mark's Gospel is Joseph introduced as "a prominent member of the Council, who was himself waiting for the kingdom of God." According to the record of Mark he "boldly" went to Pilate and asked him for the body of Jesus. He buried Jesus in a new tomb where nobody had ever been buried.

three years during his public life, he died. But now there was no one to bury his body. All his disciples left him and no one was there. In this situation a rich man called Joseph of Arimathea volunteered. He went to Pilate and asked him for the body of Jesus. Asked by Joseph, Pilate gave him the body, perhaps because he thought that he could get some of Joseph's wealth in return for this event. Joseph also knew that he had to give the governor a considerable portion of his wealth. He was a person who knew where to use his wealth valuably.

After wrapping the body of Jesus in clean linen cloth, he placed it in a new tomb. How thankful we should be to Joseph for taking care of the body of our LORD Jesus who was to be raised from the dead soon.

4. The first witnesses of resurrection

Mat.28:1-15 / Mar.16:1-11/ Luk.24:1-12/ Joh.20:1-18

Before Jesus took up the cross, he had already said that he would rise again from the dead on the third day after his crucifixion (Mat.20:17-19). And as promised, he rose from the dead in three days. In three days he destroyed the power of darkness and became the first fruit of resurrection. The one who was blameless and flawless died and rose again from the dead. He came victorious and overcame the power of death.

However, none of the disciples who heard Jesus' promise of resurrection in person came to the venue of resurrection. Only two women, Mary Magdalene and the other Mary who perhaps heard about it indirectly came to the tomb on the first day after the Sabbath and met the LORD who rose from the dead. Jesus who rose from the dead said that he would meet his disciples in Galilee, not in Jerusalem.

5. Coming to his disciples

Mar.16:12-14/ Luk.24:13-43/ Joh.20:19-chap.21

Rose from the dead, Jesus came to the disciples who were depressed in despair and grief. By appearing to the disciples various times after resurrection, Jesus made them firmly believe that he was the living God. Simon Peter and some disciples were back in their hometown. They were catching fish from their boat in the Sea of Tiberias as they had done before they met Jesus. At that time Jesus came to them.

Silently seeing Jesus, John said, "O he looks like Jesus." Upon hearing that, Peter wrapped his outer garment around his body, jumped into the sea and swam toward Jesus. Although there was some shame left in Peter who denied Jesus saying he did not know him a while ago, still it was Peter who first ran to meet Jesus. Covering their shame, Jesus again started a new relationship with his disciples. **Like this, Jesus came to those who had shame and sorrow with wholehearted passion.**

Thomas
Unlike three other gospels, the name Thomas appears in John's gospel as often as three times (Joh.11:16; 14:5; 20:24-29). Although he doubted the resurrection of Jesus, he came to believe in the LORD truly after he met him himself.

6. Jesus' ascension to heaven and sending out the disciples

Mat.28:16-20/ Mar.16:15-20/ Luk.24:44-53

The disciples who seemed to be scattered due to Jesus' death

Jesus, The name of power
"The name of Jesus" was pride and the source of power for the disciples who received the Holy Spirit. In that name of Jesus, Peter and John helped a man up who could not walk.
The wonderful authority of this name was given to all who believe the name of Jesus Christ and practiced it (Joh.14:13-14).

began to gather in Jerusalem again. When Jesus was crucified, everything seemed to have ended but the disciples who experienced Jesus' resurrection now gathered again. Jesus asked the disciples;

"All authority in heaven and on earth has been given to me. Therefore go and make disciples of all nations, baptizing them in the name of the Father and of the Son and of the Holy Spirit, and teaching them to obey everything I have commanded you." (Mat.28:18-20). "You will receive power when the Holy Spirit comes on you; and you will be my witnesses in Jerusalem, and in all Judea and Samaria, and to the ends of the earth"(Act.1:8).

This word of will became the source of power which made the disciples never fear death but preach the gospel of the kingdom of God. It was through them that the history of Church began.

Write down the contents of this lesson in the form of Tong Story

Let's pray in a loud voice so that we may be able to teach the contents of this lesson to our children

- Teach them to your children, talking about them when you sit at home and when you walk along the road, when you lie down and when you get up……so that your days and the days of your children may be many……as many as the days that the heavens are above the earth (Deuteronomy 11:19-21).
- you know those from whom you learned it, and how from infancy you have known the holy Scriptures(II Timothy 3:14-15).

Track 5 THE 4 GOSPELS

Track 6
30 years of Acts

Tong Track 6 - The atmosphere of the 30 years of Acts

The atmosphere of the 30 years of Acts is that of the extension of the Gospel from Jerusalem to the end of the world amidst the opposition between the priests and apostles. Throughout the New Testament, despite being ruled by Rome, its emperor, its governors and even Herod the king of Judah, the High Priests of Jerusalem exercised great power.

It was their manipulation of Rome which crucified Jesus. But after Jesus' death, his disciples became apostles and were even more energetic in spreading the stories of the Kingdom of God.

"Annas the high priest was there, and so were Caiaphas, John, Alexander and the other men of the high priest's family. They had Peter and John brought before them and began to question them: "By what power or what name did you do this?" Then Peter, filled with the Holy Spirit, said to them: "Rulers and the elders of the people! If we are being called to account today for an act of kindness shown to a cripple and are asked how he was healed, the know this, you and all the people of Israel: It is by the name of Jesus Christ of Nazareth, whom you crucified but whom God raised from the dead, that this man stands before you healed" (Act.4:6-10).

As such, from Acts 4 onwards, the apostles opposed the High Priest and his followers whilst preaching the gospel. The atmosphere of the 30 years of Acts is again different to the atmosphere of the 4 gospels; full of power and enthusiasm.

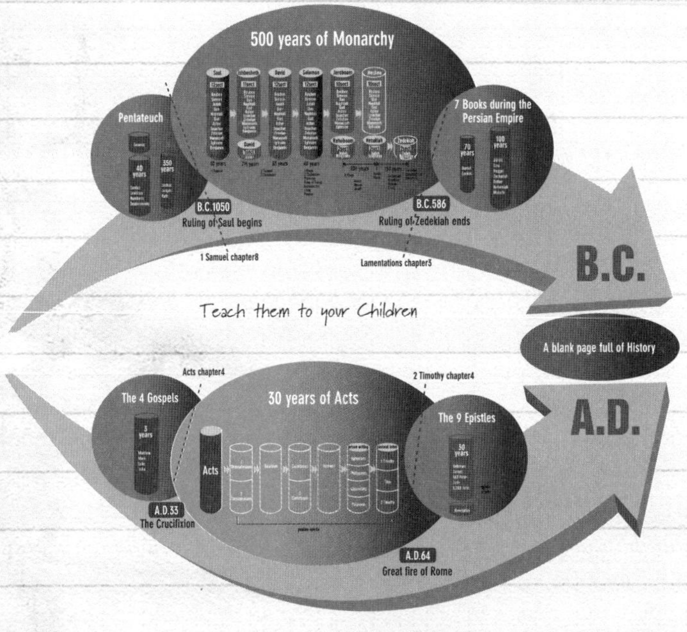

16 Session

The Disciple Era

Tong Map

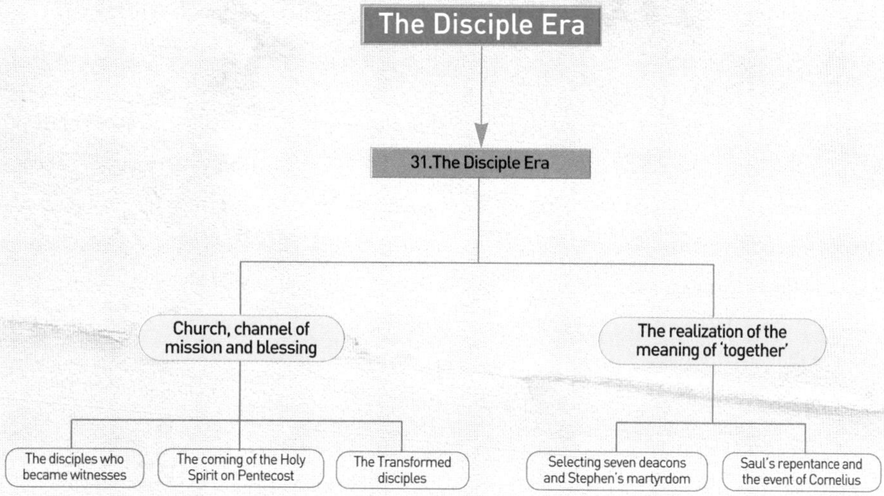

Tong Concept

- **The Disciple Era**

The Era of world missions was unfolded by the disciples who made the will of Jesus their vision. Let's observe with focus on the following contents.

- The activity of apostles including Peter
- The activity of seven deacons including Stephen and Philip
- The meaning of 'together' they finally realized through the event of Cornelius
- Apostle Paul called to be the apostle for the Gentiles

Track 6 30 YEARS OF ACTS

Tong At a glance

* Looking around the forest

Acts chapters 1-12 are the portion which was recorded with focus on Jerusalem Church and the ministry of Peter. Particulary, the event of meeting between Peter and Cornelius the Roman centurion appearing in Acts chapter 10 was very important which became a groundwork of opening the door of the ministry of Apostle Paul.

As Deacon Stephen was martyred and Apostle James was martyred by Herod (Herod Agrippa I), the gospel spreaded everywhere. Now the era of world missions began to unfold.

* Land and annual ring

We can say that the duration that became the chronological background of Acts was about 30 years, provided that Jesus ascended into heaven and the Holy Spirit came down on Pentecost in A.D.30 and Apostle Paul was put into Roman prison and wrote prison letters around A.D.61. This period was a very important period of change in Christianity. The Gospel was preached to the Jews only in the beginning and the early chruch was made up of mostly Jews. However, gradually the Gentiles also came to believe and accept the gospel. The community agreed to accept the Gentiles as Christians through Jerusalem Council of Acts chapter 15. This way Christianity came to be officially torn away from Judaism.

* Wind and Climate

Palestine in the days of Acts was under the rule of Rome. In those days the Roman Emperor was Tiberius(A.D.14-37). The Judean region was ruled by the Roman governor. From the last days of Jesus' life to the days of the early church it was ruled by Pontius Pilate(A.D.26-36), Marchelus(A.D.37-39) and Herod Agrippa I(A.D.39-44). It was none other than Herod Agrippa I who was mentioned as 'King Herod' in Acts 12:1 who martyred James the brother of John.

After Stephen and James were martyred, the gospel did not stay only in Jerusalem but rather was expanded, and Antioch Church (which was the center of Gentile missions) was established.

Tong Seeing the forest

Acts The Acts of the Apostles introduced the activity of the Holy Spirit who worked fully in the early church. After Jesus rosed to heaven, power appeared in the early church where the Holy Spirit came upon as promised, and wonderful changes happened such as believers loving one another and boldly preaching the gospel. It records in detail the process in which eventually the gospel was preached starting from Jerusalem in all Judea, Samaria and so on through the help of the Holy Spirit and dedication of the people chosen by God. Since the writer of Acts was doctor Luke who accompanied Paul in his missionary journey, the second half of the Acts was recorded with the ministry of Apostle Paul as center.

31 Lesson

The Disciple Era

Acts chap.1-12

Accumulative reading amount 87.5% 1189

The One Year Tongdok Bible Days 316-319 | Reading time 35 minutes

TongBible Story Overview

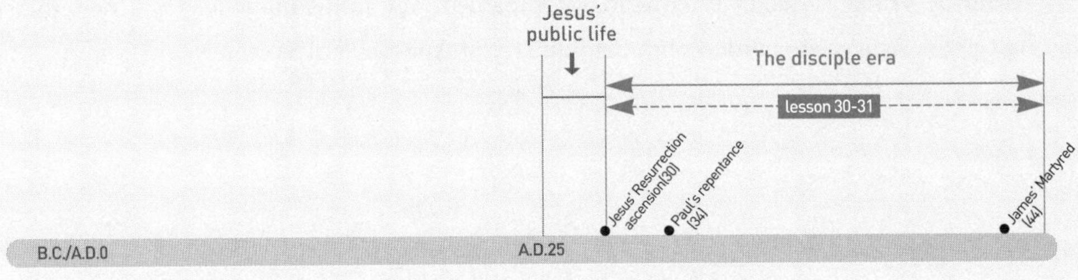

Reading the New Testament in detail in the order of history (5)

After Jesus went up to heaven, the ministry of the disciples left was launched. First, we read through Acts chapters 1 to 12. After the disciples who were called to be witnesses received the Holy Spirit on the day of Pentecost, they began to testify the gospel boldly. The gospel was made to be preached as far as Samaria beyond Jerusalem and Judea.

How to read the Disciple Era

Luke was both a physician and historian. He devoted himself to preaching the gospel all his life after meeting Paul.

Through the Acts Luke wrote, we can understand the beginning of the early church, its process of expansion and the working of the Holy Spirit who made the gospel spread to Jerusalem, all Judea, Samaria and to the ends of the earth.

Tong Point

Church, channel of mission and blessing
In Jerusalem was launched the Church, which preached the gospel of God's grace demonstrating power in the name of Jesus, by the disciples who received the Holy Spirit.

1. The disciples who became witnesses Act.chap.1

● The birth of disciple generation

Jesus left his will, "you will receive power when the Holy Spirit comes on you; and you will be my witnesses in Jerusalem, and in all Judea and Samaria, and to the ends of the earth" (Act.1:8), and went up to heaven.

● Aligning organization

In order to start fresh, the disciples chose another disciple in place of Judas Iscariot. First, Joseph and Matthias were recommended. Then after prayer they cast lots and the fell to Matthias. It was a method in which human choice and faith in the providence of God were harmonized.

The Acts of the Apostles and Christianity

The Acts is the central book which explores changes of Christianity

Stepping stones	Classification
From the gospels to the books of letter	History
From Judaism to Christianity	Religion
From law to grace	God's working
From only Jews to Jews and Gentiles	The people of God
From the kingdom of God to church	The plan of God

2. The coming of the Holy Spirit on Pentecost Act.chap.2

As requested by Jesus, "Do not leave Jerusalem, but wait for the gift my Father promised, which you have heard me speak about," the disciples gathered in one place and devoted themselves to prayer.

As said by Jesus, the Holy Spirit came down. The disciples began to preach 'the wonders of God'. It was Pentecost when the people from many foreign countries filled Jerusalem. On the day of Pentecost a wonderful work of God happened; 3,000 people heard Peter preach and repented. The apostles performed miracles and signs, boldly preached the word of the LORD and the number of people being saved increased daily.

When the Holy Spirit comes
Jesus was taken up to heaven and the Holy Spirit came. The promise he gave his disciples before his crucifixion (Joh.16:7) was fulfilled. When Peter who was filled with the Holy Spirit preached that Jesus was Christ, 3,000 people repented.

3. The Transformed disciples Act. chap.3-5

● The apostles who became channels

One day while Peter and John were on their way to the temple to pray, they saw a man crippled from birth begging at the gate called Beautiful and healed him in the name of Jesus. The name of Jesus of Nazareth became the power to heal him. To the people who saw this and gathered, Peter again preached the news of death and resurrection of Jesus Christ.

● Without fear

Priests, Sadducees and religious leaders became displeased about the changes and as a result seized the people involved as well as keeping them in custody. Though they were put in the Sanhedrin by force, they preached the name of Jesus boldly and fearlessly. They proclaimed that Jesus was the Son of God and the Savior of all the world.

Teachers of the law and elders tried to stop the disciples but failed. **The ministry of Jesus did not end with his death on**

Church
In spite of the persecution of the priests and teachers of the law, the apostles "never stopped teaching and proclaiming the good news that Jesus is the Christ" (Act.5:42). Therefore, this great system called church was able to be continued until today.

the cross but strengthened with his resurrection and the testimony of the disciples.

Tong Point

The realization of the meaning of 'together'
The disciples finally realized the meaning of 'together'. Let's remember that this way Jerusalem Church came to stand as 'Church for all nations'; the true identity as church.

4. Selecting seven deacons and Stephen's martyrdom Act.chap.6-8

Seven deacons of the early church
Stephen, Philip, Procorus, Nicanor, Timon, Parmenas, Nicolas

● The occasion of choosing seven deacons

There was one complaint during the early church where the Holy Spirit worked so powerfully that 3,000 or 5,000 people were transformed in a day. It was about 'the matter of eating.' There arose complaints amongst the people about the inequality of food distribution.

As such crisis took place in the early Jerusalem church, the disciples first considered why this crisis happened and found out that equal care was not realized.

Creative Alternative
When problems happened within the early church, the apostles responded to this in a wise manner. They first appointed 'the people' who were able to carry out the work responsively rather than renewing the existing method of relief or making new rules and the like.
Appointing the rightful people well was wisdom. The creative alternative of apostles was none other than 'the people'.

So the Apostles chose seven persons from within the community who would be able to carry out these problems. **The standard of choosing these seven deacons were "people who were known to be full of the Spirit and wisdom" and "people who were praised by others." This way seven deacons were appointed and they led the early church by playing their roles in cooperation with the twelve disciples.**

● Stephen's martyrdom

Stephen, one of the seven deacons became the first martyr of Christianity. Although a full scale persecution against the church began with Stephen's martyrdom, this event became the point in which the gospel spread around the world.

5. Saul's repentance and the event of Cornelius

Act. chap.9-12

● Saul's repentance

When Stephen was martyred, there was a man who thought that people like Stephen needed to be killed and imprisoned. This man was none other than Saul, who was to be transformed into Apostle Paul.

Paul met Jesus on his way to Damascus to seize believers in Jesus and put them into prison. As Paul was under going preparation, now the gospel was made to be spread to the Gentiles beyond the Jews.

● The event of Cornelius

However, there was a part which needed to be prepared beforehand so that Paul's ministry for the Gentiles could be carried out effectively. This was is the event of Cornelius shown in Acts chapter 10.

Cornelius was a Roman centurion and a righteous man. He feared God and devoted himself to relief work. He wanted to know God and do his will all the more. Therefore, he invited Peter. When Peter arrived at his house, he knelt before him.

Cornelius
Prayer and relief were combined in unison in Cornelius. Just as the right hand and the left hand work properly and freely in a body, the fact that prayer and relief were so well combined in him deserved to be a great model for people around him.

Abolishing discrimination
Though people judge others by outward appearance, God does not see or judge by appearance. This was said by Jesus many times when he was in this world. Jesus showed by his life that it was not right to discriminate people by gender, color of skin and the matter of wealth or poverty, that is, that God does not show favoritism.

Unlike Cornelius, Peter was very reluctant to go to his house. This was because he had a deeply rooted sense of discrimination about the Gentiles and the Jews. However, the Holy Spirit woke him up. Seeing the Gentiles receiving the Holy Spirit his prejudice of distinguishing the elect from the Gentiles dissolved. At last, the door was opened for all the people of the world to be called to become Christians.

Write down the contents of this lesson in the form of Tong Story

Let's pray in a loud voice so that we may be able to teach the contents of this lesson to our children

- Teach them to your children, talking about them when you sit at home and when you walk along the road, when you lie down and when you get up……so that your days and the days of your children may be many……as many as the days that the heavens are above the earth (Deuteronomy 11:19-21).
- you know those from whom you learned it, and how from infancy you have known the holy Scriptures(II Timothy 3:14-15).

17 Session

Extension of the Gospel with no Boundaries

Tong Map

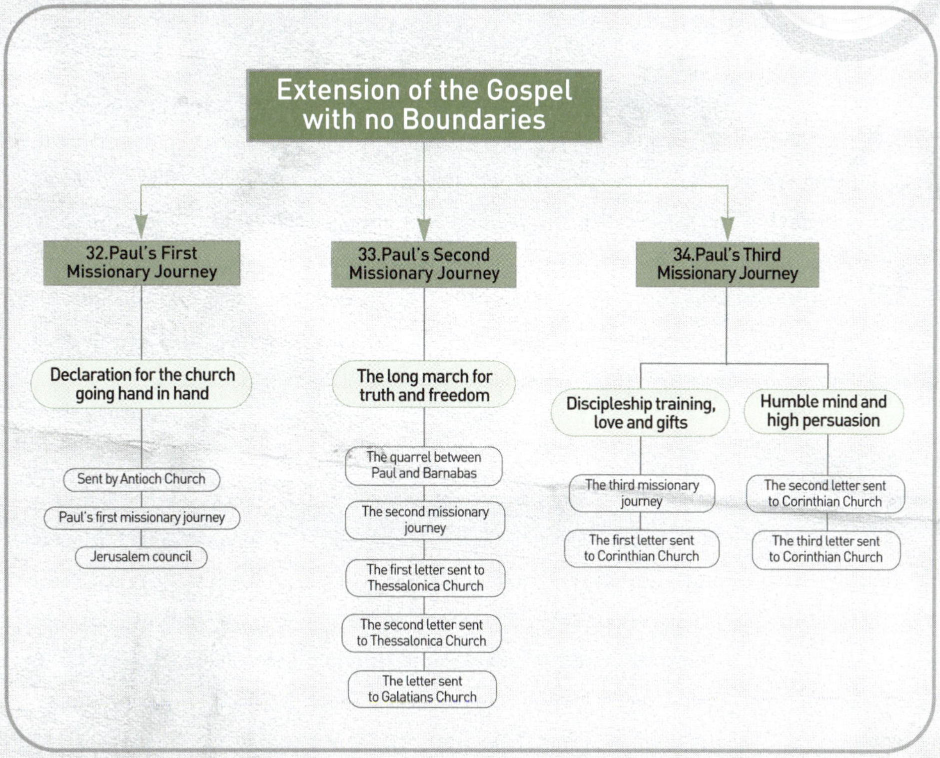

Tong Concept

- **Apostle Paul's Missionary Journey**

Apostle Paul launched the missionary journey with fellow workers. The gospel was expanded to the Gentile land beyond the boundary of Judea. We'll review with focus on the incidents that happened in each place of the missionary journey.

- **Apostle Paul's missionary journey and his letters in Tong!**

We observe the course of missionary journey by connecting Acts and letters in the order of history.

Acts	Letters	Apostle Paul's missionary journey	Lesson
chap.13-15:35		The first missionary journey	32
15:36-18:22	I Th., II Th., Gal.	Second missionary journey & letters	33
18:23-chap.19	I Co., II Co.	Third missionary journey & letters	34

Tong At a glance

＊ Looking around the forest

The disciples of Jesus who finally realized the meaning of 'together' through the event related to Cornelius now began to preach the gospel to the Gentiles. Apostles and elders who met together in Jerusalem after the first missionary journey decided not to bother Gentile believers with the frame of the law but to embrace them. Afterwards, Paul went on the second and third missionary journey with fellow workers. During the journey he heard that various happenings arose in the churches where he had preached. He ended up writing numerous letters of comfort as well as teachings.

First, he wrote to the Thessalonian church members that Jesus would come again without fail, and he taught them not to be tempted by idols in their daily lives. Writing to Galatian church, he said that all people were one in Jesus Christ and strongly advised them that there could be no condition in believing the gospel of Jesus at heart and being saved. Within the Church of Corinth, there were divisions. This church was noisy with moral problems, sexual problems and the like. About these he advised them by writing I & II Corintians. Through his letter in Romans he revealed that he wanted to be supported by the Roman Church to preach the gospel to Spain via Rome. At the time, Spain was regarded as the end of the world.

＊ Land and annual ring

The missionary journey Paul and Barnabas had set off to Asia Minor, being sent by Antioch Church, was called the first missionary journey (around A.D.46-48). After Paul and Barnabas who had finished such a long journey returned to Antioch(A.D.49), Jerusalem Council was held. Paul's second missionary journey started at Antioch as the first journey and it took about three years (A.D.50-52). Through this journey Paul came to be able to preach the gospel in Europe. Meanwhile, during his second missionary journey, Paul wrote I Thessalonians in Corinth around A.D.51-52. In those days Thessalonica was a prosperous harbor city in Macedonia (Europe). It was thought that Galatians was written at the early stage of Paul's ministry. Paul's third missionary journey is recorded from Acts 18:23 to 21:16 and it lasted about four years from A.D.53.

＊ Wind and Climate

Corinth was an important commercial center in the southern Greece. The city's population was as many as 600,000. So, this city was full of with shrines and temples where they served all kinds of gods with fornication. In Corinth were prevalent commerce and corruption. In those days the saying, "Behave like Corinthians" was synonymous to "be licentious."

Tong Seeing the forest

I Thessalonians Thessalonica was the city from which Paul was forced to be driven away due to the threat of the Jews while he preached the gospel. However, the seed of the gospel was sown there, took root and finally a church was born. It was this letter to the Thessalonians that Paul wrote to Thessalonian church members to encourage them to overcome difficulties and hardships with their expectation and hope for Jesus who would come again. The early church had more imminence in preaching the gospel while holding to the word of Jesus who said he would come again soon as he was taken up to heaven. However, as the time of Jesus' second coming delayed, their wonder about his second coming began to increase. Hearing this news, Paul wrote this letter of encouragement to them saying that Jesus would come without fail.

II Thessalonians The most serious problem in the church in Thessalonica was the 'theory of end-coming;' that Jesus would come soon due to this. Lots of saints neglected their daily routine life and became confused. Perhaps, it was the result of some having read Paul's first letter and amplified only a few verses. Paul said that although Jesus would come again without fail, we cannot know the exact time. He strongly admonished them to live everyday faithfully.

Galatians Paul sent a letter to the church in the region of Galatia. He heard the news that a false gospel came into the church of Galatia. They were Jewish legalists who claimed that people should be circumcised in order for salvation. They claimed that people should keep the law to be saved.
However, there was no condition in the gospel of Jesus Christ. Those who stressed the law still judged the people by outward appearance. They distinguished free people from slaves, men from women, the circumcised from the uncircumcised and included these things in the conditions for receiving the grace of God. In this letter is vividly described the passion and determination of Paul who tried to preserve the gospel of Jesus Christ while resisting the logic of these people.

I Corinthians News about Corinthian church reached Paul who was in Ephesus. It was none other than the news that Corinthian church members were divided into the sect of Paul, the sect of Apollos, the sect of Peter and the sect of Christ and stood against each other in conflict. I Corinthians was Paul's answer to the division of church and its various problems that appeared in the lives of saints.

Church was divided because people judged others with their own "wisdom". Paul stressed that when church admit God's wisdom rather than the wisdom of man, small difference of each other disappears. Chapter thirteen of I Corinthians, which describes love in detail that unites one another, is famous for being the 'Chapter of love.'

II Corinthians To Paul who, after sending his first letter to Corinthians wrote for the good news that the community would be harmonious, came the news that instead of their problems being solved, some people in the community questioned 'Paul's Apostleship' and attacked him. Since Paul's apostleship was questioned and it could have affected even the gospel he preached, he boldly and frankly confessed that he was an Apostle. He also confessed about the sufferings he went through while preaching the gospel. This letter can be found in chapters 10-13. II Corinthians chapters 1-9 was the letter in which he expressed gratitude and joy to Corinthian church members who repented after receiving the second letter.

32 Lesson

Paul's First Missionary Journey

Acts chap.13-15:35

Accumulative reading amount 88.02% 1189

The One Year Tongdok Bible Day 320 | Reading time 15 minutes

TongBible Story Overview

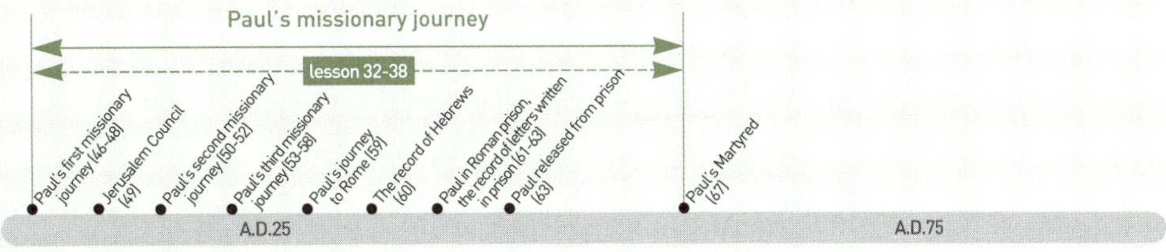

Reading the New Testament in detail in the order of history (6)

Next, we go on to read Acts chapter 13 to 15:35. Here are recorded the first missionary journey of Paul and Barnabas sent by Antioch Church and the outcome of Jerusalem Council.

How to read Paul's first missionary journey

Paul and Barnabas were sent by Antioch Church and went on a missionary journey centering around Asia Minor. This is called the first Missionary Journey(around A.D.46-48).

Paul and Barnabas finished this missionary journey and returned to Antioch (A.D.49) and then a meeting was held which was very important within Christian history. It was the Jerusalem Council. In this meeting, the early church declared separation from Judaism and that salvation was realized not by the law but by faith in Jesus Christ.

Tong Point

Declaration for the church going hand in hand
Antioch Chruch became an advance camp for mission for the Gentiles. You may think that it was a base camp for all missionary journeys of Paul. Let's remember that Jerusalem Council held that the first missionary journey was eventually "Declaration for the church to go hand in hand."

1. Sent by Antioch Church Act.13:1-3

Those who were scattered due to Stephen's martyrdom went to Antioch and preached the gospel to the Greeks. The Christians who received the seed of the gospel began to gather in Antioch. Jerusalem church which heard this news sent Barnabas to Antioch. At this time Barnabas went to Paul who was staying in Tarsus and brought him with him and began ministry together (Act.11:25).

Sent by Antioch church, Paul and Barnabas began their first missionary journey. In the beginning they preached the gospel to the Jews centering around the synagogue of each region but soon Paul came to minister to the Gentiles along with various fellow workers. Everywhere they went, the gospel of life went to spread.

Barnabas
Jerusalem church did not believe Paul's repentance easily. At this time Barnabas became a stepping stone and helped Paul. Since he sold a considerable quantity of his wealth and offered it to the church, perhaps he had a strong say in the early church. Barbabas believed and trusted Paul and became the foundation of Paul's ministry.

2. Paul's first missionary journey Act.13:4-chap.14

● Cyprus (Act.13:4-12)

Paul, Barnabas and Mark (real name: John - Barnabas' nephew) made their way to Cyprus, the hometown of

Barnabas. For the first time they preached the gospel in the synagogue of Salamis in Cyprus. Though a false Jewish prophet called Bar-Jesus obstructed them in Paphos in the middle of the island, one good news was that proconsul Sergius Paulus accepted the gospel. However, during the trip, Mark returned to Jerusalem in Perga. The missionary journey he set out with passion was too tough for him.

● Pisidian Antioch(Act.13:13-52)

After Paul's group reached Pisidian Antioch, they worshipped in the synagogue on Sabbath. At that time Paul testified that the history of Israel was oriented toward Jesus from Exodus to the times of Jesus. Many people in Antioch decided to follow what Paul said. They asked him to preach the next Sabbath also and many heard the word.

However, not all accepted the gospel. The Jews who misunderstood Jesus because of their intensive sense of being elected by God deliberately opposed Paul and Barnabas. They persecuted Paul and Barnabas by agitating the noble women and the powerful in the city and then drove them out of the city.

● Iconium (Act.14:1-7)

When Paul and Barnabas reached Iconium and entered the synagogue of the Jews and preached the gospel, many people in Iconium received the LORD. However, here also the Jews who did not believe in the LORD prevented them from preaching the gospel. The Jews came up to them to stone them. Eventually Paul's company left and went to Lystra.

● Lystra (Act.14:8-20)

In Lystra Paul performed the miracle of making a man crippled from birth walk. Seeing this, people said that gods came down, called Barnabas 'Zeus' and Paul 'Hermes' and tried to sacrifice to them. Shocked by this, the two apostles tore their clothes, narrowly dissuaded them from doing so and testified that it was not they but God who did it. But those who obstructed Paul's ministry in Antioch and Iconium came as far as Lystra. They obstructed the ministry of Paul and Barnabas, agitated the people, and dragged him off out of the city thinking he was dead. **Even stoned almost to death, Paul got up again and went to Derbe the next day to preach the gospel. Indeed he was a passionate man. As he was being stoned, maybe Paul thought of the scene of Stephen being stoned to martyrdom in front of him.**

The summary of Paul's first missionary journey

- Set out after being sent by Antioch church in Syria
- Preached the gospel in Salamis of the island of Cyprus
- Preached the gospel in Pisidian Antioch
- Preached the gospel in Iconium
- Preached the gospel in Lystra
- Preached the gospel in Derbe
- Visited again the cities he had visited
- Returned to Antioch in Syria and visited Jerusalem.

● Returning to Antioch(Act.14:21-28)

Paul visited Lystra, Iconium, Antioch and called the leaders who took care of church and told them, "We must go through many hardships to enter the kingdom of God." He stressed that there was suffering along with joy given from the gospel. Then Paul went to Perga through Pisidian Antioch and preached the gospel there, then again sailed back from Attalia to Syria Antioch and reported on the missionary journey. In this report Paul stressed "all that God had done through them and how He had opened the door of faith to the Gentiles."

Apostle Paul

Paul's name orignally was Saul in Aramaic and Paulus in Latin. Therefore, we call him Paul. He was born as Roman citizen. He said to a commander of thousand in Jerusalem "I am a Jew, from Tarsus in Cilicia, a citizen of no ordinary city"(Acts 21:39). He inherited an abundant Jewish legacy and was a successor of prospering Greek culture. He was "circumcised on the eighth day after birth, of the people of Israel, of the tribe of Benjamin, a Hebrew of Hebrews; in regard to the law, a Pharisee; as for zeal, persecuting the church; as for legalistic righteousness, faultless." He studied under Gamaliel who was a famous Pharisee in Jerusalem.

3. Jerusalem council Act.15:1-35

Paul, who finished the first missionary journey and returned to Antioch, went to Jerusalem. This was because there was an issue they had to solve for Gentile regions which was to be continued onto future.

A few Christians who had been Pharisees and came to believe in Jesus visited Antioch church and taught about the Old Testament and laws. But the problem was that they told the church members of Antioch who did not know the laws that they were in order to be circumcised to become the children of God by faith in Jesus. Among the members of Antioch church arose those who were not able to easily accept this matter.

Since this matter could not be solved within the Antioch church itself, eventually Antioch church asked Jerusalem church to resolve this matter. They asked them to reply correctly as to whether they could be saved by keeping the law of Moses including circumcision or whether they could be saved just by believing in the cross and the resurrection of Jesus Christ.

Receiving this matter, the leaders of Jerusalem church had a long discussion. Peter stoods up and testified to the event of Cornelius. He was followed by Paul and Barnabas who also talked about their mission for Gentiles they experienced in person. Finally James (Jesus' brother) who can be said to have been the chairman of the meeting at that time concluded;

"He made no distinction between us and them.", "We believe it is through the grace of our LORD Jesus that we are saved, just as they are." He said that the observance of circumcision or law could not become the standard of salvation. This was to clearly put in order the matter of distinguishing the elect from the Gentiles that had been handed down for 2000 years. **Now, it was no longer necessary to distinguish the Jews from the Gentiles in Christianity. It was not the will of Jesus that the people of Israel thought themselves as superior and elected by God that they thought the gospel of Jesus Christ was only for Israel. Our LORD Jesus already expressed his will for the gospel to be preached to the ends of the earth.**

Although the decisions made at Jerusalem council were conveyed through letters also, officially the four people, Judas, Silas, Barnabas and Paul came down to Antioch and conveyed the result of the council. Hearing this, the Gentile church members of Antioch were pleased.

The boundary between heaven and earth was broken down because Jesus was crucified on the cross. Because of the decision of Jerusalem council, the wall between the elect and the Gentiles that was built by the Jews was destroyed. The conclusion of Jerusalem council gave a great joy to not only Antioch church but also the second and the third Gentile churches.

Classification between the Gentiles and the chosen people

Long ago God gave Abraham the promise that "all the peoples of the earth will be blessed through you" (Gen.12:3). Abraham lived all his life with this promise of God. Then, God made Israel who got out of Egypt the kingdom of priests (Exo.19:5-6). Therefore, the nation of Israel naturally became the channel of blessing for all the nations. However, the descendants of Israel gradually missed the core and were captured by a prejudiced thought of chosen people.

Write down the contents of this lesson in the form of Tong Story

Let's pray in a loud voice so that we may be able to teach the contents of this lesson to our children

- Teach them to your children, talking about them when you sit at home and when you walk along the road, when you lie down and when you get up……so that your days and the days of your children may be many……as many as the days that the heavens are above the earth (Deuteronomy 11:19-21).
- you know those from whom you learned it, and how from infancy you have known the holy Scriptures(II Timothy 3:14-15).

33 Lesson

Paul's Second Missionary Journey

Acts 15:36-18:22, I Thessalonians, II Thessalonians, Galatians

Accumulative reading amount 89.24% 1189

The One Year Tongdok Bible Days 321-325 | Reading time 35 minutes

TongBible Story Overview

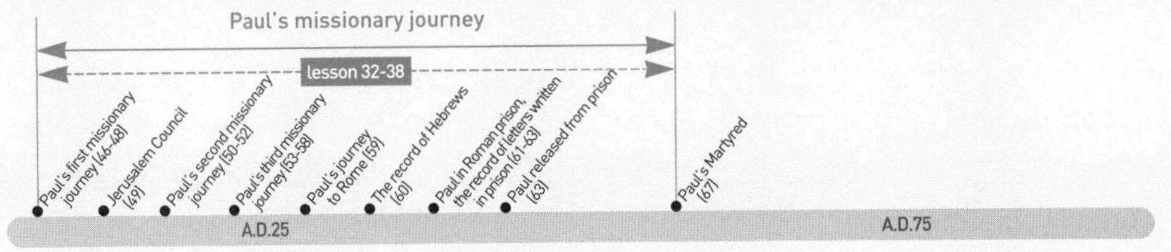

Reading the New Testament in detail in the order of history (7)

Next, we come to the second missionary journey of Paul. We read Acts 15:36-18:22. Then we read through I and II Thessalonians written by Paul while he stayed in Corinth as his last part of the second journey. We also read Galatians which was one of his early letters.

How to read Paul's second missionary journey

Like the first missionary journey, Paul's second missionary journey started in Antioch and it took about three years. Through this journey, Paul came to be able to preach the gospel from Asia as far as Europe. Meanwhile, during Paul's second missionary journey, he wrote I Thessalonians while staying in Corinth. It is thought that Galatians was written at the early stage of his ministry. It was a letter sent to the Galatia region. It reminds the readers of the decisions by the council of Jerusalem and stressed that they were not be shaken by what the Jewish legalists said but take firm roots in the gospel which was only by faith.

Tong Point

The long march for truth and freedom

Dreaming of the next missionary journey after the first one is indeed admirable. The two men who had experienced how difficult the journey was to set out for that journey again with passion for the gospel. This passion should be the prerequisite for all missionary journeys. However, the two men who agreed on this second journey came to separate from each other. It was because of 'Mark.' Barnabas insisted on taking Mark with them while Paul opposed it. The two finally decided to have following missionary teams.

- Barnabas and Mark: Cyprus
- Paul and Silas: Syria and Cilicia

1. The quarrel between Paul and Barnabas Act.15:36-41

Even after Paul decided to serve Jesus Christ as the LORD, it was not easy for him to enter the church, due to many people who doubted his repentance thinking it might be false since his past was so hostile to Christ. But Barnabas recommended Paul. The people of the early church accepted Paul on the basis of their trust in Barnabas due to his noble personality and his great contribution to the early church. Therefore, for Paul, Barnabas was a thankful benefactor. However, as they were going to leave for their second missionary journey after the first, they decided to take separate paths because of 'the matter of Mark.'

Mark gave up and returned during the previous first missionary journey. Now at the point when they were going to start their second missionary journey, Barnabas proposed that they take Mark again with them. The opinion of Barnabas who proposed that they gave another opportunity to Mark as an evangelist and the opinion of Paul who opposed it and thought they should not take him ran into each other. **It seems that Paul considered thoroughness important in the ministry of the gospel and Barnabas considered generosity important.** Their quarrelling was not for personal benefits. The two claims were in bitter tug-of-war. Eventually they agreed to form two separate evangelistic teams. So Barnabas went to Cyprus with Mark and Paul went to Syria and Cilicia with Silas. After this, Barnabas is not mentioned in Acts but we can guess that he also had a precious ministry.

Perhaps there was some sense of emptiness in the mind of Paul who left for the second missionary journey without being accompanied by Barnabas. However, Paul left with a strong step for the gospel along with new fellow workers such as Silas.

2. The second missionary journey Act.chap.16-18:22

● Re-visit to the places of the first missionary journey (Act.16:1-5)

As Paul launched the second missionary journey, he went with have a precious companion. He was a young Greek youth called Timothy, whose mother was a Jew and whose father a Greek. He was praised by people in his neighborhood. Paul's company went around the places where they visited around on his first journey, told them the contents of the decisions made at Jerusalem Council and helped the church to be able to stand right.

● God's calling to Macedonia (Act.16:6-10)

Paul's first plan was go back to and see the regions of the first missionary journey and again, make the churches stand firm as well as preach the gospel around the Asia Minor region. However, this will of Paul was not permitted by the Holy Spirit (Act.16:6-7). Paul saw the vision of Macedonia in Troas and then went to Macedonia, which he was not familiar with, for mission for the Europe region.

● Philippi(Act.16:11-40)

The summary of Paul's second missionary journey

- Visited again the places of his first missionary journey
- Was called to Macedonia
- Preached the gospel in Philippi
- Preached the gospel in Thessalonica
- Preached the gospel in Berea
- Preached the gospel in Athens
- Preached the gospel in Corinth
- Preached the gospel in Ephesus

Reaching Philippi which was the first city of that district of Macedonia, Paul met a woman named Lydia, a dealer in purple cloth and preacher of the gospel. Furthermore, Paul and Silas healed a slave girl who was possessed by a demon. However, since the master of the slave girl was making quite a lot of money through this who was a fortune teller, he falsely accused Paul and Silas and beat and threw them into prison. Even while they sat in the cold cell of the prison with their bodies beaten, they praised the LORD. Then a great earthquake struck and at once all the prison doors flew open.

Waking up from sleep and finding this out, the jailer tried to kill himself worrying that he would be punished for failing to keep prisoners. In the Roman Empire, if the jailer lost prisoners, he was to suffer the penalty of the prisoner or even executed. Then Paul loudly said, "Don't harm yourself! We are all here!" and relieved the jailer. Surprised, he came running to see Paul and Silas and fell before them. Hearing Paul saying "Believe in the LORD Jesus, and you will be saved - you and your household.", the jailer and all his family believed in Jesus and was baptized with great joy in their heart.

● Thessalonica (Act.17:1-9)

Now Paul moved down south to Thessalonica. Lots of Greeks accepted the gospel Paul preached while the Jews became jealous of Paul's preaching the gospel and stood in his way. That was why Paul was able to stay in Thessalonica only for three weeks. In spite of that short period of gospel preaching, some came to believe in Jesus and Thessalonica church was started.

● Berea (Act.17:10-15)

Arriving in Berea, Paul's company preached the gospel in the Jewish synagogue. The Bereans were gentle and studied the scriptures daily. The number of those who believed in the gospel increased significantly. However, the Jews who followed them from Thessalonica obstructed Paul there. Eventually just Silas and Timothy stayed there whereas Paul had to move on to Athens.

● Athens (Act.17:16-34)

Athens was the point of beginning of Greek philosophy. Finding the whole city filled with idols, Paul introduced God, the true owner of the world to them. The Athenians who called themselves intellectuals in those days listened to what Paul said attentively but accepted the gospel just as another kind of philosophical theory. In this place Paul came to think 'it is not right for the way of Jesus to be presented as another knowledge to those who seek the knowledge of the world.'

The couple Priscilla and Aquila
This couple originally lived in Rome. But, in those days Roman emperor Claudius commanded all the Jews to leave Rome. So they moved to Corinth. There their job was to make tents and they met Paul whose job was the same. They were maybe very happy to discover that they were mutually Christians and the people who were filled with passion to preach the gospel earnestly to somebody. Later, Paul introduced these people as the ones who were ready to risk their life for Paul (Act.16:3-4).

● Corinth (Act.18:1-11)

Paul left Athens for Corinth. There he met good fellow workers called 'Priscilla and Aquila.' Through this couple Paul received great comfort and self-confidence. Just then Silas and Timothy came down to Corinth from Macedonia. Encouraged by this, Paul preached the gospel to Jews in the synagogue in Corinth. But their response was cold. At this time, Paul made up his mind, 'to stop the passion of preaching the gospel to Jews for a while and instead to preach it to the Gentiles.'

While he stayed at the house of Crispus the synagogue ruler 'fear' came to his mind. This was since, as you'll see in detail when studying I and II Corinthians, the city of Corinth was a city which had the atmosphere of the most hostile city with the characteristics of a harbor city. That was why Paul kept silent for a while. Then the LORD came to Paul in a vision and said "Do not be silent but keep on speaking, because I have many people in this city." Obeying the word, Paul stayed in Corinth for a year and a half and the Corinthian church was established.

Those who accompanied Paul on his second missionary journey
Silas : The man who exercised a considerable influence in Jerusalem
Timothy : The man who won in the first missionary journey. Paul's spiritual son.
Luke : Believed in Jesus during the second journey and accompanied Paul

● From Corinth to Antioch (Act.18:12-22)

Paul had to leave Corinth in a year and a half; though the number of believers in Jesus increased, again slanderers hunted Paul and harassed him. They harassed Paul by using the power of the governor. Although the governor ignored their false accusation, Paul who was unable to stay there any longer returned to Antioch through Ephesus. The second missionary journey of Paul ended there.

Tong Point

The letters read alongside Paul's second missionary journey: I & II Thessalonians, Galatians

From now on, we read Apostle Paul's letters in keeping with the movements of his missionary journey. The writers and recipients of the letters forming the main part of the New Testament are clearly set out. Therefore, reading together the contents of his missionary journey and letters greatly help figure out and understand the reasons as to why the letters were written, situations and background of those days, Paul's mind contained in the letters and so on.

3. The first letter sent to Thessalonica Church I Th. chap. 1-5

It took only three weeks for Thessalonica church to be established when Paul stayed in Thessalonica. News came that the church members were faithful to Jesus. Paul was so proud of the saints of Thessalonica that he was unable to hide this joy and so he wrote a letter to Thessalonica church. That letter remains today in the name of I Thessalonians.

Letter
Apostle Paul always used the words "grace and peace" in all the letters he sent. They were the words Aaron used in chapter six of Numbers when he blessed the Israelites. Paul blessed Christians in accordance with the method used over 1500 years earlier.

Perhaps the saints who read this letter gained self-esteem and joy for being Christians. **Paul encouraged, comforted and urged Thessalonica church and told Thessalonica church members to have hope. This hope was the hope for the eternal kingdom of God.**

However, some church members failed to see the forest of this letter and became unbalanced. Reading Paul's letter, they exaggeratedly interpreted the part 'the Second Advent of Jesus' he repeatedly mentioned.

Of course, Jesus ascended to heaven after resurrection and was to return the same way he ascended. Paul emphasized this. But Thessalonian saints thought, "Since Jesus will return soon, what good is my business? What good is my study?" They interpreted only that part exaggeratedly. Having heard that a few church members in Thessaloniaca did not work but stood in the way of others' business while stressing the LORD's return, Paul grabbed his pen again and wrote a second letter.

4. The second letter sent to Thessalonica Church

II Th. chap. 1-3

II Thessalonians
II Thessalonians is the shortest among the nine letters Paul wrote to church. It records a very important fact about the end of the world. It seems that Paul wrote this letter whilst residing in Corinth with Silas and Timothy.

It was II Thessalonians that Paul wrote to Thessalonian church again for those who misunderstood his intention.

Paul advised some church members who lost control of their mind; "We hear that some among you are idle. They are not busy; they are busybodies. Such people we command and urge in the LORD Jesus Christ to settle down and earn the bread they eat" (II Th.3:11-12). He meant that they should not go from house to house and eat there. He continued, "If anyone does not obey our instruction in this letter, take special note of him. Do not associate with him, in order that he may feel ashamed. Yet do not regard him as an enemy, but warn him as a brother" (II Th.3:14-15).

Orderly living
Labor is both a noble duty and a right that God gave people. Faithfully working at one's duty is another way of godliness that God demands of us. The LORD was pleased with the one who sows in tears and reaps the sheaves with songs of joy.

Just as we should eat all kinds of food evenly for the health of our body, so should we avoid eating only certain spiritual foods to maintain spiritual health. We should not neglect any one thing from hymn, prayer, word and service. When we read the Bible, we ought to read not part but the whole and make effort to maintain balance. If you are biased to one side, you may even lose the strong points. We should

keep our life of faith sound while maintaining a balance.

5. The letter sent to Galatian Church Gal. chap.1-6

Galatians is the letter called 'a Great declaration for freedom.'

Getting around the region of Galatia, Paul preached the gospel. As a result, a church was established in the region through the grace of God. Then a news came from there; some people came to believe the saying of the Jews who stated that they could be saved only through the law and circumcision. Paul wrote Galatians to persuade the saints who were tempted by what these Jews said.

Already in Jerusalem Council (Act. chap.15) Paul received the agreement that the Gentiles could be saved by accepting the gospel of Jesus Christ without being circumcised. However, there were still some in Galatian church who claimed that they could be saved only through circumcision.

Those who stressed the laws were as good as those who still judged people by outward appearance. They distinguished the freed from slaves, man from woman, the circumcised from the uncircumcised and added those distinctions to the conditions for receiving the grace of God. **However, there was no condition in the gospel of Jesus. There can be no condition in believing in the gospel of Jesus Christ and being saved.** In the letter of the Galatians was clearly expressed the mind of Paul who tried to keep the truth that one was justified not by circumcision or law but by the gospel only.

The freedom of becoming servants

Paul told the believers to become servants for one another in love only with true freedom obtained through faith (Gal.5:13). Although the two words "freedom" and "becoming servants" look like two opposites, the beautiful harmony of these two is possible in the name of Jesus. If people use the freedom given by God to become servants for one another, God will add greater freedom to them.

Write down the contents of this lesson in the form of Tong Story

Let's pray in a loud voice so that we may be able to teach the contents of this lesson to our children

- Teach them to your children, talking about them when you sit at home and when you walk along the road, when you lie down and when you get up……so that your days and the days of your children may be many……as many as the days that the heavens are above the earth (Deuteronomy 11:19-21).
- you know those from whom you learned it, and how from infancy you have known the holy Scriptures(II Timothy 3:14-15).

34 Lesson

Paul's Third Missionary Journey

Acts 18:23-chap.19, I Corinthians, II Corinthians

Accumulative reading amount 91.67% 1189

The One Year Tongdok Bible Days 326-334 | Reading time 70 minutes

TongBible Story Overview

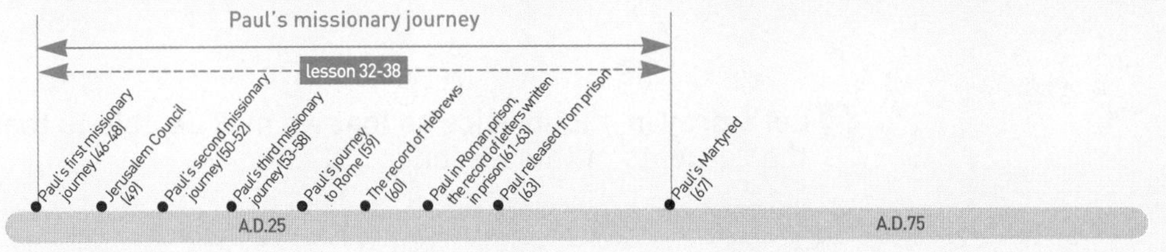

Reading the New Testament in detail in the order of history (8)

Paul departed for his third missionary journey. We read through Acts 18:23 to chapter 19. At this time Paul stayed mainly in the area of Ephesus, where he wrote I and II Corinthians to Corinthian Church.

How to read Paul's third missionary journey

The greatest difficulty in preaching the gospel was the systematic obstruction of those who misunderstood Jesus because they were gripped by the Jewish tradition. Many false teachers appeared and divided churches and even in the church the saints were not united at heart causing conflicts against one another. There were lots of issues to take care of in the church.

When Paul could not afford to go to resolve these matters himself, he usually encouraged and taught the saints by writing letters to them. If there happened to be misunderstandings because they could not see one another face to face, he wrote again to solve the misunderstandings and carried out the ministry with the mind of a father who loves his children.

Tong Point

Discipleship training, love and gifts
When Paul was in Ephesus, Apollos who pastored Corinthian Church came to him with lots of problems concerning that church. Hearing them, Paul sent a letter to the church, telling them to "become one in the power of the gospel."

1. The third missionary journey Act.18:23-chap.19

The major part of Paul's third missionary journey was his ministry at Ephesus and his writing ministry for Corinthian church.

Before Paul arrived in Ephesus the capital of Asia Minor, already a man called Apollos who was from Alexandria was teaching about Jesus. However, Priscilla and Aquila found out that he knew only the baptism of John. So they taught him the gospel they learned from Paul and helped him with his gospel ministry. Then the couple sent him to Corinthian church which still had no pastor.

By this time Paul arrived in Ephesus and called out separately those who accepted the gospel obediently and intensively taught them in the lecture hall of Tyrannus about two years. Through this education many disciples were produced. One of the disciples who learned from Paul here was Philemon who received the Letter to Philemon later.

In this situation, Paul made a new plan in Ephesus. It was none other than his plan to go to Rome the center of the world in those days. Paul who planned to stop by Jerusalem lastly and go to Rome sent Timothy and Erastus to Macedonia. Then he stayed in Ephesus a little longer. Right that time, a great riot arose in Ephesus.

In Ephesus there was a great temple where they sacrificed to Gentile gods. More and more people decided not to serve idols after hearing the gospel from Paul. So those who made idols and sold things needed for the temple of idols complained against Paul and held a rally to drive out Paul's company. Paul had to leave Ephesus again owing to this riot.

Tong Point

The letters read with Paul's third missionary journey: I & II Corinthians. Let's read them with the mind of Apostle Paul while remembering that these letters he sent to Corinthian Church were high standard persuasion toward slow minds.

2. The first letter sent to Corinthian Church

I Co. chap.1-16

While Paul was still in Ephesus, Apollos who pastored in Corinthian church visited Paul. According to the news Apollos brought, there were lots of problems in Corinthian church. Since Apollos was unable to solve the church problems at all by himself, he came to Paul in Ephesus and frankly told him all those problems.

During his second missionary journey, Paul stayed in Corinth about a year and a half, preached the gospel and established Corinthian church. Then he left and Apollos came to pastor the church. Those who uniquely liked Apollos formed

Corinth
It was said that Corinth had about 600,000 people at the time of Paul and the number of free men of them was 200,000 and there were about 400,000 slaves. Corinth, the capital of the regions of Achaia was the most active commercial center in Greece.

a club named "CLA", which was, "club for those who love Apollos." At that, others said, "Though Paul was not handsome and eloquent as Apollos, it was Paul who preached the gospel to us the first time. It was not right to neglect him." So they formed a club, "CLP." Soon after that, others said, "If possible, let's go to Peter who is a direct root of Jesus." and formed "CLPE." Then those who could not belong to any club got together and formed "CLC" saying "Let's become followers of Christ." After these clubs were formed, different opinions were expressed for every event according to each sect. Then there was a sign of church division as time went by.

Hearing this news, he wrote to Corinthian church members, **"become one in the power of the gospel" Paul stressed that though he planted the seed of the gospel in Corinth, Apollos watered it, but it was only God who made it grow.**

Then, Paul wrote solutions one by one for the problems of Corinthian church that Apollos conveyed. Particularly, Apostle Paul stressed that the head of church was Jesus, and the saints who were the body and members should take care of one another. I Corinthians chapter 13 is well known as 'love chapter' where he mentioned love as the greatest gift for Corinthian church members who were quarreling with one another while boasting the gifts of the Holy Spirit.

As he closed his letter, Paul asked them to take part in relief offering to help the saints of Jerusalem church. Paul was passionate in collections for the poor saints. Although Paul was engaged in mission at his own expense not to stand in the way of the gospel, he urged the church to help the saints positively.

Paul wrote this letter and sent it by the hand of Timothy. At

Teachings of Paul's First letter to Corinthians

1. The dispute in the church (chap.1-4)
2. Sex and marriage (chap. 5; 6:9-7:40)
3. litigation (6:1-8)
4. Food sacrificed to the idols (8:1-11:1)
5. Women in the church (11:2-16; 14:34-36)
6. The LORD's Supper (11:17-34)
7. The gifts of the Holy Spirit (chap.12-14)
8. The resurrection of the body (chap.15)

Imitate me

Paul told Corinth Church to imitate him (I Co.11:1). It meant that they should imitate him in his labor, sweat, tears and service for churh. He said, "If somebody seems to be weak, I become weak. If someone's faith is shaken due to the matter of eating meat, I won't eat meat." He said that he was willing to give up anything if it helped increase faith in community.

this time, Paul encouraged Apollos to go back to Corinth several times. But Apollos said that he did not want to do so. It seemed that Apollos really had a tough time in Corinthian church.

3. The second letter sent to Corinthian Church

II Co. chap.10-13

II Corinthians is regarded as a book where two letters were combined. When we read in an order different from what it was, we can understand much better. The second letter which was written earlier was II Corinthians chapters 10-13 and the third one was I Corinthians chapters 1-9.

Among the saints of Corinthian church who read I Corinthians that was hand-carried by Timothy, there were those who accepted what Paul wrote whereas there were others who opposed him all the more. Reading Paul's letter, some even doubted his apostleship. Hearing it, Paul became very sad. That was why he wrote his second letter which was II Corinthians chapters 10-13, which was written after I Corinthians.

"Are they servants of Christ? (I am out of my mind to talk like this.) I am more. I have worked much harder, been in prison more frequently, been flogged more severely, and been exposed to death again and again. Five times I received from the Jews the forty lashes minus one. Three times I was beaten with rods, once I was stoned, three times I was shipwrecked, I spent a night and a day in the open sea, I have been constantly on the move. I have been in danger from rivers, in danger from bandits, in danger from my own countrymen, in danger from Gentiles; in danger in the city, in danger in the country, in danger at sea; and in danger from false brothers. I have labored and toiled and have often gone without sleep; I have known hunger and thirst and have often gone without food; I have been cold and naked" (II Co.11:23-27).

Paul disclosed in detail of what kind of suffering he had gone through. Seeing Corinthians criticizing him nonsensically with the claim that he was not an apostle and even distorting the contents of the gospel he preached, he wrote in this way to prevent this thing from happening further by every means. **For Paul, being a Hebrew and well versed in the law was not something to be proud of. Rather, the standard of his being a worker for Christ was 'how much he has suffered for Christ.'** When we see from the position of a later generation, we come to know through this letter how much Paul suffered during the course of his missionary journey.

Those who resisted Paul attacked him saying he lacked spiritual experience. As their attack got stronger, he was forced to tell them his experience of having been to the third heaven. However, he talked about this spiritual experience not to boast of his spiritual power but to reveal the great God who worked through his weaknesses. This time he had the letter containing these contents hand-carried by Titus. Fortunately, reading this letter, all the Corinthian church members regretted their wrong-doings greatly.

Titus

"Titus" was Greek. Titus who repented during Paul's first missionary journey was sent to Corinthian church and carried out the ministry and later pastored in the island of Crete (Tit.1:5). He was a son of Paul by faith and an able, sincere pastor. He was also the recipient of Paul's letter to Titus.

4. The third letter sent to Corinthian Church

II Co. chap. 1-9

Paul went to Macedonia from Ephesus. He planned to go to Corinth through there. Then Titus brought up the good news that Corinthian church members repented. Paul who heard the good news from Titus while in Macedonia wrote again to Corinthian church members expressing gratitude and joy and that letter was II Corinthians chapters 1-9.

Though Paul worried and grieved due to Corinthian church, at the end he found himself filled with thankfulness to God. Then he praised God who comforted him in the midst of tribulation. He helped their misunderstanding be solved by telling them that though he really wanted to visit their church in person to help solve various problems of the church, one of the reasons that plan did not work out as he willed was the suffering he had in Asia.

Then Paul asked Corinthian church for the collection again in his letter. In fact, he was misunderstood so much on this matter. It was a shocking misunderstanding; that Paul said he served the LORD at his own expense but he secretly used money selfishly. **However, Paul did not give up serving the poor saints of other areas by receiving the collection of Corinthian church. Paul who was able to give up all his privileges for the gospel was the kind of person that could so thoroughly persuade church to give offering for needy saints.**

Law vs. gospel(II Co. Chapter 3)

Law	Gospel
Old covenant	New covenant
The letter of the law	spirit
Kills	Gives life
The duty of condemning	The duty of righteousness
There is glory	There is more glory
Will pass away	will last forever
Hidden as when towel is worn	Clear as when towel is taken off

Write down the contents of this lesson in the form of Tong Story

Let's pray in a loud voice so that we may be able to teach the contents of this lesson to our children

- Teach them to your children, talking about them when you sit at home and when you walk along the road, when you lie down and when you get up……so that your days and the days of your children may be many……as many as the days that the heavens are above the earth (Deuteronomy 11:19-21).
- you know those from whom you learned it, and how from infancy you have known the holy Scriptures(II Timothy 3:14-15).

18 Session

Eternal Crown and handed-down Request

Tong Map

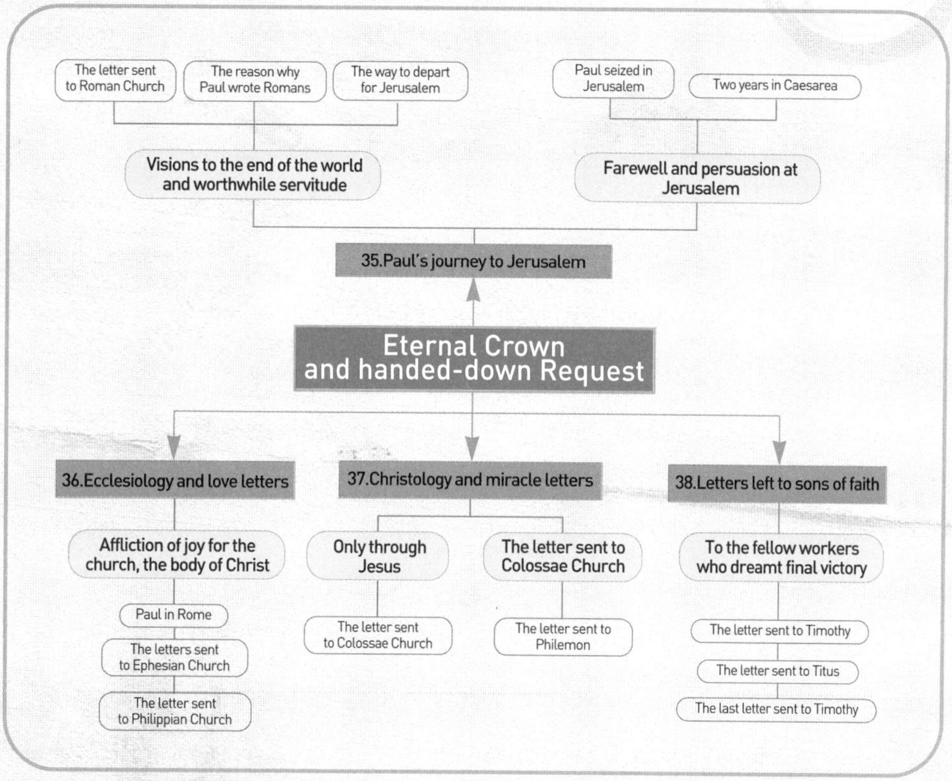

Tong Concept

- **Apostle Paul's journeys and his letters in Tong!**

We observe Paul's journey to Jerusalem and Romans using the Tong method and his imprisonment in Rome and his prison letters.

Acts	Letters	Apostle Paul's missionary journey	Lesson
chap.20-26	Rom.	His journey to Jerusalem/Rome & letters	35
chap.27-28	Eph., Phi., Col., Phi.	His prison letters written in Rome	36, 37
	I Ti., Tit., II Ti.	His fourth Missionary journey & pastoral letters	38

Track 6 30 YEARS OF ACTS

Tong At a glance

* Looking around the forest

A team of 40 assassins was formed who decided not to eat or drink until they killed Paul. Seized in Jerusalem, Paul spent two years in Caesarea and then came to leave for Rome where he was sent as criminal.

Arriving in Rome, he was made to stay there for two years under house-arrest(around A.D.61-63). Although Paul was unable to go around freely during this period, he was able to meet people who came to see him. He wrote many letters in this prison. Among them, Ephesians, Colossians, Philippians and Philemon are called four great prison letters. I Timothy and Titus are pastoral letters and II Timothy was a letter that can be said to be his final will.

* Land and annual ring

Roman emperors related to persecution against Christianity appearing in Acts were Claudius(A.D.41-54) and Nero(A.D.54-68). During the rule of Claudius, Roman government did not distinguish Christians from Jews but regarded them as Jews altogether.

Since Christians and Jews often quarelled with each other, Emperor Claudius ordered Jews to leave Rome. In A.D.64 a great fire broke out and continued in Rome for six days. At this time Emperor Nero held Christians responsible for this fire. From this time on persecution of Rome against Christians was accelerated.

* Wind and Climate

Ephesus was considered to be a great city in the Roman Empire. There was Artemis temple there, one of seven wonders of the world. You will remember that Paul was caught in a great uproar here(Act.19:23-41).

During his second missionary journey, Paul visited Ephesus. On his way back from his third missionary journey which he finished(Act.19:1) he stopped by Ephesus and trained the disciples in the hall of Tyrannus for about two years. He wrote Ephesians to the Ephesian church members there. Also afterwards he wrote I Timothy to young pastor Timothy so that he would be able to defeat false doctrines and supervise Ephesus Church well.

Meanwhile, Colossae was a Roman colony in Asia Minor and people there worshipped so many gods. False teacheres showed up in the church, came up with new thoughts which were strange mixture of Gentile religions and Jewish statutes and tempted Christians. Paul explained in detail who Christ was to Colossian Church which was faced with this kind of situation.

Tong Seeing the forest

Romans Paul's final goal was to go to Spain which was regarded as the end of the earth in those days and preach the gospel there after going through Rome. For this purpose he wanted to be supported by the Roman church. Through this letter Paul preached that Jesus Christ was the one who saved human beings, set people free from the law and death and broke down the wall of sin that separated people from God.

Ephesians This was one of the prison letters written by Paul in Roman prison who had worked for the church all his life. Paul defined what church was through this letter sent to Ephesian church. While praising this providence of God; the working of the Holy Spirit, he defined that church was 'Jesus Christ's body and the fullness of God who filled everything in every way while creating all the world.'

Philippians Paul who was in prison rejoiced. His joy was the one bound with his suffering. The joy of suffering for the gospel was the joy of Paul and of Philippian church he preached the gospel to. Although he was in prison, rather he comforted the mind of Philippian church members who were worried about him and sent them his letter of love writing each word heavy-heartedly.

Colossians When seen from the forest of Paul's life, he defined what church was in his letter to the Ephesians after he had worked hard for the church. Through this letter to the Colossians which was written in the similar period, he explained who Jesus was. Jesus who Paul met for the first time met him in when he was foolish and sinful and on his way to Damascus. Having lived serving Jesus since then, Paul became sure that Jesus was God the creator who created all things. He wanted to tell this fact to Colossian church members as well.

Philemon Philemon was a case of Paul's effort to restore the relationship between a slave he met and his master. Paul preached the gospel to Onesimus who was a slave and fled from Philemon, who happened to be his disciple. Now he sent him back to Philemon. Paul wrote this letter to ask Philemon to accept Onesimus as brother in Christ, not as a slave. This was a shocking thought that could never be thought of in the situation of those days. It was the letter of "Miracle" sent by Paul who believed in Jesus Christ to Philemon who believed in Jesus Christ for the sake of Onesimus who believed in Jesus Christ.

I Timothy Paul encouraged Timothy who did not take care of his weak body but did his best to preach the gospel. He told him to fight the good fight of faith. This letter is also called pastoral letter along with Titus. It records in detail things such as how a pastor should take care of church and how workers should be appointed to fill each position and cooperate together.

Titus Paul used the title 'my true son' to Titus also as to Timothy. Paul and Titus enjoyed such a deep trust between them that when Paul could not go in person to where there was difficulty in connection with the gospel, he always sent Titus there. Paul who was in prison wrote this letter painstakingly and sent it to Titus to encourage him and give him right instructions. Titus is also classified as pastoral letter as II Timothy is.

II Timothy Paul who was in prison in Rome was released briefly and then was put back into prison by Emperor Nero. Sensing that his life was near the end, he wrote this letter to Timothy his son in faith as his will. Although he knew by experience how great the suffering was that he received while preaching the gospel, he entrusted Timothy with preaching the gospel after him because he believed it to be the most blessed work.

35 Lesson

Paul's journey to Jerusalem

Acts chap.20-26, Romans

Accumulative reading amount 93.75% 1189

The One Year Tongdok Bible Days 335-341 | Reading time 60 minutes

TongBible Story Overview

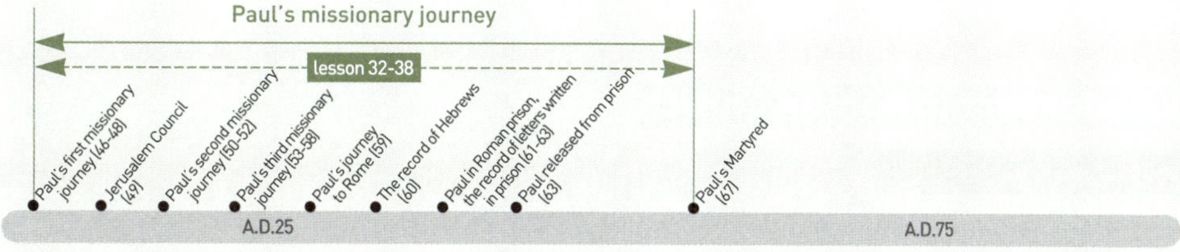

Reading the New Testament in detail in the order of history (9)

After Paul finished the third missionary journey in about four years, he left Ephesus, came to Corinth and stayed there for about three months. This record is found in Acts 20:1-3. It was right this time that Paul wrote Romans and had Deaconess Phoebe hand-carry it to the Romans. After he stayed in Corinth for three months, he came to Miletus via Troas. Before he left for Jerusalem from there, he met with the Ephesian elders and tore himself away from them for good. Upon arriving in Jerusalem, he reported the outcome of the missionary journey to the elders of the early church. All this story is depicted in Acts 20:4-21:26. Then we read from Acts 21:27 to Acts chapter 26. Here is contained the story of what happened in connection with Paul from the time he was caught in Jerusalem until he had spent two years in prison in Caesarea.

How to read Paul's journey to Jerusalem

Paul planned to go to Spain after his last visit to Jerusalem. Before going to Jerusalem, he moved ahead with his plan to go to Spain which was regarded as the end of the world in those days. By the time Paul finished his third missionary journey, he visited Corinth and stayed there for three months(about A.D.58). In those days he wrote Romans and had Deaconess Phoebe hand-carry it to Rome.

Meanwhile, Paul went to Jerusalem from Corinth. However, a team of 40 assassins who swore they would kill Paul by all means waited for him. Yet, Paul's passion for Jesus Christ was much stronger than their determination and so he was able to move forward boldly.

Tong Point

Visions to the end of the world and worthwhile servitude.
The following is the course of Paul who was on his way to Jerusalem after his third missionary journey: Ephesus-Corinth-Philippi-Troas-Assos-Mitylene-Chios-Samos-Miletus-Kos-Rhode-Patara-Tyre-Ptolemais-Caesarea-Jerusalem.
The second part of Acts is a book of precious stones which contains the fervent passion and Paul's thorough plan of toward the gospel. We read this part along with Romans.

1. The letter sent to Roman Church

Act.20:1-3/ Rom. chap.1-15:13

After Paul left Ephesus and arrived in Corinth, he stayed there for about three months. At that time he wrote Romans.

First he introduced himself as "a servant of Jesus Christ." Then he told them about Jesus he met and said that his reason for writing was to share the grace he received. He also told them clearly that he really wanted to visit Rome but was unable to as he wished.

After greeting them like this, he sedately wrote down the contents about the way of salvation, being saved by Jesus Christ and justification by using the space up to the middle of Romans chapter 15. He said that all were sinners and there was no one righteous, not even one. Therefore, nobody could avoid the penalty of sin. **The only way sin could be forgiven was the way of righteousness that was possible by believing in Jesus Christ whom God sent to this world. This righteousness meant the righteousness that was available to the one who believed in Jesus Christ whom God set up as offering of**

Justification by faith
- **Justification:** The one who believes in Christ has been made to be called righteous by holy God
- **Redemption:** Christ purchased believers from their bondage to sin by dying for them and paid the price of redemption so that they may be free from the penalty of sin.
- **Reconciliation:** The blood of Christ satisfied the requirement of the righteous.

fellowship. As Paul previously said in Galatians, he stressed that we could only be saved only by faith.

Furthermore, Paul said that anything in all creation would not be able to separate us from the love of God. Paul who received the power of the Holy Spirit who set us free from sin, death and law, praised God for the fact that God's amazing love would never be cut off from his chosen people.

However, even Paul who had this conviction in his heart and lived an abundant life had a great sorrow.

"I speak the truth in Christ and I am not lying. My conscience confirms it in the Holy Spirit that I have great sorrow and unceasing anguish in my heart. For I could wish that I myself were cursed and cut off from Christ for the sake of my brothers, those of my own race"(Rom.9:1-3).

Seen from the overview, the heart of Paul who preached the gospel to the Gentiles was filled with not only his eager wish to preach the gospel to the Gentiles but also his wanting for the Jews (his fellow nation) to be able to enjoy the abundant grace of Christ.

2. The reason Paul wrote Romans Rom.15:14-chap.16

Now, from the second half portion of Romans chapter 15, Paul began to explain why he wanted to go to Rome and why he needed to go there.

Paul wrote Romans in order to introduce himself to Roman church members and to be supported by them to go to Spain. His preaching the gospel so far was fully supported by Antioch church. However, as he wanted to preach the gospel in farther places, it would have been more effective for him to be supported by Roman Christians. If so, why did Paul intend to go to Spain so eagerly? According to the geo-political knowledge of the first century at the time, Spain was right 'the end of the earth.' **Holding on to Jesus' will as said, "Go to Jerusalem, and all Judea and Samaria, and to the ends of the earth and tell them that I love all people"(Act.1:8), Paul wanted to fulfill that will of Jesus in his own generation. Now his age was over mid 50's and close to 60's. Yet, he wanted to go as far as Spain. Indeed his passion was never ending.**

Then Paul asked Roman church members to pray for him. Now at last he intended to go to Jerusalem. He received the news that disobedient Jews planned to assassinate him. Paul who heard this fact asked them to pray for him so that he would be delivered from the death threats. It was because of his dream that he was to go to Spain (the end of the earth) to preach the gospel.

His second prayer subject was "that my service in Jerusalem may be acceptable to the saints there" (Rom.15:31). One of the purposes of Paul's visit to Jerusalem was to give Jerusalem church the offering money collected already to help the poor saints of the church. Paul feared that in the process of handing over the offering money, Jerusalem church members may feel burdensome receiving it or feel offended. He prayed that those who received might share in what God gave so that they would feel worthy to receive it.

At the end of the long letter (Rom.chap.16), Paul greeted

Spain
It was the western most end of European Peninsular during the period of the Roman Empire. It was the region of current Portugal and Spain. It was also assumed to be Tarshish where Jonah intended to go to run away by sailing from Joppa.

Apostle for the Gentiles
Although Paul was an apostle for the Gentiles, he also had salvation of the Israelites in mind.
If we read Romans carefully, we can feel Paul who eagerly wanted his fellow Jews to be saved. As an apostle for the Gentiles Paul was a man of God who was equipped with fervent passion of salvation for the Jews and Gentiles. God used such apostle Paul as a faithful servant and worker.

many people. We are able to get a glimpse of the relationship Paul had with his fellow people. Paul did not work alone. We learn that only when we keep our relationship both with God and with neighbors right, we are true Christians.

3. The way to depart for Jerusalem Act.20:4-21:16

Paul who wrote Romans while staying in Corinth three months planned to go to Spain after visiting Jerusalem as his last visit. However, Paul heard that the degree of Jewish obstruction against him became so extreme that a team of assassins was formed to kill him. Yet, Paul did not compromise in spreading the gospel.

When Paul arrived in Miletus before going to Jerusalem, he asked the elders of Ephesus to go there. Perhaps they knew that it was hard for them to see one another again. He earnestly pleaded with the elders to care for the church, knelt down and prayed together. When it was time for Paul to depart, everyone threw their arms around Paul's neck and wept loudly. **Though he knew some people were trying to take his life, Paul departed and the elders of Ephesus still let him go. This meant that both Paul and the elders harbored the mark of love of Jesus.**

4. Paul seized in Jerusalem Act.21:17-chap.23

Paul could have gone to Rome straight from Corinth. The

reason he planned to get there by way of Jerusalem was that he wanted to have a final greeting with the community of Jerusalem church before going to Spain. Before leaving for his missionary journey which was unable to promise anything for the future, he intended to report to Jerusalem church the work of Gentile mission he had done for a long time and to connect the church with Gentile churches.

Arriving in Jerusalem, Paul testified how God made Gentiles believe in Jesus through him. The elders who got together gave glory to God after hearing Paul's report.

A few days later, when Paul went into the temple, the crowds quickly ran to him and tried to drag him out of the temple and kill him. In that situation, Roman soldiers in charge of public safety of Jerusalem delivered Paul right before he was about to get killed. Then Paul who was being dragged off by soldiers suddenly turned around and asked the commander to do him a favor. He asked him for an opportunity to speak to the Jews. Granted by the commander, Paul persuaded his fellow nationals for the last time. First he explained how he had lived for the last thirty years. He first disclosed that he used to study under Gamaliel (a great scholar of the law) as his best disciple. He said that not only his teacher but chief priests and their associates recognized his future. **Then he met Jesus. He proclaimed that he found Jesus Christ to be the real way.**

Paul lastly persuaded them with all his soul and energy. Hearing Paul, however, the crowds said, "We need to hear him no longer. Let's kill him." In this desperate situation, the commander got Paul out of them first and let him escape. Knowing Paul was a Roman citizen, the commander wanted to

Great uproars in Jerusalem
- When Jesus entered Jerusalem and was crucified
- When Stephen who was a worker of the early church became the first martyr by being stoned
- When Paul who wrapped up his third missionary journey returned to Jerusalem

Sanhedrin
: Council(Act.23:15)
The Greek word for 'Sanhedrin' meant a place where particular people gathered together. The Aramaic expression of this word was 'Sanhedrin.' It was the highest decesion-making organization of the Jews in the New Testament era. It was composed of chief priests, teacher of the law, Pharisees and Sadducees whose total number was 71.

know why they were eager to kill him and held the Sanhedrin. Even in the Sanhedrin, Paul's life was in danger and he narrowly escaped.

However, the Jews were determined to kill Paul by any means. A team of assassins was formed who swore they would neither eat nor drink until they killed Paul. Knowing this, the commander decided to send Paul to Caesarea where the governor lived. He arranged a detachment of two hundred soldiers, seventy horsemen and two hundred spearmen as a military escort of total 470 persons. Paul who met Jesus and did his best for preaching the gospel of Jesus Christ over 30 years never returned to Jerusalem after leaving the city that night.

5. Two years in Caesarea Act.chap.24-26

Paul was made to stay in Caesarea for about two years. Paul who managed to escape the Jewish threat and was transported to Caesarea was to be attacked by the Jews even there. Paul who stood before governor Felix due to the accusation of high priest Ananias came to have another opportunity to defend himself. But Paul's unfair situation was not solved right away and was on hold for a while. Governor Felix protected Paul, sometimes called him and wanted to hear about Jesus Christ. On the other hand, he wanted to receive bribe from Paul.

Two years after Paul was put into prison in Caesarea, Festus was appointed as new governor in place of Felix. New governor Festus' attitude was not much different from that of the former governor Felix. He was also interested in just winning the hearts of the Jews and tried to hand over Paul to them. Sensing this, Paul took his last legal measure as a Roman citizen. He requested a trial for him by the Roman emperor Caesar. This way, though Paul was transported as prisoner and was not free until trial, he was able to get an opportunity to go to Rome.

Opportunity for evangelism
King Agrippa and Bernice who came to greet new governor Festus after Felix heard about Paul and wanted to see him(Act.25:13, 22). Although he was in chains like a criminal, Paul got another opportunity to preach the gospel through another channel prepared by God.

Write down the contents of this lesson in the form of Tong Story

Let's pray in a loud voice so that we may be able to teach the contents of this lesson to our children

- Teach them to your children, talking about them when you sit at home and when you walk along the road, when you lie down and when you get up……so that your days and the days of your children may be many……as many as the days that the heavens are above the earth (Deuteronomy 11:19-21).
- you know those from whom you learned it, and how from infancy you have known the holy Scriptures(II Timothy 3:14-15).

36 Lesson

Ecclesiology and love letters

Acts chap. 27-28, Ephesians, Philippians

Accumulative reading amount 94.79% 1189

The One Year Tongdok Bible Days 342-345 | Reading time 30 minutes

TongBible Story Overview

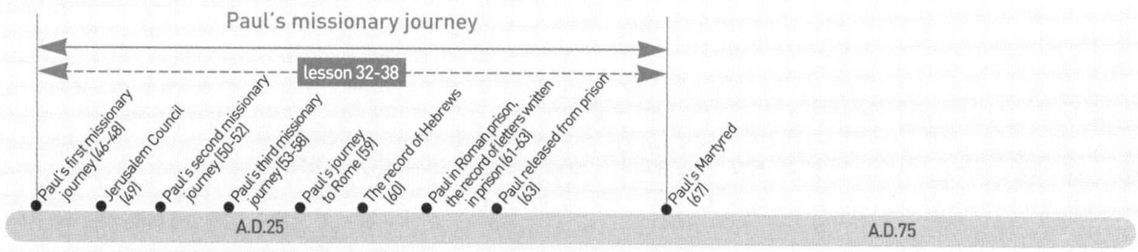

Reading the New Testament in detail in the order of history (10)

We read Acts chapters 27-28. Paul got caught in Jerusalem and had stayed in prison in Caesarea for two years. Then he made on his way to Rome by asking to stand trial before the Roman emperor. Here is contained that story. It makes up the last part of Acts. Acts 28:30, For two whole years Paul stayed in his own rented house refers to the two years he spent in prison in Rome. Paul wrote many letters while imprisoned in Rome. Among them were Ephesians, Philppians, Colossians and Philemon which are called four great prison letters. Let's read these letters with the mind of Paul who was imprisoned but free in the gospel.

How to read prison letters

As a prisoner Paul was made to go to Rome to stand trial before Roman Emperor. In this journey to Rome Paul was accompanied by Luke, the author of the Acts. In Rome Paul stayed in a house under house arrest for two years. Though he was unable to go around freely and meet people, he was unable to meet people that visited him. He wrote many letters in this prison. Among the letters he wrote in the Roman prisonwere , Ephesians, Colossians, Philippians and Philemon.

Track 6 30 YEARS OF ACTS

Tong Point

Affliction of joy for the church, the body of Christ
Let's read letters written by Paul whilst in prison from his perspective.

1. Paul in Rome Act. chap.27-28

Finally Paul reached Rome and met the Roman church members in person. Paul waited for the trial of the emperor and testified to the kingdom of God diligently.

Luke closed the Acts with the words, "For two whole years Paul stayed there in his own rented house and welcomed all who came to see him. Boldly and without hindrance he preached the kingdom of God and taught about the LORD Jesus Christ"(Act.28:30-31). **But Paul did not stop his gospel ministry there. Though he was bound in prison, he was able to meet people that visited him freely and spent each day busily in encouraging and teaching many church saints with many letters he wrote.**

Acts which was not over
Though it was guessed that Paul was martyred under the rule of Emperor Nero, Luke did not finish Acts with the death of Paul. Because Paul's ministry had to be handed down to other people, just as the ministry of Jesus was handed down to Paul and other apostles. Acts of the Apostles was the Acts of the Holy Spirit which was still not over. The Bible is inviting us to join the disciples' march toward the ends of the world.

2. The letters sent to Ephesian Church Eph. chap.1-6

Since Paul intensively trained his disciples early in Ephesus for two years, he had a special love for Ephesus church. Now, Timothy who was a disciple of Paul ministered in Ephesus. Paul wanted to teach Timothy in detail what church was by writing him a letter. Paul who worked for the church with all his life defined church in his letter to the Ephesians.

When Christianity and Judaism were compared, Christianity seemed to lack something. It neither had synagogues nor a long tradition like the laws of the Jews. There were many visible things in Judaism but there was nothing except Jesus in the church. **However, Paul stressed that for the church only Jesus was enough. Regarding the salvation of believers, he made a wonderful declaration that there was our God's preparation before the creation of heaven and earth. Tracing back the course he has followed, he found out that there was God's providence in all the courses.** Tracing back the hand of God, he discoverd that it began before the creation of the world (Eph.1:3-5).

In Ephesians Paul **defined, "The church is his body, the fullness of him who fills everything in every way."** Then he asked church to do four things.

His first request was to promote the concord of church. To seek this purpose, the practice of humility, love and peace was requested.

His second request was to edify as Christians.

His third request was to establish Christian homes. Christians were to make homes where masters and slaves loved one another, husbands and wives love one another and parents and children.

His fourth request was to put on the full armor of God that God gave. Truth, righteousness, gospel, faith, salvation, the word of God was taught to become the energy that will enable us to resist easily and stand right when the day of evil comes.

Church

In those days when somebody became a Christian, one hardship he had to suffer was to tear himself away from the community of the Jews. Excommunication was awful. Perhaps Paul had been asked many questions including what Christianity was, why there was real truth in Christianity, not in Judaism and the like. In Ephesians he answered to the question 'What is church?' and in Colossians he answered to the question 'Who is Jesus?.'

Tong Point

Philippian church
During the second missionary journey, Paul came to minister in Philippi due to 'the calling of a Macedonian'(Act.16:8-10). At that time, Lydia and a few people came to receive Jesus Christ. Although Paul and Silas were flogged and imprisoned, because of this the prison captain of Philippi was transformed. During Paul's third missionary journey, he again visited Philippi. When Philippian church heard that Paul was put into Roman prison, they sent financial support to him through Epaphroditus (Phi.4:18).

3. The letter sent to Philippian Church Phi. chap.1-4

Though Paul considered all churches as precious as his own body, we can say that compared with other churches, the Philippian church had a particular deep relationship with Paul personally. Since Paul carried out his ministry at his own expense, he did not get honorarium from churches. But it was different with the Philippian church. Paul enjoyed a private relationship with the church that he was glad to receive a little of their financial support without feeling burdensome.

Now Paul was imprisoned in Rome. For that reason, his financial situation became more and more difficult. At this time Philippian church collected their love offering for Paul and had their pastor Epaphroditus hand-carry it. Paul thankfully received it. Like that, the relationship between Paul and Philippian church saints was equivalent to family relationship.

Epaphroditus, who brought to Rome the love offering the church members collected painstakingly, talked with Paul about the matters of the church and then disclosed that in the church the sect of Euodia and that of Syntyche were in

Jesus described by Philippians

- The source of fruits of righteousness(1:11)
- The reason for joy(1:18)
- The one who will be exaled in my body(1:20)
- The one who lives in me(1:21)
- The one who has the form of servant(2:6-7)
- The name which is above all other names(2:9)
- The body of the greatest knowledge(3:8)
- The one who strengthens me(4:13)

confrontation with each other and the like. And then for some reasons like the fatigue he had pastoring church plus the fatigue he got traveling, Epaphroditus got sick there. Paul worried much for the reason. Fortunately, Epaphroditus restored his health and got to return to Philippi. Paul became so relieved and wrote Philippians and sent it through Epaphroditus.

Paul talked about joy in this letter. Some preach Jesus Christ out of competitive spirit to boast before others while others do it in honest heart. However, Paul expressed his joy for the fact that the gospel of Jesus was preached anyway whether it was outwardly or inwardly. Although he was in prison, Paul said that he was happy that Epaphroditus restored his health, and that he was happy that Philippian church members sent painstakingly the love offering and he was very happy that Philippian church thought of God and neighbors. Talking about this joy, Paul urged Euodia and Syntyche to humble themselves and to amount to the full measure of faith in Christ just as Christ humbled himself.

There were some in the church, though not many, who both criticized Paul and the church messed up and slandered Paul. Some of them exalted themselves boasting that they were circumcized. To them Paul responded by his confession of faith that he considered everything a loss in Jesus Christ. "I considered everything a loss compared to the surpassing greatness of knowing Christ my LORD, for whose sake I have lost all things. I consider them rubbish, that I may gain Christ and be found in him....."(Phi.3:8-9).

Paul was a thorough Christ-centered person. He was ready

to give up everything for Jesus.

Paul said, "Rejoice in the LORD always. I will say it again: Rejoice!" Then he exhorted them by saying that if they let God know all anxieties by prayer, the peace God gives would come upon them.

Write down the contents of this lesson in the form of Tong Story

Let's pray in a loud voice so that we may be able to teach the contents of this lesson to our children

- Teach them to your children, talking about them when you sit at home and when you walk along the road, when you lie down and when you get up……so that your days and the days of your children may be many……as many as the days that the heavens are above the earth (Deuteronomy 11:19-21).
- you know those from whom you learned it, and how from infancy you have known the holy Scriptures(II Timothy 3:14-15).

37 Lesson

Christology and miracle letters

Colossians, Philemon

Accumulative reading amount 95.14% 1189

The One Year Tongdok Bible Days 346-347 | Reading time 10 minutes

TongBible Story Overview

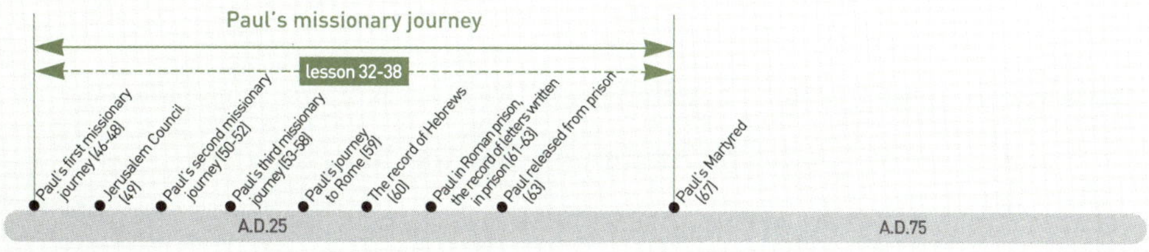

Reading the New Testament in detail in the order of history (11)

We go on to further study the prison letters. We read Colossians and Philemon.

How to read prison letters

Colossians was a prison letter of Paul sent to the church in Colossae which Epaphroditus pastored. Philemon was Paul's personal letter written to Philemon (who was a disciple of Paul). Serving Colossian church, Paul wrote in order to send Onesimus a servant of Philemon back to him.

Tong Point

Only through Jesus
Tychicus who was the special messenger of Paul did the work of conveying the situations and conditions of Paul to fellow missionaries. Thanks to him, Paul was able to give and take this many contents through letters. We read Paul's letters thinking that they were the letters of love and joy that contained his heart.

1. The letter sent to Colossae Church Col. chap.1-4

Colossae was a small capital of Asia Minor. Around it there were the small cities of Laodicea, Hierapolis and the like. In those times in Colossae were prevalent all kinds of philosophies and heresies ranging from Gnosticism to utilitarianism, mysticism, asceticism and so on. In Colossian church, with this kind of environment, Epaphras who was one of Paul's disciples pastored.

Paul who spent all his life participating in the sufferings of Christ explained who Jesus was through Colossians. "He is the image of the invisible God, the firstborn over all creation ...... And he is the head of the body, the church; he is the beginning and the firstborn from among the dead, so that in everything he might have the supremacy"(Col.1:15-18). **Since there is no lack with Jesus Christ, we do not need other vain customs or philosophies.** He exhorted Colossian church members "to continue in their faith and to be established firmly on the foundation" and encourages them "to grow in the knowledge of God."

Here we come across a man called 'Tychicus.' "Tychicus will tell you all the news about me. He was a dear brother, a faithful

Colossian Church
It is obvious that Epaphras established Colossian Church (Col1:4-8, 2:1). During his third missionary journey Paul spent almost three years in Asia centering around Ephesus. It seems that Epaphras probably came to Christ this time. Years later he visited Paul when he was in prison in Rome (Col.4:12-13; Phm.1:23).

The Christ whom the Letter to the Colossians talks about
- "He is the image of the invisible God." (1:15)
- "He is the firstborn of all creation." (1:15)
- "He is the head of the church which is his body." (1:18)
- "He is the glory of mystery, the hope of glory." (1:27)
- "He is the Christ who is the mystery of God." (2:2)
- "He is the head of all rulers and authority." (2:10)
- "He is the Christ who is our life." (3:4)
- "He is the Christ who is all, and is in all." (3:11)

minister and fellow servant in the LORD" (Col.4:7). Though the man called Tychicus was not a pastor in charge of a certain church, he was a much appreciated follower of Paul's who played the role of mail deliverer, informing Paul about circumstances and vice versa.

Tong Point

The letter sent to Colossae Church
Paul wrote a letter for a man named Onesimus with all his heart. We will have to take note of the ministry of Paul who wrote even at the risk of his personality for a slave who was regarded poorl socially in those days.

2. The letter sent to Philemon Phm. chap.1

While in prison in Rome, Paul met Onesimus who was a young man. As he talked with him and fellowshiped with him, he knew that he was a very highly intelligent person.

One day he visited Paul and confessed his past. Paul found out that he was a slave. And that he was one of slaves of Philemon who was a disciple of Paul. Philemon was a disciple he taught in the lecture hall of Tyrannus while he was in Ephesus. Now that man's slave escaped to Rome. By accident he met Paul, accepted the gospel and became a Christian.

After agonizing much, Paul decided to send him back to Philemon. Onesimus also decided to go back to his master after being persuaded by Paul. It meant that he was ready for death. Because in those days it was only natural for a master to kill his runaway slave. Sending such Onesimus back, Paul painstakingly wrote a brief letter with much prayer and had him hand-carry it. That letter was none other than Philemon.

Reading down Philemon, we can feel how painstakingly Paul wrote each word. He sent back Onesimus through Tychicus. If Philemon would ever kill Onesimus, from Paul's standing it would be a terrible matter. That was why Paul pleaded with Philemon eagerly. Perhaps Paul sent back Onesimus because he trusted the good nature of Philemon .

"Therefore, although in Christ I could be bold and order you to do what you ought to do, yet I appeal to you on the basis of love. I then, as Paul - an old man and now also a prisoner of Christ Jesus - I appeal to you for my son Onesimus, who became my son while I was in chains" (Phm.1:8-10).

He explained his circumstance as much as possible and attached the word 'son' before the name of Onesimus. "Formerly he was useless to you because he fled as slave. I know it. But now he has been transformed in the gospel and become useful both to you and to me. How about regarding him as no longer a slave but a brother?"

In those days this was a revolutionary story. According to an information of word of mouth, Onesimus became a great leader of the early church.

Onesimus

In Hebrew 'Onesimus' meant 'beneficial person.' Paul wrote; "Formerly he was useless to you, but now he has become beneficial both to you and to me." When we see this in light of original language, it was a language raveling that used the name of Onesimus. Thinking that this letter would be read in a tense situation where the slave who had fled returned, Paul wrote considering the situation. We can feel his heart taking pains for Onesimus.

Write down the contents of this lesson in the form of Tong Story

Let's pray in a loud voice so that we may be able to teach the contents of this lesson to our children

- Teach them to your children, talking about them when you sit at home and when you walk along the road, when you lie down and when you get up……so that your days and the days of your children may be many……as many as the days that the heavens are above the earth (Deuteronomy 11:19-21).
- you know those from whom you learned it, and how from infancy you have known the holy Scriptures(II Timothy 3:14-15).

38 Lesson Letters left to sons of faith

I Timothy, Titus, II Timothy

Accumulative reading amount 96.01% 1189

The One Year Tongdok Bible Days 348-350 | Reading time 25 minutes

TongBible Story Overview

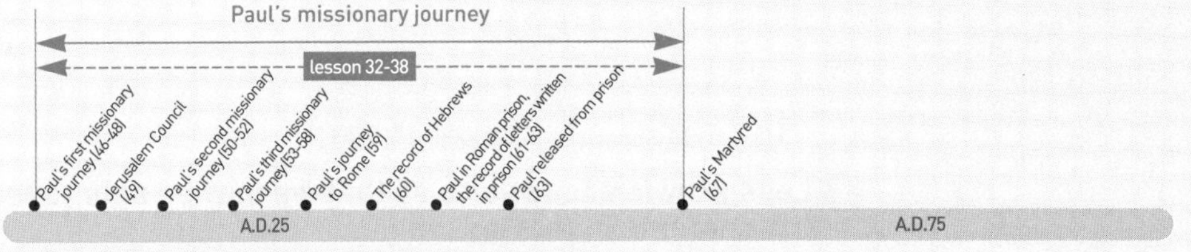

Reading the New Testament in detail in the order of history (12)

After two years, Paul was made free briefly and again planned to depart for another missionary journey. The letters written by him around this time were I Timothy and Titus which are called pastoral letters. However, Nero the Roman emperor again had Christian prisoners imprisoned. At this time Paul who sensed the last days of his life approach wrote II Timothy and sent it to Timothy.

How to read pastoral letters.

Paul met Timothy during his second missionary journey. He was accompanied by Timothy, who became his disciple. Their relataionship was so deep that Paul regarded him as a son in faith. Now Timothy was not with Paul but was pastored in Ephesus. However, in Ephesus there were many problems such as Gnosticism, corrupted Judaism, faked asceticism and so on. Finding this out, Paul wrote to young pastor Timothy to help him shun false doctrines and supervise Ephesus church well. Titus participated in Jerusalem council with Paul, conveyed Paul's letter (II Corinthians) to Corinthian church and so on. He was one of Paul's trusted disciples. He ministered in a place called Crete. Paul wrote and sent the letter Titus to convey the teachings that would be helpful in caring for Crete church.

Paul was put into prison again by the decree of emperor Nero. Right this time, sensing the flow of times and knowing his life was near the end, he left a letter with Timothy as his will. At the point of time when his life came to an end, Paul wrote II Timothy to Timothy his son in faith, saying, "suffer with the gospel."

Tong Point

To the fellow workers who dreamt of final victory
Let's figure out and observe the feelings conveyed to fellow workers by Paul who consistently walked on the way of the preacher of the gospel.

1. The letter sent to Timothy I Ti. chap.1-6

Titus and I Timothy
Titus and I Timothy were very similar in terms of time, situation and purpose. Both contain teachings about the qualification of leader, how to deal with fake teaching, the necessity of right doctrines and deeds. Both contain encouragement and advice but Titus focuses more on the deeds of saints. It was more concise than I Timothy, more official and less personal.

Timothy was a disciple Paul held dear as he called him a son in faith. Since I Timothy taught what a church was and recorded various advices to aid ministry, it is known as 'pastoral letters' along with Titus.

Originally, it was Paul's personal letter to Timothy (who cared for the Ephesian Church) but it records in detail about the leadership and organization of church. **I Timothy contains two kinds of contents about what church was. First, the body of Christians who are loved by God is the church.** About this Paul wrote in detail in Ephesians. **The second was the church as organization; he taught about church by appointing elders or deacons.** The qualification of bishops or deacons who were to serve as representatives of the church was very important. First, they needed to rule their home well and be also persons who were respected morally. Leaders needed to be well spoken of not only within the church but also outside the church. There had to be many clauses that was dealt with the qualification of leader but what was important was that they needed to live a model life without shame.

Concerning the attitude of minister, Paul said two things: first he told Timothy to be on his guard against false doctrines and second, he advised him to be nurtured with good teachings as worker of the gospel and church and practice godliness. Also he taught him in detail about discerning false teachers, how to treat older saints, widows, elders and the like.

Finally, he asked him to live the life of self-sufficiency and godliness and urged him to fight the good fight of faith. God who called Paul (who was a sinner) and entrusted him with the precious ministry also called Timothy and entrusted him with mission. So Paul asked him to devote himself with passion and do his best.

2. The letter sent to Titus Tit. chap. 1-3

Paul wrote many letters to many churches. Particularly, he wrote more passionately to churches that were in hardship or shaken by problems. Titus conveyed a special command to stabilize the church community wavering in the region of Crete.

First, Paul, who knew moral depravity which was prevalent among Cretans, stressed the necessity of righteousness of Christians in this letter. Because false teachers, especially 'circumcision sect' spoke vain words and deceived people. One of the heretics that came into being at the early stage of Christianity was Circumcision sect. They were legalists and added the condition of 'keeping the law' to the salvation by believing in Jesus Christ. This claim was that the grace of the cross of Jesus Christ was not enough to fulfill salvation. Apostle Paul called these "the men who speak myths and reject

The island of Crete
When Peter preached the gospel in Jerusalem on the day of Pentecost, there were a few Jews who came from the island of Crete(Act.2:11). Some of them may have believed in Jesus and it is very possible that they preached this gospel to the people of the island. One thing that is clear is that perhaps Paul did not have an opportunity to preach the gospel when he stopped by the island of Crete on his way to Rome (Act.27:7-13). It was 'Island of Crete.' It was a civilized city which had stone buildings in B.C.2,000 and was a city of culture more advanced than that of mainland Greece. Due to the great earthquake of around B.C.1350 and the invasion of mainland Greece, it declined. When conflict within the church was at its height owing to the serious circumcision sect, Titus was dispatched there as pastor and resolved the problems of church.

the truth and claim to know God, but by their actions deny him and detestable." In order to abolish their false doctrines and make the church stand right, Paul advised pastor Titus; " In everything set them an example by doing what is good. In your teaching show integrity, seriousness and soundness of speech that cannot be condemned, so that those who oppose you may be ashamed because they have nothing bad to say about us."

The heart of Paul's teaching was generosity and gentleness. As he saw, the church in Crete also needed generosity of accepting one another as entities of character worthy of respect just as Corinthian church did. This was an important virtue to leaders and an extremely important one to each individual.

Released briefly from prison in Rome, Paul was now on a missionary journey. It seemed that he had this letter hand-carried by Zenas and Apollos who departed from Corinth and was to stop by Crete on a trip. Since Paul planned to winter at Nicopolis that year and leave Nicopolis the next spring and go to Spain, it seemed that he wanted to be accompanied by his trusted fellow worker Titus.

3. The last letter sent to Timothy II Ti. chap.1-4

Paul who was released from Roman prison briefly prepared for Nicopolis evangelistic meeting with fellow workers. When the evangelistic meeting was being prepared, a decree was issued from Rome that all prisoners, particularly all Christian prisoners be arrested and put in prison again. So Paul was put in prison again. Sensing this time that he would be killed, Paul wrote a letter akin to his will and that was II Timothy. The contents of this will was (in a word): "Suffer with the gospel." Paul told him to suffer with the good news of Jesus.

The Gospel and suffering cannot be separated from each other. However, if ordinary people are asked to suffer with the gospel, they throw away even the gospel because they do not like suffering. Yet, since this suffering is a blessing, Paul told us to suffer with the gospel. Here Paul takes the examples; that no one serving as a soldier gets involved in civilian affairs, that an athlete does not receive the victor's crown unless he competes according to the rules and that only a hardworking farmer will receive a share of the crops and the like. For Paul, Timothy and Titus were as good as his own sons. No father wants to give his sons trouble. Paul did not ask Timothy to suffer because he was not his father in flesh. Paul was a real father who advised his spiritual son to go on the way of true joy. Paul had been trained through so many days of hardship and now he taught Timothy that lifestyle.

"Preach the Word; be prepared in season and out of season; correct, rebuke and encourage - with great patience and careful instruction (II Ti.4:2)." Such a strong request as "Preach the Word; be prepared in season and out of season" meant that he taught Timothy the life attitude of gospel preacher and asked him to live by it just as he had pursued only the one way as gospel preacher. The picture of Paul putting in order his life in prison was greatness of gospel preacher who had overcome hardship. After Paul ran over a wide area and was about to finish his life, he left the gospel of Jesus Christ with his spiritual son Timothy and then left this world. This way the mission of

Leaving behind what is valuable

There are times when we need to leave behind what we have valuably achieved to someone. When such time approached, Paul, left the most important task of preaching the gospel to Timothy. The church which had been handed down and down this way is our church today.

evangelism was handed down to Timothy from Paul.

Write down the contents of this lesson in the form of Tong Story

Let's pray in a loud voice so that we may be able to teach the contents of this lesson to our children

- Teach them to your children, talking about them when you sit at home and when you walk along the road, when you lie down and when you get up……so that your days and the days of your children may be many……as many as the days that the heavens are above the earth (Deuteronomy 11:19-21).
- you know those from whom you learned it, and how from infancy you have known the holy Scriptures(II Timothy 3:14-15).

Track 7

The 9 Epistles

Tong Track 7 - The atmosphere of the 9 Epistles

The atmosphere of the 9 Epistles (Hebrew, James, I&II Peter, Jude, I&II&III John, and Revelation) is that of the attainment of the Kingdom of Heaven under the persecution of the Roman Empire. From A.D.30 to A.D.64, the thirty or so years of Acts suffered under the opposition of Christianity by the Jewish authorities.

However, in A.D.64 immediately after the great fire of Rome, Christianity was scrutinized under the Roman Empire incomparable to that of the Jewish authorities. This was due to Rome pointing their fingers at Christians as culprits for starting the fire. At this point, St. Paul sent a letter to Timothy from inside his cell, which brought about yet another change in the atmosphere.

"For I am now ready to be offered, and the time of my departure is at hand. I have fought a good fight, I have finished my course, I have kept the faith: Henceforth there is laid up for me a crown of righteousness, which the LORD, the righteous judge, shall give me at that day: and not to me only, but unto all them also that love his appearing" (II Ti.4:6-8).

St. Paul did not despair at his death but rather became the driving force behind the righteous fight against the Roman Empire and other heterodoxies. In the end, in A.D.313, Christianity prevailed by triumphing after 250 years of Rome's scrutiny.

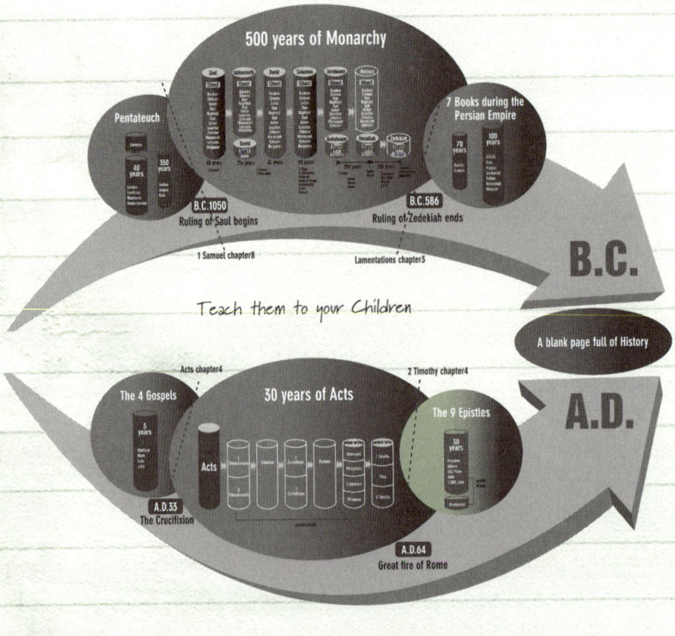

19 Session

Letters for the Righteous Fight

Tong Map

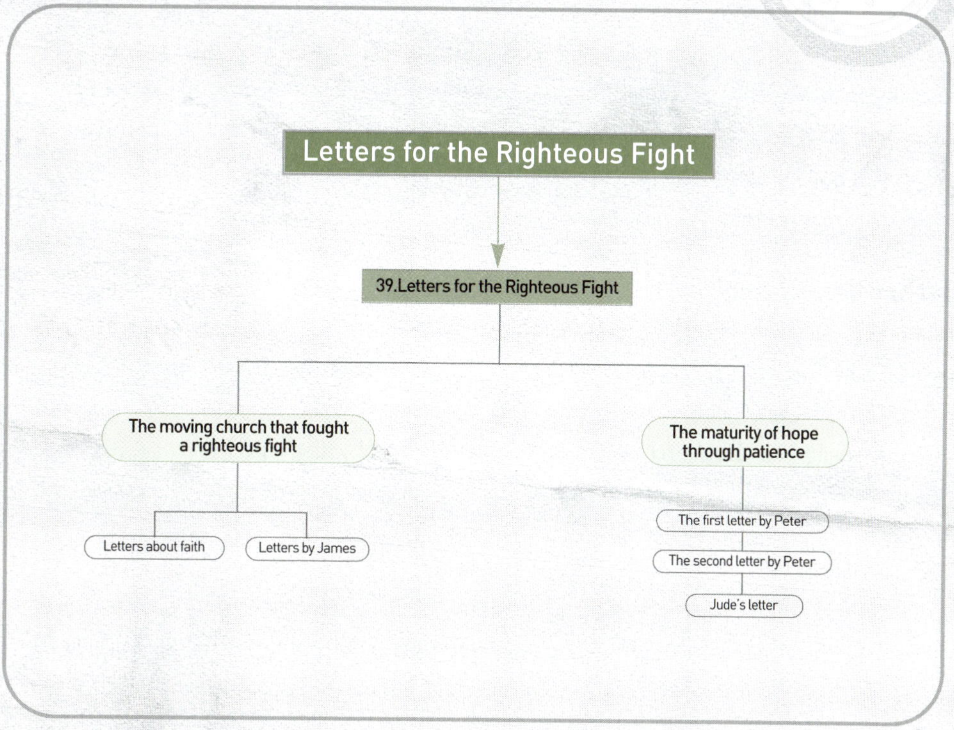

Tong Concept

- **General letters! Letters for good fighting!**

Here we observe general letters which unfold for us the viewpoints with which we can see by faith the fact that saints suffered for the gospel and sometimes were even martyred in the midst of great trials of church community.

Tong At a glance

✻ Looking around the forest

After Christians were held responsible for the great fire in Rome in A.D.64, persecution and oppression against the saints in the empire gradually became stronger. Even worse, false teachers came into the church and made the saints (who were weak in faith) confused. Therefore, apostles had to carry out the duty of having to comfort, encourage and teach saints to keep faith with courage.

Hebrews, James, I Peter, II Peter, Jude, I John, II John, III John …… all these letters were the letters which contained labor, sweat and effort of apostles who have served with all their souls. They are called 'general letters.' The recipients were not particular people but general readers except for II John and III John.

✻ Land and annual ring

Once Roman empire's persecution against Christians was launched, many Christians tried to return to Judaism or even some determined to betray Christianity. It was the time when various heresies came into being in response to this and confusion became greater. The apostles who were responsible for the church began to write letters to solve these problems.

✻ Wind and Climate

One of the heresies which were prevalent in the days of the early church was Gnosticism in which they had the dualistic thought of seeing materials as evil and spirit as good. They claimed that the body of Jesus was not real but only had outward appearance because if Jesus had body, it would be evil, according to them.

However, this was against the Bible. I John stressed that it was an unshakable truth that Jesus was both perfect God and a perfect man. At the same time I John contains a wonderful intuition that 'God is love.'

Tong Seeing the forest

Hebrews Hebrews shows us where the root of faith began by tracing the history from the Old Testament to Jesus Christ and from Jesus Christ to the people of those days. Though the writer is not known clearly, there is an opinion that perhaps Paul wrote it.

James General letters including James were written on the premise of great persecution. Since the situation of those days was as such, there were always tempting apostacy that told believers to deny Jesus Christ. In such times, there was need of faith that did not give up but endured to the end; faith that worked in action. James insisted that the kingdom of God came upon this world not by the people who were tossed here and there by the waves and winds of this world but by the Christians who were equipped with firm faith and specific practice.

I Peter This was written to give energy and encouragement to saints who endured suffering and persecution. He said that the person who had strong hope and vision for future had the power to be able to turn present trial and suffering into joy. Stressing this fact, he told a true hope in Jesus Christ to churches in Asia Minor.

II Peter Seen from the forest of the whole Bible, Satan had tried to shake all those who had faith in God with temptation and blasphemy. He tempted Adam, made the people of Noah's days stumble and tempted Job and still is working without rest.
However, God saved Noah and delivered Israel out of Egypt. Stressing that the help of God was with those who keep faith to the end amid much temptation and trial, Peter encouraged them to keep faith to the end. This was written to comfort the saints in hardship and to give them energy.

Jude Jude is the precious word that teaches how church should keep firm faith in the midst of the field of spiritual war where church was persecuted and some saints turned away from faith.

39 Lesson : Letters for the Righteous Fight

Hebrews, James, I Peter, II Peter, Jude

Accumulative reading amount 97.92% 1189

The One Year Tongdok Bible Days 351-357 | Reading time 55 minutes

TongBible Story Overview

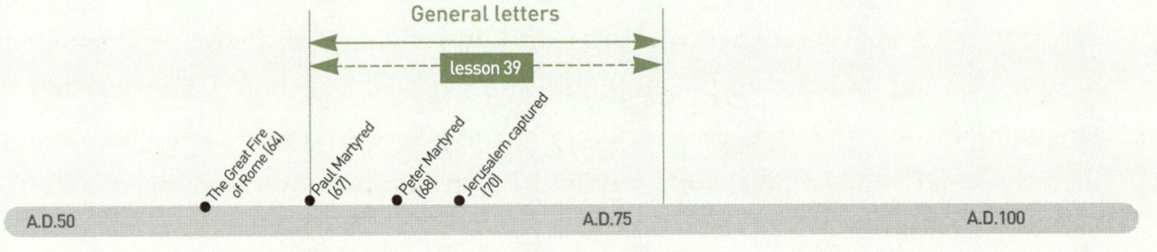

Reading the New Testament in detail in the order of history (13)

After we have finished reading all the letters of Paul, we come to read general letters. Let's read through while thinking about the messages, circumstances of writers and recipients of each letter(Hebrews, James, I Peter, II Peter and Jude).

How to read general letters

We can see that an erudite knowledge about the Old Testament was the foundation of the letter of Hebrews. James makes us feel as if we are looking at Proverbs of the Old Testament. I Peter was the letter of Peter written to comfort all the saints who were looked down on, misunderstood and persecuted in the Roman empire in those days. Coming next, II Peter is like a written will of Apostle Peter. He wrote this to point out the evils of Gnosticism, a religion of mystic philosophy that began to arise in the church in those days and to warn the saints against false teachers. Jude was a warning against Gnosticism that was prevalent in those times, which claimed that materials are evil and spirit was good. Jude strongly claims that Jesus was a perfect God and a perfect man.

Tong Point

The moving church that fought a righteous fight
Christians who were held responsible for the great fire in Rome in A.D.64 were put into a situation where leaders were martyred. There also appeared false teachers and heretic thoughts in and outside of church community. At this time the general letters written for saints to overcome persecution Show that saints suffered for the gospel and sometimes were even martyred. Literally, they were 'letters for the righteous fight.' We should to read 'general letters' on the premise of these contents.

1. Letter about faith Heb. chap.1-13

Faith(Heb.11:1)
Here the writer of Hebrews the word 'faith' many times to stress the faith of believing in God. He said that we cannot please God without faith (Heb.11:6).

As persecution and hardship came more severely upon the saints of the early church who believed and confessed Jesus was the Savior and became Christians, there formed those who gave up Christianity and returned to Judaism. Therefore, church leaders had to help them make their faith in Jesus Christ by persuading and encouraging them.

Judaism which had the consciousness of being elected by God did not propagate their religion. However, the reason God made the people of Israel a kingdom of priests was not because they were more excellent than other nations. They were so prejudiced that they misunderstood God whose plan was to first choose them, make them know and experience God and then make them serve all the people of the world. In Judaism the Jews hold on to the supremacy of their nation and consider knowledge of laws and tradition important. However, the heart of Christianity is to have to preach to the ends of the earth that all have been saved by Jesus Christ who bore their sins while dying on the cross. That was why Christians preached even amid hardship and persecution and stressed change.

The writer of Hebrews tells believers to be on their guard against the folly of returning to the past because of external dangers after having found what was genuine. Therefore he taught by comparing Judaism with Christianity. He listed what are considered important in Judaism and tried to help Christians' faith by telling them that Jesus was above all.

Tong Point

Judaism vs. Christianity

Judaism	Stresses tradition and ceremony	Consciousness of being God's chosen people	Stresses strengthening solidarity of members	Stagnant community	Welcomed by people around them	Do not tell people to join
Christianity	Stresses changes and life	Thought of equality	Stresses expansion of community through evangelism	Dynamic community	Persecuted by people around them	Evangelize even with the risk of life

Judaism did not evangelize due to their consiousness of being chosen but Christianity did its best to spread the gospel to the ends of the world.

● Prophets of Judaism and Jesus : Though the prophets of the Old Testament preached the word to the people of Israel when required while influencing them, their word was completed. However, Jesus the Son of God came as perfector of the word.

● Angels and Jesus : Angels are beings with which Jews have been familiar. The writer declared that Jesus was more outstanding than the angels.

● Moses and Jesus : Moses was the great leader and was held in honor by the Jews. However, Moses was a servant in God's house.

● Joshua and Jesus : Because Joshua who led the Canaan Conquest War guided them into the land of Canaan it did not mean they enjoyed true rest. However, in Jesus we can lay down our burdensome loads and enjoy true rest.

● Legitimate priest and Jesus : God exalted Melchizedek who blessed Abraham more highly than the priest of Levite division who was regarded as absolute one by the Jews. Therefore, he explained that Jesus in the division of that Melchizedek was beyond the law and higher than that authority. Now what was not made perfect by the law which was the old covenant was completed as perfect salvation by Jesus Christ who was the new covenant.

● Temple and Jesus : True temple is not on this earth and is in the eternal world of God. Jesus was the one who offered his blood as sacrifice of redemption for sinners once and for all in the greater and perfect tabernacle not made by hand; but in the heavenly sanctuary.

Christ the letter of Hebrews describes
Hebrews describes Christ as God-man, prophet, priest and king. It emphasizes his divinity and human nature equally and explains his attributes and accomplishments by using more than 20 positions such as apostle, high priest, mediator and so on.

● Sacrifice and Jesus : Jesus was the last high priest that God appointed. The previous priests sacrificed on every feast whenever the people wanted, but Jesus sacrificed himself to redeem the sin of all mankind once and for all. This was the way of expressing the absolute love of God who wanted to save all the people.

The writer of Hebrews says that therefore Christianity is the truth and therefore it is natural that Christianity will suffer hardship and persecution.

Hebrews emphasizes faith: "Now faith is being sure of what we hope for and certain of what we do not see. This is what the ancients were commended for"(Heb.11:1-2). "And without faith it is impossible to please God, because anyone who comes to Him must believe that He exists and that He rewards those who earnestly seek Him"(Heb.11:6).

The long letter that exhorted and encouraged the saints who struggled to overcome the temptation of apostasy and persecution came to an end with the word of hope and request that there would be victory of resurrection at the end of the hard-to-endure suffering of the followers of Jesus.

2. Letter by James Jam. chap.1-5

James told the saints who lived scattered in many places being persecuted and tempted to consider the suffering joyful. Like Apostle Paul, James was the one who knew that the testing of faith developed perseverance and suffering was also blessing. To those who went through much hardship and trial, James confirmed the promise of hope that God would give them the crown of life. ''Blessed is the man who perseveres under trial, because when he has stood the test, he will receive the crown of life that God has promised to those who love

James

James (the author of the letter of James) was Jesus' younger brother who was born between Joseph and Mary after Jesus was born. He did not accept the word of Jesus until he rose from the dead and appeared to him in person (I Co.15:7). James and his brothers were among the saints who earnestly hoped for the coming of the Holy Spirit on Pentecost(Act.1:14). Soon James became a respected leader of Jerusalem church. He showed up as a central figure in Jerusalem Council (Act.chap.15).

Him"(Jam.1:12).

James stressed deeds, telling even "faith by itself, if not accompanied by deeds, was dead." Seemingly at a glance these contents look contrary to the word "to be saved only by faith" in Romans or Galatians. However, seen from the forest of the entire Bible, it never is. **Paul taught us to receive the gospel of Jesus Christ into the heart. On the other hand, James taught us to reveal the gospel out of us. Paul said the source of faith. James spoke of the fruit of faith.** He said that already saved saints should show deeds as fruits of faith. Deeds do not save us. However, at the same time we also should not know the life and work of Jesus only by head. As there was the way of cross on which Jesus walked shedding tears and sweat, so should his followers have specific traces of life. **Because to serve and to love only by tongue cannot help our neighbors at all and Christians without deeds cannot emit any light and fragrance in this world.**

James unceasingly emphasized the importance of deeds along with faith. The words of general letters also ask Christians today for the same faith. Today the kingdom of God comes upon this land through Christians who do not live tossed by winds and waves of this world but are equipped with firm faith and specific practice of their faith.

Tong Point

The maturity of hope through patience
Peter talks about 'suffering' and 'hope' in I Peter and II Peter by combining them. When we think of tomorrow's glory amid affliction, wisdom appears. We should become mature amid affliction, not arrogant when we are in glory and should dream of the possibility of being developed amid blessing. We should be able to control our behavior, endure and be patient in the midst of affliction and think of mission, tears, labor and affliction in the midst of glory.

3. The first letter by Peter I Pe. chap.1-5

In A.D.64 Roman Emperor Nero held Christians responsible for a great fire, and persecution against Christianity became very severe speedily. Persecution was both cruel and severe. In this situation, Peter could not help worrying about the future of the church.

Peter's letter was written to give strength and encouragement to the saints who endured suffering and persecution. Though it was very hard for saints to endure suffering, it also made their faith much stronger. Hope requires patience. The person who has tomorrow needs patience. The man who has a strong hope for future has power to be able to turn present trial and suffering into joy. Peter wrote about the right attitude of Christian's life on the basis of the hope in Jesus.

● Love : The word of Jesus Christ who told us to love even our enemies was explained only by God's love. Since we have already received the great love of Jesus Christ who died vicariously for us, we are debtors to his love.

Peter

Peter was one of the best the disciple of Jesus. While Jesus was alive, he was the head of disciples. He confessed his faith; "You are the Christ, the Son of the living God." The meaning of his name was 'rock.' He once denied Jesus, but gained trust again. Later, he confessed "love covers over a multitude of sins." He experienced Jesus covering all his sins. In the relationship with Cornelius he broke down the wall, contributed to helping the Gentiles and the elect break down their wall and became a leader of the early church.

- Set examples of goodness : Those who have received grace first should play the role of priests with the mind of indebtedness and responsibility. It meant that just because they were first saved they should not separate themselves from the world and live locked within their own fence but set good examples all the more in society.

- Watch your speech : One of the secrets to get blessings in life is to control the word of mouth. Peter urged saints to live reaping the fruits of righteousness with peace and mercy by speaking words of blessing and praise rather than those of exposing faults of other people.

- Be examples to the flock : The attitude of all those who served in the church was not to become greedy, but to gain but a cheerful will. Those who had positions in the church were to not take the attitude of asserting their views, but only to become examples to the flock.

4. The second letter by Peter II Pe. chap. 1-3

The contents of II Peter was to ask them to be on their guard against the matter of false prophets. They were known to lead saints into falsehood. Peter warned about the teaching of such false teachers.

Some time after Jesus was taken up to heaven, there began to be some in the church who doubted the ministry of Jesus. But Peter clearly stated that the ministry of Jesus and his death on the cross and his resurrection were not fake made-up stories. "We did not follow cleverly invented stories when we told you about the power and coming of our LORD Jesus Christ, but we were eyewitnesses of his majesty"(II Pe.1:16). Peter also advised, "It is easy to distort the Scripture if we try to interpret it by our own wisdom. Don't interpret it by your own wisdom" (II Pe.1:20-21; 3:16).

To those who hoped for the promise of God and endured each day, false teachers said deceitfully, "Jesus will not come again." Among those who heard it, there were be some who felt that the promise was delayed. But Peter awakened them again by saying that the day of salvation that God promised would surely come. He said; "The LORD is not slow in keeping His promise, as some understand slowness." "With the LORD a day is like a thousand years, and a thousand years are like a day." **Though the promise is slow, it will be fulfilled surely. Because God promised and He will fulfill.**

Only brief suffering

Peter saw oppression as brief agony. He encouraged saints to tolerate, endure and bear oppression. What he stressed the most was that saints should not fall into fear when facing fierce trial but depend on God with prayer and supplication. Because the power to overcome oppression is given only by God.

Themes of I and II Peter

I Peter
- "suffering"
- Explaining new birth through the word of life
- hope

II Peter
- "knowledge"(empirical awareness)
- Emphasizing the necessity of growth in the grace and knowledge of Christ
- Eradication of heresies

5. Jude's letter Jude

Jude is a letter that was written to urge saints to maintain strong faith through the hard times. Affliction and persecution came upon saints. Jude heard the news that the church came to be in trouble and they fought hard. At this, Jude exhorted them to fight the evil power groups to keep the way of faith. Jude warned that woe would come upon false teachers and said that their sin was like the crookedness of Cain who killed his younger brother Abel due to his jealousy, of Balaam who

Faith that overcomes temptation
Since the creation of the human race, Satan has tempted Adam, made the people of Noah's times stumble and seduced Balaam. However, God delivered Noah and led Israel into Canaan. There are also a lot of temptations today. However, God will lead into eternal salvation and rest those who keep faith and righteousness to the end and are equipped with the wisdom of discerning falsehood with the standard of the Bible.

coveted the unrighteous wages and of Korah who resisted Moses. These men were grumblers and fault finders; they followed their own evil desires; they were full of language of boasting and flattering. Jude told believers not to go on the way of these false teachers by remembering the words the apostles of Jesus Christ.

The event of Jesus Christ's resurrection has an important meaning in that all his believers gained victory. However, fighting is not finished. Therefore, we need mutual encouragement, prayer, our own will and endeavor. One fact that can not be changed, however intense the fight may be, is the fact that eventually all Christians will participate in the victory of Jesus Christ.

Write down the contents of this lesson in the form of Tong Story

Let's pray in a loud voice so that we may be able to teach the contents of this lesson to our children

- Teach them to your children, talking about them when you sit at home and when you walk along the road, when you lie down and when you get up……so that your days and the days of your children may be many……as many as the days that the heavens are above the earth (Deuteronomy 11:19-21).
- you know those from whom you learned it, and how from infancy you have known the holy Scriptures(II Timothy 3:14-15).

20 Session

Song of Victory Pre-received

Tong Map

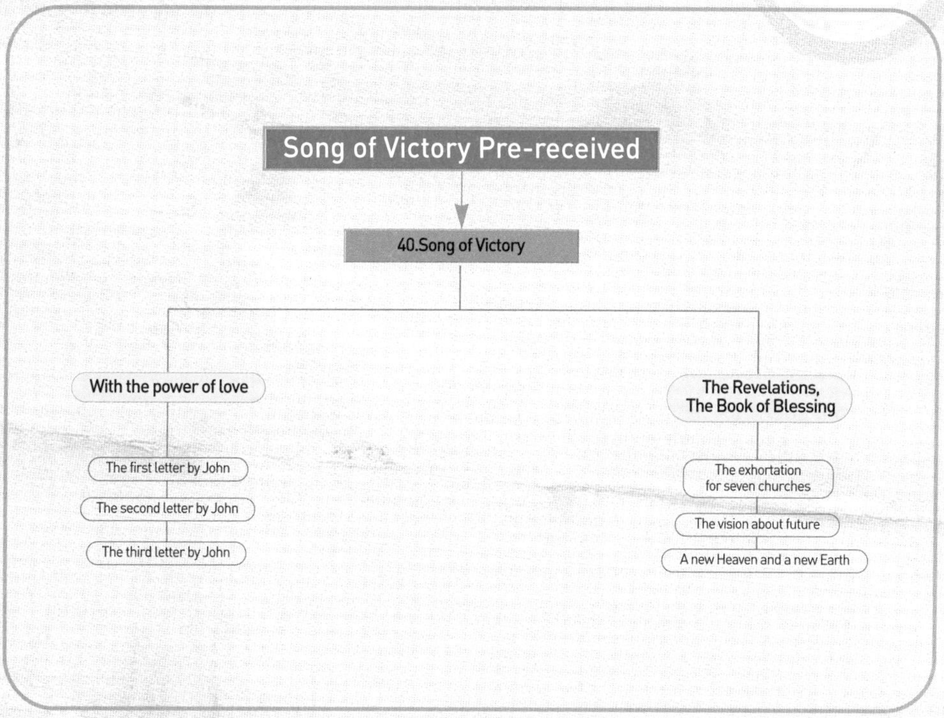

Tong Concept

- **John's letters! Loving God and loving neighbors**

We observe that 'God is love' through I John, 'harmony between love and truth' through II John and 'Gaius who deserves to be commended' through III John.

- **The Revelation, the song of victory received in advance.**

The Revelation was the word of revelation that new heaven and new earth would be given as gift eventuallly to the saints of the early church who were to keep faith to the point of being ready to be martyred in front of the sword of the Roman Empire. It explains in such a way that we may be able to hope for the day of hope rather than interpret the letters themselves.

Tong At a glance

✻ Looking around the forest

In the era which became the background of the Revelation, the persecution of Roman Empire was very severe. In the early days of Roman Empire unfolded a generous policy for the foreign religions. However, after Emperor Nero seized power, he began to oppress religions in the form of 'emperor worship' as he saw national discipline weaken.

Although Nero's oppression was fearful, it was temporary. However, later the oppression of Emperor Domitian was systematic and lasting. Previously they had worshipped the dead emperors but Domitian was the first to order people to worship the sitting emperor who was alive. As Christians refused to worship the sitting emperor, they were all the more oppressed. That the Revelation had many symbolic language and vision has a deep relationship with this kind of situation.

✻ Land and annual ring

Among John's letters II John and III John were the letters sent to particular persons except for I John. It is thought that they were written in A.D.85-95. There is a strong possibility that the Revelation was written around A.D.95-96 when Roman oppression against Christianity became public.

During the rule of Domitianus the Roman Emperor(A.D.81-96) the oppression against Christians was at its height, which created a great confrontation between Roman Empire and Christians. John preached the word of prophecy to the seven churches in Asia under Roman rule.

✻ Wind and Climate

After the oppression of Domitianus, it was Trajan the Roman Emperor(A.D.98-117) who continued to oppress Christians. Under his rule Christians were already distinguished from Jews and regarded as a secret group.

Under Roman rule, just because someone was found to be a Christian he was not killed immediately. Any seized Christian was given opportunity to deny and give up his faith. But this meant that he or she had to swear to worship the image of emperor and curse Christ. This condition was not acceptable to Christians at all and those Christians who refused this condition had to be martyred right away.

Tong Seeing the forest

I John In John's Gospel he showed how Jesus lived as the light of the world whereas in I John he tells us how Christians who follow Jesus, who is the light of the world, should live as the light of the world.
Apostle John confirmed that "God is love" and stressed that we should know His love and live practicing love by following him.

II John II John says that Christians should love brothers and also told saints to take firm measures against those who did not follow right truth but denied Jesus Christ. This was not saying that they were to distinguish people in the church from those outside of church. Church were to embrace all people of the world with the mind of Christ whether they were believers or not. However, John warned saints to turn away from false teachers who tried to make believers stumble with wrong doctrines.

III John This was Apostle John's letter of gratitude to Gaius who opened his house for gospel preachers, who had preached from place to place, and treated them with food so that they could preach the gospel again with new energy.
In his earnest prayer for Gaius, John expressed his mind of wishing he may enjoy good health and that all may go well.

Revelation Revelation is filled with many visions because, for the early church saints of 2,000 years ago, they were figures of speech easy to understand. In a critical situation where more believers gave up faith in the midst of suffering and went on the way of apostacy, Revelation says that there was ultimate hope for the one who endures present suffering and waits.

40 Lesson

Song of Victory

I John, II John, III John, Revelation

Accumulative reading amount 100% 1189

The One Year Tongdok Bible Days 358-365 | Reading time 60 minutes

TongBible Story Overview

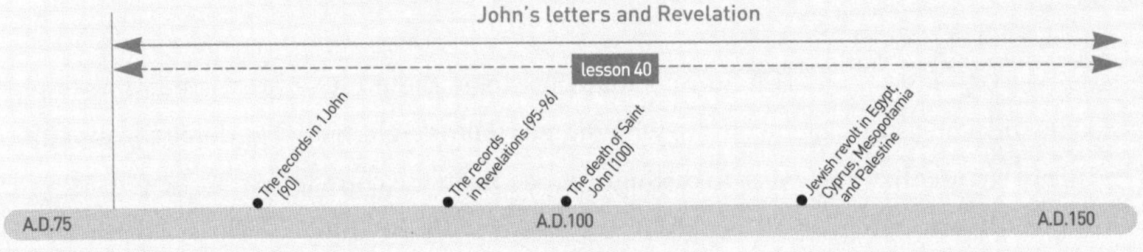

Reading the New Testament in detail in the order of history (14)

The books we are going to read through from now on are the letters written by John. We read I John, II John and III John with the mind of Apostle John who lived the longest among Jesus' disciples and took care of churches and saints. And finally we read the Revelation which is the last book of 66 books of the Bible. Although we may not understand Revelation right away, it is the blessed word to all 'those who read it, hear it and take it to heart.' After we have read it, let's confess, "Amen. Come, LORD Jesus" with overflowing feelings as Apostle John did.

How to read John's letters and Revelation

John, who lived the longest among Jesus' disciples was responsible for churches and cared for the saints, thought about Jesus over and over and again. As a result, he deeply realized that Jesus Christ (the real entity of love) came to this earth to love us and even gave his life. Afterward, apostle John was sent to the island of Patmos on exile, saw the visions of new heavens and new earth and wrote Revelation. Since the contents were about the hope that persecuting Rome would be destroyed and the eventual day of victory, that is, the day when freedom of religion would be allowed will come, difficult parables were used so that Romans could not understand them even while reading them.

Tong Point

With the power of love

The churches in the days when John's letters were written were amidst repeated confusion due to lots of wrong teaching. There were occasions when they destroyed Christian truths by interpreting Christianity with the worldview, lifeview and the way of thinking of the Gentile society. There were also occasions when they clouded the purity of Christianity by adding something to the gospel or subtracting something from it. Apostle John strongly urged saints to utterly reject the teaching of these false prophets and to overcome everything with the power of love as saints who were loved by God(I Jo.4:1-4).

1. The first letter by John I Jo. chap.1-5

Apostle John
- The one who was loved by Jesus
- Had a great brotherly love(elder brother James)
- Had lots of special experience with Peter and James while Jesus was alive.
- Jesus told John to look after his mother Mary
- Writer of John's Gospel, I, II, III John and Revelation
- Lived the longest among twelve disciples

John declared, "God is love." The theme of I John is fellowship with God and fellowship with neighbors. John called faith fellowship between God and man and fellowship between man and man. He said that completion of fellowship was love. And true fellowship with God was possible only through Jesus Christ who redeemed our sins on our behalf.

And this love required labor. Love should not be expressed just by speech but in the form of action. Believing in Christ is revealed when we practice love for our brothers. Jesus' love for people also took labor. There should also be labor in our love. John said that whoever does not love does not know God (I Jo.4:8).

Apostle John declared at the end of this letter that everyone who is born of God overcomes the world. When John's letters were written, the churches were in confusion due to many wrong teachings. Apostle John told saints to utterly reject the teachings of these false teachers and overcome everything with the power of love as saints who received the love of God. This is because with the power of God's love we can overcome any temptations.

The theme of the Bible which I John clearly shows was that he who believes in Jesus is saved; that the LORD gives eternal life. Whoever believes in the Son of God has eternal life, but whoever does not cannot have eternal life. Though the world is overflowing with so many kinds of thought and belief, the way that gives us salvation and eternal life is only Jesus.

Contrast of concepts found in I John

light	darkness
truth	falsehood
love	hatred
Loving the Father	Loving the world
Christ	Antichrist
God's children	The devil's children
Righteousness	Sin
God's spirit	Antichrist's spirit
life	death

2. The second letter by John II Jo. chap.1

This letter seems to be a personal letter sent to a woman. In those days the teaching of Gnosticists came into fashion in the early church and made Christians stumble. They stressed Jesus as the Son of God so much that they did not consider Jesus' sweating ministry as man. They denied the incarnation of Jesus. John who enjoyed intimate love with Jesus closely while living with him for three years stressed that believers should not follow such false teaching. He asked those who had already been elected and became the LORD's children to keep themselves from these false teachings.

Furthermore, he told them not to let heretics come in their house while warning them against them. "If anyone comes to you and does not bring this teaching, do not take him into your house or welcome him" (II Jo.1:10). Only by doing so can the power of truth be made to last in the church.

Gnosticism

The teaching of the heresy called Gnosticism was as follows;

1. Knowledge is superior to virtue.
2. Salvation is given only to some people chosen by unknown God who has nothing to do with the material world directly.
3. Divinity cannot be combined with material like body, and they cannot believe the incarnation of Jesus.
4. There is no such a thing as resurrection of body.

The dualistic thought of Gnosticism about spirit and flesh was revealed in two different forms; The first is extreme asceticism that prohibits all meat eating and sexual intercourse. The second, on the other hand, is ethical dissipation that it is all right even if you become lascivious claiming that flesh is totally useless.

3. The third letter by John III Jo. chap.1

The purpose of III John
1. To protect truth and commend Gaius who treated well the evangelists John sent
2. To encourage Gaius to keep supporting evangelist brothers
3. To reproach the arrogance and bad behavior of Diotrephes
4. To recommend Demetrius
5. To inform Gaius that John planned to visit personally and deal with these matters in person

"Dear friend, I pray that you may enjoy good health and that all may go well with you, even as your soul is getting along well" (III Jo.1:2).

This beautiful word of blessing was the word in the letter that apostle John wrote to a man called Gaius. In those days evangelists had to experience much difficulty. Since accommodations were not developed like today, it was very difficult to eat and sleep during the journey. However, a man called Gaius let his house be used by evangelists; he invited them, fed them, let them sleep in his house and helped them with travel money. He warmly welcomed evangelists who became travelers for the gospel of the LORD. All these things edified the church greatly and furthermore helped greatly the preaching of the gospel. The evangelists who stayed at the house of Gaius praised him at the church. Hearing this, Apostle John wrote a letter to him.

Tong Point

The Revelation, The Book of Blessing
It may be hard to understand all the contents of the Revelation right away. But God said, Blessed is the one who reads the words of this prophecy, and blessed are those who hear it and take to heart what is written in it(Rev.1:3). Because this word is the word that becomes comfort and strength to those who keep firm faith and the word given for the victory of Christians and church. So we can say that the Revelation is 'anthem of final victory of Christians.'

4. The exhortation for seven churches Rev. chap.1-3

John who became an old man was on the island of Patmos on exile. However, he still encouraged and strengthened churches which were the fruits of Christ's precious sacrifice.

God gave the words of prophecy to the seven churches in Asia and furthermore to a great number of churches through the enthusiasm of John. It may be hard to immediately understand every letter and vocabulary of this word. However, **God declared, "Blessed is the one who reads the words of this prophecy, and blessed are those who hear it and take to heart what is written in it"(Rev.1:3). God gave the word of this revelation for the the victory of Christians and churches. Therefore, we can call Revelation 'the anthem of victory of Christians.'**

The victory of Jesus Christ was fulfilled already on the cross. Now only the victory of Christians themselves remains. Although God Himself guards and protects churches, He gave this word so that churches may be blessed. This word is the love of God who hopes that each Christian and church will become victorious in the last days by keeping their mind faithfully.

God commanded John, who was to receive this song of victory in advance, to write "what you have seen", "what is now" and "what will take place later." This was the command that John was to receive the already prepared news of victory, tell it to the saints and leave it for later generations in the form of writing.

According to the word of God, John came to write and send

The island of Patmos
The island of Patmos, which is thought to be the place where Revelation was written, was an island where political prisoners were sent on exile during the Roman period and its circumference was about 27km. There was a quarry there during the period of Rome where seemingly political prisoners suffered forced labor.

the revelation of the Holy Spirit he saw through visions to seven churches in Asia. **We can say that the seven churches in Asia, that is, Ephesus, Smyrna, Pergamum, Thyatira, Sardis, Philadelphia and Laodicea were representative of the conditions of faith which were prevalent in those days.**

The first was Ephesus church whose love cooled down.

The second was Smyrna church which was promised the crown of life.

The third was Pergamum church which indulged in the teaching of the Nicolaitans.

The fourth was Thyatira church which allowed idolatry and immorality.

The fifth was Sardis church which had a reputation of being alive but was actually dead.

The sixth was Philadelphia church which kept the word and did not betray it.

The seventh was Laodicea church which was not at all passionate.

God spoke to these seven churches not to reprove, rebuke and punish but to help them overcome suffering.

5. The vision about future Rev. chap.4-20

John heard a voice from heaven that commanded him to come up. In the heaven John saw seated on the throne the one who died on the cross, rose from the dead and was taken up to heaven. Around it there were four creatures and 24 elders. Day and night they praised God ceaselessly. "Holy, holy, holy is the LORD God Almighty, who was, and is, and is to come"(Rev.4:8).

In the right hand of God who was seated on the throne was a scroll sealed with seven seals. Though an angel asked who was worthy to open the scroll and break the seals, no one in this world could either open the scroll or look at it. Who can understand God's providence and plan perfectly? Apostle John wept and wept because no one was worthy to open the scroll. However, one of the elders said "the Root of David has triumphed. He is able to open the scroll and its seven seals." The Root of David was none other than Jesus Christ the Lamb of God. Only he was worthy to open the seven seals.

From Revelation chapter 6 is recorded a long list of visions John saw about future. The figure '7' often appears throughout Revelation. Finally, the lamb begins to break off the seven seals that are to bring in judgments. Everytime a seal is broken off, a tribulation of huge scale strikes. Generally it is thought that the first seal stands for war, second seal stands for civil war, third famine, fourth pestilence, fifth religious oppression and sixth natural disaster. Seals are broken off and the whole world is put into tribulation but there is no one who can stop that authority.

Then is recorded the situation of the time when the seventh seal was broken off. The first half hour after the seventh seal was broken off, it was very silent just like the night before a great storm. However, the silence was a sign of the great disaster that was to follow.

The seventh seal was followed by seven trumpets, and seven prepared angels sound seven trumpets. Everytime each angel

Jesus revealed in the Revelation

- The one who deserves to open seven seals(5:5)
- The Lamb who has seven horns and seven eyes(5:6)
- The one who is worthy to receive power, wealth, wisdom, strength, honor, glory and praise(5:12)
- The one who is the Alpha and the Omega, the First and the Last, the Beginning and the End(22:13).
- The one who is the Root and the Offspring of David(22:16)
- The bright Morning Star(22:16)

sounded his trumpet, disaster stroke the world (Rev. chap.8-9). When the first trumpet was sounded, hail and fire mixed with blood burn a third of the earth. When the second trumpet was sounded, a third of the sea turned into blood. When the third trumpet was sounded, a star named Worm-wood falls from heaven and made a third of the waters bitter. When the fourth trumpet was sounded, a third each of the sun, the moon and stars turned dark and a third each of day and night turned dark. When the fifth trumpet was sounded, a star that fell from the sky opens the Abyss. The locusts that came up out of the Abyss received the power to harm people and harass those who did not have the seal of God on their foreheads. When the sixth trumpet was sounded, a third of mankind were killed by the disasters of fire, smoke and sulfur.

Even amid the history of this dark world were God's patience and mercy overflowing. Though church suffers affliction in the tribulation of the world, the work of faith and the work of martyrdom were together in it. God's grace for the chosen saints was continued as ever to the end.

The adversaries of God appear in Revelation chapter twelve. The adversaries, who were represented by dragons, blaspheme a male baby who was to rule all the nations according to God's plan and at the same time persecute the woman who had given birth to the baby. God drove blasphemers out of heaven to earth by sending His angels. It was difficult for Christians to endure the oppression of Roman empire in those days. Keeping on keeping faith in those days was as hard as being ready to die at any point. The vision that God would surely judge the power of evil became comfort and encouragement to the saints who kept faith.

As the seven seals were followed by the seven trumpets and then followed by seven bowls, the disasters to come to judge became greater gradually. Though God extended love without reservation to mankind to the point of giving His only begotten Son, He also judged those who were mired in sin and live foolishly. Satan who blasphemed God would be thrown into the Abyss and sealed a thousand years. While the root of evil is seized, the people of God will reign with Jesus Christ. After those thousand years have passed, Satan would be thrown into the lake of fire and sulfur and be tormented forever. The power of Satan would be powerless before the judgment of God eventually and the reign of God would be fulfilled finally.

No man can escape the judgment of God. Judgment is waiting after death as appointed by God. The grounds of judgment are 'books' where all the deeds that people have done are recorded without missing anything. If the saints were to remember that they would be judged according to the books where their deeds were recorded, they would be able to keep on keeping their faith even in the midst of tough circumstances. The faith that truth is alive and eternal, though evil is prevalent, is the energy that makes us hold on to the word firmly.

Praising the Lamb
Beautiful is the song of praise given to God and the Lamb who is seated on the throne of God. Awesome is the praise sung not for the thrones of the world but for God who is the superintendent of history and Jesus the Lamb.

6. A new Heaven and a new Earth Rev. chap.21-22

In the end he who sat on the throne said, "I am making everything new!"(Rev.21:5). Who indeed in this world can say this? Only God can make everything new. There unfolds the sight of the new Jerusalem which was the beautiful work of God. In John's view the new Jerusalem was like a bride beautifully dressed for her husband. This sight was the Heart of God (who created the universe and was pleased) in the beginning fully fulfilled and restored. Can you imagine the joy of God that indwells all things of this universe?

Hope is not made in us. Hope begins in the covenant of God, that is, the promise that Jesus Christ the Lamb will come to this world and restore everything. **The prophecy of a new heaven and a new earth that God shows in the last part of Revelation is a vision which was already given through the prophets of the Old Testament. God will keep this long-awaited promise without fail.**

There are things we can no longer see in new Jerusalem; a new heaven and a new earth. We can see the temple, the sun and the moon no longer. This is because God and Jesus who is the Lamb are not only the temple but also the lamp which shines with glory. Parables or symbols about God are needed no more. We can simply neither misunderstand nor pretend to not know God, because God is with us right where we are. **Living with God eternally is the joy of the kingdom of heaven.**

The saints who overcame suffering and became victors would see the glory of God here and live an honorable life with the

Genesis vs. The Revelation

The first creation of Genesis	New creation of the Revelation
Creating Heaven & Earth(Gen.1:1-2:3)	Creating new Heaven & new Earth (Rev. chap.21-22)
Adam ruled the Garden of Eden(Gen.1:26)	Jesus Christ rules(Rev.21:5)
Got separated from the Tree of Life (Gen.2:9, 3:22)	Can see the tree of life(Rev.22:2)
Were cursed due to sin(Gen.3:17-19)	Tears, curse & death don't exist (Rev.21:4, 22:3-5)
Satan seduced man(Gen.3:13)	Satan is destroyed forever(Rev.20:10)
Hid from the face of God(Gen.3:8)	Serves God and sees His face(Rev.22:4)
Life with suffering and labor(Gen.3:18-19)	Life of victory of reigning like king(Rev.22:5)

authority of God. God will give a new country of new heaven and new earth as gift to those who kept the fidelity of faith with the mind of loving God.

Finally he who testifies to all these things says;

"Yes, I am coming soon!"

We respond with;

"Amen. Come, LORD Jesus!"

Write down the contents of this lesson in the form of Tong Story

Let's pray in a loud voice so that we may be able to teach the contents of this lesson to our children

- Teach them to your children, talking about them when you sit at home and when you walk along the road, when you lie down and when you get up……so that your days and the days of your children may be many……as many as the days that the heavens are above the earth (Deuteronomy 11:19-21).
- you know those from whom you learned it, and how from infancy you have known the holy Scriptures(II Timothy 3:14-15).

The Song of TongBible
통通성경 노래

Lyrics Byoungho Zoh(작사: 조병호)
Composition Tong Orchestra(작곡: 통오케스트라)

경통독』 20마당의 제목으로 만든 노래입니다.

TONGDOKWON

Tong Note